AMBIVALENT NATION

CONFLICTING WORLDS

New Dimensions of the American Civil War

T. Michael Parrish, Series Editor

AMBIVALENT NATION

HOW BRITAIN IMAGINED
— THE —
AMERICAN CIVIL WAR

Hugh Dubrulle

Louisiana State University Press
Baton Rouge

Published by Louisiana State University Press

Manufactured in the United States of America
First printing

Designer: Michelle A. Neustrom
Typeface: MillerText
Printer and binder: Sheridan Books, Inc.

Library of Congress Cataloging-in-Publication Data
are available at the Library of Congress.

ISBN 978-0-8071-6880-6 (cloth: alk. paper)
— ISBN 978-0-8071-6881-3 (pdf) — ISBN 978-0-8071-6882-0 (epub)

Chapter 3 is a revised version of an essay published as Hugh Dubrulle, "'If it is still impossible . . . to advocate slavery . . . it has . . . become a habit persistently to write down freedom': Britain, the Civil War, and Race," in *The Civil War as Global Conflict: Transnational Meanings of the American Civil War*, ed. David T. Gleeson and Simon Lewis, 56–84 (Columbia: Univ. of South Carolina Press, 2014). Used with permission.

An earlier and much different version of chapter 5 was published as Hugh Dubrulle, "A Military Legacy of the Civil War: The British Inheritance," *Civil War History* 49, no. 2 (June 2003): 153–180. Copyright 2003 by The Kent State University Press. Used with permission.

All images courtesy of "The Civil War in America from the *Illustrated London News*": A Joint Project by Sandra J. Still, Emily E. Katt, Collection Management, and the Manuscript, Archives, and Rare Book Library and the Louis H. Beck Center for Electronic Collections at the Robert W. Woodruff Library at Emory University.

The paper in this book meets the guidelines for permanence and durability of the Committee on Production Guidelines for Book Longevity of the Council on Library Resources. ♾

In memory of my father, Augustin Albert Edouard Dubrulle (1935–2016),
who knew of "old, unhappy, far-off things" firsthand

CONTENTS

ACKNOWLEDGMENTS

In "Why I Write," George Orwell asserted that "writing a book is a horrible, exhausting struggle, like a long bout of some painful illness." "One would never undertake such a thing," he continued, "if one were not driven on by some demon whom one can neither resist nor understand." While I did not experience these sensations with quite the same intensity as Orwell, I have a very good idea what he meant.

As with some sort of chronic condition, I have lived with this project since I started working on my dissertation years ago. It is here that I must begin recounting the debts I have incurred in writing this work and pay tribute to the books I read by people I never met. In graduate school, I was interested in the Civil War's influence on British military thinking before World War I. This train of thought led me to *The Military Legacy of the Civil War: The European Inheritance*, by Jay Luvaas. Luvaas's book is a gem. In *The Face of Battle*, John Keegan described it as a "glittering example" of a work that connected "thought and action." However, as I began to consult the writings of Britons who visited America during the Civil War, I came to understand that *The Military Legacy of the Civil War* was limited in its focus. Luvaas's work sought to determine the influence of the war without considering the larger context within which that influence emerged. As I realized that British military observations formed only part of a panoply of attitudes, I tried to study that panoply and wrote a dissertation about it. In addition to looking at the military lessons Britons extracted from the conflict, I investigated British attitudes toward American politics, society, and nationality during the war. The dissertation that resulted sat squarely within the "traditional interpretation" of British opinion.

The limitations of my approach became evident once I read R.J.M. Blackett's *Divided Hearts: Britain and the American Civil War* and Duncan Andrew Campbell's *English Public Opinion and the American Civil War*—both of which were published a few years after I completed my dissertation. I cannot adequately summarize here the impact of these books on my thinking. Suffice it to say that they forced me to reconceptualize my own project and discover a new way to theorize British opinion during the Civil War. In looking at the question with fresh eyes, I found a new appreciation for older works such as D. P. Crook's *The North, the South, and the Powers, 1861–1865,* Douglas Lorimer's *Colour, Class, and the Victorians,* and Martin Crawford's *The Anglo-American Crisis of the Mid-Nineteenth Century:* The Times *and America, 1850–1862.*

Throughout this long bout, though, I have relied on more than books. In *A Letter to a Whig Member of the Southern Independence Association,* Goldwin Smith defended what was widely perceived as a materialistic American culture by asserting that although "man does not live by bread alone, he must have bread to live." I am very grateful for the financial support I have received over the years. The Institute on Global Conflict and Cooperation, which serves the University of California system, provided the necessary funds for my initial research trip to Britain in 1996–1997. I also have Saint Anselm College to thank for repeated summer research grants issued in 2003, 2007, 2011, and 2015. These grants not only funded trips to Britain but also provided time and resources for writing.

At the same time, I am indebted to a large number of people who helped me with this book, provided inspiration, or supplied support of various kinds. Throughout my various visits to archives in the United Kingdom, the Republic of Ireland, and the United States, I was met almost invariably with helpfulness and courtesy. Two archivists who stood out for their kindness and solicitude were Peter Day, Keeper of the Devonshire Collection at Chatsworth, and Eamon Dyas at the News International Record Office in London. I also would like to thank the Trustees of the 10th Lord Monson and the Lincolnshire Archives for granting me permission to quote from the Monson Papers.

I also enjoyed the assistance of a number of mentors. Alfred Gollin was my advisor before he retired midway through my time in graduate school at the University of California, Santa Barbara. He taught me to make sure I knew what I was talking about before I dared to say it, and he demanded that all of his graduate students think big. John Talbott, also at the University of California, Santa Barbara, oversaw the completion of my dissertation. I found him ever thoughtful and unerring in his judgment. What is more, his prose became to me a model of concision that I could never seem to equal. As a visiting assistant professor working in various departments, I also had the good fortune to receive advice from a number of people who encouraged me in my work. These included Joseph Fracchia and David Frank at the Robert D. Clark Honors College at the University of Oregon as well as David Smith at the University of Puget Sound. For about fifteen years, my past and present colleagues in the History Department at Saint Anselm College have helped create a wonderful and supportive working environment. Poppy Fry (now at the University of Puget Sound), Sarah Hardin, Matt Masur, Andy Moore, Phil Pajakowski, Sean Perrone, Beth Salerno, Silvia Shannon, and Fr. William Sullivan (recently retired) have all put up with my antics and made the department feel truly like an academic home. Sue Gagnon, who headed Interlibrary Loan at Saint Anselm College's Geisel Library while I was writing this book, deserves a shout-out for enthusiastically hunting down hard-to-find newspapers, books, and pamphlets.

I should also thank the people who made it possible for bits and pieces of this book to appear in various venues over the years. A very early version of chapter 5 appeared in *Civil War History*, and I must express my gratitude to William A. Blair, who was then editor of that journal, along with the anonymous readers who looked over the manuscript.

A special thank you also goes to Simon Lewis and David T. Gleeson, who hosted the Civil War—Global Conflict Conference put on by the Carolina Lowcountry and Atlantic World Program at the College of Charleston in 2011. At this wonderful conference, I presented a paper that was later published as an essay in *The Civil War as Global Conflict* (also edited by Lewis and Gleeson). This essay, with some revisions, eventually became chapter 3 of this book.

To those who read the book manuscript, I must extend my deepest appreciation. Aaron Sheehan-Dean looked over about two-thirds of the first draft. All of his comments were spot-on. He not only exposed various weaknesses in the organization and argument of my work but also provided much needed encouragement to carry on. I am left with enormous respect for his judgment. Amanda Foreman, Jay Sexton, and Nimrod Tal all read completed drafts of the manuscript, and I cannot thank them enough for their thoughtful responses.

I must also express my gratitude to Louisiana State University Press, particularly T. Michael Parrish (editor of the Conflicting Worlds: New Dimensions of the Civil War series) and Rand Dotson (executive editor in history). Both have taken great pains to guide and reassure me throughout the process of producing this book. At this point, though, I ought to issue the usual disclaimer that the shortcomings of this work are my responsibility entirely.

Finally, I must thank my family, who have suffered alongside me throughout the "exhausting struggle" that culminated in this book. I use the word *suffered* because everyone in my household pointed out that long sessions of writing made me distracted and grumpy. Still, my wife, Elizabeth, not only continued to serve as a fount of good judgment and practical sense but sustained her role as my number one cheerleader. I am not sure how I would have made it as far as I have without her support. My son, Jackson, and my daughter, Vivien, did not in any way contribute to this book. Rather, they were unwittingly engaged in the very important task of reminding me that there are things much more important than books. And for that, I am more thankful than they can know.

AMBIVALENT NATION

INTRODUCTION

How Britain Understood Mid-Nineteenth-Century America

> The character of a people has such a complexity of aspect, that even the honest observer knows not always, not perhaps after long inspection, what to determine regarding it. From his, only accidental, point of view, the figure stands before him like the tracings on veined marble,—a mass of mere random lines, and tints, and entangled strokes, out of which a lively fancy may shape almost *any* image. But the image he brings with him is always the readiest; this is tried; it answers as well as another; and a second voucher now testifies to its correctness. Thus each, in confident tones, though it be with a secret misgiving, repeats his precursor; the hundred-times-repeated comes in the end to be believed; the foreign nation is now once for all understood, decided on, and registered accordingly; and dunce the thousandth writes of it like dunce the first.
>
> —HARRIET MARTINEAU, QUOTING THOMAS CARLYLE, 1837

> The error lies in that summary process of generalization, which extends, without inquiry, to all, the peculiarities which are observable in a few. . . . It is almost impossible for one at a distance, in contemplating a moral picture so diversified as is that presented in America . . . to distinguish at all times between a local peculiarity and a general characteristic.
>
> —ALEXANDER MACKAY, 1849

BRITAIN AND THE AMERICAN CIVIL WAR: PASSIONATE AMBIVALENCE AND POSTCOLONIALITY

In March 1861, shortly after disembarking in New York, William Howard Russell, *The Times*' special correspondent, wrote about his first impressions of the United States to John Thadeus Delane, the paper's editor. "The chaos of opinions into which I was at once plunged over head & ears," Russell wrote, "[was] all so opposite & so violent that like opposing forces they produced at the unhappy centre . . . complete absence of motion."[1] Upon the American Civil War's conclusion, Russell eagerly and disingenuously claimed to have supported the North all along, but for much of the conflict he expressed mixed feelings about both sides. His attitude was not characterized by a cold neutrality. Rather, he expressed a passionate ambivalence that recognized the conflict's significance for both the United States and Britain. In other words, Russell's position exemplified the bulk of British opinion toward the American crisis.

The two main scholarly approaches to the study of British attitudes toward the American Civil War have found it difficult to come to terms with this passionate ambivalence. The "traditional interpretation" has stressed a sociological examination of British opinion to determine who supported which side.[2] Perhaps, in a nod to Alfred Cobban's groundbreaking work about the French Revolution, the expression "social interpretation" is somewhat more appropriate.[3] The scholars who founded this tradition originally opted for a simple class-based view of British opinion that pitted the "gentlemen" (partisans of the Confederacy) against the "masses" (advocates of the Union).[4] The most recent work in this vein, R.J.M. Blackett's *Divided Hearts* (2001), presents a far more sophisticated and nuanced view of opinion that accounts not only for the influence of social class but also political creed, the abolitionist tradition, racism, diplomatic considerations, economic interests, and national feeling. Blackett argues that, generally, these considerations arrayed Radicals, advanced Liberals, Dissenters, and the working class on the side of the North against the aristocracy, the Church of England, and elements of the professional classes who supported the Confederacy. While he recognizes that the "complexity and subtlety of reactions to the war are staggering," Blackett still expresses the tendency of this tradition to divide Britons into partisans of one belligerent or the other.[5] In other words, there is a stress on passion at the expense of ambivalence.

"Revisionists" emphasize the degree to which the British policy of neutrality reflected what was generally an uncommitted public opinion.[6] D. P. Crook, who articulated this position best, recognized that "partisans existed" but warned against dividing British opinion into "distinct blocs, set into more or less antagonistic postures for the duration of the war." Rather, British public opinion toward the conflict was led by men of the "center" who "were not deeply committed, [and] whose approach was essentially pragmatic."[7] More recently, in *English Public Opinion and the American Civil War* (2003) Duncan Andrew Campbell has declared that "most English observers, irrespective of class, wished to remain neutral in the struggle and distrusted (and even disliked) both sides."[8] In this case, the emphasis on ambivalence has drained all the passion out of British opinion.

The foregoing suggests that a true estimate of British opinion cannot dwell exclusively on *who* believed *what*; rather, it must also expend some effort in studying *how* Britons believed. Addressing the *how* requires creating a model of mid-Victorian Anglo-American relations that allows for a methodical analysis of the way British opinion of the United States formed during this period. Until recently, scholars had not developed this model partly because their study of the nineteenth-century Anglo-American relationship was episodic. As Fred Leventhal and Roland Quinault have lamented, historians have tended to focus "on episodes of conflict or partnership between the two nations in the international arena, but their preoccupations with such topics has fostered a view of Anglo-American relations as discontinuous, rekindled only at moments of disagreement or co-operation."[9] For example, those who have studied British attitudes toward the American Civil War have not shown sufficient interest in the way antebellum relations might have shaped reactions to the conflict (Martin Crawford being a notable exception).[10] Mid-Victorian Britons themselves were guilty of this very propensity. Indeed, in 1862, as the Civil War intensified, the *Saturday Review* pointed out that when something noteworthy occurred in another part of the world, whether it be "Turkey, or India, or America, or Italy," most Englishmen "are sure to think themselves bound to have an opinion about the matter." Unfortunately, "while Turkey or America keeps quiet, people take no heed to its affairs, and, therefore, when the disturbance comes, they have no notion of the causes of the disturbance."[11]

We need not look far to find a model that allows us to understand how Britons thought, shows the way their mode of thinking had developed over a period of time stretching back well into the antebellum era, and explains the passionate ambivalence of British opinion toward America during the war years. If we recognize the degree to which the Anglo-American relationship was still postcolonial by mid-century, we can employ a series of ideas from postcolonial studies that help explain the way in which Britons thought about Americans. Recent works have made much of America's postcolonial position in the first half of the nineteenth century (although they look mainly at the American end of the transatlantic relationship), but scholars have long understood this point.[12] More than twenty years ago, Peter Hulme argued that "if 'postcolonial' is a useful word, then it refers to a process of disengagement from the whole colonial syndrome," something he believes the United States did not accomplish until the Spanish-American War.[13] More recently, Jay Sexton has claimed that "nineteenth-century America was a 'postcolonial' entity" because Americans struggled well into the 1800s to "consolidate their independence."[14] Due to the old imperial connection, British observers felt compelled to recognize Americans as an Anglo-Saxon yet subsidiary people. The former status implied American equality, the latter, British superiority. Britons, then, could not look toward the United States without feeling, alternately, proud and patronizing—accompanied almost always by a sense of wonder. It was this contradictory dynamic that accounted for the passionate ambivalence which characterized British opinion toward the American Civil War.

The postcolonial nature of the transatlantic relationship is not merely the invention of contemporary historians; during the mid-nineteenth century, a number of British observers believed the United States had not fully freed itself from the old imperial connection. There was, of course, the seemingly endless flow of British capital, goods, and labor across the Atlantic that led *The Times* in 1859 to describe America casually as "a commercial if not political province of England."[15] Yet even more important to British observers was America's cultural and political immaturity that made it reliant on the old mother country. For example, in an 1863 speech to his constituents in Bridgwater, Alexander William Kinglake, the travel writer, historian, and MP, claimed that despite Americans' constant references to the Declaration of Independence, "that independence is not complete" because he found Americans "looking constantly to England."[16]

That being the case, even though it rubs shoulders uneasily with history, postcolonial studies has much to offer an interpretation of the Anglo-American relationship during the Civil War era. The ideas associated with this field should be used with some caution, but they have come a long way since Edward Said's *Orientalism*.[17] Scholars working in this area have generated a series of concepts that are much more sophisticated, nuanced, and flexible than those presented in Said's pioneering but flawed work. If we apply these ideas to the Anglo-American relationship, we can clearly see that Britain's great material interests in the United States inspired British writers to assume a position of superiority and authority when it came to discussing all things American. This position allowed them to judge, instruct, and correct the United States with the intent of guiding American development according to British norms. In other words, they expressed the "will to dominate and not be dominated, to impose change whilst remaining unchanged," which is the hallmark of cultural imperialism.[18] Grudging and resentful as they might have been, many Americans felt the force of British judgments because, as Ralph Waldo Emerson observed, "If there be one test of national genius universally accepted, it is success; and if there be one successful country in the universe for the last millennium, that country is England."[19] To mangle Harold Macmillan's phrase somewhat, Britons, along with many Americans, believed that Britain served as America's Greece *and* Rome. Yet, we should not overstate the case; British literature did not merely express a single will to power, and authors were not imprisoned by a monolithic, hegemonic, imperialist discourse. Writers brought a diversity of experiences and interests to their writings that led to the articulation of competing discourses, often within the same work.[20] As we shall see, while postcolonial discourses explain a great deal, they always competed with those shaped by class, gender, race, and other important forces.[21]

We can say something analogous about the "archive of information" or "tradition of representation"—key concepts in postcolonial theory—that were produced by these discourses and which weighed heavily on those who wrote about America. Clearly, what previous authors had written about America influenced each writer who was new to the task.[22] This weight is reflected in the way writers often tackled the same topics in the same way: the problems of slavery, the place of women in society, the nature of the republican experiment, the relationship of manners to American political arrangements, the workings of federalism, the mainspring of American patriotism, the state of religion, and so on. This consistency extended to the description of small things as well—for instance, the speed with which Americans inhaled their meals, the peculiar nature of boarding house culture, the prevalence of chewing tobacco, and the unique American arrangements associated with rail travel.[23] However, in the same way that they were not imprisoned by a single imperial discourse, authors were not held absolutely captive by the various tropes that had become prominent in the representation of America. They possessed sufficient autonomy to present novel viewpoints or synthesize material in original ways, especially as circumstances changed.[24]

The influence of the "tradition of representation" is also reflected in the self-referential nature of much British writing about America. Before voyaging across the Atlantic, British visitors to America invariably read the works of their predecessors (interestingly enough, as we shall see, Alexis de Tocqueville's *Democracy in America* was perhaps the most influential), and this reading fundamentally shaped the way they understood their experiences.[25] Moreover, much evidence supports the view that the British distrusted American sources of information about the United States. There was a widespread impression that Americans were not "objective" about their country and that their newspapers were trash. And yet, it is also clear that Britons found Americans indispensable in constructing images of the United States. Moreover, Americans could and did represent themselves to British audiences, although the latter did not always appreciate these interpositions.[26]

Finally, postcolonial analysis helps illuminate the character of the "Other." During the antebellum period, Americans clearly became a sort of Other, an "underground self" (to use Edward Said's phrase) on whom all sorts of British conflicts, anxieties, and shortcomings were projected.[27] It was against this figure that Britons could define themselves. British commentary about American uniformity, philistinism, materialism, mob rule, lynch law, vulgarity, slavery, violence, mediocrity, dishonesty, and envy, then, all reflected some concern about domestic developments.[28] What made the Anglo-American case especially complex was that while Americans were different from Britons, they were awfully similar; it was difficult to detect where Britain ended and America began. Several of Homi Bhabha's concepts are particularly relevant in this case. His ideas regarding "hybridity" stress the ambivalence of the imperial encounter. On the one hand, imperialist discourses sought to capture the Other, describe him, and render him knowable in text. On the other hand, such texts portrayed the Other as alien, incomprehensible, and unknowable in an attempt to emphasize his differences so as to legitimize imperial rule. The tension between these conflicting objectives contributed to a fundamental insecurity and instability in imperialist discourses that led to constant repetition of stereotypes in a vain attempt to anchor the Other once and for all. What made this task especially difficult in the case of the Americans was that they were the ultimate "mimic men"—colonized peoples whose close resemblance to the colonizer threatened to expose the fundamental conflict that lay at the heart of all imperial discourses.[29]

All of these elements of postcolonial studies seem well suited to capture the strange amalgam of discordant elements found in British representations of America during the Civil War—the intimacy, insecurity, repetition, hostility, anxiety, affability, and aloofness—all of which overlay a desire to shape the destiny of a kindred people. In short, they explain the conflicted feelings with which Britain observed America during these years. There is no better way of illuminating the expression of these themes in a preliminary sort of way than through reference to two incidents that, together, reveal the bifurcated view that Britons held of America shortly before the Civil War.

RAILWAYS AND REVOLVERS IN GEORGIA: THE GEORGIA RAILWAY HOAX, 1856

On October 15, 1856, *The Times* printed a remarkable and lurid letter purporting to be an eyewitness account of a railway journey from Macon to Augusta, Georgia, that had taken place in late August of that year.[30] In the letter, entitled "Railways and Revolvers in Georgia," the anonymous author claimed that an argument over a woman led to a series of fatal altercations during the ten-hour nighttime trip. Of the twenty-five or so travelers gathered in the lone passenger car of the train, five were killed in duels, and another passenger, a six-year-old boy, was murdered. The author closed by stating, "In Augusta I heard a person say that these were not uncommon incidents, and that scarcely a week passed without some fatal encounter on that road."[31]

On October 16, a day after releasing this letter, *The Times* printed an equally remarkable editorial. It marveled at the commonplace nature of such events and the casual way in which Americans "engaged themselves for this dance of death quite as freely as at our own county balls, and on as slight an introduction." After joking about how American railroad companies ought to make better accommodations for duels by providing shooting stations, ammunition, and surgeons for passengers, *The Times* explained why widespread violence was bad for the South, the United States, and Britain. The paper had little sympathy for the southern states, which had recently earned bad press; Charles Sumner had been caned in the Senate only several months before by Preston Brooks, and southern border ruffians had made a mockery of free elections in Kansas. If southern "public advisers preach pistol-law against their political opponents in the North," *The Times* explained, "they must be prepared for the inevitable consequences among themselves." As for the United States, frequent duels did not promise much in the way of future progress and civilization. Indeed, "there is something very grand in a whole nation pairing like a main of fighting cocks, but then it is the *finale* rather than the foundation of empire." Finally, from the angle of British interests, the dueling in Georgia was bad news because "we are sorry to see our customers killing one another so fast."[32] As one can see from the quotes, the language of the leader was characterized by a patronizing and dry jocularity. *The Times* represented Americans as deviant, incomprehensible, and foreign when judged against British norms. And yet, *The Times* assumed a kind of familiarity with Americans because they were, after all, kin and customers.

It is easy to understand why *The Times* persisted in claiming the story was true, even after the letter was challenged as a hoax from many different quarters. But why did the newspaper fall for this preposterous tale in the first place? For one thing, *The Times* had obtained "satisfactory vouchers for the writer's respectability, sanity, and truthfulness." Moreover, the "plain narrative" presented in the letter, apparently unembellished by melodramatics, told in favor of its truthfulness.[33] Finally, the letter seemed plausible because it employed a number of American images developed by travel literature with which a British audience would have been familiar.[34]

One of these images consisted of the passenger car as a setting for the strange manners and conventions associated with American democratic society. British travel literature made much of the fact that, unlike the British, who divided their first- and second-class passenger cars into compartments, the Americans had only one class of passenger whom they seated in an undivided car.[35] British visitors took this arrangement as a reflection of America's commitment to equality. Crammed together in a common car, white American men (there were separate cars for women and blacks) expected democratic sociability and openness from their fellow travelers.[36] Accustomed to these images of American democratic sociability, it would not have required much of a stretch for British readers to imagine how a private quarrel over a woman could easily become a public matter involving everyone in an American passenger car. Indeed, *The Times* appeared to stress Americans' social promiscuity when it commented on how the passengers freely issued challenges to one another on "as slight an introduction" as those requesting a dance at an English country ball.

At the same time, the American train served as a symbol of recklessness in Britain, something that also contributed to the plausibility of the hoax. American railways seemed unrestrained by the kinds of regulations imposed in Britain.[37] The conspicuous absence of safety precautions along with the willingness to accept accidents as a part of doing business suggested a terrible callousness on the part of Americans, especially when a dollar could be made.[38] The Americans' obsession with size, speed, strength, and wealth—in other words, their materialism—so the argument went, had blunted their moral sensibilities and undermined consideration for their fellow men.[39]

Finally, the hoax's setting in the South also contributed to its believability, because British travelers had long described the region as a scene of violence. Here, many travelers agreed, an imperious slave-owning culture, habituated to the employment of coercion, held sway. According to British visitors, since slavery appeared to produce a gentry of sorts in the South, quarrels often took the gentlemanly form of duels.

The Times' response to the Georgia railway hoax shows how the United States could look from the British end of the postcolonial relationship. The newspaper seemed quite comfortable in its role as arbiter of things American—the United States was easily and glibly understood. The newspaper's editorial expressed a sense of superiority and criticized the United States while describing Americans as alien, exotic, and irrational. In so doing, it referred to several tropes that readers would have understood if they were at all familiar with the traditions governing the representation of America.

The denouement of the incident, however, revealed another side of the Anglo-American relationship. The hoax sparked an extensive transatlantic conversation between a large number of American newspapers and *The Times*. Many Britons and Americans participated by writing letters, including Richard R. Cuyler, president of the Central Georgia Railroad, who eventually produced depositions from the conductor, mail agent, enginemen, flagmen, and fireman who served on the now infamous train to Augusta. The pursuit, detection, and unmasking of the letter's author, John Arrowsmith, an expatriate English cotton factor living in New Orleans, was truly an Anglo-American venture. Journalists on both sides of the Atlantic participated in the chase while collectively and thoughtfully musing on the larger significance of this episode for Anglo-American relations.[40]

BLOOD IS THICKER THAN WATER: JOSIAH TATTNALL BEFORE THE TAKU FORTS, 1859

If the Georgia railway hoax stressed the distance between the United States and Great Britain, an incident three years later appeared to emphasize the intimacy of the Anglo-American relationship. Another Georgian, Flag Officer Josiah Tattnall, made a positive impression in Britain that could not have differed more from the widely circulated image of his bloodthirsty, Augusta-bound compatriots.

In late June 1859, Tattnall, commander of America's East India Squadron, found himself aboard the shallow draft steamer *Toeywan* at the mouth of the Hai (Peiho) River. John Ward, a fellow Georgian, accompanied him as the recently appointed U.S. minister to China. A nearby British fleet of fifteen vessels under Admiral Sir James Hope lay at anchor supported by a French frigate and gunboat. Aboard were Frederick Bruce and Alphonse de Bourboulon, the British and French ministers to China, respectively.

According to the Treaty of Tianjin, signed with China in June 1858, the British and the French were supposed to exchange formal ratifications of that agreement with the Chinese in Beijing by June 25, 1859. For that reason, both Bruce and Bourboulon were determined to make their way to the Chinese capital via the Hai. Reluctant to admit foreigners to Beijing, however, the Chinese sought to delay the inevitable through a variety of ploys. These included stringing a series of booms across the Hai and refusing to allow the British and French ministers to proceed to Beijing. Frustrated by Chinese delays, Bruce delivered an ultimatum: if the Chinese did not clear the booms from the river by June 25, the Anglo-French fleet would push its way through by force.

Not wishing to be associated with British and French efforts, the American government ordered Ward and Tattnall to pursue an independent and neutral policy. On June 24, pretending they knew nothing of the Anglo-French ultimatum, Ward and Tattnall pushed the *Toeywan* to the mouth of the Hai in an attempt to contact Chinese authorities and obtain unobstructed passage to Beijing. Unfortunately, their vessel ran aground in the shallow, muddy river, only a few hundred yards from the Taku forts that guarded its mouth. Quickly grasping what had happened, Hope ordered a British gunboat to free the Americans. Unfortunately, the tow chain on this vessel snapped, and Hope sent another gunboat. This time he invited Tattnall to hoist the American ensign and take command of the British vessel. Tattnall declined the courteous offer. While stranded on the mudbank, he opened negotiations with the Chinese, who refused him passage. Several hours later, after a favorable wind and a high tide freed the *Toeywan,* the Americans retired behind the Anglo-French fleet, which had obviously begun to prepare for action.

On the next day, when it became clear that the Chinese had no intention of complying with the Anglo-French ultimatum, Hope readied his fleet to push through the booms. At 2:30 P.M., his flagship *Plover* passed over the first boom, partially disabled by British sailors the night before. Shortly thereafter, the Taku forts, a series of earthen batteries that ran along the river's banks, suddenly opened fire at close range. For much of the afternoon, as they engaged the Chinese fortifications, the British gunboats took a fearful pounding. Hope was badly wounded and, after changing flagships several times, ended up on the *Cormorant.* Despite their difficulties, the British began to silence the Chinese batteries, and an amphibious assault looked practicable against the outer bastion of the south fort. British reinforcements waited at the mouth of the river in a number of junks, but the tide was so strong that they could not reach the mudflats in front of the bastion and disembark an assault force of Royal Marines. Having learned of Hope's condition and the terrible losses among the British fleet, Tattnall and Ward decided to depart from their government's neutrality by towing British reinforcements toward the forts. It was at this moment that Tattnall supposedly declared, "Blood is thicker than water!" Significantly, he swore, "I'll be damned if I'll stand by and see white men butchered before my eyes." "No sir," he added, "old Tattnall isn't that kind, sir. This is the cause of humanity."[41]

After having towed British reinforcements to the hottest part of the action, Tattnall remembered that he had not acknowledged Hope's kindness of the day before. Under heavy fire, he directed his launch to the *Cormorant* and paid his respects to the wounded admiral. In the meantime, a substantial number of American sailors made their way to the British gunboats, slipped aboard, and began providing what assistance they could. After taking a British bark back to his own vessel (by this point his launch had been sunk),

Tattnall himself helped evacuate a number of British wounded to the hospital ship *Assistance.*

As night began to fall, Royal Marines and French sailors launched an amphibious assault on the Taku forts. The attack failed, and fighting finally petered out late that night. In the end, three British gunboats were a total loss. The British also suffered 450 casualties among their sailors and Marines. The battle had been a disaster for British arms.[42] Tattnall, however, won nothing but praise from British sailors and Marines. Lord John Russell, Britain's foreign secretary, officially conveyed his thanks to Tattnall, while the American government and British newspapers showered Tattnall with praise.

As reported in the British press, Tattnall's behavior before the Taku forts provided reassurance that Americans were not only Englishmen but also saw themselves as such. This reassurance proved comforting because antebellum Anglo-American diplomatic relations were perpetually fraught.[43] Neither side pursued a belligerent policy in the sense that it inclined toward war as a solution to diplomatic problems, but American diplomats, much like British ones, often used bluffs, threats, and informal pressure that looked very warlike to contemporaries.[44] Although most British commentators displayed little compunction about vigorously upholding British interests in the face of American challenges, some still felt discomfort about the character of diplomatic relations between the two supposedly kindred nations. In 1846, for example, during the dispute over the Oregon territory, *The Times* editorialized that while parties on both sides of the Atlantic possibly desired war, "commerce—the affections of kindred—identity of origin, of language, and laws—the common pursuit of similar objects, the common prevalence of similar sentiments, and the common deference to the same principles of moral action" bound Britons and Americans together. *The Times* concluded, "we are two people, but we are of one family."[45]

What Tattnall's actions promised was that the natural affinities of these two peoples would overcome the self-interested calculations of diplomats. In an essay recommended by *The Times* as relating both the "tale" and the "moral" of the battle before the Taku forts, *Blackwood's Edinburgh Magazine* commented that "the calculating long-backed diplomatists of the United States" had forgotten "that there were certain promptings of the heart which override all selfish considerations." Tattnall had reminded them of this truth when he claimed "blood is thicker than water," doing more that day to bind the two countries together than all of America's "lawyers and pettifogging politicians have ever done to part us."[46]

According to this view, Americans and Britons would be brought together as kindred lovers of liberty and propagators of civilization. In a world ruled by Oriental despots, absolute monarchs, dictators, primitive savages, and *caudillos,* republican America, for all of its faults, was widely perceived in Britain as the only other great free society in the world. Writing in 1859, John Roebuck, the maverick Radical MP, stressed the bonds between Britons and Americans as "the only free people on the earth, united heart and hand against despotism and bad government, wherever found."[47] The United States was also considered an apostle of world progress that had done yeoman's work on the North American continent. For example, in a review of Sir Charles Lyell's works on America, the *North British Review* explicitly connected westward expansion with British imperialism, referring to the two Anglo-Saxon peoples as "fellow-workers" in a "sublime mission" that would "diffuse among nations, now steeped in ignorance, those glorious truths, secular and divine, which are destined to effect the reformation of the world."[48] Through a common struggle on behalf of world progress that involved commerce, moral influence, and military force, the British and Americans could recognize and reinforce their sense of Anglo-Saxon kinship.

In a November 1859 editorial that was one of the last to comment on the subject, *The Times* summarized the British response to Tattnall's gracious actions and explained how these fit in the overall scheme of Anglo-American relations:

> There is always on this side of the Atlantic a strong kin-like feeling towards the people of our own blood who dwell on the other side. We are jealous of their affection, and hurt when we find their sympathies turned from us, perhaps to be lavished upon despots with whom they have nothing in common, and barbarians who have one word for them and for us. We are irritated also when they are querulous and tetchy with us, and when, having abundance of gentlemen to choose from, they set the most ill-bred swaggering adventurer they can find to insult us and wrong us. But we are never happier as a nation in our relations with the American people than

upon those rare occasions when we are going cordially together, never better pleased than when we have some act of courtesy, or, still better, some act of kindness, to thank them for, as in this affair of the Peiho.[49]

In this passage, a sincere tenderness replaced the sardonic tone that had characterized *The Times*' coverage of the Georgia railway hoax. Americans had been transformed from the Other into kinsmen. And yet, as the foregoing suggests, Americans were expected to act in accordance with British standards. Among other things, doing so required moving in conformity with the interests of world civilization and progress—which the British frequently confused or conflated with their own interests.

CONCLUSION: THE TONE WHICH BEFITS EQUALS

As the preceding anecdotes suggest, the stock figures with which Britons populated the American landscape could oscillate in nature from one pole to the other according to the requirements of the situation. For example, as we have seen (and shall see), when a southerner committed a transgression and required correction, the dynamics of the postcolonial relationship frequently required that he become a violent, dueling slaveowner, but when he acted in accordance with British norms, he became a gracious gentleman or an emblem of Anglo-American comity. In these ways, the Georgia railway hoax and Tattnall's actions before the Taku forts are equally indispensable to understanding the way in which the British came to terms with America during the antebellum and Civil War eras.

While representations of Americans could switch as circumstances dictated, the discourses that underpinned them could also change as the British responded to shifts in the distribution of power within the Anglo-American relationship. During the antebellum years, British observers had developed a powerful apparatus that, for all its contradictions, provided ready answers for questions about the United States. It was with this apparatus that they continued to study America during the Civil War. Over the course of the war, however, the Americans conjured up such awesome power, wrought such devastation, and initiated such sweeping changes that many Britons felt compelled to speak of America in a different language that indicated a newfound respect. As the *Spectator* pointed out toward the end of the war, American strength and greatness required the British "to adopt the tone which befits equals, to listen as well as declaim, to give the adversary fair credit for motives, to make all those allowances men so readily make for equals and with such difficulty to inferiors."[50] If British observations about the Civil War relied on discourses associated with a postcolonial relationship, the war itself played an important role in changing those discourses and dissipating the postcolonial spell.

1

ANTEBELLUM AMERICA IN THE BRITISH IMAGINATION

> It has been truly observed that a reliable book on
> the United States yet remains to be written.
> —ISABELLA BIRD, 1856

BRITAIN'S UNITED STATES: NO PAST, AN UGLY AND PROSPEROUS PRESENT, BUT SUCH A FUTURE

While sailing down the Nile in late 1849, Florence Nightingale wrote in her journal that Europeans were fond of using the words "Past" and "Present" because "they generally present a cheerful view of things." An Englishman looking back to the medieval period or even the days of Charles II, she wrote, could only feel pleasure at the moral and material progress that had taken place since those times. In Egypt, however, the words "Past" and "Present" were "above all that you can conceive strange and painful." The Egyptians had once possessed "almost all our civilization . . . our philosophy, and . . . our art and science," but now these were "entirely lost." Nightingale asserted Egypt was characterized by "the savage, sensual, childish life." She believed that Egypt provided a signal lesson to Britain, but she found it difficult to decipher. She could not believe that "all nations shall fall after a certain number of years." Indeed, she clung to the idea that the Egyptians must have broken one of God's laws to suffer such degradation. Yet, she wondered, "Are all nations to sink in that way?" Or would a nation one day discover "the laws of God by which she may make a steady progression"? It was in the context of these thoughts that Nightingale sought to highlight the East's character by searching for its opposite—and found America. In the East, "there is such a Past, no Present, and, for a Future, one can only hope for extinction!" In

America, on the other hand, "there is no Past, an ugly and prosperous Present, but such a Future!"[1]

Nightingale's comments were entirely characteristic of British attitudes toward both regions. If the East conjured up images of decay, the United States was associated with growth and especially material progress. And indeed, it appears that a number of Americans shared her view. In 1862, during the journalist Edward Dicey's visit to the northern states, "the ablest of American novelists" told him, "We have no past, we have no present to be proud of, and, if we lose our faith in the future, we have nothing worth living for."[2] If such thoughts proved disturbing for Americans, they were hardly comforting or unproblematic for Britons. Nightingale's observations indicate that they raised fundamental questions about the Anglo-American relationship. Where exactly did Britain fit in America's past, present, and future? Britain was an undeniable part of America's past, but Nightingale's formulation, which was a common one, indicated that the past did not matter in the United States. Would the historic traditions associated with British civilization and culture, then, guide Americans as they moved forward from their "ugly and prosperous" present? As for the present, that appeared to belong to Europe, particularly Britain. But Nightingale accepted this position as only temporary. How should Britain, the greatest of all present nations deal with, to use Christopher Mulvey's phrase, "the best of potential nations"?[3] Finally, the future also presented difficult questions. Many European commentators accepted that America's future would become the civilized world's; Britain would inevitably come to resemble the United States. How would Britain change, and what could Britons do to prepare themselves for this transformation? These questions about the American present and future proved most interesting to British commentators. As Anthony Trollope claimed in *North America* (1862), the study of the United States was "the best means of prophesying . . . what the world will next be, and what men will next do."[4]

According to British observers, America indicated that the world would next be a bourgeois democracy, and men would next live in social equality. In other words, America was the middle-class nation that Britain would soon become. Not everyone, however, agreed entirely with this assessment. Tocqueville, who became extremely influential in Britain, believed that since circumstances in Europe were far different from those in America, equality of conditions would not manifest itself in exactly the same way.[5] Nevertheless, most British commentators not only insisted that the United States had fallen under the rule of a middle class that resembled their own, but also cited Tocqueville in support of this thesis. For example, in his famous review of *Democracy in America* (1835, 1840), John Stuart Mill asserted that Tocqueville had implicitly linked America's present with Britain's future.[6] Mill foresaw the American spirit becoming "ascendant" in Britain because Britain's government was increasingly a popular "*régime* of the middle class." For all intents and purposes, this regime constituted a democracy since "the government of a numerous middle class is democracy." In that respect, the British system had started to resemble the democracy of America because "what is called universal suffrage in America," Mill argued, arose "from the fact that America is *all* middle class; the whole people being in a condition, both as to education and pecuniary means, corresponding to the middle class here." Indeed, the American middle class resembled nothing so much as an "exaggeration" of Britain's own bourgeoisie.[7] D. P. Crook has identified this rhetorical strategy of Mill's as a means of rendering the American experiment less radical and therefore less threatening to a middle-class British audience.[8] Although Mill was alive to the widely perceived weaknesses of the transatlantic middle class, particularly its materialism, poor education, and lack of culture, he then viewed its ascendancy with some optimism.[9]

Not everyone saw matters as sanguinely as Mill. Since so many British observers believed America was ruled by a middle class that resembled their own, their visions of the United States were often colored by the ambivalence they felt toward their own bourgeoisie. Matthew Arnold presents an excellent example of this phenomenon. In 1861, just as he started his career as a social critic, Arnold wrote an introduction to his *Popular Education of France* entitled "Democracy" that discussed how Britain ought to prepare for the impending social and political ascendancy of the bourgeoisie. Throughout this discussion, Arnold implicitly saw Americans as an exaggerated version of Britain's middle class and expressed mixed feelings about this class's nature and potential. For Arnold, the United States showed both the strengths and weaknesses of a society where an untutored middle class assumed preponderance. Arnold used the verb "Americanise," a "short and significant expression which everyone understands," to describe this process by which a bourgeoisie obtained untrammeled power. If Britain experienced the rise of a similar bourgeois regime, "the dangers of America will really be ours." While the middle class advanced the causes of liberty and industry, it was also "conscious of no weakness, no inferiority" and lacked culture and dignity. It only felt "ardour for the ideas it already possesses"; like the Bourbon royal family, to paraphrase Talleyrand, it learned nothing and forgot nothing. If it came to power without undergoing some transformation for the better, this middle class "will rule [Britain] by their energy, but they will deteriorate it by their low ideals and want of culture."[10] In the British mind, these attributes became indissolubly associated with the New England Yankee, who was widely considered the most characteristic American type.

Starting from similar premises but reaching different conclusions, Mill's and Arnold's ruminations reveal that fixing the Americans relative to Britain proved problematic. They remind us, to quote John Brewer's review of Linda Colley's *Britons,* that "the Other was always within."[11] Those Britons who sought to evaluate the United States found themselves simultaneously dwelling on American distinctions while also recognizing American likenesses and Britain's destiny as an Americanized society. Within this strange relationship, British observers found both freedom and limits while developing various images of Americans. Observers could choose a variety of conventions and tropes according to the circumstances, their inclinations, and their experiences. At the same time, the instabilities of these conventions and tropes produced many contradictions and much ambivalence. As we shall see, in the years before the Civil War, this situation led British travelers to envision the United States as populated by a diverse collection of standard yet incongruous types. It was with these types in mind that Britons imagined the American conflict.

BRITAIN'S SEARCH FOR THE AMERICAN CHARACTER: YANKEES, WESTERNERS, AND SLAVEOWNERS

In Britain, at least until the mid-1850s, travel writers took the leading role in studying and producing images of the United States that commentators like Mill and Arnold employed in sweeping generalizations. Regardless of their particular interests and motives for traveling, authors of travel literature understood that the genre required informed and enlightened analysis of a national character that provided a glimpse of the British future. To catch this glimpse, writers did an American version of what Max Berger called the "Grand Tour."[12] They took the obligatory stroll down Broadway in New York; surveyed the magnificent spectacle of Niagara Falls; floated at a leisurely pace along the North's many canals; studied the alien rituals associated with America's unique boarding house culture; visited factories, waterworks, schools, lunatic asylums, prisons, and institutions for the blind; sized up the incomplete capital city of Washington, D.C.; observed the behavior of their fellow passengers as they covered vast distances by train; investigated the plantation system of the slave states; toured the hot springs of western Virginia; stayed in the small, languid port towns of the South; survived near-fatal mishaps that resulted from the fearsome combination of poor roads and reckless coach drivers; took steamboats down the Alabama and up the Mississippi; and viewed the great expanses of the Midwest's vast prairies. Traveling, when done in the purposeful fashion of most Victorian writers, was hard work. It is no wonder that one Georgian sizing up Alexander Mackay guessed, "I don't think you're in the commercial line . . . and you don't look as if you was travelling for pleasure neither."[13]

The writing itself proved no easier than the traveling. As they struggled to delineate the American national character, British authors issued occasionally incoherent, sometimes contradictory, and frequently ambivalent statements. For these reasons, Americans often appeared in travel literature as paradoxical figures. British visitors experienced great difficultics wrestling with the apparent conflicts and inconsistencies of the American character. These difficulties had much to do with both objective realities and subjective perceptions. There was the problem of generalizing about a diverse people strewn across a vast continent. Contradictions in representations of the American character also stemmed from the problem of American hybridity mentioned in the introduction. As Henry Hart Milman claimed in a *Quarterly Review* essay on Sir Charles Lyell's *A Second Visit to the United States of North America* (1849), America was a transatlantic England, "yet we can never forget that it is Transatlantic": "the points of resemblance and dissimilitude—of kindred, and of departure from the original stock—of national sympathies and national peculiarities—are equally striking; and give at once the interest of that which is native and familiar, and the freshness of a strange and untrodden land."[14] Thus, in the words of Linda Colley, Americans became to Britons a "mysterious and paradoxical people . . . engagingly similar but irritatingly different."[15] At the same time, representations of America were subject to the requirements of various domestic British needs.[16] As the 14th Earl of Derby (who visited the United States between 1824 and 1825 and led the Conservative Party during the Civil War) wrote, since the American Revolution the United States had become in Britain a theme of "political animosity, & the watchword of political parties," with Conservatives execrating the United States, Whigs conceding it possessed certain redeeming features, and Radicals praising it.[17] Social, economic, and cultural changes played a similar role in influencing British views of America.

When compounded with oscillations in the Anglo-American relationship (which went far beyond diplomatic relations), these changes led to fluctuations in the tone of British travel writing about America. In *American Social History as Recorded by British Travellers* (1923), probably the earliest scholarly study of British travel literature about America, Allan Nevins saw several distinct eras, each characterized by different outlooks and moods (for example, "Utilitarian Inquiry," "Tory Condescension," "Unbiassed Portraiture," etc.). While the tone might adjust fairly quickly, images of America were much slower to change; the weight of tradition and the exercise of power imposed a number of limits. Clearly, though, a mildness in the character of British commentary appeared to sink in during the 1850s as British observers self-consciously attempted to strengthen the transatlantic relationship.[18] British visitors still criticized the United States, but they took pains to avoid doing so in an offensive or acerbic manner. In *Letters from the Slave States* (1857), one of the better works of this period, James Stirling counseled the British press to embrace moderation when discussing America, but as *The Times* pointed out in a review of the book, such advice sounded "not a little singular" from an author who told "sensitive Americans many unpalatable truths."[19]

In the antebellum period, travel literature may have changed, but images of America manifested an underlying consistency. This consistency not only expressed itself across time, but also across the political spectrum. Travelers frequently concurred on Americans' attributes and deficiencies. Where they disagreed was on the relative importance of these attributes and deficiencies as they sought to gauge whether or not America had "succeeded." In other words, they much more frequently disagreed on the relative significance of various facts than on the facts themselves. Accordingly, this chapter surveys the multitudinous and often contradictory elements associated with various

American types rather than tracing the manner in which their relative importance fluctuated during the antebellum era.

Any analysis of antebellum British discussions about American national character must begin with the Yankee, widely considered a central figure in America's past, present, and future. Most travelers believed the middle-class democracy that gave the United States its character originated in New England, and the Yankee served as the foundation of the American bourgeois regime. Tocqueville argued that it was in New England "that the two or three main ideas which constitute the basis of the social theory of the United States were first combined." These principles spread to neighboring states, he believed, and would eventually come to dominate the entire country. As he put it, this civilization "appears to be the common standard, to which the whole nation will one day be assimilated."[20] For that reason, the appellation "Yankee" applied to New Englanders in particular and Americans as a whole. As Thomas Colley Grattan explained, "Although the genuine Yankee is only he who belongs to the part of the country called New England, the term 'Yankee,' as the cognomen of the entire national family, is now as appropriate to the natives of the Union at large as are the distinctive national appellations given to the people of other countries. Yankeeism is the general character of the Union. . . . Yankee connections and interests are spread throughout the land, and are gradually neutralizing all opposing forces."[21] The New England Yankee was not yet the sole type or character in America. Nonetheless, most British visitors saw New England as the cradle of American middle-class civilization and the Yankee as the quintessential American. As we have already seen, British commentators readily compared the Yankee's American middle-class culture to that of Britain's bourgeoisie. The Yankee, then, was a kind of Briton and therefore a known quantity. For this reason, he fell under the jurisdiction of British cultural norms. Yet his shortcomings, which were very much the same as those of the British middle class, contributed to the Yankee's difference, at least from the travelers' perspectives. On these grounds, British travel literature represented him as an exotic and oftentimes incomprehensible Other. Tocqueville noticed the irony of this situation, pointing out that while "the English make game of the manners of the Americans," it was "singular that most of the writers who have drawn these ludicrous delineations belonged themselves to the middle classes in England to whom the same delineations are exceedingly applicable." He continued, "these pitiless censors . . . do not perceive that they are deriding themselves, to the great amusement of the aristocracy of their own country."[22]

Explanations concerning the origins of the New England civilization that became the basis for American culture betrayed these tensions. British travel writers could not agree if continuity or a fundamental discontinuity characterized the emergence of this culture. Tocqueville was perhaps the most prominent and articulate exponent of the idea that American middle-class democracy was the product of a long, drawn-out process that had begun in Europe itself. He asserted that the English Puritans who first settled in the northeast were not only educated and propertied, but also possessed traditions of liberty and involvement in local government. They had no aristocratic element (and as he put it, "the soil of America was opposed to a territorial aristocracy"), while their religious doctrine "corresponded in many points with the most absolute democratic and republican theories." Through their combination of the "spirit of Religion and the spirit of Liberty," Tocqueville claimed, these original settlers of New England brought the "germ" of democracy to American shores.[23] The American Revolution, like all great modern revolutions, he believed, only intensified an existing desire for equality in America.[24] American history, like the history of the civilized world, revealed the gradual advance of democracy through the ages.

Not everyone agreed with this version of events. A number of British visitors claimed that a recent, sudden, and revolutionary process had thrown up American democracy. Up until the American Revolution, so the argument went, America had been governed by a moderate and conservative aristocracy. A combination of events, developments, and forces—including the emergence of "Gallic ideas," the overthrow of the monarchy, the widespread distribution of property, various laws, and social flux—had destroyed this de facto American aristocracy and produced a much more democratic world.[25] A middle-class civilization had now taken hold, and the prospects of an aristocratic resurrection were exceedingly bleak.

This disagreement concerning the origins of American civilization and the Yankee was not a matter of antiquarianism (in Tocqueville's case, America's Puritan, New England origins lay at the very foundation of his entire argument). Indeed, the dispute centered on whether the Yankee and the America he had created belonged to the mainstream of modern civilization's historical development or not. On one side, Tocqueville suggested that the rise of middle-class democracy was a natural and inevitable growth in the civilized world. On the other side, those who disagreed with Tocqueville on this issue portrayed the Yankee world as a contingent aberration produced suddenly by revolution and unfounded in the historic order of things. In other words, Yankee culture was strange, marginal, and not entirely civilized.

Of course, only the most bilious observers could claim that the United States had not made important contributions to the material progress of civilization. In that particular sense, Americans did indeed express what British visitors saw as the spirit of the age. Traveler after traveler marveled at American dynamism, ingenuity, optimism, and determination as farms and factories replaced prairies and forests at an extremely rapid pace. Visiting the United States upon the outbreak of the Civil War, Sir George Bell wrote a typical paean to American energy when he asked his readers to "see what has been done by perseverance and industry in two hundred years." America's hills and valleys were "covered with cattle, fruit trees, gardens, orchards, and abundant harvests of all sorts of the best" while the landscape was dotted with "a thousand prosperous and thriving towns . . . where wild forests and jungle grew fifty years ago." New York, the jewel in this crown of industry, possessed "beautiful streets, squares, churches, public buildings, and elegant houses; hotels not to be equaled in the world; shops containing merchandise from China, Java, Hindostan, Arabia, and all parts of the world. . . . [and] harbours all crowded with ships and steamers coming and going like bees on a sunny day."[26] It should come as no surprise that British visitors saw the United States in this light. As Arnold had claimed, one of the outstanding virtues of the middle class with which Britons identified America was industriousness.

If the Yankee's contribution to material progress was undoubted, his moral and cultural attainments, however, seemed suspect. Indeed, criticisms of moral and cultural shortcomings appeared with monotonous frequency when travelers analyzed American society. Discussions on this topic were characterized by a strange paradox not easily resolved: in the United States, society appeared both weak and strong. On the one hand, British visitors clearly believed that the relentless pursuit of the almighty dollar—a typical fault of the middle class—had led to the atomization of American society and threatened it with disintegration. George Combe remarked that such travelers "who blame the Americans for worshipping an aristocracy of wealth, appear to me to forget the practice at home," yet few shared his views.[27] Even Harriet Martineau, who often looked at Americans in a sympathetic light, declared that "an aristocracy of mere wealth is vulgar everywhere," but "in a republic, it is vulgar in the extreme."[28] Frances Trollope quoted an Englishman long resident in the United States who "had never overheard Americans conversing without the word DOLLAR being pronounced between them." Trollope went on to comment, "such unity of purpose, such sympathy of feeling, can, I believe, be found nowhere else, except, perhaps, in an ants' nest."[29] Ironically, according to many travelers, this particular unity of purpose led to the dissolution of society as it undermined the ideals that made men realize their common humanity. As each individual sought his own material gratification, so the argument went, he neglected his responsibilities to his fellow men. One of Dickens's greatest criticisms of Americans was the "Universal Distrust" that went hand in hand with "love of 'smart dealing.'"[30] James Silk Buckingham complained that "all the softer feelings of love, friendship, humanity, and benevolence . . . have become absorbed and overpowered by the intense love of gain . . . which swallows up every minor feeling, and leaves only a concentration of selfishness."[31] Among other things, that selfishness contributed to callousness and disorder as individuals engaged in a war of all against all.

On the other hand, many of the same British visitors believed an oppressive tyranny of the majority imposed a conformity and order that was characteristic of a bourgeois social dictatorship. Although Tocqueville did not believe a tyranny of the majority existed in the United States yet, he thought there was no guarantee against such a tyranny erecting itself in the near future. Already, he asserted, Americans had begun to suffer from a social and moral despotism that restricted independence of mind, curtailed freedom of discussion, and enforced conformity. British travelers dwelled relentlessly on this problem. Fanny Kemble complained how "vulgar dread of vulgar opinion" pervaded the United States, while Martineau worried about the "worship of Opinion" and "fear of singularity" that characterized American life.[32] One can detect the frustration of Dickens, a man habituated to caricaturing others, when he moaned that in America, "the people are all alike. . . . There is no diversity of character."[33] Grattan also complained that, "Character seemed moulded . . . into one regular standard. . . . One unvarying cut and pattern was seen throughout . . . and it was . . . of a very ordinary kind. . . . Equality was more present than liberty. . . . The movements of all were as nearly as possible alike. It was . . . a most curious specimen of living mechanism, completed and brought into action by the irresistible force of public opinion and general habit."[34] This phenomenon led to a leveling downward of standards. While explaining why President Andrew Jackson had felt compelled to admit riffraff to the White House for a presidential levee, Thomas Hamilton pointed out that "wealth and intelligence are compelled to bend to poverty and ignorance, to adopt their prejudices, to copy their manners, to submit to their government."[35] Similarly, Frederick Marryat complained bitterly that the following ethic seemed to govern American society: "if you cannot rise above another by your own merit, you can at least so far equalize your condition by pulling him down to your own level."[36] Conformity to mediocre standards ensued.

Tocqueville and other travel writers did not seem unduly troubled by the difficulty of reconciling the claim that American society had begun to descend into anarchy with the idea that this same society was characterized by a tyranny of the majority. Tocqueville tried to square the circle by arguing that the relationship between tyranny and anarchy was sequential, not simultaneous: tyranny led its victims (often a minority) to rebel, giving rise to anarchy.[37] British travelers, many of whom had read Tocqueville, did not, however, follow his lead. It was entirely conceivable to these authors that a disorderly, laissez-faire, dog-eat-dog world could exist comfortably within a middle-class social and cultural dictatorship. One has only to look at Thomas Carlyle's *Past and Present* (1843), John Stuart Mill's *On Liberty* (1859), or Matthew Arnold's *Culture and Anarchy* (1867–1868) to see that such ideas were prevalent in the minds of Britain's leading intellectuals throughout the early and mid-Victorian period. Even if contemporaries could reconcile these visions of American society (and bourgeois society as well) as weak and strong, this reconciliation did nothing to erase the sense that such a society lacked all the elements that constituted a true civilization.

The perception that the United States suffered from the typical faults of bourgeois society colored the investigation of all topics associated with American culture, which was central to travel literature's task of analyzing national character. Indeed, British travelers almost universally assumed that American standards in this area were not as high as they could be. At the same time, however, their views were also dogged by contradictions, paradoxes, and exceptions as visitors struggled with the difficulty of fixing the American character.

Criticisms of American culture were of long standing. In 1820, Sidney Smith, the prominent reviewer for the *Edinburgh Review,* wrote a blistering criticism of American culture:

> During the thirty or forty years of their independence, they [the Americans] have done nothing for the sciences, for the arts, for literature, or even for the statesmanlike studies of politics or political economy. . . . In the four quarters of the globe, who reads an American book? Or goes to an American play? Or looks at an American picture or statue? What does the world yet owe to American physicians or surgeons? What new substances have their chemists discovered, or what old ones have they analysed? What new constellations have been discovered by the telescopes of Americans? What have they done in the mathematics?[38]

Echoing Smith, Basil Hall asserted that nearly all of American letters, art, and science "still continues to be imparted from us."[39] The assumption was that the exclusively practical bent of the Yankee middle-class mind militated against the emergence of high culture. *Blackwood Edinburgh Magazine*'s review of Tocqueville's first volume claimed Americans consisted of "*one industrious class*" in which "all understanding higher than a mechanical one" had been "banished . . . from [the] soil."[40] For this reason, as Dickens commented, "It would be well . . . for the American people as a whole, if they loved the Real less, and the Ideal somewhat more. It would be well, if there were . . . a wider cultivation of what is beautiful, without being eminently and directly useful."[41] In this kind of world, Mackay commented, "the really intellectual man holds a position of comparative isolation."[42] Moreover, if the tastes of the many dictated the nature of American literature, so the argument went, little could be expected from this field. In a comment that echoed Tocqueville, Martineau declared that "if the American nation be judged by its literature, it may be pronounced to have no mind at all."[43] Yet the very same pages produced much evidence that implicitly contradicted these claims. British visitors frequently provided descriptions of interviews with notable American statesmen, authors, and scientists. Almost every visitor admitted to encountering educated, intelligent, and well-mannered American gentlemen.

Ironically enough, it is hard to escape the conclusion that these very American elites supplied British visitors with the many criticisms of American middle-class culture that appeared in British books.

British criticisms of American education reflected the same types of criticisms and contradictions. British visitors were impressed by the public school system in New England and the sheer number of people who knew the three "Rs." Grattan commented that "almost all native-born Americans are able at least to read, write, and cipher, while the great majority have received much more than . . . those primary acquirements." He judged that "education is the strongest point in the social condition of America."[44] Lyell concurred, writing that Americans could feel justly proud of their public education because "it is the most original thing which America has yet produced."[45] At the same time, they found American notions of education circumscribed by a lack of interest in any intellectual pursuit that did not have immediate practical applications. For instance, Hamilton could not foresee America "becoming a mental benefactor to the world" because "while the steps of youth are studiously directed to the base of the mountain of knowledge, no facilities have been provided for scaling its summit." "Not only is there an entire absence of learning, in the higher sense of the term," he continued, "but an absolute want of the material from which alone learning can be extracted."[46] Even those who sought to scale Hamilton's "summit" by obtaining a post-secondary education came in for criticism. As Sir John Acton pointed out after visiting Harvard College, "Nothing is studied for its own sake, but only as it will be useful in making a practical man." For that reason, Americans pursued useful studies like rhetoric and some of the sciences, but otherwise "there is no demand for learning."[47] In other words, American education responded exclusively to bourgeois needs, and high culture—often in the form of "classics, science, the fine arts, letters, taste, and refinements," as Hall described them—suffered accordingly.[48] Yet, again, the obviously large number of educated Americans whom British visitors accepted as gentlemen made many of these assertions questionable.

British travelers' attitudes toward American religion betrayed a similar character, although these were complicated by British discussions concerning the utility of an established church. American religion reflected the weaknesses of American bourgeois society as a whole in which a tyranny of the majority and anarchy existed side by side. On the one hand, Harriet Martineau claimed American ministers suffered from an "idolatry of opinion" that led them to adapt "the truth to the minds of the hearers."[49] Likewise, Lyell worried that ministers were too dependent on their flocks and felt compelled to defer "outwardly to many theological notions of the vulgar with which they have no real sympathy."[50] Yet, on the other hand, some of the same travelers claimed that outlandish cults had proliferated because many ill-educated people, to quote Lyell, had learned "a docile, submissive, child-like deference to the authority of churchmen."[51] The relentless pullulation of sects, including groups like the Mormons, Millerites, and Shakers, had led to the dissemination of what British visitors believed was much nonsense. Moreover, these visitors also recoiled from what they saw as the dangerous effusiveness associated with such groups. Buckingham wrote that a Methodist revival "was like being in an assembly of maniacs," and Lyell complained that such events drove people "to the very verge of distraction" with the "application of such violent stimulants."[52]

British travelers' representations of American manners betrayed many of the same tendencies we have seen in discussions of other elements associated with American culture. Exceptionally, there was much more explicit disagreement and ambivalence on this issue than on others. Frances Trollope famously condemned Americans out of hand: "I do not like them. I do not like their principles, I do not like their manners, I do not like their opinions."[53] If Trollope's wholesale denunciation of American manners was unusual, many travelers still frequently complained about undue familiarity, boastfulness, hypocritical distinctions, nasty habits (namely tobacco-chewing), the absence of standards, and a host of other behaviors associated with provincial, middle-class boorishness. Tocqueville believed that as a rule everyone's status in a democracy was doubtful, which led to "pride but seldom dignity of manners." Widespread mobility also contributed to a lack of coherent standards. In the end, democratic manners were mediocre, like everything else in middle-class America; they missed "the coarse oaths of the populace [and] choice expressions of the nobility."[54]

Such sentiments, however, did not characterize all of British travel literature. A number of travelers positively praised American manners. Dickens, who criticized the United States harshly in a number of areas, made an exception of manners. "Travellers," he wrote, "have grossly exaggerated American rudeness and obtrusion. . . . I have never once encountered a man, woman, or child, who has asked me a rude question, or made a rude remark."[55] Even more interesting in this case (as in others), however, is the extent to which British comments were fundamentally conflicted on this subject. Martineau believed "The manners of the Americans (in America) are the best I ever saw," yet she felt the fear of opinion in the United States produced a "want of social confidence" that was "little short of disgusting."[56] Buckingham "felt . . . perpetual disgust" at the many infractions of etiquette that he witnessed during his travels, but when he measured the manners of Americans by their intent, he found them very good: "[Americans] are almost uniformly decorous, civil, obliging, willing to yield in any manner for the accommodation of others, quiet, orderly, and inoffensive; and neither at the hotels, nor in the steamboats, or on railroads, is the ear so often offended as it is in England, by oaths, vociferations, quarrels, complaints, bickerings among equals, and abuse of inferiors."[57]

It was this vexed subject of manners more than any other that brought home to many British visitors the overall difficulties of assessing American society. Although he was repulsed by much of what he saw, Buckingham refused to condemn American manners because "that cannot be *vulgar* which is almost universally practiced in any nation. . . . And that cannot be *rude,* which does not originate in a disregard to the feelings of others."[58] In other words, different standards obtained in different countries. Likewise, Hall, a conservative writer who disliked American voluntarism, noted the deficiencies of American education, and decried the state of American politics admitted that on the subject of American manners, "It is scarcely fair to judge one nation by the conventional standards of another."[59] This question of standards was troubling in that it got to the heart of problems associated with the Anglo-American relationship and hybridity. If Americans and their manners were really so different, the Americans were not British, they were not liable to judgment by British standards, and they therefore fell outside of British cultural jurisdiction.

Although the middle-class Yankee character had begun to prevail in the United States and fundamentally shaped American development, it had not completed its conquest. A number of other distinct types still remained on the American scene. One of these was the westerner. In his work on the European image of the American frontier, aptly entitled *Land of Savagery, Land of Promise* (1981), Ray Allen Billington asserted that Europeans believed that the characteristics that set westerners apart from Americans "were exactly those that distinguished Americans from Europeans, appearing now in exaggerated form." These characteristics included hospitality, materialism, wanderlust, inventiveness, optimism, and a strong work ethic. In other words, to quote Lord Bryce, "the West was the most distinctly American part of America."[60] If the Yankee's claim to civilization was somewhat questionable, then, the westerner's was even more tenuous. Although the westerner performed a great service for civilization on the frontier, he was suspect for a number of reasons. Despite his important contributions, the westerner was ephemeral and in other ways marginal. Unlike the Yankee, he did not belong to a well-defined ethnic group with its own history and culture, however flawed. The westerner had no pedigree, past, or tradition; his culture consisted of no culture at all. At the same time, he had no future. British travelers foresaw the time when Americans would conquer the frontier, when, for instance, the Mississippi River valley would become the actual, not potential, center of the world. By that point, the westerner would disappear, replaced in all likelihood by the Yankee, who would bring his civilization. Most important of all in this context, the westerner was tainted by the process of conquering nature. Mackay voiced the concern among many observers that serving as a missionary for progress took its toll on the westerner: "As man civilises the wilderness, the wilderness more or less brutalizes him. In thus elevating nature he degrades himself. And thus it is with the pioneers of civilisation in the American wilds."[61] Not all westerners were the same, but they did share this ironic predicament of serving as the chief agents of spreading civilization even as the task called their own civilization into question.

British travelers detected several distinct types of westerners. George Featherstonhaugh's *Excursion Through the Slave States* (1844), which detailed travels through the Arkansas Territory in 1834 and 1835, provides perhaps the clearest and most entertaining sense of the differences between these types. For Britons, the West was by far the most "exotic" part of America, and Featherstonhaugh's account, like many that described this region, adopted a tone similar to that employed by travelers in Africa and the Middle East. From this perspective, the West was populated by miscellaneous tribes of white men who, like the Yankee, were simultaneously knowable and incomprehensible. Each also represented different degrees of civilization. The first consisted of backwoodsmen, hunters, and squatters. A few travelers, inspired by James Fenimore Cooper's romanticism, insisted on portraying these frontier folk as noble savages of a sort—strong, independent, honest, forthright, and without affectation. Most British visitors, however, expressed a low opinion of these people because they had almost completely surrendered to nature and contributed nothing to civilization. Living mainly by hunting, their food was inedible, their housing squalid, their personal hygiene disgusting, and their health precarious. Happily, they provided excellent subject matter for humorous anecdotes. In the Arkansas backcountry, Featherstonhaugh encountered a remarkable and decidedly unfeminine Mrs. Barkman who chewed tobacco, smoked a pipe, drank whiskey, and swore like a backwoodsman, "doing quite as much vulgarity as four male blackguards could do." Her brother, who had been raised on "fat bar's meat," was dressed in the skins of animals he had killed and lived "*al fresco*" in a wretched, unfinished cabin.[62] Typically, Featherstonhaugh claimed, such people did no farming, keeping only a cow that emerged from the woods every so often for salt and who yielded only a "teaspoonful of milk." A typical visit to such a household led to the following encounter:

> When you arrive, the owner of the mansion is not at home, and in his place you find six or seven ragged wild-looking imps, and a skinny, burnt up, dirty female who tells you that he is "gone to help a neighbor to hunt up an old painter that's been arter all the pigs; he ain't been hum in a week, and I reckon he's stopt somewhar to help shuck the corn. . . . We han't got nothing in the house but a little corn that I pounds as I uses it, and a couple of raccoons jist to sarve us till he gets back."[63]

In this case, British readers were brought face to face with the incongruous image of white people as savages.

Second, and more threatening, were the dangerous riffraff—dishonest peddlers, con artists, outlaws, gamblers, bargemen, and the like—who sought refuge from the law in a territory where proper society was not well established. Especially appalled by the state of things in Little Rock, Arkansas, Featherstonhaugh asserted that the region was infested with "many timid and nervous persons" against whom the laws of the United States and Mexico "had a grudge," including, "*Gentlemen,* who had taken the liberty to imitate the signature of other persons; *bankrupts,* who were not disposed to be plundered by their creditors; [and] *homicides, horse-stealers,* and *gamblers.*"[64] These miscreants had erected a paradoxical society of sorts that subscribed to antisocial tenets. As Featherstonhaugh explained, "where an absolute majority within a community consisted of criminals, gamblers, speculators, and men of broken fortunes, with no law to restrain them, no obligation to conceal their vices, no motive to induce them to appear devout or act with sobriety, it was not surprising that such men should indulge openly in their propensities."[65] Like the savage Mrs. Barkman and her brother, this society of criminals living according to their own lights could exercise only a dubious claim to civilization.

The third type of westerner, and more promising for the future of civilization than the others, was the farmer. On his travels, Featherstonhaugh met a Mr. Prior, whom he found an agreeable and "refined" companion. Eventually they reached Prior's farm, which Featherstonhaugh described as "truly an oasis in the desert." Prior had cleared several acres of forest around his "villa" and a series of detached buildings. He had laid a fence around it, using more fencing to subdivide his property neatly. Featherstonhaugh could hear a piano playing within the main house and marveled that such a thing was possible "within ten miles of a Mexican province." Prior had obviously exerted the necessary effort to conquer nature. Featherstonhaugh commented that serious farmers in Arkansas "are hard-working enterprising men, always busy, fencing, ploughing, chopping timber, setting traps for the wolves, hunting the panthers that destroy their calves and swine, and are continually occupied without a moment's relaxation."[66] More than anyone else on the frontier, these men resembled the Yankees of the East.

Yet these farmers could not be Yankees because the West had its own distinct atmosphere. In the West, where civilization was incomplete, according to British observers, freedom and struggle characterized daily life. A new and unsettled society weighed lightly on the individual who pursued his own interests by his own lights. This freedom contributed to the peripatetic nature of westerners (another feature that made them appear somewhat untrustworthy in British eyes). Instead of choosing the advantages of progress associated with a settled civilization, they constantly moved forward with the frontier. This freedom also led to a kind of forthrightness and honesty found nowhere else; everyone could be himself. The West was without pretension, artifice, or hypocrisy. Martineau praised the "universal freedom of manners" in the West, claiming, "the people of the west have a comfortable self-complacency, equally different from the arrogance of the south, and the timidity of the north. . . . They are the freest people in America."[67] James Alexander advised the conceited youth to make a tour of the American frontier because "Affectation is unknown there, and he will soon acquire a natural manner of acting and thinking."[68] At the same time, however, the unremitting struggle against the land, Indians, wild animals, and criminals made the westerner a hard, violent, and—despite Mr. Prior's piano—generally uncultured man. Minor disputes often culminated in violence, and everyone felt he had to stick up for himself to avoid being trampled. The hardships of frontier life led to what Featherstonhaugh referred to as an "indifference of everybody to what we call personal comforts."[69] There was little room, then, for music, literature, or the arts in the West. If, as Alexander commented, "the people of the West are very plain in their manners," they also "dislike all pretensions to singularity, or to superior refinement"—hardly a situation under which high culture could thrive.[70]

The westerner did not present as much of a challenge to Yankee values as the southerner and his distinct culture did. The southerner had a long and proud history, like the Yankee, that produced a traditional society based partly on time-tested principles. But like the westerner, the southerner appeared to have no future; from the British perspective, the march of progress would probably doom slavery and therefore the South. Although British visitors could not foresee the circumstances of slavery's collapse, they believed it was destined to fail because it ran so contrary to the course of progress. As Martineau wrote, "slavery was not always an anomaly; but it has become one. Its doom is therefore sealed; and its duration is now merely a question of time."[71] They could not predict how it would end, but they were united in condemning it out of hand; there was no waffling here about the need to develop new standards of measurement as with the Yankee.[72] Indeed, the frequency with which most British travelers employed elements of free labor ideology's criticism of slavery is impressive. From this perspective, slavery was, to use William Seward's concise statement, "morally unjust, politically unwise, and socially pernicious."[73] With its chief social institution characterized and corrupted by coercion, the South appeared uncivilized in its own way. Indeed, the prevalence of violence gave the South something in common with the West. Despite British travelers' near-universal hostility to slavery, the South elicited mixed feelings. If southern slavery served as an obstacle to the moral and material progress that otherwise characterized the civilized world, it also contributed to great refinement and culture unattainable elsewhere in the United States. It was this refinement, produced largely by the widely perceived social inequality of the South, that set this region apart from bourgeois conformist New England and the rude, egalitarian West. Like the other types, then, the southerner was British and not British, civilized and not civilized, known and unknown.

Visitors could not clearly establish if the South's aristocratic society produced slavery or if slavery produced the South's aristocratic society. Tocqueville unequivocally defended the latter proposition. He claimed the introduction of slavery was "the main circumstance which has exercised so prodigious an influence on the character, the laws, and all the future prospects of the South." "The influence of slavery," he continued, "united to the English character, explains the manner and the social conditions of the Southern States."[74] A number of writers, particularly those who believed in the Cavalier myth of southern origin (often peddled by southerners themselves), thought otherwise.[75] These authors believed the South's Cavalier society preceded slavery and that southern aristocrats had adopted the peculiar institution to sustain their way of life in the New World. In what was an otherwise hard-headed, sensible, and perceptive look at the South, Stirling's work sentimentally stressed these aristocratic origins in determining the nature of southern society. Virginia and the Carolinas, he asserted, had been "settled mainly by English gentry, with a sprinkling even of the nobility." These people brought their "aristocratic feelings," "aristocratic laws," and aristocratic spirit. Stirling continued by claiming that the "aristocratic nature of Southern society, by dishonouring labour, has tended, even more than the climate of the South, to perpetuate slavery." It was, then, the "aristocratic tendencies of the people that preserved slavery in the South when it was abandoned in the North."[76]

Whatever the case, from the British vantage point the relationship between slaveowner and slave proved central in defining the South's distinct culture and society while explaining the region's strengths and weaknesses. This relationship produced a society that was fundamentally violent. Indeed, the frequency with which southerners employed coercion against their slaves inured them to violence in all of their relationships. Buckingham attributed "the frequent affrays, duels, street-fights, shootings, stabbings, and assassinations" in the South to the influence of slavery.[77] Stirling believed the connection between master and slave was similar to that produced between lord and serf in Europe: "there is the same imperious will, the same impatience of restraint, the same proneness to anger and ferocious strife."[78] Southern "unconsciousness of guilt" led Martineau to state that "one of the absolutely inevitable results of slavery is a disregard of human rights; an inability even to comprehend them."[79] Mackay commented, "It is only under a system [slavery], which promotes a laxity of habits, blunts the moral perceptions, engenders leisure, and fosters pride, that could arise those quick resentments, that morbid sensitiveness, that proneness to quarrel, and that indifference to human life."[80] In his chapter on slavery, Dickens presented page after page of runaway slave advertisements that detailed the brutality of slavery (much like those found in abolitionist tracts), along with newspaper clippings describing routine violence among whites whose character "was formed in slave districts, and brutalized by slave customs."[81] Buckingham presented a short tale illustrating the dreadful influence of slavery on southern whites. A Louisville tailor and a Mississippi judge named Wilkinson fell into a dispute over the "fit of a coat." The argument grew in acrimony until the judge brought his brother and a friend to town. The tailor rounded up his allies, a hatter and a barkeeper, and threatened to whip the judge. The six men settled their dispute in a bar, where the hatter and barkeeper met their demise, the Mississippians "leaving the one with his bowels protruding from his body on the bar-room floor, and the other weltering in his blood." The judge and his accomplices went on trial for murder. Their defense attorney argued before the jury that the "law of Kentucky instinct," a law not found in statute, but "a law that emanates from the hearts of the people of Kentucky, and is sanctioned by their heads," dictated that "the man who is attempted to be cowhided, not only may, but must . . . kill the man who attempts to degrade him." As Buckingham explained, the cowhide was "employed only to correct slaves." A whipping was the ultimate degradation for a white man, and he was compelled to avoid it all costs, even if that meant the use of deadly force.[82] Wilkinson and his confederates were found not guilty.

While British visitors wrote much about the *slave system,* they had little to say about individual *slaves.* Encounters with slaveowners and poor whites received much attention, but accounts rarely detailed interactions with slaves.[83] There are a number of reasons for this omission. First, British travelers visited the South as the guests of slaveowners, and it is hard to see how they could have managed tours through slave districts otherwise. Such a circumstance placed visitors in a delicate situation. Slaveowners carefully controlled access to slaves during such visits, especially since they suspected all Britons of abolitionism. At the same time, following a universal convention of their craft, travel writers sought to avoid abusing the hospitality extended to them by their hosts. Writers rarely published descriptions of specific events that could reflect badly on the slaveowners who had accommodated them. Consequently, as Fanny Kemble pointed out, "it is morally impossible for any Englishman going into the Southern states except as a *resident*, to know any thing whatever of the real condition of the slave population."[84] Second, British visitors clearly found the raw experience of slavery extremely disturbing and uncomfortable; the accounts of those who recorded their reactions indicates why many probably chose not to subject themselves to these unsettling situations. While attending a slave auction in Washington, D.C., Hall "felt my pulse accelerating at each successive offer, and my cheek getting flushed—for the scene was so very new that I almost fancied I was dreaming." When called up to make a bid, Hall blurted out "with more asperity than good sense or good breeding,—No! No! I thank God we don't do such things in my country!"[85] Instead of undergoing such an ordeal, it was much easier, like Grattan, to "consider slavery as an abstract moral question" because such a stance made close observation of slaves unnecessary.[86]

Even if they often conceived of the slave as an abstraction, British visitors recognized his real impact on southern society, particularly the extent to which his degradation led ineluctably to the degradation of all labor. While discussing slavery, Martineau presented it as an axiom that "wherever there is a servile class, work is considered a disgrace, unless it bears some other name, and is of an exclusive character."[87] Fanny Kemble wrote, "Industry, man's crown of honor elsewhere, is here his badge of utter degradation; and so comes all by which I am here [in Georgia] surrounded—pride, profligacy, idleness, cruelty, cowardice, ignorance, squalor, dirt, and ineffable abasement."[88] Buckingham believed the "slave system" was a "powerful cause" of the "general indolence and dirtiness of the whites, among the farmers and peasantry of the South," because industry was "distasteful" to this class.[89] Indeed, British travelers believed that slavery had produced a class in the South referred to variously as "poor whites," "white trash," "pinelanders," "mean whites," or "crackers" that found labor abhorrent. Kemble described this population as "the direct growth of slavery"; they would not work as it "would reduce them to an equality with the abhorred Negroes." She described them as "the most degraded race of human beings claiming an Anglo-Saxon origin that can be found on the face of the earth—filthy, lazy, ignorant, brutal, proud, penniless savages" who fiercely defended slavery "because it is the barrier that divides the black and white races, at the foot of which they lie wallowing in unspeakable degradation."[90] Stirling found the emergence of this class "the most remarkable and important feature of Southern civilization," and attributed its origins simply to the fact that "the white poor man disdains to 'work like a nigger.'"[91] Although Hall "was well satisfied" with them because they had "less of that frigid, uninviting formality" and "sometimes understood a joke," Buckingham described them as "generally dissipated, their language coarse, and their amusements barbarous." Overall, Buckingham found they were "reckless, dirty, dissipated, and vulgar."[92] Here again, as with certain types of westerners, British readers were brought face to face with white men as savages.

This aversion to labor contributed to an economic backwardness that was immediately evident to most British travelers in southern landscapes.[93] Tocqueville famously contrasted the left and right banks of the Ohio River in pointing out slavery's affects. On the Kentucky side of the river, "the population is rare," there were "half-desert fields," "the primaeval forest recurs at every turn," and "society seems to be asleep, man to be idle, and nature alone offers a scene of activity and of life." In free Ohio, however, "a confused hum . . . proclaims the presence of industry; the fields are covered with abundant harvests; the elegance of the dwellings announces the taste and activity of the labourer; and man appears to be in the enjoyment of that wealth and contentment which is the reward of labour."[94] This type of comparison became a familiar trope in British travel literature. Along with making the very same comparison between Kentucky and Ohio, Buckingham also juxtaposed eastern and western Virginia in the same manner, to the former's disadvantage.[95] In a similar vein, Stirling compared Illinois and Georgia.[96] In fact, British visitors appeared to be particularly struck by such comparisons, because they commented relentlessly on the South's dilapidated appearance. Traveling between Washington, D.C., and Fredericksburg, Virginia, Dickens observed,

> In this district, as in all others where slavery sits brooding . . . there is an air of ruin and decay abroad, which is inseparable from the system. The barns and outhouses are mouldering away; the sheds are patched and half roofless; the log cabins . . . are squalid in the last degree. There is no look of decent comfort anywhere. The miserable stations by the railway side; the great wild wood-yards, whence the engine is supplied with fuel; the negro children rolling on the ground before the cabin doors, with dogs and pigs; the biped beasts of burden slinking past: gloom and dejection are upon them all.[97]

Mackay likewise commented, "It requires no anti-slavery predilections, no jaundiced eye, no European prejudices, to recognise the two states of activity and inertness between which the Potomac intervenes, like an impassable gulf." The difference between the North and Virginia, he believed, was "as great as is the change from the activity of Lancashire, to the languor and inertness of Bavaria." Virginia, he lamented, "seems to be afflicted with some ineradicable blight."[98]

Slavery and the South's aversion to labor also produced a fundamentally unequal society that suffered from a lack of social mobility. Stirling argued that unlike Britain or the North, the South could not recruit an "easy, affluent, well-educated, and law-abiding class" from the lower orders because "men of industry, integrity, and intelligence" could not "rise to a condition of independence."[99] For all its talk of democracy and republicanism, the South was fundamentally aristocratic, hierarchical, and static. As Tocqueville commented, if the North possessed "the characteristic good and evil qualities of the middle classes," the South had the "prejudices, weaknesses, and the magnanimity of all aristocracies."[100] This aristocracy dominated a society that was fundamentally unequal in power, wealth, and status. Stirling commented that in the South, unlike the North, there was not "the same appearance of equably disseminated comfort" because one missed "the neat farm-houses that dot the landscape of New England, and speak of comfort, equality, and intelligence." The North, he continued, possessed "a population of comfortable yeomen" while the South had "rich planters and poverty-stricken peasants." The South, then, was an "Aristocracy, nay, an Oligarchy; for in addition to aristocratic feeling, there is also an anti-democratic inequality of fortune." Under this semi-feudal scheme of things, "the South is ruled by its leaders; the poor of the community, the 'white trash,' go with their lords."[101]

Despite these criticisms, almost all travelers testified to the superior refinement and cultivation of southern planters, whom they often likened to English gentry. Grattan claimed that the terror and violence that characterized the relationship between master and slave made it impossible to speak of aristocratic refinement in the South. "When we look at an American cotton-planter, or tobacco-grower," he argued, "in the midst of his brutified and trembling slaves, how repugnant is the picture to our sense of all that is ennobling and affecting!" Indeed, the so-called southern aristocracy was nothing but "cattle-dealers, without any of the attributes of the nobility they would emulate."[102] Most British travelers, however, did not agree; even those who expressed criticisms of slavery felt compelled to concede the merits of the southern aristocracy. Lyell was impressed by the "perfect ease and politeness," "warm and generous openness of character," and "dignity of manner, without stiffness which is most agreeable" that he noticed among southern planters, whom he compared to "English country gentlemen."[103] Buckingham remarked that "the graceful ease and quiet elegance of the southern families make their visitors feel that they are in the society of well-bred and recognized gentlemen and ladies."[104] These gentlemen and ladies were more "thoroughly educated in the classics and polite literature" and "so much more polished in their manners" than northerners. Hamilton believed southern gentlemen distinguished themselves by their "high-mindedness, generosity, and hospitality."[105] On estates that resembled English manors, even a visitor with radical proclivities like Mackay found that "one much more frequently meets with the conventional lady and gentleman in the slave, than in the free states; the latter being not only more polished in manner than his northern countryman, but also presenting a higher standard of intellectual cultivation." Mackay attributed this difference between South and North to the fact that "in the latter, activity takes the place of refinement; in the former, refinement takes the place of activity." Mackay added, however, that "In this one particular of refinement alone is the result of slavery on southern society in the least degree favourable."[106] Even Kemble conceded that slaveowners possessed better manners than New Englanders (at least on the surface), but she dismissed this attribute by claiming that "good manners have an undue value for Englishmen."[107]

In the British mind, the South was a land of gross contradictions. If aristocracy and slavery were intimately intertwined in the British mind, they were also fundamentally incompatible. Stirling found aristocratic refinement and the barbarity of slavery on which it rested irreconcilable. He argued that "The governing class of the south is too highly-civilized to co-exist with slavery. . . . Slavery and high civilization are a contradiction, a monstrosity, an absurdity. . . . Strangers have concluded that the South was barbarous, because she holds by a barbarous institution, while the South herself exalts slavery as a powerful element of her high civilization. Both are wrong: the South is a refined community, but it is in spite of slavery; and the contradiction between her social system and her state of culture is so gross that it cannot long continue."[108] Like a number of thoughtful travelers who looked to the future (except for Martineau, who claimed a beneficent American public opinion would compel the peaceful abolition of slavery), Stirling believed slavery would probably collapse in some sort of bloody cataclysm. Slaves, he thought, had already shown signs of increased restlessness. With time, they would grow more violent. Slaveowners had already responded to this violence with more repression, but Stirling found such a policy misguided: "Curfew laws, passes, increased police, 'mounted patrols'—all will not avail so long as the generating cause of discontent exists. The only way to extinguish slave disaffection is to extinguish slavery." Stirling saw no reason why white southerners could not get on with liberated blacks with the passage of time, but he also understood that slaveowners were unwilling to part with their slaves. If southerners did not find a solution to slavery, he predicted, "God will find one for them, and that, trust me, will be a violent one." For that reason, he likened the South to "one of her cotton steamers": "Filled from the hold to the topmost deck with the most inflammable matter; everything heated up to the burning point, a furious draught blowing from end to end, and a huge high-pressure boiler in her belly, pressed to bursting."[109]

Mackay foresaw a similar situation developing. Using a metaphor of his own, he claimed slavery was the "Ireland of the Americans."[110] The "antipathy of race" along with uncertainty about what do with liberated blacks made it unlikely that southerners would ever emancipate their slaves. Whether southerners freed their slaves or not, "the war of races is an event in the certain future." Mackay believed blacks would certainly lose such a war and suffer expulsion from the continent, but only after "untold miseries on all sides."[111]

Tocqueville served as the inspiration for much of this thinking; both Stirling and Mackay had clearly read *Democracy in America.* Tocqueville believed that as slavery retreated southward in the face of progress, the Gulf States would become inundated with slaves. Southerners in these areas faced a difficult dilemma: "either to emancipate the negroes, and to intermingle with them; or, remaining isolated from them, to keep them in a state of slavery for as long as possible." The South had obviously opted for the latter, but Tocqueville believed such a course was unsustainable in the long run. In the civilized world, slavery was besieged by Christianity, the doctrines of political economy, and democratic liberty. Moreover, while conflict between southern whites and blacks was perhaps "remote," it was also "inevitable." "By the choice of the master, or by the will of the slave," slavery would cease; "and in either case great calamities may be expected to ensue."[112]

WORK WHICH CANNOT BE REGARDED AS BADLY DONE?: ASSESSING BRITISH TRAVEL LITERATURE ABOUT ANTEBELLUM AMERICA

In a review of Said's *Orientalism,* Albert Hourani defended Orientalists by claiming that they had "produced a body of work which cannot be regarded as badly done."[113] Determining the extent to which this description fits British travel literature about America is difficult. Writing in 1837, Martineau seemed to indicate that British travel literature complacently believed that it had "once for all understood" America, but a number of her contemporaries clearly found this body of work repetitive and unconvincing.[114] As early as 1829, Sir John Barrow complained in the *Quarterly Review* that although "a vast number of travellers have visited America of late years . . . none of them have contributed to inspire any great confidence in the European public."[115] Some years later, Thomas Hood was still complaining in the *New Monthly Magazine and Humorist* that "numerous had been the writers on the land of the stars and stripes . . . without hitting . . . the jack." In fact, an "impartial account of America and Americans was still to seek."[116] This strange situation where literature repeated itself despite (or because of) a sense that it was somehow inadequate certainly seems consistent with Homi Bhabha's claims about hybridity. British writers sought to capture, for instance, the

Yankee as an expression of power (his manners and mental peculiarities were thoroughly understood), but the Yankee had to remain unknown to justify the exercise of that power (his actions were at times incomprehensible). The only way to resolve this contradiction and the unease that arose from it was through constant repetition of received truths.

One cannot attribute the shortcomings and contradictions of British travel literature about America exclusively to the instabilities associated with British discourses about the United States. Even contemporary Britons realized that the task of delineating the American character was an extraordinarily difficult one. As William Empson pointed out in the *Edinburgh Review,* "a theory of national character, deduced as the positive effects of certain causes, is perhaps the most complicated and baffling subject which man in a state of society presents."[117] In any event, British authors were not equal to this arduous enterprise because they did not devote the necessary time, effort, and thought to it. Unlike Orientalists, who "made a career" of the East, most British authors did not make a career of America. The study of America became just one of many projects undertaken in the course of their lives. Many assumed that the similarities between Americans and Britons meant that observation of the United States required no specialized training or intellectual apparatus.[118] To put it another way, if familiarity often bred contempt for Americans, it also bred contempt for the serious study of the United States. Harriet Martineau was perhaps the only British visitor who attempted to study the United States in a systematic, objective, scientific, and rigorous manner.[119] Martineau believed that America ought to become one of the primary subjects of the new field of sociology and, at one point, was prepared to devote her life to that pursuit.[120] Like everyone else, however, she moved on to other endeavors.[121]

Oddly, it was Tocqueville, a Frenchman writing for other Frenchmen, who exerted the greatest influence on both British writers' and readers' perceptions of America.[122] Tocqueville worked on *Democracy in America* for almost ten years, and this book reveals what was possible if an author set out to make a serious study of the United States. In comparison to this work (and that of the Orientalists for that matter), the great bulk of British travel literature about America seems slapdash, amateurish, and haphazard. For years afterward, educated Britons considered *Democracy in America* the gold standard of American studies. As the *Quarterly Review* commented in 1864, "Tocqueville gave to the study of American character and institutions as many years as English tourists give months," and the result was that "his insight into and comprehension of his subject were unrivalled." At the same time, the *Quarterly Review* remarked that "it is far from refreshing to reflect that out of the few French books on America there is hardly a bad one; while out of the many English books on the same subject there is hardly a good one."[123]

Clearly, Tocqueville's background as a Frenchman was an important source of *Democracy in America*'s strengths. Basil Hall, author of *Travels in North America in the Years 1827 and 1828* (1829), knew Tocqueville and touched on these strengths in a review he wrote of the French aristocrat's work in the *Quarterly Review*. First, Hall argued, Tocqueville assumed nothing and took nothing for granted. The institutions, practices, and language of the United States were so different from those of France that Tocqueville did not make the inapt comparisons so prevalent among British travelers. "The Englishman never suspects that he is taking up a wrong idea"; Hall observed, "the Frenchman distrusts himself, and inquires." Since everything looked somewhat familiar to the Englishman, he facilely missed "those very points of distinction upon which the real merits of the question turn," but "to a Frenchman . . . the whole is so new, that he studies without any bias one way or the other." Second, since Tocqueville came from a country that had recently experienced far more turbulence and instability than Britain, he often exercised more patience with American shortcomings than his British counterparts did. As Tocqueville apparently told Hall himself, "Had you, like me, been bred up in the midst of revolutions and counter-revolutions, despotisms, restorations, and all the miseries of insecurity, political and personal, you might have learned to view the worst that passes in America with calmness!" Hall reasoned that these circumstances inspired Tocqueville to survey the United States with "uniform composure," "good humor," and "kindly forebearance." Third, although Tocqueville had visited the United States like other travelers, his book resembled political philosophy more than the travel literature that characterized most British investigations of America. According to Hall, *Democracy in America*'s "philosophical manner" made it quite unlike any British work. Indeed, Hall could not "recall . . . any work similar to this, in which there is no narrative, nor any other enlivening circumstance to give it animation, and yet in which the interest is sustained from beginning to end without once flagging."[124] What this praise of Tocqueville seemed to suggest was that the easy position of authority, superiority, and familiarity which British travelers assumed when they surveyed America rendered them incapable of achieving any profound insight.

Despite its prominence and singularity, *Democracy in America* was assimilated to conform to a British sensibility in a number of ways. For one thing, Henry Reeve, who translated the book into English, gave it a Whiggish, aristocratic, and British coloring that made Tocqueville uncomfortable.[125] For another, British readers, to use Stanley Fish's formulation, used their own "interpretive framework" to write or make meaning from Tocqueville's text.[126] We have already seen how Mill rendered Tocqueville's arguments in a way that would appeal to British audiences. Tocqueville himself understood how British readers had appropriated his text when he lamented that they "want to make me a party man. . . . They ascribe to me passions when I have only opinions. . . . Democratic and aristocratic prejudices are alternately ascribed to me."[127] What facilitated these reactions was the complex, sophisticated, and nuanced nature of *Democracy in America*; Tocqueville frequently took with one hand what he gave with the other, giving readers the opportunity to see what they wished to see.

In these ways, *Democracy in America* became part of the British canon about America, and that canon had reached some important conclusions about the United States well before the outbreak of the Civil War. Americans may have possessed one government, but they were divided in spirit. Northerners and southerners (westerners did not figure as prominently in the national calculus) lived under fundamentally different and irreconcilable political, economic, social, and cultural systems. Whether it was a cause or consequences of these differences, slavery was the most important expression of the division between the antebellum North and South. These attitudes are well reflected in a story that Grattan related in his *Civilized America* (1859). In 1842, while serving as the British consul in Boston, he met Sir Charles Bagot, who had just been appointed governor general of Canada. An experienced diplomat, Bagot had served as British minister to the United States between 1815 and 1819. Upon receiving an invitation from an American acquaintance to see Bunker Hill, Bagot turned to Grattan and asked, "What the devil *is* Bunker's Hill?" This anecdote seems hard to credit, but Grattan believed Bagot's comment "afforded another proof of the insignificance attached by a certain idiosyncrasy of mind in England, regarding everything connected with America, beyond the facts that it was once an English colony, which waged a successful rebellion; and is an independent state, with rival interests, uncongenial feelings, and a cotton-growing, tobacco-chewing, sherry-cobler drinking, Lynch-law practising, and slave-holding population. This was, I firmly believe, until very lately, the sum and substance of many a well-informed, highly educated Tory mind (and such was Sir Charles Bagot's)."[128] Grattan appeared to imply that the state of knowledge about America had improved "lately" and that, perhaps, liberal minds were somewhat more informed than "Tory" ones. Yet Bagot was not only "well-informed" and "highly educated," but he had also lived in America for four years. Grattan's text could be read in two different ways. On the one hand, it shows how shockingly obtuse an Englishman could be with regard to America. On the other, it indicates that even a shockingly obtuse Englishman was well-versed in common British stereotypes about Americans.

As the sectional crisis in the United States progressed, British travel literature about the United States prepared readers to anticipate and even accept a political division between Americans. Once the secession crisis began to unfold, travel literature also shaped British understandings of Americans' behaviors. Images of northerners and southerners developed during the antebellum era were pressed into service. Each type that populated the American landscape consisted of contradictory elements, and as we shall see, during the Civil War, each of these elements assumed prominence according to its ability to explain particular American circumstances. On one side stood a middle-class democracy—or was it a bourgeois tyranny? The contradictory qualities of Yankees that leapt to the fore depended on the circumstances. They could either be the characteristics that contributed to material progress or those that inspired moral backwardness. There was less confusion about the other side; almost all agreed that the South was dominated by a slave-owning oligarchy. As we shall see, once the war got under way, there was less concurrence about which set of qualities associated with this oligarchy outweighed the other. Was it the refinement and leadership skills associated with a leisured class? Or was it the savagery, unscrupulousness, and relentless will to power of a slaveowning cabal? Underlying and informing the answers to all of these questions was the degree to which Americans—northerners and southerners alike—could (and ought to) be retained within the British sphere of influence.

2

THE FORMATION OF BRITISH ATTITUDES TOWARD THE CIVIL WAR

It is, indeed, scarcely possible to speak in public without a notice of the American war. . . . The spectacle is too conspicuous and too powerfully interesting to be readily passed over in silence.

—*SATURDAY REVIEW*, 1862

What a war of wonders it has been!

—*DAILY TELEGRAPH*, 1864

A TALE OF *THE TIMES*: WILLIAM HOWARD RUSSELL AND THE CIVIL WAR

When William Howard Russell disembarked in New York in March 1861 as *The Times*' American correspondent, he was the most famous journalist in the world. Through his fluent pen, his penetrating judgment, and his association with *The Times*, Russell had risen from obscurity to become a transatlantic celebrity. A seasoned journalist, he had covered a number of important events during the 1840s and 1850s, including Daniel O'Connell's trial in Dublin, the rise and fall of "Railway Mania," the Irish famine, the Duke of Wellington's funeral, and Lajos Kossuth's visit to Britain. By the early 1850s, his admission to the Garrick Club, where he mingled with the likes of William Thackeray and Charles Dickens, indicated that he had attained a certain measure of success. It was not until *The Times* sent him to cover the Crimean War in 1853, however, that Russell truly achieved fame as the world's first war correspondent. His dramatic, well-written accounts of combat captured the British reading public's imagination and elicited much sympathy for the hardships of the rank and file. At the same time, appearing as they did in Britain's most influential newspaper, his powerful indictments of the military blundering and the logistical inefficiency of the British army exerted an extraordinary political influence. Russell clearly contributed to the crisis that led to the fall of Lord Aberdeen's coalition government in January 1855.[1] Undoubtedly, the impact of Russell's scribblings added not only to his own prestige but to the status of *The Times* as well. In late 1857, Russell reprised his role as war correspondent when he traveled halfway around the world to cover the Indian rebellion. His eyewitness accounts of events in India fascinated his readers, but his criticisms of the uprising's brutal repression proved unpopular.

It is a mark of the significance *The Times* attributed to the secession crisis that it sent a reporter of Russell's stature and caliber to the United States. As *The Times* truthfully claimed in a leader, sending Russell to America was "the best pledge that we could have given of our desire to procure the most accurate information at first-hand."[2] Russell was not without his biases and flaws, but among British journalists he produced some of the most evenhanded reporting of the war. When he arrived in America, he claimed that he had "no theories to uphold, no prejudices to subserve, no interests to advance, no instructions to fulfill" and that he sought to report "without fear, favor, or affection of or for anything but . . . the truth."[3] While British visitors frequently made such professions, Russell earnestly tried to live up to this declaration. This evenhandedness led Russell to present a complex view of both the North and the South to his British readers. At the same time, Russell's journalism was typical of British opinion, in that his views of the war were mixed and often moved with events.

Russell's passionate but disinterested commentary did not sit well with Americans.[4] It was only a matter of time before Russell became the victim of a deterioration in Anglo-American relations that he inadvertently helped precipitate. It was his famous (or perhaps infamous) account of the northern rout at the First Battle of Bull Run that irrevocably damaged his position in America, later making it almost impossible for him to discharge his duties to *The Times*. Russell reached the battlefield just as Federal forces began their retreat. He provided a graphic and unattractive portrayal of a panicked army on the run (he described the behavior of some officers and men as "scandalous"), concluding that the defeat had resulted not so much from cowardice as from bad discipline and poor leadership.[5] When Russell's account of the battle reached the United States around the middle of August, he earned the sobriquet "Bull Run" Russell and immediately became the most unpopular man in the North. Northerners channeled their frustrations with the war and British opinion against poor Russell. His acquaintances among northern political and military leaders shunned him. People in public casually insulted him.[6] The New York press attacked him remorselessly, and he received an endless torrent of hate mail and death threats for the remainder of his stay.[7] At a camp near Washington, D.C., a sentry of German origin leveled a rifle at Russell and roared in a heavy accent, "Pull-Run Russell! You shall never write Pull's Run again!" He pulled the trigger, but the weapon misfired.[8] Russell did not help his cause when, during the Trent affair, an indiscretion of his made the *New York Herald*'s charges of insider trading look plausible.[9] Not wanting "to show a white feather," Russell kept up a brave front.[10] In September 1861, Sir George Bell found Russell in Washington, D.C., "fat and jolly, all alive, eating his breakfast as if he was not going to be paid off by Judge Lynch and Co.!"[11] Clearly, however, Russell was miserable and feared for his life. From that period onward, Russell sent home an unending stream of querulous letters to Mowbray Morris, the manager of *The Times,* implying that he was looking for an honorable exit from his American assignment.[12] He complained of northern attacks on his character while asking *The Times* to moderate its editorial stance, which had grown increasingly critical of the North. Russell pleaded with Delane, "I don't want to ask you to sacrifice the policy of the Times to me, but I would like you if possible not to sacrifice me . . . to the leaders in the Times."[13]

By March 1862, Morris had become exasperated and seriously contemplated withdrawing Russell from the United States.[14] Accusing Russell of having "lost heart" and "thrown us overboard," Morris demanded, "*You must either go to the front or come home.*"[15] At this point, Russell had obtained a pass from General George McClellan to accompany the Army of the Potomac in the field as it prepared for the Peninsula Campaign. At the last minute, however, Edwin Stanton, the secretary of war, revoked Russell's pass. Russell briefly considered using his connections to smuggle himself into the Confederacy but decided against it. It was at this point that Russell seized upon Morris's ultimatum as a pretext to leave America; since he could not go to the front, he claimed he was under orders to go home.[16] In April 1862, Russell boarded a steamer for Britain. Deprived of their sole correspondent in America just as the spring campaign season commenced, *The Times*' management was furious. Eventually Russell patched up his relationship with *The Times,* but he witnessed the rest of the war from Britain as the editor of the *Army and Navy Gazette.*

Russell's experiences and circumstances are significant in understanding the formation and character of British opinion toward the war. Russell was associated with a new, more influential journalism that had emerged in the 1850s and 1860s. As the most visible figure in a process that saw newspapers replace travel literature as the main means of representing the United States in Britain, Russell helped conduct the communication that sustained the Anglo-American relationship. While the press inherited many of the traditions and tropes developed by travel writers in the antebellum period, features of the new journalism and the very nature of periodicals modified the expression of British discourses concerning America significantly.

Encouraged by a number of reforms and technological advances, the newly confident management of newspapers began to display a more capitalistic attitude, greater partisanship, and a strong sense that the press had a vital role to play in the political education of its readers. Editors embraced novel styles of presentation that included more reliance on vivid, "you were there" correspondence in which the doings of the reporter became news. Russell's depiction of the Federal retreat at Bull Run is an excellent example of this new style. For instance, his famous account included the following dramatic exchange: "'Stop,' cried I to the driver of one of the carts, 'everything is falling out.' '— you,' shouted a fellow inside, 'if you stop him I'll blow your brains out.'"[17] At the same time, as Russell himself realized when he published *My Diary North and South* (1863), the day-by-day perspective that characterized a diary—as well as a newspaper—constrained what both media could express. Writing to John Bigelow, he admitted that he was "not at all pleased" with the work because "the form of a diary is quite destructive to any sustained interest and I will never be a slave to my daily nonsense and hasty observations again."[18] All of these factors modified British discourses, producing more sensational and more superficial images of America.

The British press had changed dramatically, and the resulting expansion of circulations made Britain's metropolitan dailies more influential than ever. Russell's celebrity was clearly bound with the recognized power of his employer, *The Times,* even if Americans, and many Britons, exaggerated that newspaper's significance. As a journalist with many barely reputable acquaintances, Russell himself still stood on the margins of good society. When his name was omitted from the guest list of a function at the British legation, a miffed Russell wrote that "it was considered that I was not good enough company." Yet, as he recognized in the next line, it was solely his role as the correspondent of *The Times,* or "the unaccredited ambassador of the people," as he more grandiloquently put it, that made him the equivalent of Lord Lyons's other guests.[19] President Abraham Lincoln's statement upon meeting Russell only confirmed the source of Russell's fame: "The London *Times* is one of the greatest powers in the world—in fact, I don't know anything which has more power,—except perhaps the Mississippi. I am glad to know you as its minister."[20] As Lincoln's words made clear, he paid homage to a representative of *The Times,* not the man himself.

Yet, as Russell's correspondence indicates, so far as coverage of America was concerned, the new journalism still owed much to traditional representations of America established by antebellum travel literature. In both the route he took and the manner in which he reported his experiences, Russell's visit to the South between April and June 1861 resembled the tours of prewar British travel writers. Russell's diary, which he published upon his return to Britain, read very much like a traditional piece of travel literature—with the exception that it was somewhat less discreet than usual efforts of that sort. Moreover, Russell explicitly and implicitly relied on Tocqueville throughout much of his correspondence, indicating that *Democracy in America* was still widely considered the standard work on the subject.[21] Not surprisingly then, Russell still employed many of the same tropes and images associated with antebellum traditions of representing the United States.

If Russell was a glamorous symbol of the synthesis between the new and the old, he was also extremely well placed to witness and even participate in the fraying of Anglo-American relations that reshaped British views of the United States during the Civil War. As Martin Crawford has argued, British correspondents during the conflict served as the indispensable links in the transatlantic line of communication that bound Americans and Britons together, and in the first year of the war Russell himself was perhaps the most important of those links.[22] *The Times* was not far off the mark when it claimed that Russell's letters from the Confederacy "gave almost the only description we have of the state of [Southern] society since Secession."[23] Because he occupied this vital position, however, Russell found himself subjected to immense pressures from both sides of the Atlantic as relations between Britain and the United States deteriorated; each nation felt the other's reaction to the secession crisis posed a threat to its vital interests. A variety of factors, including the postcolonial nature of the transatlantic relationship, the influence of domestic political considerations, and the intervention of the new partisan press, only exacerbated a perceived conflict of interests between the two nations.

Occupying the point of contact between Britain and America, Russell was acutely aware of the extent to which opinion in one country reacted to that in the other and how this dynamic worsened relations between the two. He saw how the British press, which naturally assumed the role as arbiter of things transatlantic, not only grew frustrated with a Federal policy that was perceived as ineffective, impervious to British wisdom, and reckless of British interests, but also impatient with "the irritation and ill-feeling existing against England on the alleged grounds of want of sympathy with the North."[24] He also believed this frustration and impatience had become intertwined with British partisan politics through criticisms of American institutions—with dangerous results. Russell was convinced that his newspaper was using the opportunity presented by the war to discredit parliamentary radicalism in Britain, namely by associating John Bright, Richard Cobden, and the Manchester School with the perceived failure of the United States.[25] These types of attacks, along with the British habit of writing *de haut en bas* (Sumner complained that Russell's correspondence was "not friendly . . . and that you write down on us") created enormous resentment in the North, where people were already "in a passion."[26] As *The Times*' correspondent in America, he was thus placed in an impossible position. To John Thadeus Delane, the editor of *The Times,* he wrote, "The tone of The Times has been regarded with anger & indignation—it is considered by the Federals as entirely antagonistic & embittered & I am looked upon as the main agent in producing that disposition on the part of the paper."[27] Russell concluded that he was not merely hated as a correspondent of *The Times* but as the "only English thing they [northerners] can vent their anger on."[28] Ground down between northern and British public opinion, Russell left the United States. Both sides lost as honest a broker as they could find under the circumstances; succeeding correspondents from *The Times* would prove far less measured in their reporting. Undoubtedly, Russell's departure was an important step in the deterioration of Anglo-American relations and heralded worse times to come.

While in many ways Russell's position and role were extraordinary, in other ways he was entirely typical. For instance, Russell's ambivalence toward the war was representative of British opinion in general. As with many other British observers, this ambivalence was produced by mixed feelings not only toward specific American circumstances, but also the general social and political principles implicated in those circumstances. Russell believed hierarchical societies preserved order and sustained elevating influences better than more egalitarian arrangements.[29] Yet he also felt that there was much that was "really good and wholesome in American Democracy."[30]

Not surprisingly, then, Russell's position toward the belligerents was hard to sort, and his experience highlights the difficulty of dividing Britons simply into supporters of one side or the other. During his stay, northerners vilified him as a Confederate sympathizer. Yet a number of his acquaintances identified Russell as pro-northern, a reputation he was more than happy to own up to when the Federals had won the war. Confusing the issue still further, Russell's public and private correspondence was somewhat contradictory. Perhaps Edmund Monson, who then served on Lord Lyons's staff at the British legation in Washington, D.C., put it best when he claimed of Russell, "He don't seem enamoured of the South, any more than he is of the North."[31] As in the case of most other British public figures, Russell found himself balancing a series of interests and considerations as he struggled to define his opinion toward the war. From Russell's perspective, both sides suffered from besetting sins, and many of his criticisms echoed those made by British travelers during the antebellum era. Northern bourgeois democracy, he contended, contributed to low cultural standards, an anarchic tyranny of the majority (that would eventually lead to despotism), and low military effectiveness. Moreover, the North's struggle to restore the American federation by force was futile; a defeated and embittered South would never freely consent to rejoin the Union.[32] At the same time, Russell believed that in the South, social aristocracy had partially compensated for the deficiencies of political equality.[33] While he admired the southern gentry and its leadership, he found slavery abhorrent and indefensible.[34] For that reason, he concluded that although he felt "a sincere regard and liking for many of the Southerners who I have met, I cannot say their cause, or its origin, or its aim recommends itself to my sympathies."[35] Despite his great interest in the war, it is not clear that Russell himself knew whom he favored.[36]

Like those of his countrymen, Russell's impressions of the American Civil War may have proven mistaken. Yet a survey of Russell's story reminds us of the extraordinary and difficult conditions under which various Britons labored to understand the conflict and attempted to formulate its lessons. Russell's attitudes were typical, but his perspective was not; few Britons observed the war so closely or bore the brunt of northern anger so directly. Moreover, the important position he occupied astride Anglo-American lines of communication provided him with an extraordinary vantage point from which to perceive the great forces that shaped British images of the conflict. Although he was conscious of these forces, a sensitive, conscientious, and perceptive man like Russell could not transcend them. What hope was there that other observers would succeed where Russell failed?

A FUGITIVE LITERATURE ON THE TOPICS OF THE DAY: THE BRITISH PRESS AND THE CIVIL WAR

Scholars studying British attitudes toward the war have mentioned the press's impact on both British and American opinion and recognized the deleterious effect newspapers had on transatlantic relations during the Civil War. Yet they have not investigated the important changes that took place among periodicals throughout this period that made such influence possible. Historians of the British press have traditionally argued that the repeal of various imposts that had made dailies expensive—the abolition of the advertisement duty (1853), the stamp tax (1855), and the paper duty (1861)—radically changed newspapers and journalism. The repeal of these "taxes on knowledge," as they were known, certainly lowered the price of newspapers and permitted the rapid expansion of circulations, but this legislation does not fully account for the important qualitative and quantitative changes that took place in the press during in this period. The advent of the telegraph and the railroad, along with technological advances in printing, facilitated the collection of information as well as the production and dissemination of news.[37] Changes in British politics also played an important role; politicians and centralizing party organizations became increasingly interested in using newspapers to formulate programs and mobilize support among the electorate through the use of the press.[38] Finally, important and sensational foreign events, such as the Crimean War, the Indian rebellion, Italian unification, and the American Civil War, which created demand for up-to-date news in Britain, played to newspapers' strengths and further encouraged the expansion of circulations. Some thirty years after the Civil War, in a work that looked back on the major developments of modern civilization, Sir Hugh Gilzean-Reid and P. J. MacDonnell claimed, "the modern Press, as we know it, may be said to date from the year 1861" because it witnessed "the removal of the paper tax" and "the outbreak of the American War."[39] It seems hard to avoid the conclusion that if the press helped make the American conflict extremely important in Britain, the conflict performed the same service for the press.

The concatenation of these developments led to several important changes among British periodicals. First, it killed off what remained of the old, unstamped (and illegal) radical press.[40] Second, it contributed to the rise of healthy and active provincial newspapers.[41] Third, and most important for our purposes, it precipitated the emergence of metropolitan dailies that enjoyed unprecedentedly large circulations.[42] These dailies warrant the most attention since the size and territorial range of their circulations, along with their prestige, made them the closest thing to national newspapers that Britain possessed. Moreover, the scale of the resources at their disposal and their proximity to the corridors of power meant they possessed the means and will to dominate the collection of foreign news.

The London daily of the 1860s was new in a number of ways. It generally sold many more copies than in the past. In the mid-1850s, *The Times,* priced at 3*d.*, enjoyed a daily circulation of sixty thousand—roughly three times that of the rest of the daily London press combined. Less than ten years later, although *The Times* still sold the same number of papers, penny dailies like the *Daily Telegraph* and the *Standard* regularly sold well over one hundred thousand copies. By that point, working-class weeklies like *Reynolds's Newspaper* probably enjoyed circulations of over two hundred thousand. As Charles Bowen commented in 1862, the rise of penny papers had "materially affected" the influence of *The Times,* which until recently had enjoyed the status of a monarch in the press world. *The Times* had been forced to reduce its price, and Bowen foresaw a time when further reductions "may convert the monarchy of letters into a republic."[43] Even more important than ending the supremacy of *The Times,* the rise of metropolitan penny papers both reflected and created the vision of newspapers not only as highly profitable commercial ventures, but also as dependable political tools. The large capital investment required to start a daily, the relentless push to expand the market, and the resultant commodification of the newspaper all seemed to indicate that this industry had entered a new capitalistic phase. At the same time, politicians moved quickly to associate themselves with this new forum so they could broadcast their ideas, and the press grew increasingly partisan. Every major faction in Parliament was connected to at least one London newspaper, and a number of important political figures enjoyed an intimate relationship with a proprietor or editor. Many scholars of the press have emphasized the tension between the commercial and political objectives of these newspapers, claiming that journalists were not totally free to indulge their partisanship for fear of offending readers and advertisers.[44] Yet it appears that commerce and politics could just as frequently further one another. Certainly, the new commercial success and political influence of newspapers conferred upon them an unprecedented respectability. These developments allowed dailies to begin dominating British print culture. Not every newspaper had a correspondent in America, but its various strengths, including an ability to cover fast-moving events, made it possible for the press to replace travel literature as the most important source of information about America during the Civil War.

Although the forces acting on this newly powerful press changed the way it expressed prevailing discourses about the United States, in many ways images of America remained remarkably consistent. Russell perpetuated traditional images of Americans, and Francis Lawley, Russell's successor in America, who became *The Times*' southern correspondent, employed many of the same ideas. He described the origins of the war in terms developed during the antebellum period: "Two races have come into collision," he asserted: "On one side an aristocracy, agricultural, sparsely settled, given to field sports, living in the saddle; on the other, a democracy, which has been travelling downwards for 80 years . . . which breathes only an atmosphere of dollars, and has no aspirations beyond commercial gain."[45] Again, Lawley employed the classic antebellum depictions of the southerner divested of his vices and the Yankee deprived of his virtues.

This consistency was probably due to the lingering influence of antebellum travel literature, particularly Tocqueville's work, which had become something of a gold standard in analysis of America. In an 1864 essay for the *Quarterly Review* Lawley displayed a thorough familiarity with this literature, referring not only to Dickens, Thackeray, Lyell, Martineau, Tocqueville, Mackay, Stirling, and Grattan, but also to wartime visitors like Russell and Trollope.[46] The close relationship between the periodical and book trades also probably helped sustain these traditions in the press. Scholars have claimed that the press increasingly developed a unique way of doing things and have even hinted at its de facto professionalization during this period. Yet the worlds of periodicals and books overlapped significantly because the same people often wrote both. Such was especially the case among the weeklies, monthlies, and quarterlies that did the bulk of profound thinking in the periodical press. The big book publishers—including William Blackwood and Sons, Macmillan and Co., Richard Bentley, and John Murray—produced periodicals to advertise works and provide employment for their authors. This close relationship was highlighted by the fact that many of the mid-Victorian era's most important books first appeared as serials in such publications: John Stuart Mill's *Utilitarianism,* Walter Bagehot's *English Constitution,* Matthew Arnold's *Culture and Anarchy,* and James Fitzjames Stephen's *Liberty, Equality, Fraternity.*[47] And indeed, a number of the better known British accounts of the war, including Edward Dicey's *Six Months in the Federal States* (1863), Lieutenant-Colonel Arthur James Lyon Fremantle's *Three Months in the Southern States* (1863), and Heros von Borcke's *Memoirs of the Confederate War for Independence* (1866) were produced by authors who had started out writing a single article or series of articles in a monthly. These types of connections extended well into the daily press: between 1860 and 1865, George Augustus Sala, who produced leaders for the *Daily Telegraph* and served as that newspaper's American correspondent during the war, also founded (as well as edited and owned) the monthly *Temple Bar* and wrote *My Diary in America in the Midst of War* (1865). The world of literature—and contemporaries included periodicals in that category—was small, well integrated, and unified by similar practices.

While newspapers shared much with the rest of periodical literature, which, in turn, was closely associated with book publishing, dailies were strikingly different in one manner that modified the expression of discourses about America. Unlike the travel writer (or even the author of an essay in a monthly) who folded his experiences and thoughts into one coherent and broad synthesis, the journalist daily recorded fleeting impressions that he could never assemble into a seamless whole. To use an expression by Eneas

Sweetland Dallas, a Scots journalist and author, in an 1859 article for *Blackwood's Edinburgh Magazine,* newspapers produced a "fugitive" and "ephemeral" literature, a "creature of the day" calculated for "rapid sale and immediate effect." Although Dallas denied that such a literature was "superficial," the newspaper's very frame of reference militated against wide-ranging or profound thought.[48] Using press coverage of the Civil War as an example, James Fitzjames Stephen (then a journalist, but later a prominent jurist and High Court judge) asserted that since journalists had to refer to the "topics of the day," they could only deal with subjects "under the forms in which the subjects present themselves." For that reason, the journalist "hardly ever gets the chance, even if he had the power, of taking a comprehensive view of the whole subject, reducing the whole matter to order and principle, and setting before his readers something like a real judgment upon it." Consequently, "If M. de Tocqueville were now writing in *The Times,*" Stephen surmised in a thought experiment, the Frenchman could probably provide opinions about the military prospects of the belligerents, "but he would not be able to impress upon the public at large his philosophical theories about the strong and weak points of democratic institutions." Under such circumstances, articles could never display much coherence. They "never form a connected whole," partly because they were "completely the creatures of the particular circumstances which suggest them."[49] For these reasons, Britain's daily press produced a more impressionistic and less nuanced view of America than the travel literature of the antebellum period.

Stephen went on to liken journalists to barristers since both spoke "from a particular point of view, and with the purpose of effecting a particular result." This assertion points to another way in which the daily press changed discourses about the United States during the war. If travel literature was often overtly ideological, it was rarely partisan. Although editors often fought to maintain their independence and newspapers were not reliable party instruments, the daily press was more closely related to parliamentary parties than ever before. As Stephen asserted with regard to British reporting of the American conflict, "the conclusion being given, the premisses are to be shown to fit into it."[50] In other words, the newly powerful and partisan daily press, which relentlessly used current events to obtain domestic political advantage, had a tendency to strip American images of their nuance and render them simply, vividly, and starkly. This partisanship frustrated many British readers.

For instance, the influential *Times* came in for much criticism from Radicals who had long disliked its editorial policy. Like William Howard Russell, they believed that "The Thunderer," as it was nicknamed, had endangered Anglo-American diplomatic relations for the sake of political point-scoring at home.[51] To use just one example, the *Bee-Hive* asserted that the "*Times* has labored hard to embitter the feeling between England and America, and embroil the two countries in a bloody war," labeling the newspaper a "base and lying journal." Only a few months later, the *Bee-Hive* charged that *The Times* had "prostituted" itself to glorify principles "utterly opposed to Christianity, freedom, and humanity."[52] These types of frustrations eventually culminated in *The "Times" on the American War* (1865), an extensive catalog of grievances written by Leslie Stephen (brother of James Fitzjames Stephen) that charged the daily with simultaneously leading and following a perfectly ignorant British opinion. The newspaper's coverage, he charged, was characterized by a "vague cluster of associations, compounded of Mrs. Trollope, *Martin Chuzzlewit,* and *Uncle Tom's Cabin,*" a "few commonplaces about democracy," and perfect ignorance of American history and geography—in other words, "mere random assertions about unknown quantities."[53] A number of Stephen's charges were unfair and contradictory (for example, *The Times* was inconsistent *and* unwilling to change its stance on the conflict), but more important, they could have been—and often were—leveled at other newspapers.[54]

It is important to remember, however, that despite this partisanship, newspapers did not speak with one voice. Normally, either an editor or proprietor exerted tight control over the drafting of leaders, but there were important exceptions. During this period, Harriet Martineau's editorials in the *Daily News* were never rejected and rarely revised, while Robert Lowe, who had been Delane's tutor at Oxford, enjoyed a moral ascendancy over his editor that allowed him to write pretty much what he wanted at *The Times.*[55] Foreign correspondents also proved much more difficult to control. Editors expected these journalists to agree with the political slant of the newspaper and often provided them with extensive instructions both before and after they departed. As George Sala explained, "frequent and protracted were the conferences between the proprietors of the *Daily Telegraph* and myself as to how my mission to America in the midst of war was to be carried out."[56] Yet the problems associated with managing a correspondent thousands of miles away (and sometimes marooned behind the Federal blockade) often proved insuperable. This issue of management was extremely important since correspondence provided material necessary for well-informed editorials and also legitimized the positions of these editorials in the eyes of readers. Not surprisingly, then, *The Times*' archives are full of frustrated letters from Mowbray Morris seeking to correct and guide his various correspondents. Charles Mackay, *The Times*' correspondent in New York, provides perhaps the most dramatic example of how badly matters could turn out between a newspaper and a reporter. James Fitzjames Stephen, who was by no means a northern sympathizer, described Mackay as an "unscrupulous advocate, carefully reporting to his employers, every statement and every fact which could create contempt and disgust against the conduct, the principles, and in general the cause of the North." Mackay's correspondence described the Federals as "tyrants, marauders, curs, who bought Irishmen and Germans to fight their battles, fraudulent bankrupts, and odious hypocrites."[57] Throughout Mackay's tenure, however, Morris had sent mixed signals to the journalist, alternately praising and criticizing him. Yet once the North had won the war and Mackay had embittered northern opinion against the newspaper, Morris felt compelled to fire the writer. In a letter to Mackay, Morris claimed that the correspondent's willingness to "persistently & wilfully shut your eyes to all facts & signs which did not tend to the support of your foregone conclusions" led to a situation in which *The Times* "has suffered in reputation . . . & . . . readers have been misled by your statements to take an erroneous view of the current of events." Moreover, Morris accused, Mackay's "wild declamation" had "contributed very largely to . . . the exasperation which you allege to exist in the American mind against the English." Indeed, Mackay had made himself "so unpopular that no government of the United States" would tolerate him "except under a sort of protest."[58]

As Morris's reference to the Federal government intimates, the rise of a technologically sophisticated, mass-circulation political press in Britain had contributed to an increasingly popular transatlantic communication and diplomacy (such a press and diplomacy already existed in America). This new diplomacy, which was closely associated with a changing political system in Britain, further complicated Anglo-American relations. Whether he was inspired by Anglophobia, a calculating brinkmanship, or both, William Seward, the U.S. secretary of state, crafted foreign policy with an eye on domestic consumption—something that worried British diplomats, who believed that one day Seward would prove unable to control the popular forces he had unleashed. In contrast, Max Beloff has described Lord Palmerston, the British prime minister, as "firmly in control" of a "traditional diplomacy, unheroic and unmoved by sentiment" during the Civil War; public opinion, Beloff argues, only began to exert an influence on British foreign policy after Palmerston's death.[59] Palmerston, who privately charged Seward with practicing a crass and vulgar diplomacy, would probably have agreed with Beloff, but as we shall see, more recent scholarship has stressed the extent to which Palmerston himself pioneered a new popular foreign policy in Britain that successors like William Gladstone would pursue with even greater enthusiasm.[60] Certainly Palmerston was fully aware of the press's power, and he attempted to use it. For instance, in 1863, even though he was not "personally acquainted" with the louche George Augustus Sala, Palmerston wrote a letter of introduction for him to Lord Lyons because "he [Sala] is going out to America as the Correspondent of the daily Telegraph a Paper which has I believe the most extensive Circulation of any daily Paper printed in London."[61] Intimately associated with a press it could not fully control while speaking simultaneously to audiences at home and abroad, this popular diplomacy was dangerous as well as unpredictable.

For one thing, the press was heavily and consciously implicated in the postcolonial nature of the relationship between Britain and the United States—a situation that only exacerbated tensions. For instance, in a *Fraser's Magazine* assessment of Anglo-American relations, James Fitzjames Stephen argued that Americans were "keenly alive" to the British press's "praise or blame" because that press was far superior to their own. He maintained that "we have the upper hand in literature," particularly periodical literature, because it occupied "a higher relative position in England than in America" and was the profession of a higher class. Moreover, Americans "were deeply persuaded that the most highly educated class" for which this press wrote was "better instructed, more accomplished, [and] more polished than any class in the United States."[62] In other words, Americans' sensitivity was an acknowledgment of Britain's right to judge them. Stephen stressed this point when he claimed Britons, in contrast to the Americans, "never condescend to plead to any jurisdiction whatever."[63] Even if Stephen was wrong about American attitudes, he certainly revealed something about the sensibilities of British writers who sought to lay down the law to domestic and foreign audiences during periods of great transatlantic tension.

Another problem was that although the press frequently cooperated with politicians like Palmerston, it was independent and often pursued objects of its own—regardless of diplomatic consequences. Bowen implied that *The Times*' attacks on the *New York Herald,* which had done so much to worsen relations between the United States and Britain, were inspired by a desire to retain market share against increasingly aggressive penny papers, "the best of which are by no means wanting in ability and moral elevation."[64] Even if such attacks were inspired by ideology rather than the bottom line, they were hardly calculated to advance Palmerston's policy of neutrality.

The dangers associated with the new press's involvement in popular diplomacy became most manifest in the aftermath of William Gladstone's infamous October 1862 Newcastle speech, delivered during a triumphant tour of northern England that was emblematic of the new popular politics. Carried away by the Tyneside's enthusiastic reception, Gladstone, then chancellor of the exchequer, proved rather careless with his words, claiming Jefferson Davis "and the leaders of the South . . . have made a nation."[65] Widely reported in the British and American press, the speech horrified his colleagues by appearing to intimate that the British government was preparing to recognize the Confederacy—a course of action the cabinet had not agreed upon.[66] The *Saturday Review* captured the difficulties inherent in playing to the electorate on foreign policy issues, pointing out that an argument which could be safely expressed in the cabinet was not always suitable for public consumption.[67] Gladstone's speech, of course, caused enormous consternation among northerners. From New York, August Belmont, the financial agent for the English Rothschilds, reported to his superiors in London that the speech "is very severely criticised" in the North because "it is considered an actual declaration of hostility against our Government & I hope it will not be followed by the action on the part of England, which foreshadows viz. a recognition of the Southern Confederacy."[68] As we shall see, after the war the speech was used against the British government during negotiations over the *Alabama* claims.[69] Ironically enough, Gladstone had been inspired by a friendly desire to spare northerners further "bloodshed and greater calamity."[70] Amplified by the press, however, which constituted an integral part of the new popular politics in which Gladstone participated, the Newcastle speech only embittered northerners and undermined Anglo-American relations still further.

OPEN THEIR EYES AND EARS AND KEEP THEIR MOUTHS SHUT: BRITISH SOURCES OF INFORMATION ABOUT THE CIVIL WAR

From the start of the American crisis, British commentators showed a decided mistrust of American sources. Much of this mistrust stemmed from a postcolonial unwillingness to let Americans represent themselves. During the antebellum era, this attitude had manifested itself partly through a denigration of American newspapers, which had earned a reputation for low quality and mendacity. This image of the American press continued well into the Civil War years. During the war, Sir George Bell referred to American dailies as "flimsy lying rags" while George Augustus Sala described them as "brief, careless, declamatory, and scurrilous."[71] That Americans on both sides seemed determined to use information as a weapon in the struggle to influence British public opinion only exacerbated this suspicion of their press. The *Saturday Review* complained that in America "Truth is hard to get at when facts are weapons of war," because "every Northerner and every Southerner who wishes for the success of his country's arms has an interest in making every misrepresentation which can give aid and comfort to his own side."[72] In this war for British opinion, the Confederacy appeared to suffer from a huge disadvantage; for all its porousness, the Federal blockade greatly diminished the outflow of information from the South. For these reasons, *The Times* complained that only the northern "face of affairs" was presented to Europe, while "the Southern side is almost as much concealed from us as the half of the moon that is never turned to the earth."[73] British wartime visitors to the South often justified their travels by referring to the Confederacy's isolation and the unreliability of northern reports concerning that region. Lieutenant-Colonel Sir Arthur James Lyon Fremantle, who wrote *Three Months in the Southern States* (1863), explained that because of the blockade, "the truth can with difficulty be arrived at, as intelligence coming mainly through Northern sources is not believed."[74] *The Times* claimed that it sent Lawley to the South because "whether the North is deceived or only wishes to deceive us, the effect is the same: we cannot trust the accounts that reach us through the Northern press, and an independent source of information is most desirable."[75] As always, a reluctance to allow Americans to speak for themselves was compromised by the necessity of obtaining information that only Americans had. To use perhaps the most obvious example, Henry Hotze, officially the Confederacy's commercial agent in Britain, proved particularly effective in influencing the British press. While his newspaper, *The Index,* did not prove terribly influential (with its small circulation, it could not survive without a subsidy), Hotze used it to assemble a collection of British journalists whom he educated in the Confederate point of view and who went on to promote the southern cause at a number of powerful dailies, including the *Standard.*[76] Still, most Britons would have agreed with Edward Dicey, who wrote *Six Months in the Federal States* (1863) after having visited the North as a correspondent for the *Spectator* and *Macmillan's Magazine:* "as far as political matters are concerned, we English bystanders judge American affairs more impartially than the actors do themselves."[77] In other words, the task of obtaining intelligence about America and assessing it was best left to Britons.

Through William Howard Russell's experiences, we have already witnessed how British journals collected information in the United States. For all of its advertised power as the "Fourth Estate," however, the press overlapped and cooperated with other networks in the collection and distribution of information. The most important of these networks were associated with the British government. As Lucy Brown pointed out, foreign correspondents often relied on British diplomats for assistance.[78] In the American case, Russell enjoyed a fairly close relationship with Lord Lyons. Lyons frequently invited Russell to dine at the legation, allowing the journalist to meet a number of important British and American figures. At the same time, Russell frequently shared intelligence with Lyons; for example, when Russell toured the South in the spring of 1861, he sent the British minister a series of letters detailing the situation he found there.[79]

Leaving journalists like Russell aside, Lyons and the British government possessed ample means and opportunities for collecting information about the American conflict. Unfortunately, the personnel on which Britain relied operated under circumstances that either limited their effectiveness or bent their judgment. In part, these shortcomings began at the top. Lord Palmerston, the prime minister, had served as foreign secretary for years and had dominated British foreign policy since about 1830. Palmerston was much more familiar with European affairs, which he considered more important than developments in the Western Hemisphere. For that reason, he was not particularly comfortable in dealing with the United States, for which he felt an implacable hostility on both diplomatic and ideological grounds. This discomfort was reflected in his comment to Edmund Hammond, the under-secretary of state for foreign affairs, that "these American People are So difficult to deal with So uncertain from Time to Time as to the way in which they may think it useful to make Questions with foreign Governments."[80] According to Palmerston, the Federal leadership was a "Swaggering bullying Set of men. . . . Who have no Sense of Honor and who are Swayed by the Passions of irresponsible masses, and by a reckless desire to hold their Positions by all and any means."[81] Shaped by almost thirty years of Palmerston's leadership, much of the Foreign Office shared this outlook.

It is a measure of the insignificance that the Foreign Office traditionally attached to the United States that, in 1859, Lord Lyons became the British minister in Washington, D.C. Lyons possessed almost twenty years of diplomatic experience, but he had obtained almost all of it in Greece and Italy (with a brief stint in Saxony).[82] He had attained ministerial status for less than a year in Florence when he was assigned his position in the United States. Lyons has received much praise from historians for defending British interests in a discreet and sensible manner, but he was ill-suited for the collection of intelligence.[83] Almost pathologically shy, he busied himself primarily with Chancery work. He rarely mingled with northern society, and he never lived up to his profession that a minister in the United States ought to "visit, from time to time, the principal cities"; he left the capital only infrequently.[84] Russell observed that the minister "has no personal influence in Washington because he never goes into American society."[85] Although his dispatches were full of social and political commentary (much of it very guarded and commonplace), Lyons generally left the gathering of intelligence to others.[86]

The legation staff was somewhat more active in this respect. Many of them hobnobbed with a motley collection of British visitors (including many journalists) and American notables. H. Percy Anderson, the head of the Chancery, accompanied McClellan's army for part of the Peninsula Campaign, toured several western states to speak with governors about protecting British subjects from military service, and visited New York to confer with leaders of the

Democratic Party. William Stuart, the secretary of the legation and sometime chargé d'affaires, also toured various sections of the North. Like Lyons, however, the staff frequently found itself too busy with Chancery work to gather intelligence.[87] Moreover, the members of the legation suffered from a great deal of turnover; since most foreign service officers viewed Washington, D.C., as an unpleasant, second-rate appointment, they left as soon as decently possible.[88] What is striking about many of these diplomats is their animosity toward the Federal government. Edmund Monson, who served in the legation during the early years of the war and later became an ambassador to France, wrote in a letter home, "This Govt [the Federal] are such blackguards that all the Corps Diplomatique are praying for their downfall. . . . They are atrociously vulgar and have not the redeeming virtue of honesty. . . . Old Abe is a mean coward. . . . The Northern policy is to the last degree fatuous."[89] The staff openly teased Lyons's personal secretary for being the only member of the legation to hold pro-Union views.[90] These were the men closest to Lyons who supplied him with much of his intelligence.

British consuls in major ports throughout the North and the South were very well placed to provide invaluable information to their superiors. Since they played a vital commercial role in the towns where they served and often stayed put for many years, they frequently figured prominently in the social life of these areas. Lyons, the Foreign Office, and the British government were all particularly interested in obtaining intelligence from consuls who served in the Confederacy.[91] Not surprisingly, most of these people, who had long resided in the South, sympathized with their neighbors. When William Howard Russell visited the area, he was convinced that "our consuls are nearly to a man Secesh."[92] With only a couple of exceptions, they did not appear particularly insightful, and many were too busy with a variety of tasks to submit lengthy observations. By 1863 it became increasingly difficult to send correspondence out of the Confederacy (consuls throughout the South sent their dispatches to the consulate in Charleston, where a Royal Navy sloop picked up the material for forwarding, but the siege of that city eventually made the arrangement unworkable). In any event, frustrated by the British government's unwillingness to confer recognition, the Confederate government stripped the British consuls of their credentials in October 1863, and information from this source completely ceased.

In the North, the Foreign Office proved most interested in extracting intelligence from the New York consulate. Lyons believed it was "so much the best place for obtaining a knowledge of what is going on in the political world," and many Britons saw it as the true social and economic capital of the United States.[93] Edward Archibald, the consul in New York, began the war as an earnest supporter of the Federal cause. The ferocity of party strife and the strength of Peace Democrats in the state, however, colored Archibald's perceptions, leading him to question the North's commitment to the conflict. Years later, Archibald enjoyed telling northerners that he had held fast to the Federal cause, but his correspondence reveals his opinion—like that of many Britons—as fundamentally mixed.

On several occasions Lord Lyons and the Foreign Office asked the British army for assistance in gathering intelligence. Both officially and unofficially, British officers played a very important role in collecting and broadcasting information about the war. Much like those in the foreign service, soldiers tended to view the Federal government as a likely enemy. Indeed, both of the official military missions sent to the United States were inspired by a wish to know more about an army the British might soon find themselves fighting. A widely circulated letter by Colonel Frederick Eardley-Wilmot, R.A., praising the rifled artillery of the Army of the Potomac, which he saw while on leave in November 1861 (in the midst of the *Trent* crisis), prompted the first mission.[94] After reading the letter, Major-General William Fenwick Williams, commander of British forces in North America, who hated "Yankee insolence" and looked forward to what he saw as an inevitable war with the United States, eventually organized a mission to find out more about this potential enemy's artillery.[95] Between May and July 1862, this mission, consisting of three officers (including Williams's aide-de-camp), visited Federal forces in the field as well as northern fortifications and foundries before producing a report that focused mainly on weapons technology.[96] Fearful that war would break out with the United States at any moment, Lyons instigated the second mission in November 1863 when he asked Lord Russell, the foreign secretary, to send out some British officers to take the measure of the Federal armies.[97] Earl de Grey, the secretary of state for war, authorized two officers to report on American artillery and fortifications. Between February and June 1864, these officers made the rounds of northern camps, fortifications, and foundries, but

Edwin Stanton, the secretary of war, revoked their passes to accompany the Army of the Potomac in the field. This mission's report focused mainly on technical subjects.[98]

As Stanton's behavior reminds us, although these were ostensibly friendly visits, they occurred in an atmosphere of suspicion and hostility. Lieutenant-Colonel T. L. Gallwey, who constituted part of the second mission, found himself charged by Lyons with writing a report prognosticating what course a war between the United States and Britain would take.[99] One can capture something of the attitude of these observers by reading Palmerston's special instructions to the second mission: "If our Military Officers are to join the federal Forces in the Field, They Should be Strictly cautioned not [to] make any Criticisms which might be useful to the Federals in pointing out to them Faults or Imperfections. . . . The Federals are luckily too vain to attach much value to the opinions of Englishmen, but our officers might be told to open their Eyes & Ears and keep their mouths Shut."[100] It is hard to avoid the conclusion that the threat of war during this period influenced the comments of most civil and military travelers in America.

A large number of private visitors supplemented the observations of journalists, foreign service officers, and soldiers. Many consisted of officers on leave from duty in Canada, but they also included politicians, authors, businessmen, and gentlemen—all of whom tended to be well connected. Drawn by curiosity, a desire for adventure, and (oftentimes) southern proclivities, many of them reached the Confederacy or at least tried. British soldiers in particular displayed a weakness for southern leaders, whom they recognized as fellow English gentlemen. For instance, in January 1863 a Captain Bushby of the British army visited the Army of Northern Virginia's headquarters near Fredericksburg bearing an English saddle for General Robert E. Lee, a breech-loading carbine for General J.E.B. Stuart, and an "india-rubber bed" for General "Stonewall" Jackson. As he was signing an autograph for Bushby, Jackson spilled some ink on the paper and discarded it before starting over; the British officer, however, took great pains to retrieve the ruined sheet and "carefully treasured it."[101] A number of factors probably explain why British visitors to the South sympathized with the Confederacy. Before he became a partisan of the Confederacy and smuggled himself southward through the "underground route," Frank Vizetelly, the correspondent for the *Illustrated London News,* observed, "it would be difficult, indeed, to travel among a people [southerners] so confident of the justice of their cause, without becoming to a certain extent a convert to their opinions."[102] Lawley, Vizetelly's boon companion in the South and a supporter of the Confederate cause, saw matters in a different light. No doubt remembering Russell's fate, he feared offending his southern hosts and thus avoided "topics which will be calculated to ruffle the amour proper & awaken the jealousies of one of the most susceptible people & Governments on earth."[103] The staunchly abolitionist *Reynolds's Newspaper* put the same problem somewhat differently: "when a man gets into a robbers' den, he cannot be expected to be very eloquent in his reprobation of robber practices."[104] No doubt, the Britons who headed south of the Mason-Dixon Line were a self-selecting group; it is hard to see why one would submit himself to the rigors of running the Federal land and sea blockade unless he felt some interest or sympathy in the Confederate cause.

Many of these visitors broadcast their observations through informal networks of acquaintances, the periodical press, or both. As we shall see in chapter 5, Lieutenant-Colonel Henry Charles Fletcher of the 2nd Battalion, Scots Fusilier Guards, was able to spread his observations of both the North and South's military capacities through an extended network of well-positioned Britons, including Lieutenant-Colonel Edward Neville (cousin of William Gladstone, then chancellor of the exchequer), H. P. Anderson (head of the Chancery at the British legation), William Stuart (chargé d'affaires at the British legation), Francis Lawley, and Lieutenant-Colonel Henry Charles Eden Malet (whose family was very well-connected in the foreign service). In a number of cases, these figures forwarded Fletcher's observations to their acquaintances. Fletcher also enjoyed a wide circle of correspondents who forwarded his letters. By such means, Fletcher's letters themselves reached Major-General Sir William Fenwick Williams, Major-General Lord Frederick Paulet (commander of the Brigade of Guards), Earl de Grey (then under-secretary of state for war), Lord Lyons, and Lord John Russell (foreign secretary). Returning to Britain, Fletcher wrote a *Report on the Military Academy at West Point, U.S.* for the War Office, "A Run Through the Southern States" (1863) for the popular *Cornhill Magazine,* and a massive three-decker *History of the American War* (1865–1866), published by Richard Bentley.

The number of his well-placed acquaintances, the extent of his correspondence, and his voluminous publications made Fletcher somewhat unusual. Yet surviving documents indicate that many other private British visitors employed personal connections as well as the press to circulate news and information about America during this period. Like the travel writers of the antebellum period, these independent individuals were free agents who could do or say whatever they wished. The more partisan among them found the press and the influence it promised very attractive, but once they began writing for periodicals, like journalists, they partially lost their independence. John Blackwood's correspondence provides a good idea of the extent to which a proprietor could exercise tight control over contributors who were not professional writers. A self-described southern sympathizer, Blackwood ceaselessly looked for Britons recently returned from the South so he could "obtain some enthusiastic account of how they [the Confederates] have fared."[105] Once he obtained these accounts, however, he rewrote them extensively for both literary and political reasons. In fact, inspired by a desire to help the cause, he forwarded a number of manuscripts to James Mason, the Confederacy's envoy in Britain, seeking suggestions for revisions.[106] In dealing with the press, it was impossible to escape the battle for public opinion waged by partisans of either the North or the South.

THE CONTOURS OF BRITISH OPINION ABOUT THE CIVIL WAR

Generalizing about the overall nature of British public opinion is extremely difficult because evidence points in a variety of directions. For instance, in August 1861, while discussing the American crisis, *The Times* editorialized, "Never was there a war in which the people of this country took a greater interest. We watch with the utmost solicitude all the proceedings of the belligerents, and observe not only the operations of their armies, but the manifestations of popular feeling, with sentiments which no other struggle could excite."[107] Almost four years later, the *Saturday Review* claimed, "The distinction between Federal and Confederate sympathizers [in Britain] is one of the most marked political divisions of the day."[108] Such claims indicate that British opinion was characterized by great interest, certainty, and partisanship.

Yet, we can easily find contemporary statements that indicate a much different state of affairs. In December 1861, Edward Horsman, the influential independent Liberal MP who sat for Stroud, delivered a speech on the American crisis that the *Spectator* found indicative of British opinion: "He is . . . like the British public, unable at once to combine so many divergent influences into opinion, and falls back in sheer despair on the great English first principle, that our flag is to be left alone."[109] The next year, the *Economist* complained that it was "very difficult" to understand the war and that "in dealing with a subject of the details of which we know so little, and with a people whose character we so imperfectly understand, we must speculate very much in the dark."[110] Several years of war did not provide much clarity for Sir Roundell Palmer, MP for Richmond and the recently appointed attorney general, when he told his constituents in October 1863 that "if a fair balance was struck it would puzzle any one to say on which side our sympathies lie."[111] Observations such as these express a confusion and frustration that pushed observers toward neutrality.

These conflicting sets of statements—which were all true in their way—indicate that the passionate ambivalence that characterized British attitudes toward the United States during the antebellum period persisted during the Civil War years. Many of the same postcolonial discourses continued to influence British perceptions of the United States. Traditional tropes, images, and representations of Americans were employed in an attempt to make sense of the conflict. To take only one example, the Confederacy's military victories in the East during the summer of 1862 inclined a number of observers (who otherwise knew very little of the Confederacy) to explain this development by referring to qualities associated with the well-established antebellum image of the southern gentleman.[112] The image of a southern aristocracy as an explanation for military victory became one element among several in pro-Confederate propaganda, but it also exerted a powerful influence outside this quarter.

As usual, Americans remained known and unknown, sometimes acting in accordance with British desires and sometimes not. Only now, the war both supercharged and complicated these discourses because Britain suddenly became aware of how much the American crisis had imperiled a wide variety of great interests. As we shall see later in the chapter, the swift crumbling of the Anglo-American relationship and the frightening possibility that all of the United States or part of it could slip out of the British sphere of influence also played an important role. In other words, the stakes threatened by the deterioration of the Anglo-American relationship seemed much greater—but more difficult to disentangle—than ever before. No one could survey events in America without contemplating a host of issues as disparate as the Morrill Tariff, the cotton famine, the seemingly parlous state of American finance, the Federal blockade, Canadian security, and so on—all of which were tied to Britain's well-being. Indeed, in the British mind, America became a kind of vortex that seemed to suck *all* British interests in its direction. *The Times* explained in October 1862, "Everything leads to the American war: the Revenue, Armstrong guns and plated ships, Lancashire, the French Treaty, the Income-tax, and even Italy, all naturally converge in that one point."[113]

As the foregoing suggests, opinion on the American war usually issued from a weighing of various interests. The results of this balancing were not always predictable, nor did they lend themselves to easy categorization as pro-northern or pro-southern. For instance, as Michael Churchman explained some years ago, Walter Bagehot, the prominent editor of the *Economist,* was moved by five distinct issues: concern for commerce, particularly the cotton trade; "anti-slavery sentiments"; a love of liberty and a dislike for democracy; a hatred for "the wastefulness of war"—particularly one he believed the North could not win; and a "smug Englishness."[114] E. D. Steele has characterized Gladstone's attitude toward the war as a similar amalgam of conflicting feelings: a dislike of slavery; a sense that united and determined as it was, the Confederacy would be impossible to destroy; fear of social unrest in Lancashire should the cotton famine persist; a regard for what he took to be an "authentic manifestation of nationality" in the South; and a skcpticism of American democracy.[115] Stephen Meardon writes that the war confronted Richard Cobden with a quandary in which he had to choose between three dear but (in this case) conflicting principles: peace, free trade, and antislavery. Where Cobden's partner, John Bright, compromised his free trade principles by accepting the Federal blockade for the sake of ending the war and obtaining emancipation, Cobden "did not acknowledge the trilemma and refused to choose."[116] These characteristic mixtures of expedience, idealism, and prejudice capture the complex nature of the calculations that helped produce what was a typically ambivalent but complicated British opinion.[117] A multiplicity of discourses played a role in reaching these decisions rather than a single-minded will to power.

Indeed, no single issue, not even slavery, proved decisive in influencing British opinion or policy.[118] In the summer and fall of 1862, when the cabinet seriously contemplated intervention in the war, it indicated repeatedly that slavery constituted no obstacle to recognition of the Confederacy.[119] Earl Russell, the foreign secretary, went so far as to say during his Blairgowrie speech in October 1863 that hostility to slavery could not become a primary consideration in guiding policy toward the Confederacy. Although he considered slavery "one of the most horrible crimes that yet disgraces humanity," he doubted "whether it would be expedient or useful for humanity that we should introduce that new element of declaring that we will have no relations with a people who permit slavery to exist among them."[120] What went for slavery went for other issues. William Schaw Lindsay, the great shipowner, Confederate supporter, and MP for Sunderland, might have argued that a single issue—northern tariffs—had caused the war (and determined his position), but a perusal of his correspondence reveals that a number of other factors conditioned his sympathies.[121]

In an environment where opinion was dependent on a wide variety of factors, attitudes could shift rather rapidly with events in the same way that a complex pattern could change dramatically with a quarter-turn of a kaleidoscope. Such was especially the case in 1861, when a torrent of unprecedented American developments confronted the British public and attitudes had not enjoyed sufficient time to solidify. D. P. Crook has referred to a "disenchanting march of events" that took place in the United States during the first six months of the conflict that tended to disaffect British opinion and undermine the Anglo-American relationship. These included the apparent paralysis of the Federal government as one state seceded after another, the Morrill Tariff, the imposition of the blockade, the American reaction to the Queen's Neutrality Proclamation, and the defeat at Bull Run.[122] All of these events had important implications for British interests since the length of the war, the developments that issued from it, and its outcome would impinge on the British people in a variety of ways. Later events, such as the *Trent* affair and the Emancipation Proclamation, also told with the British public. The military situation, which seemed much more fluid to British observers toward the beginning of the war, exerted an influence on British attitudes that scholars have not always fully appreciated. For a number of British commentators, Federal defeat at the end of the Peninsula Campaign in July 1862 brought to a close the North's last, best chance to stamp out the rebellion.[123] Federal persistence in the aftermath of this reverse seemed futile and alienated opinion, which groaned at the continuation of a war that seemed hugely disruptive of British interests. Observers did not find their minds changed solely by the great events of the war; vivid or instructive personal experiences also played an important role as well. For example, in June 1862 Frank Vizetelly, illustrator and correspondent for the *Illustrated London News,* who had hitherto sympathized with the Federals, converted after he visited newly occupied Memphis and found no Union feeling whatsoever. His eyes were opened to the idea that "there is more bitterness of feeling evinced toward the North by Memphians than I ever saw displayed by Italians to the Austrians," that the Confederacy was "unanimous," and that reconstruction was "impossible." He asked, "what is to be the result of all this bloodshed?"[124] Vizetelly became a partisan for the South and soon had himself smuggled into the Confederacy.

What a survey of the factors that influenced British opinion should make clear is that commentators were moved mainly by British interests. While sorting his thoughts about Confederate recognition, William Gregory, MP for County Galway and one of the South's foremost supporters in the House of Commons, wrote, "I must . . . observe that when I speak of Southern interests, I consider English interests indissolubly connected with them."[125] Likewise, when justifying Confederate recognition before his Sheffield constituency in 1863, John Roebuck claimed, "I can tell you that it is to me an entirely English question" since "what I have to consider is what is for the interest of England."[126] In the same year, Colonel Edward Bruce Hamley, who frequently wrote about American affairs in *Blackwood's Edinburgh Magazine,* complained that both belligerents in America "profess to be outraged by England's selfish regard for her own interests," but, as he asked pointedly, "since when has self-interest become so little important in international questions?" Indeed, he argued, "the welfare of his own country is the first and most legitimate consideration of a statesman."[127] In other words, British opinion was not pro-northern or pro-southern as much as it was pro-British. As we shall see throughout this book, this attitude could sometimes inspire postcolonial dreams of using the Civil War as an opportunity to reforge the Anglo-American relationship and reconstruct the North and the South in conformity with British interests.

It would seem natural that political ideology and social class influenced understandings of Britain's interests—and therefore attitudes toward the war. Such has been one of the core tenets of the traditional interpretation of British opinion, and a number of British commentators at the time saw opinion in much the same way.[128] The influence of politics and class, however, did not always operate in a straightforward way. Clearly, some important working-class papers, such as the *Bee-Hive* and *Lloyd's Weekly Newspaper,* asserted that the upper classes supported the Confederacy because "the spectacle of a dismantled and shivered republic may be a lesson to the odious radicals who want an extension of the suffrage, the ballot, the abolition of church rates, &c."[129] Such claims may have been a matter of political point-scoring, but it is clear that these views were widespread at the time. Middle-of-the-road Bagehot, for example, who disliked Radicals and the Federal government's behavior in equal measure, saw British opinion dividing along similar lines. As he described it, abolitionists, merchants, Radicals, and "the Democracy of Britain" supported the North because they dreaded "the discredit of Republican institutions," believed Federal victory "would be the shortest way to peace," and thought emancipation would naturally follow from northern success. Against this alliance was arrayed "the governing classes as a whole, the Conservatives generally, and probably the majority of the middle classes, and most statesmen certainly" who wished for the independence of the South.[130] Yet much evidence points to the fact that political beliefs and social position influenced opinion in far different—and unpredictable—ways. As Royden Harrison pointed out years ago in his attempt to save the traditional interpretation (even as he inadvertently undermined it), considerations of class interest among workers did not necessarily point sympathy to one side or the other.[131] Harrison's thesis explains why *Reynolds's Newspaper,* one of Britain's great working-class journals, could relentlessly demand that the Royal Navy break the Federal blockade one year and then claim the United States was a shining example of what common people could achieve "without crowned monarchs, hereditary nobles, or privileged classes of any kind" in another.[132] The stance on the blockade would have favored the Confederacy, while the comments about democracy formed part of an encomium for the North; both, however, seemed consistent from a working-class perspective.

Another relationship that did not appear to operate in a straightforward way was the link between Britons' sympathies and their attitudes toward government policy. Support for one side or the other most often did not indicate a desire to dispense with Britain's policy of neutrality. In other words, contrary to the intimations of revisionists, policy did not reflect British attitudes toward both sides. Indeed, a number of politicians repeatedly and publicly distinguished between the "direction the sympathies of people took" and "the line of conduct which [the] country as a whole pursued."[133] While the people indulged their feelings, they recognized that the government had to consider interests.[134] British commentators repeatedly stressed the separation between sympathy and policy. In 1861, the *Spectator* made this very distinction when it asserted in the wake of the Queen's Neutrality Proclamation that "the *policy* of England is neutrality, but its *bias* remains to be defined."[135] In his famous *Fraser's Magazine* article of 1862, John Stuart Mill clearly saw the difference between Britain's official political stance of neutrality and its "moral attitude."[136] Almost all agreed that no matter what the public's feelings toward the American war might be, the policy of neutrality was best. In 1863, Bagehot, in the *Economist,* claimed of Britons that "though singularly divided in our *sympathies* on this matter [the war], we are singularly united in our *intentions* and decision. We all of us know so distinctly what we shall do, that we feel no scruple in expressing with equal distinctness what we *think.*"[137] Toward the end of the war, *The Times* stated essentially the same thing, claiming that in Britain there were "many wellwishers both to North and South, but though opinion is divided on this subject we believe there is an almost universal approval of the observance by this Government of the strictest and most impartial neutrality."[138] All in all, as the *Spectator* asserted, in assessing British opinion of the American question, it was a mistake to confound "calm with indifference."[139]

This distinction between sympathy and policy was related to an important discrepancy in the expression of opinion: prominent politicians and journalists often wrote or said different things in private and public. In private, they felt the freedom to express their personal sympathies, but in public they often felt an obligation to weigh their words lest they damage the Anglo-American relationship and harm British interests. British visitors to the United States during this period were especially wary of issuing statements that would make them targets of American harassment. The experience of Russell weighed especially heavily on journalists. Lawley presents a particularly good example of a correspondent who kept his true feelings to himself. In a private letter to William Gregory, he lamented that "the Demon of Cupidity" had infected the South and that after a Confederate victory, "the old scramble for wealth, the old levelling downwards" would completely eradicate the disinterested ethos associated with the Cavalier. "Pour moi," he concluded, "I despair of this continent."[140] Lawley, however, never spoke in such terms to southerners because he feared retaliation.[141] Moreover, antagonizing southerners would conflict with his self-appointed task of propagandist for the Confederacy. Whatever his feelings about the South's limitations, he sincerely supported the cause; in 1863, while accompanying the Army of Northern Virginia as it invaded Pennsylvania, Lawley antagonized a Unionist crowd in the lobby of a Chambersburg hotel by "showing them a twenty-dollar Confederate note" and crowing that "in a month it would be worth more than all their greenbacks in the North put together."[142] Lawley was not alone in his conflicted expressions. In an 1862 article, Hamley complained that the "deprecatory tone adopted by our journalists and public speakers" which sought to conciliate the Americans did not at all match the much harder sentiments often expressed in "private life."[143] The same inconsistency characterized the expressions of politicians, especially members of the government. Lord Palmerston felt nothing but loathing for Lincoln's administration, and privately he used harsh language when mentioning the Federal government. In a private missive to Lord John Russell (made Earl Russell in July 1861), he explained why the low quality of the Federal leadership was no accident: "The History of the world in all Times and Countries shows that Power in the Hands of the Masses throws the Scum of the Community to the Surface and that Truth and Justice are Soon banished from the Land—we Should all fare in the Same way under the Sway of [John] Bright and his associates."[144] Yet, these sentiments never found their way into his speeches, and there is no evidence that these feelings influenced Palmerston's official conduct toward America.

Still, according to American and particularly northern tastes, Britain did not show sufficient restraint. The harsh judgments of British newspapers and the clumsy comments of British public figures led to much anger in the United States. Lord Stanley, MP for King's Lynn (and son of the 14th Earl of Derby, leader of the Conservatives), understood the damage done by British commentary, telling his constituents that "I do not wonder at the annoyance which Americans sometimes feel and express at the summary way in which we here undertake to settle their affairs for them."[145] For this and other reasons, the Anglo-American relationship suffered from a serious crisis that had important implications for British opinion. From the perspective of many Britons, the North's repeated failures, its tenacity in an apparently impossible cause, its heedlessness of the damage that the war inflicted on British interests, and its unwillingness to accept the counsel of the transatlantic community's leading nation made it a source of enormous frustration. This frustration manifested itself in acerbic criticisms and advice. By December 1862, *The Times* threw up its hands in despair, claiming that "it is of little use to counsel America, if we are to reason from facts, and she from dreams and hallucinations."[146] The Anglo-American relationship had entered a vicious spiral, and British opinion was sucked down this vortex.

As the war continued, northern hostility toward Britain grew rapidly. Under these circumstances, American commentators had begun to call the nature of the entire postcolonial relationship into question. A July 1862 *New York Times* editorial well captures the degree to which northerners believed Britain had not lived up to the obligations demanded by such a relationship. The newspaper admitted that in the past, when British orators had spoken about "'common blood, common liberties, common literature,' and all that," Americans had believed them, and a special relationship had bound the two countries together. Wartime developments, however, had taught Americans that "nations have no sympathies; that in the great family of peoples, whether of 'common blood' or of the most diverse blood, as in the great family of nature, the success in the 'struggle for life' is only to the strong, and that power and success are alone considered in the relations of Governments." It was clear, then, that Britain believed there were no special relationships, just power. And when a great imperial state like Britain advised Americans to let the South go in peace for the sake of "British manufactures," northerners could only see such comments as the most cynical hypocrisy. The British press lacked even the most elemental empathy necessary for maintaining a relationship that went beyond mere power politics. British newspapers had made no effort to undertake a "generous and intelligent understanding of a terrible foreign difficulty" and had not bothered to put "themselves historically or politically in our places, to get at our stand point."[147] An enormous gap had opened up between Americans and Britons in the way they perceived the war.

One can measure the size of this gap by reading an exchange of letters between Gladstone and Cyrus Field, the American entrepreneur who laid the first transatlantic cable. Hoping to convert Gladstone to a more sympathetic view of Federal policy, Field mailed his friend a copy of William Stevenson's *Thirteen Months with the Rebel Army* (1862) in late 1862. A New Yorker in Arkansas on business during the secession crisis, Stevenson found himself forced to join a Tennessee infantry regiment and serve the Confederacy for a little over a year before he managed to desert. The main theme of his work, as Stevenson put it, was "that if the North had known the whole truth as to the *power, the unanimity, and the deadly purpose* of the leaders in the rebellion, the government would have been far better prepared for promptly meeting the crisis."[148] Undoubtedly, Field wished to impress on Gladstone the extent to which the South was rude, violent, illiberal, and ruled by the mob. As he put it in a letter to Gladstone, Field was "sure that if you have facts, you will draw correct conclusions from them."[149] Unfortunately for Field, Gladstone read the work very differently, asserting that it only confirmed his views. The South's unity and commitment to secession, "proved by every page of this Book," made northern success an "impossibility" and the war itself, therefore, "unjust."[150] Gladstone forwarded the book to Sir George Cornewall Lewis, who found it "one of the most interesting narrations I have ever read," but who also believed that "it shows how united & determined the South are, and what an impossible task the North have undertaken."[151]

The Federal government was determined to persist in this task, as evidenced by the Emancipation Proclamation, which, as the British recognized, heralded a new, harder phase of the war. A novel, if controversial, sense of purpose in the North was matched by the growth of is armed force as well as the emergence of better military leadership. British images of northerners reacted in several ways to the deterioration of the Anglo-American relationship, the growth of Federal military power, and the increasing violence of the war. In some cases, British commentators dispensed with the usual ambivalence and chose to distance themselves from the Yankee by decisively fixing him as a savage Other. For instance, at a breakfast held by Gladstone in 1864, Lord Stanley remembered someone claiming, "with general assent," that the war "had exhibited quite a new phase of American character—recklessness, not only of life, but of money, and a kind of volcanic force not before suspected to exist." Applying a traditional image to this unprecedented development, James Anthony Froude, a prominent historian, responded, "Scratch an American, and you find a Red Indian."[152] The problem with this attitude was that it ineluctably led to the disowning of the Americans, abandonment of the postcolonial relationship, and loss of British influence. A number of commentators, however, were quite prepared to take this step. In a January 1862 essay in *Blackwood's Edinburgh Magazine*, Hamley explicitly disavowed the transatlantic connection. No one, he claimed, "talks about 'our Transatlantic kinsmen,'" and he dismissed those who used the phrase "our American cousins" as "twaddling sentimentalists." Nobody, he argued, "desires to claim peculiar ties with the performers in the absurd and barbarous dances which the American nation executes round its idols of the hour, any more than with the worshippers of Mumbo Jumbo."[153] It is significant in this case that Hamley, through his reference to "Mumbo Jumbo," explicitly compared Americans to the Mandinkas, a West African people. The attempt to render Yankees as bizarre and exotic creatures who saw the world in their own idiosyncratic way also led to the creation of "Manhattan" (a pseudonym for James A. Scoville, John C. Calhoun's former private secretary), the *Standard's* New York correspondent.[154] The *Standard* itself described him as a "notoriety" and a "vulgar American," while the *Saturday Review* portrayed him as a "clever buffoon who . . . acts the part of the drunken helot" and whose writing was "absurd to the pitch of raving insanity."[155] At the head of his correspondence, the *Standard* consistently ran a disclaimer: "We continue to publish 'Manhattan's' letters, notwithstanding some of his statements may be offensive to English ears, believing that it is desirable our readers should have reliable information from the powerful section of the American community of which he is the representative."[156] The letters themselves were declamatory and strangely written, but without further evidence it is hard to determine if Scoville wrote this correspondence in earnest or if he was perpetuating a joke designed to pander to British prejudices.

Others sought to restore the relationship on British terms. Whether they supported the North or the South, they believed that Britain still possessed the power to influence American affairs for the better. For example, John Elliott Cairnes, the classical political economist, protégé of Mill, and author of *The Slave Power* (1862), called for a deliberate renewal of this relationship. He suggested that British Radicals could improve northern behavior and save the transatlantic connection by guiding the "better and more influential minds of the Republican party."[157] Indeed, some British Radicals used their status as partisans of the North and employed their connections in the United States to influence various northern statesmen. The extensive correspondence between John Bright and Richard Cobden on the one hand, and Charles Sumner (the Republican senator from Massachusetts and chairman of the Committee on Foreign Relations) on the other, is a good example of this influence. Edward Horsman saw a different route to restoring British influence. In his December 1861 speech to his constituents in Stroud, he asserted that the failure of democracy and the Union would compel northerners to return to British norms—indeed, the strength and familiarity of the British example meant they could not do otherwise. Their eyes opened to the weaknesses of their constitution, northerners would revert to "old English law" and form a "stronger Government" where "the few will govern and the many obey, instead of every man governing and no man obeying." Once the North had embraced such "sound and rational" principles of government, Horsman predicted, "you will then see a new empire start forth with a new future before it—with a higher intelligence, with a sounder morality, with a purer patriotism—and then if old England is fallen or decayed she may still live again in the blood and the sinews of a young Anglo-Saxon giant, who inherits her energies and perpetuates her language, her civilization, and religion to nations and ages yet unborn."[158] The war, then, would prove a salutary lessons for the Americans, leading to a rebirth and blossoming of the postcolonial relationship with Britain. The two nations would become one, and even should Britain die, it would live on in America. This vision was a fantasy, but it shows the degree to which the postcolonial idea still generated much enthusiasm in Britain.

With a better sense, perhaps, of what was possible, still other British commentators recognized that the time had come to rework the Anglo-American relationship and stop speaking to Americans as if they were former, current, or potential colonial people. We have already seen in the introduction how the *Spectator* believed that the waxing of American power meant Britain had "to adopt the tone which befits equals" and "make all those allowances men so readily make for equals and with such difficulty to inferiors."[159] Even more important, the weekly conceded that the war had either revealed or developed a new American national character that could no longer be defined with reference to Britain. "The American," the *Spectator* admitted, "is not simply an Englishman in his shirt sleeves, but that and something more."[160] Leave it to Benjamin Disraeli, then leader of the Conservatives in the Commons, to put the matter in grander terms during his oft-quoted response to the Speech from the Throne in 1863. Before the war, he argued, the United States had been "colonies." The conflict, however, had actuated a number of latent forces for change that had precipitated a "great revolution." It was clear to Disraeli that a different America would emerge at the end of the fighting. He predicted that this new country would be "an America of armies, of diplomacy, of rival states and manoeuvring Cabinets, of frequent turbulence, and probably of frequent wars." Moreover, he assumed that American events were not "of a mere casual character." Rather, they would exert as sustained an influence on European affairs as the French Revolution.[161] Disraeli was wrong in his apparent assumption that the Confederacy would win its independence, but his statement is important because it indicates a recognition that Americans had undergone a great transformation. They were no longer colonists or "Anglo-Americans," as Tocqueville had described them. Nor were they an adjunct nation. Rather, they were now a distinct and unique people like other civilized peoples who would speak the language of power and exert great influence on European affairs.

Once the Federals won the war in 1865, British journalists and politicians worked swiftly to repair the Anglo-American relationship. Southerners and northerners were recognized as honorary Anglo-Saxons, the former for their gallantry against long odds, the latter for their perseverance and discipline. The British press, which had vilified and ridiculed President Abraham Lincoln for much of the conflict, wrote handsome eulogies (sometimes grudgingly) about the assassinated American leader. In 1867, at a public breakfast for William Lloyd Garrison, Earl Russell, who had been foreign secretary during the war, apologized for not having done justice to the difficulties facing Lincoln and the United States in wiping out slavery.[162] And by 1872, the British government eventually settled the *Alabama* claims, paying the United States over $15 million for the destruction inflicted on American shipping by Confederate vessels built in Britain during the war. For the rest of the century, when referring to the United States, British public figures continued to use the language of kinship, family resemblance, and a common race. America, as numerous observers pointed out, still had important lessons to teach, especially since many agreed with Lewis that the war was the "greatest political event which has occurred in the political world since the definitive fall of Napoleon in 1815."[163]

Yet close observation of Americans during the war revealed the extent to which the United States was no longer comparable to Britain. As we shall see, the war disclosed that white Americans and Britons increasingly saw eye to eye on race, but on other topics there was not as much of a meeting of the minds. Observers came to recognize that American politics and society were so different from what obtained in Britain that analogies could no longer be made between the two nations, and British standards were increasingly difficult to apply. Largely because of their unique political and social systems, the Americans waged their war in a way that seemed insupportable to many British observers. Finally, British commentators frequently proved unable or unwilling to understand the workings of an American nationalism that seemed so similar yet different from their own.

In late April 1865, as the Civil War was winding down, Delane had the nerve to ask Russell if he was interested in entering "upon the congenial task of describing the process of re-construction" for *The Times*. Proposing that Russell make a six-month visit to the United States, Delane believed his star correspondent would now face few obstacles. "Your Federalism is well known," he asserted, and "there is no longer any question of Stanton's permission." The only difficulty would consist of "adjusting the many interests which have grown up during the contest to be weighed & discussed."[164] Russell's response dwelled mainly on financial matters. To Morris, he wrote, "If I could afford to make the sacrifice which an acceptance of the terms you offer me . . . would impose I would make my interests subsidiary to sentiment, but my circumstances do not permit me to yield to my feelings." Russell enclosed a short memorandum showing how much more he could earn at home.[165] This memorandum must have seemed pointed since Russell and *The Times* had still not yet settled his expense account from the 1861–1862 visit. Obviously, finances were important to Russell, but it is hard to imagine that he did not consider the thirteen harrowing and uncomfortable months he had already spent in America. He liked many of the individuals he had met, looked upon American institutions as a noble experiment, and admired the "real & prodigious power & energy of this people in spite of all their bunkum." Yet halfway through his stay he concluded that northerners were "so very French I can not cotton to them" and the South "was not fit for me."[166] That Russell used such expressions to describe Americans not only shows how far Britain and the United States had drifted apart, but also corresponds in part with Disraeli's vision of America's future. Not surprisingly, Russell declined *The Times*' offer.

3

BRITAIN, THE CIVIL WAR, AND RACE

> No doubt, it is common to hear the disclaimer—"Of course we don't approve of slavery!" but I think it will generally be found that this is but the prelude to a discourse showing how much is to be said for the institution.
>
> —JOHN ELLIOTT CAIRNES, 1862

> It is a remarkable fact to reflect upon that we have had the Negro so long before us now, and yet that there is so little agreement as yet upon his intellectual character and capabilities—upon what can ultimately be made of him. The phenomenon is before us, but is not yet explained.
>
> —*THE TIMES*, 1863

THE KEMBLES, THE BUTLERS, AND BLACK AMERICANS

Perhaps the best measure of changing transatlantic attitudes toward race during the mid-nineteenth century consists of a comparison of the ideas expressed by Fanny Kemble, a prominent British actress, and her daughter, Fan Butler. In December 1838, Fanny Kemble arrived on Butler Island, Georgia, with her husband, Pierce Butler, one of the state's greatest slaveowners. Butler and others had led her to believe that his Georgia estates possessed a reputation for enlightened management.[1] Kemble had left the family residence in Philadelphia "prepared to find many mitigations in the practice to the general injustice and cruelty of the system—much kindness on the part of the masters, much content on that of the slaves."[2] Nonetheless, she headed South "prejudiced against slavery," for as "an Englishwoman . . . the absence of such prejudices would be disgraceful."[3] Kemble believed that the shortcomings of African Americans were due to their circumstances, not to their race.[4] Anticipating that her time in the South would constitute a test of her principles, she kept a travelogue in the form of letters to Elizabeth Sedgwick (sister-in-law of the novelist Catharine Sedgwick), her intimate abolitionist friend. Kemble would eventually publish these letters in *Journal of a Residence on a Georgian Plantation in 1838–1839* (1863), an extraordinary book that provided far more of an insider's view of slavery than any other work by an antebellum British visitor.

What Kemble saw first on Butler Island and then at Hampton Point on St. Simons Island only confirmed her views; slavery, not race, accounted for the shortcomings of black slaves.[5] Indeed, one of the main themes of her journal was that the "detestable qualities, which I constantly hear attributed to them [slaves] as innate and inherent in their race, appear to me the direct result of their condition."[6] Although she did not shy away from describing the physical hardships of slavery, it was the moral degradation of the institution that appalled her.[7] Realizing that she was implicated in the slave system, she could not view it as a disinterested spectator. As she explained, "with shame and grief of heart I say it, by their unpaid labor I live—their nakedness clothes me, and their heavy toil maintains me in luxurious idleness."[8] Kemble attempted to reform practices at the estates, but her husband refused to countenance her projects. She drew parallels between herself and the slaves; both were subject to the same master, who was unwilling to ameliorate the wretchedness that surrounded them. After Butler refused to accept any more petitions from slaves, Kemble wept with frustration "for them, for myself, for US."[9]

The visit to Georgia dealt a fatal wound to her already troubled marriage.[10] Upon their return to Philadelphia in May 1839, Kemble threatened to leave Butler if he did not cease living upon the labor of slaves. The marriage staggered onward for several more tempestuous years. In 1845, however, fatigued by her "great energy of will" and "decided preference for her own judgment and opinions," both of which were compounded by her vision of marriage as a "companionship on equal terms," Butler finally ejected her from the household.[11] Four years later, a Philadelphia court granted him a divorce.

In March 1866, Butler and one of his daughters by Kemble, Fan, headed back to his Georgia estates to repair his fortunes. These properties had fallen into decay under Federal occupation, but many of his former slaves—now freedmen—had wandered back to the Sea Islands looking for work. Fan became Butler's indispensable helpmate until his death in 1867, when she took over management of his estate. Like her mother, Fan eventually published an account of her experience, *Ten Years on a Georgia Plantation since the War* (1883)—based mainly on contemporary letters that sought to serve as an antidote to her mother's account.

For almost a decade Fan waged an unremitting struggle against flood, drought, labor troubles, lack of capital, armyworm, fluctuating rice prices, and an uncertain political situation to save her patrimony and livelihood. In the end the struggle proved too much for her, and in 1876 she and her husband, James Leigh, an English clergymen, abandoned the properties, left their oversight to an agent, and moved to Britain. In retrospect, Fan partly blamed her black laborers for her failure. Initially she had sought to perpetuate the indulgent paternalism that she believed traditionally characterized the Butler estates. Such a policy not only served as a kind of tribute to her father, but also accorded with her view (based on "hard ethnological facts") of blacks as "children" by "nature and character."[12] Yet these views became unsustainable in the long run as it became clear that her workforce had taken advantage of her paternalism to gain the upper hand in a test of wills.[13] Frustrations with her freedmen led Fan to yearn for greater authority over her workforce. She eventually inclined toward a defense of slavery stripped of sentimentality. She confessed that she was "utterly unable to understand them [her black workers], and what God's will is concerning them, unless He intended they should be slaves."[14]

As one observer who knew both women commented, Kemble believed slavery accounted for all the South's problems, while Fan thought blacks were responsible for the region's difficulties.[15] Where Kemble attributed the behavior of blacks to their status as slaves, Fan claimed that their race determined their nature. Their differing experiences highlight the dramatic shift in racial attitudes that occurred within the Anglo-American world during the mid-Victorian years.[16] Kemble wrote her journal during the heyday of abolitionist sentiment in Britain, when sympathy for the black slave was at its height, and many believed he could be inculcated with British values.[17] Fan Butler wrote in an era when white disappointment with emancipated slaves was palpable and growing, leading to increasing doubts about the capacities of black people and the belief that they were fundamentally different. Although she was somewhat unusual in defending slavery, Fan's assumption that blacks absolutely required white guidance had become increasingly prevalent. In the thirty years that passed between Kemble's and Fan's stays in Georgia,

American and British attitudes toward people of color had begun to move toward one another. The major transatlantic event of this period, the Civil War, must have played a role in transforming British ideas, but what exactly was that role? Did the conflict merely provide an occasion for the expression of existing racist ideas, or did it actually inspire new contributions to racist discourses in Britain?

It appears that the war witnessed the uncovering of a British racism that had been formed during the antebellum period. Masquerading as anecdotal truth and scientific fact, this racism was nonetheless ambivalent. Much like white Americans, African Americans were widely perceived in Britain as possessing a Janus-faced nature. As several commentators understood at the time, however, British racism was uncertain in its understanding of African Americans, and these people remained just as much a mystery at the end of the war as they had at its beginning.

"SYMPATHIES . . . MULTIPLE AND PERVERSE": ANTEBELLUM BRITISH VISIONS OF AFRICAN AMERICANS

Scholars have long recognized that changes in racial attitudes exercised a significant influence on British opinions toward the Civil War. For instance, as early as 1925 Ephraim Douglass Adams hazily referred to "a decay of general humanitarian sentiments" that took place after 1850.[18] Yet Adams never paid much attention to this issue, and succeeding historians of British opinion toward the Civil War have experienced some difficulty in discussing how British racism played a role in shaping responses to the American conflict. To his credit, R.J.M. Blackett recognizes the increasing prevalence of racism in Britain during the 1850s.[19] His interests, however, revolve around reform and abolitionism, while his story concerns itself with the way in which class, religious, and political affiliations influenced British attitudes toward the conflict.[20] Because he views the topic from this perspective, Blackett does not fully integrate racism into his narrative. Meanwhile, Duncan Andrew Campbell admits that by the 1860s "Britain was beginning to emulate American views on race," but he seems determined to minimize the extent and intensity of racist feeling in Britain during the conflict. According to Campbell, the "decisive incident" in the development of British racial thinking only occurred after the Civil War, with the Morant Bay Rebellion (1865) in Jamaica. Nonetheless, in the course of this discussion, he drops the aside that "ideas usually take time before they become widespread," an inadvertence that suggests racist feelings had gained momentum in Britain well before 1865. The main difficulty with Campbell's treatment of this subject is that while pursuing the thesis that slavery constituted "the millstone around the neck of the Confederacy" in Britain, he conflates attitudes toward race with those concerning slavery; if Britons were hostile to slavery, so his argument goes, they could not have been very racist.[21]

In Britain, the rise of racism and the decline of abolitionism were thoroughly intertwined in many different ways; it is impossible to understand one without the other. An animus toward slavery, however, was not synonymous with color-blindness. By looking through a lens that only picks up various intensities of abolitionism, scholars of British opinion during the war have not always detected these different hues of racism. Emphasizing British attitudes toward race during this period is fraught with difficulty. If students of British opinion toward the war have frequently avoided fully coming to terms with the question of race, scholars of race have often gone to the other extreme. As Douglas Lorimer has complained, contemporary scholarship, particularly postcolonial discourse theory, has a tendency to colonize the mid-Victorians as a racist Other. In an attempt to define themselves against this racist past, these academics have tended to drain it of nuance and complexity.[22] British thinking about race during the mid-Victorian period, however, was characterized by conflict, ambiguity, and change.

As soon as racism became more prevalent in Britain, it immediately found itself challenged from without and contested within.[23] From without, the Christian humanitarian discourse associated with abolitionism perpetuated the belief in "particularism-generalism"—that all men were different, but all men were brothers in the eyes of God.[24] Interwoven with British national identity and the evangelical movement, this discourse proved immensely strong.[25] At the same time, as Peter Mandler has argued, the evangelicalism that served as a foundation for abolitionism also contributed (along with Scottish conjectural history) to the emergence of a "civilisational perspective" that stressed the extent to which all people—regardless of their nationality or race—could progress toward civilization.[26] Such attitudes were buttressed by the sciences, particularly the ethnology associated with James Cowles Prichard, who emphasized the common origin of men, attributed their variety to environmental factors, and stressed linguistic and cultural differences rather than physical ones.[27]

At the same time, racial theorists were badly divided. As George Fredrickson, one of the leading historians of race, has lamented, for all the modern discussion of the topic, the word "racism" has long been unstable and ill-defined.[28] The mid-Victorian period was no different, with James Hunt, the controversial founder of the London Anthropological Society, famously pointing out in his 1863 inaugural address that there were "hardly two persons [who used] such an important word as 'race' in the same sense."[29] Discussions of race were also complicated through their intersection with discourses concerning gender, class, nation, and empire.[30] Proponents of the new race science also employed concepts that differed from those used by common people, and British writers not only dismissed American scientific racism but remained ignorant of developments in French racial theory.[31] It is not surprising, then, that racists like Thomas Carlyle and Anthony Trollope did not see eye to eye on very important issues.[32] Moreover, individual racists often felt much ambivalence about the subject. For instance, William Thackeray's attitude toward blacks was inspired by conflicting elements: English abolitionism, an Indian upbringing, and a reaction against his mother's evangelicalism. Not surprisingly, to quote Deborah Thomas, these elements inspired in Thackeray "powerful and contradictory" attitudes toward blacks and slavery.[33]

Regardless of these challenges and difficulties, racism clearly grew more powerful in Britain throughout the 1850s. Carlyle's "Occasional Discourse on the Negro Question" (1849) might have been the product of a cranky maverick, but Trollope's *The West Indies and the Spanish Main* (1859), in which he referred to West Indian blacks as members of a "servile race" and "inferior species," cannot be so easily dismissed.[34] The abolitionist idea of a man and a brother—a supplicant who suffered from heathenism, but was nonetheless a man and a brother for all that—was slowly but surely faltering before a new vision of an incorrigible alien and inferior. The mid-Victorians themselves were well aware that their views had changed and commented upon this phenomenon extensively. In 1862, the *Saturday Review* claimed that a "great revolution" in British attitudes toward blacks had taken place in the previous generation: "Interest in our 'black brother' continued some time after his emancipation but gradually began to die away, and finally was to some extent replaced by contemptuous indifference and indignant depreciation."[35]

To some extent, abolitionists themselves were to blame for this revolution. Some members of the movement displayed patronizing attitudes toward blacks and reduced them to passive subjects who required British assistance.[36] Widespread abolitionist propaganda also inadvertently led the British public to identify blacks with slavery. As an 1853 essay in *Fraser's Magazine* put it, "there is some cloudiness in the perception of John Bull which induces him to consider every man with a black face as a slave, and one entitled to his, Mr. Bull's, especial protection."[37] This association of African Americans with slavery and degradation facilitated the habits of mind that automatically linked blackness and debasement. Indeed, abolitionist images and tropes often became unmoored from their original context and served sinister ends. Meanwhile abolitionists and other reformers did not achieve their overly ambitious goals of promoting improvement overseas. Perceived failures in these areas, particularly in the West Indies, led many Britons to question the abilities of people of color.[38]

Various domestic social and cultural developments also may have contributed to the rise of racism. Lorimer has posited that as social mobility slowed and widespread poverty refused to succumb to the progress of the age, Britons' attitudes toward class became more exclusive. As a more tough-minded disposition toward the lower orders emerged and blacks became automatically associated with these lower orders, elites proved less susceptible to appeals based on sentimental humanitarianism and more inclined toward authoritarianism.[39] Catherine Hall has also suggested that as Dissent moved from the peripheries to the center of political power, it became less inclined to identify with other outsiders—such as blacks overseas—to form part of a universal brotherhood. Instead, Dissenters' identity was increasingly defined by a discourse of exclusion that revolved around white, independent manliness.[40] Both deliberately and unconsciously, a variety of mass media also helped promote racism. Several scholars have drawn a link between the information explosion of the mid-nineteenth century and the growth of racism.[41]

American slavery also figured prominently in British discussions of race. This contribution to the British conversation was complex and difficult to interpret, largely because it was filtered through a series of discourses associated with the Anglo-American relationship, national identity, the meaning of freedom, and the worth of democracy. As Sidney Smith's famous 1820 rant in the *Edinburgh Review* suggests, attacks on American slavery were often linked to assaults on American claims to distinction and pretensions to liberty.[42]

It was in this context that minstrelsy constituted the single most important American influence on British representations of the African American during the antebellum era. Undoubtedly, this form of popular culture did incalculable harm in Britain to the image of the American slave by depicting him as lazy, happy, mischievous, sly, careless, irresponsible, impulsive, pretentious, uneducated, sentimental, and inferior.[43] The extent and nature of this harm, however, remains difficult to ascertain. Michael Pickering has made a strong case that minstrelsy provided Britons with a black Other, a subterranean self that helped define English national identity and justify imperial expansion overseas.[44] Yet a number of factors probably blunted minstrelsy's pernicious racial influence. As several scholars have argued, Britons embraced the form, made it their own, modified it according to their own traditions, and drained it of racial content.[45] Even more important is the question of minstrelsy's fundamentally ambivalent and contested nature. Contemporary students of minstrelsy are unanimous in arguing that while the form denigrated African Americans, it simultaneously used blackface as a shield from behind which to engage in social protest—a way "to laugh at social pretension, posturing and pomposity, and to mock the holders of authority and power."[46] Minstrelsy, as Eric Lott has asserted, carnivalized race, which meant that its "ideological production became more contradictory, its consumption more indeterminate, its political effects more plural than many have assumed."[47] Impossible to control, minstrelsy, like British racism, was never "monolithic or simply hegemonic."[48]

Another related import from America that has often been associated with influencing British views of race is Harriet Beecher Stowe's *Uncle Tom's Cabin; or, Life among the Lowly* (1852).[49] The diversity and complexity of British reactions to the book were due partly to the fact that it owed a great deal to minstrelsy for its dialog and characterizations. Readers of the novel, as Sarah Meer claims, "could harbor sympathies as multiple and perverse as those of any blackface audience."[50] It is easy to see how the "plethora of tie-ins and spin-offs" associated with Tom-mania led to a "fragmenting and diversifying" of the public's understanding of the book.[51] Meer claims the combination of blackface, sentimentality, patriotism, and antislavery attitudes that characterized *Uncle Tom*-inspired plays "made for a very strange cocktail" in which audiences "wept for stage slaves, cheered at their rebellions, reflected smugly on the superiority of British laws and attitudes, and also laughed at images of dim, deceitful, and inherently comical blacks."[52]

These American imports exposed the risks inherent in Britain's postcolonial relationship with the United States; while Britain felt obliged to engage with cultures under its sway, it ran the risk of becoming contaminated by the values of these other cultures. Frederick Douglass recognized this dynamic in 1860 when he spoke to a Newcastle audience about the "reciprocal influence" between the two nations. Globalization had brought these two countries ever closer, and the "proximity to and intercourse with the United States . . . endangered the high moral purity of England on the question of slavery." Where once Britain had been color-blind, Douglass now found "American prejudice" in "nearly all" of Britain's "commercial towns."[53]

The extent to which Americans could control the representation of their slaves within this relationship indicated how much power they exercised in relation to Britain. Americans made it very difficult for British visitors to report on the nature of the African American slave. As we have seen in chapter 1, southerners carefully controlled access to slaves, while British visitors were reluctant to criticize the slaveowners whose hospitality had made visits to the South possible in the first place. Consequently, as Fanny Kemble pointed out, "it is morally impossible for any Englishman going into the Southern states except as a *resident,* to know any thing whatever of the real condition of the slave population."[54] In any event, many travelers clearly did not want to witness slavery firsthand because they found it too distressing.[55] Instead of undergoing such an ordeal, it was much easier to think of the question in the abstract.[56] For these reasons, travel literature was filled with discussions of the slave system and its political, social, and economic consequences, but it rarely examined slaves themselves. A British metropolitan population that rarely encountered black people, let alone African Americans, was left to form its image of the slave from literature, lectures, and popular entertainment.[57]

The African American lecturers who toured Britain throughout the antebellum period constituted the great exception to this rule. They were popular, accomplished, and, especially after the passage of the Fugitive Slave Act in

1850, numerous. As Blackett claims, they possessed a "legitimacy" and "authenticity" that made them "bona fide" representatives of the more than 3 million black Americans who remained in chains. Few of these lecturers, however, sought to counter British racism because they feared such a tack would distract from their main mission, which consisted of building a moral cordon around the United States. Meanwhile, it is not clear what British audiences learned from these encounters. That British newspapers in one issue could praise lectures by Douglass and William Lloyd Garrison and in the next encourage readers to visit a traveling minstrel show indicates that Britons possessed a far from straightforward attitude toward African American slaves.[58]

British reactions to John Brown's raid in 1859 provide an interesting means of gauging this complex stance toward slaves on the eve of the Civil War. Initially, newspapers portrayed the raid as a servile insurrection, conjuring up images of slave rebellions in ancient Rome and more recent uprisings in Haiti. From this perspective, black slaves played the role of vengeful savages prepared to commit the worst atrocities in a fight to the finish against their masters. When it became clear that Brown's plans had failed, the image of the slave reverted to the passive and harmless creature who, enervated by slavery, required white guidance. Attention subsequently focused on Brown, the man who had attempted to mislead them. British reporting of the incident indicates, as Seymour Drescher argues, that the image of the slave was "sharply bifurcated."[59] This bifurcation was due, partly, to the many discourses that collided in any discussion of African Americans. As *The Times* pointed out, the events at Harper's Ferry were connected with "the growth of cotton in India or West Africa, with the instincts of the Anglo-Saxon race, with the intellectual powers of the African, with the principles of self-government, with the theory of the American Constitution."[60] Clearly, imperial concerns never lay far away from British considerations of American slaves.[61]

When the Civil War broke out, British views of African Americans—as well as of all people of color—were contradictory and increasingly negative. Lorimer has rightfully referred to the "the many-sided stereotype of the Negro" that portrayed African Americans simultaneously as children and savages.[62] They could play the roles of passive Christian martyr and untamed heathen. They could serve as vehicles for critiques of bourgeois values and justifications for imperialism. They could be objects of pity and of fear. They could be the paradoxical Other that served as an object against which to define national identity while also acting as a "subterranean self." What is more, they could be all of these things at once.[63] W. T. Lhamon has likened the reception of minstrelsy to the curious sensation associated with Ludwig Wittgenstein's "duck-rabbit," and it appears that in mid-Victorian Britain the African American's image resembled this curious creature.[64]

Moreover, with the Civil War's outbreak, a number of intelligent British observers realized that racism was increasingly an "Anglo-Saxon" problem rather than a uniquely American one; it had become an imperial issue that faced all of Greater Britain. In 1862, while discussing northern racism, Edward Dicey, correspondent for both *Macmillan's Magazine* and the *Spectator*, referred to the treatment of the "native Irish," the "Chinese in Australia," the "New Zealanders by the colonists," and the "Hindoos under the Company's rule" while arguing that Anglo-Saxons had "shown a uniform intolerance of an inferior race." In so many ways, America was "the complement of England," and in race, as on other issues, "the national virtues of the New World are very much those of the mother country, developed on a different and a broader scale."[65]

BRITISH DIFFICULTIES DISCUSSING RACE DURING THE CIVIL WAR

It would seem that the war ought to have clarified British thinking about African Americans. As northern forces penetrated Confederate territory and outsiders enjoyed unprecedented opportunities for unimpeded views of slaves, there was a sense in Britain that the true nature of the African American would finally become apparent. John Malcolm Forbes Ludlow, the prominent Christian Socialist, argued in an 1864 pamphlet that before the war the British public had to rely on "the representations of masters and of their friends," the "overcharged" accounts of abolitionists, and the depictions of escaped slaves whose knowledge "was at best local and limited, presumably tinged with passion, resentment, habits of falsehood, [and] likely to represent only extreme cases." Now, he wrote, northern armies had overrun "the domain of the slave-power . . . well nigh from end to end" and "what the white man may have failed to see, the black man has told." These circumstances had "cast a flood of light upon the condition of the American slaves."[66]

These opportunities, however, produced more smoke than light, partly because the topic of slavery prompted the collision of several powerful, related, and yet contradictory discourses. Abolitionism still retained great power in Britain during the war, and a postcolonial discourse led Britons to believe they had a special role to play in the resolution of the "negro question" in America. For one thing, slavery was a legacy of the old imperial connection, and Britain had a special obligation to assist Americans in destroying the institution.[67] By emancipating its own slaves, Britain had also earned a moral superiority that reinforced its right to counsel the United States on this topic.[68] Certainly, the *National Review* hoped, Britain's good name would never be "marred by the accusation of having helped to fasten upon the greatest of her descendants that bondage and curse which, by an almost superhuman effort, she had cast from off her own shoulders."[69] These types of arguments had the benefit of perpetuating Britain's cultural imperialism by keeping Americans within Britain's moral orbit.

Yet as the foregoing indicates, Britons who discussed slavery and the capacities of the African American were also involved in an imperial discourse that focused on questions concerning the labor and raw materials on which British commerce and industry depended. From the beginning of the American conflict until its end, British commentators fretted about how the war would affect the labor force that produced cotton for Lancashire's mills. Early in the secession crisis, *Lloyd's Weekly Newspaper* pointed out that "when the Lancashire mill-owner or operative feels his blood boil at the indignities and cruelties heaped upon the coloured race" in America, "he does not always remember that to the slave states . . . he owes his all; that it is to his advantage the negro should wear his chains in peace. . . . Lancashire depends on slavery."[70] This concern inclined many British observers against anything that might throw southern society into turmoil and disrupt the production of cotton—including secession and sudden emancipation.[71] While considering the cotton supply in the fall of 1861, the *British Quarterly Review* felt less worried about the Federal blockade than by a slave insurrection that would turn "thriving plantations into deserts."[72] Belonging as they did to a great empire that relied on cheap, disciplined labor, British observers of the American scene felt they had another important interest in the outcome of the secession crisis: they wondered if a new labor system might emerge in the South after the war that could serve as a model for British possessions. Indeed, in this context, the South was discussed as if it were a part of the British Empire. In a survey of secession's origins that he wrote for the *Edinburgh Review* in April 1861, Sir George Cornewall Lewis, then the home secretary, explored this imperial dimension of the "negro question." According to Lewis, the Anglo-Saxon race thrived in "temperate regions," but proved less successful in "hot countries." In these latter areas, the Anglo-Saxon had been "forced to avail himself of the labour of an inferior race." Three different arrangements had been employed to extract that labor: "One is the negro slavery of the Southern United States; another is the free labour of negroes in the British West India Islands; the third is the system of British India, by which the ownership and cultivation of the soil remain in the hands of the natives, and the entire governing power is vested in Englishmen temporarily resident in the country." None of these arrangements, Lewis argued, was entirely satisfactory, and he hoped events in America might point the way to a better labor system.[73] As Lewis's statements indicate, the empire had a great stake in defining "inferior" peoples and contriving to make those peoples serve British economic interests more effectively. These interests limited what British observers were willing to approve of in America.

Throughout the war, these competing abolitionist and imperial discourses sat uneasily with one another. British journals demanded more than nominal liberty for the slave but were unwilling to countenance freedom from some type of disciplined regime. This conflicted attitude became particularly evident in British reactions to General Order No. 23, issued in February 1864 by Major General Nathaniel Banks, then Federal commander of the Department of the Gulf. Banks's order sought to codify arrangements regarding the recruitment and employment of freedmen that had emerged in the previous year.[74] Banks hoped to conciliate white opinion in Louisiana for the sake of facilitating Reconstruction. This inclination was augmented by his lack of military success in the region. While Banks created a paternalistic labor system in which planters and freedmen were bound to one another through mutual obligations, "it placed much tighter controls on the workers" and proved extremely unpopular among black laborers.[75] Historians have frequently compared Banks's general order to the infamous "black codes" that emerged shortly after the war's end.[76] Interestingly enough, the British press more or less greeted the general order with approval. The *Spectator* congratulated Banks on reconciling "an utter social change with perfect social order—the emancipation of a slave proletariat with continued labour, a state of conquest with the Yankee arrangement of society, the authority of a dominant army with freedom of commerce, of manufactures, and of agriculture."[77] Other journals were somewhat more backhanded with their compliments. The *Economist* made sport of Banks and the North for their hypocrisy in dispensing so crassly with American ideals such as liberty and democracy but concluded that the labor arrangements made sense because freedmen would not work without compulsion: "It is in direct contradiction to every notion of personal freedom, and renders the word 'emancipation' a mockery and a nullity:—but that is all. That passed by, it is sensible and fair enough."[78] The *Saturday Review* took the general order as proof that the scales had fallen from northern eyes with regard to the character and capacity of freedmen. Banks's plan of "negro serfage," it argued, rightfully left "to the negro very little beyond the name of freedom" because no serious person could give "the slightest adhesion to a principle which makes the negro the social equal of the white man."[79] Somewhat less caustically, *The Times* made the same point, lauding Banks for teaching freedmen the value of work and for avoiding "the platitudes usually employed in addressing the negro race," although the newspaper expressed concern that black labor had been reduced to "predial instead of personal slavery."[80] While these journals favored nominal freedom for black laborers, they did not support social equality because they felt the African American character required some form of extraordinary discipline or compulsion.

If the collision of imperialist and abolitionist discourses created some ambivalence about African Americans (to say the least), the manner in which British partisans of either belligerent conducted their debates—particularly with respect to slavery—led to a neglect of race. In April 1862, *The Times* complained that although attention was fixed "on the fierce encounter between the North and South," of American blacks "we hear little" even though they had "a deeper interest in the conflict than any other portion of the community."[81] Abolitionists did not refer much to race and never made a concerted effort to convince the British public that African Americans were equals. Abolitionists partly took this tack because they found the point irrelevant: slavery was wrong or pernicious regardless of the African American's capabilities. For evangelicals and dissenters reared in the antislavery tradition, the slave was a brother in Christ, and slavery was a sin. For those classical political economists who employed a free labor critique of slavery, the system was, as the *Economist* put it, "an economic blunder," "a social stain," "a moral wrong," and "detestable" because of its pervasive social effects. For many others, it was simply a violent, barbarous, and intolerable system. Edward Dicey described slavery as a "gigantic . . . attempt to reduce oppression to a system, and to establish a social order of which the misery of human beings is to be a fundamental principle."[82] Yet, at the same time, abolitionists probably refrained from discussing race because there was a great diversity of opinion among them on the topic; many abolitionists, including Dicey, were racists. Circumstantial evidence seems to suggest abolitionists recognized that much of the British public would not be receptive to claims of equality between blacks and whites. Certainly, no one would accept that blacks and whites were the same. As the *Saturday Review* commented, "It has been the fashion to speak of the negroes as if they were English free men with dark skins, who had been kidnapped and reduced to slavery by men of the same race. They are nothing of the sort."[83]

Supporters of the South tended to neglect the topics of slavery and race, either because they earnestly believed the institution had nothing to do with the conflict or because they sought to avoid what they saw as an embarrassing topic. Pro-southerners could maintain this pretense largely because the Federal government was initially unwilling to declare a war of emancipation.[84] John Worden explained British confusion regarding slavery's relationship to the war as part of a semantic problem. Britons did not regard slavery as relevant to the conflict because they instinctively identified a "slavery question" as an "abolition question," but since the Federal government had not embraced emancipation in the first couple years of the war, many Britons assumed slavery was not a significant factor.[85] Southern sympathizers, then, could plausibly portray the war as a fight over tariffs, a political battle, or a clash of cultures—anything but a struggle associated with slavery. *The Times* observed that this manner of portraying the war originated in the Confederacy: "Free Trade, foreign policy, national sovereignty, social superiority, even civilization—anything rather than the old watchword of domestic rights has been the shibboleth of the Secessionists."[86] Such a depiction of Confederate motives became prevalent among southern sympathizers in Britain. *Lloyd's Weekly Newspaper* claimed that those supporting the Confederacy had shown themselves to be "good tacticians" because they had convinced many European politicians that the war "was not in the least connected with slavery."

The weekly concluded that partisans of the South had thus wisely avoided arguing that "it was righteous and moral to buy and sell" human beings because "such an argument could not be made acceptable to any liberal-minded man in Europe."[87] This stance, however, involved much dissembling. As the *Spectator* charged, British supporters of the Confederacy suffered from the disadvantage that they could not "display the focus of their case at all" because "they are obliged to keep it as decently out of sight as may be."[88]

The intensity of the debate between southern and northern sympathizers also led to the spinning of information about African Americans if not outright obfuscation. During the antebellum period, reviewers scrutinized travel authors' biases and accepted information accordingly. Unfortunately, during the Civil War, the supercharged atmosphere in which discussions took place not only led reviewers to produce very different readings of the same work, but also tempted partisans to discredit opponents by making dishonest charges of partiality. The *Saturday Review* made a great show of evenhandedness by claiming that "it is not enough to take the testimony of the advocates of slavery who depict [the slave] as little better than a brute beast, or that of Abolitionists of the *Uncle Tom* stamp, who paint him as rather lower than the angels."[89] By drawing a specious equivalence, this statement provided cover for a very skewed discussion of African Americans.[90] For instance, the *Spectator* gave Frederick Law Olmsted's *Journeys and Explorations in the Cotton Kingdom* (1861) an excellent notice, claiming, "we know of no book in which significant but complex social facts are so fairly, minutely, and intelligently photographed—in which there is so great intrinsic evidence of impartiality."[91] The *Saturday Review,* however, described Olmsted's classic work as "clever pleading" akin to a "political pamphlet" in which his facts deserved as much credence as those presented by "a first-class Old Bailey barrister retained for the defence of a wealthy client on trial for his life."[92]

Finally, the fundamental question British commentators posed about African Americans contributed to great difficulties: was the slave degraded because of his condition or his race? As the *Saturday Review* put it in 1861, "Undoubtedly, the negroes in the Slave States are lower in the scale of being than the Anglo-Saxon race. This might be owing to a natural inferiority; but it may quite as reasonably be attributed to the fact of their being slaves."[93] The association of degradation and blackness—largely a result of the abolitionist argument that slavery was bad because it degraded the slave—was responsible for much of this confusion. That so many observers—regardless of their opinions concerning abolition—claimed the slave was degraded limited the conversation about race that could take place in Britain. Even abolitionists could not argue otherwise, unless they wished to risk legitimizing slavery. When Harriet Martineau suggested in an 1864 *Edinburgh Review* essay that slaves had inadvertently received a "training for freedom" over the previous "one or two generations," the *Saturday Review* gleefully retorted that slavery could not be all bad since in a short time it had, according to Martineau, "elevated the negroes to a condition which their African ancestors had never approached during thousands of years of indigenous freedom."[94] As we shall see, it became impossible for British travelers to separate the effects of environment from race when studying slaves or newly emancipated African Americans.

FROM "CONTRABAND OF WAR" TO "DOMESTIC LIFE IN SOUTH CAROLINA": BRITISH REPRESENTATIONS OF AFRICAN AMERICANS DURING THE CIVIL WAR

At least initially, difficulties associated with the British discussion about American slavery and race prevented the emergence of any definitive evidence or arguments. As Lorimer argues, the British did not possess "an intimate knowledge of race relations in the South." For that reason, British discussions about race showed much continuity with antebellum fantasies.[95] James Spence's *The American Union; Its Effect on National Character and Policy, with an Inquiry into Secession as a Constitutional Right, and the Causes of the Disruption* (1861) is a good expression of these continuities. The book turned Spence, a small-time dealer in "plate and iron repair commissions" from Liverpool, into a mainstay of the Confederate propaganda effort in Britain.[96] Spence attributed all of the Americans' political and social ills to the federal union and dismissed slavery as a cause of the war. Having brought up slavery, however, he defended it through a number of traditional means. Spence paid lip service to the abolitionist tradition by commencing his survey of slavery with the routine declarations that the institution was a "lamentable evil" and a "great human wrong," but it eventually became clear that he was more worried about the influence of the institution on whites, not blacks.[97] Slaves, he argued, were well housed, well fed, and well treated. They fared better than the coal miner or agricultural laborer in England. The steady population growth of slaves in America indicated they were neither "ill-used" nor "overtaxed."[98] So far as "animal comforts" were concerned, they were not deprived.[99]

Spence denied that slavery had degraded African Americans because "the amount of degradation resulting from any cause must be limited by the height from which there was room to fall." Indeed, the "African" was already degraded because of his race. Spence opined that "nature has ordained a difference in the mental powers of man, as marked and ineradicable as any of the physical distinctions of race."[100] Due to this law of Nature, the "mind of the negro may be improved and instructed, but it cannot be raised to the level of the European."[101] The African was born a slave and found such a position natural. Under these circumstances, "it is difficult to see what injury has been inflicted upon the negro by taking him from slavery to a savage in Africa, to place him under a civilized master in America." Spence wanted slavery abolished, but he clearly desired "laws carefully devised" that would compel blacks to work and keep them under white control in a post-emancipation world.[102]

Overall, *The American Union* proved successful because it employed a number of traditional ideas with which the British public was already familiar. The case was no different when Spence discussed race. Much of his argument was grounded in a partisan reading of important antebellum works of travel literature (including Tocqueville, Martineau, and Stirling), leaned on old ideas associated with white labor slavery, employed the critiques of "telescopic philanthropy" that had appeared most famously in Charles Dickens's *Bleak House* (1852), and relied on Carlyle's ideas about nature and hierarchy while engaging in the same kind of reckless generalization. Almost all of Spence's notices conceded the force of his work, even if reviewers did not agree with his thesis. Few took *The American Union* to task for its racist, proslavery views. Even the *Economist,* which disagreed with Spence, admitted that few books had "done more to mould into definite form the floating mass of public opinion on the right or wrong-doing of the Southern States in the matter of Secession."[103]

The racist views espoused by Spence, however, were conflicted. Although Spence and like-minded observers wrote with confidence about the African American, they experienced great difficulties fixing his character, and nowhere was this problem more evident than in discussions about the potential for servile insurrection in the Confederacy, especially after the promulgation of the Emancipation Proclamation.[104] Some British commentators stressed the savage nature of the slave, but they did not always clarify if this savagery was due to slavery or race.[105] While contemplating the possibility of a great slave uprising in the South, *Reynolds's Newspaper* clearly believed that slaveowners "will but reap what they have sown—the bitter cup of negro vengeance is of their own concoction," but few other journals were prepared to place exclusive responsibility for such an insurrection on white slaveowning shoulders.[106] *Reynolds's Newspaper*'s references to Santo Domingo in this context were a familiar trope in this discussion. Lurid thoughts on the topic were clearly inspired by the great Caribbean slave revolts of the early nineteenth century as well as the Indian rebellion. Richard Cobden was not the only observer to see events unfolding in America "à la St. Domingo," while the *Standard* believed, like many others, that the Emancipation Proclamation sought "to make a Cawnpore of Charleston [and] a Delhi of New Orleans."[107] The influence of antebellum travel literature was also responsible for stoking such fears. Tocqueville, whom many British writers followed, had intimated that a race war was a likely event in the South's future.[108] Racism was often associated with these kinds of forecasts, and journals frequently mentioned the significance of "differences of race and color" (or the pitting of "a lower race against a higher") in contributing to the ferocity of such conflicts.[109] These visions were difficult to reconcile with other prevalent images of African Americans, such as the carefree, improvident figure or the simple, devout slave. In defending the slave from charges that he would engage in atrocities, the *Morning Star* used the familiar picture of the passive and religious supplicant. "If the negro be the harmless, docile, faithful creature his masters have sought to make us believe he is," it surmised, he would shed little blood. Instead, he would "lift up eyes of gratitude and hope to heaven—rejoicing" that he was free.[110]

Various commentators' struggles to assemble contradictory images of the slave into a coherent whole prove particularly interesting. At the beginning of the war, the *Saturday Review* claimed that the only way to reconcile the conflicting evidence from planters and abolitionists about slaves was to conclude that "the character of the coloured race is one of astonishing plasticity," but such a statement only revealed the extent to which that journal's own views—

as well as those of many others—were inconsistent.[111] Like many other observers, George Alfred Lawrence, the novelist (and a visitor to the United States during the war), produced incongruous images of the slave, writing that immediate emancipation would turn "a quaint, simple, childish creature—prone to mirth, and not easily discontented if his indolence be not taxed too hardly, susceptible, too, of strong affection and fidelity to his master . . . —into a sullen, slothful insolent savage, never remembering the past, except as a sort of vague excuse for the present indulgence of his brutal instincts."[112]

The art of Frank Vizetelly strikingly illustrates the same phenomenon that characterized these discussions of race: the difficulty of combining discordant antebellum ideas in a harmonious fashion during the war. An experienced draftsman, Vizetelly served as the American correspondent and graphic artist for the *Illustrated London News* from 1861 to 1865. Initially a supporter of the North, he eventually became a Confederate sympathizer and smuggled himself into the South in the fall of 1862.[113] Relying mainly on themes associated with minstrelsy, Vizetelly portrayed African Americans in variety of incongruous ways that served different needs.

Minstrelsy clearly exerted a great influence on Vizetelly's depiction of slaves. In describing the conversation of one "aunty" as she awaited the Federal naval assault against Charleston in April 1863, Vizetelly rendered her speech in typical minstrel style: "Lor-a-mussy, boss! Is dem cussed bobolitionists gwine to shoot dar big guns mongst us women folk? . . . Praise de Lord be joyful, I'se ready to die, but I ain't no way fixed to go de long road to hebbun, and dat's what's de matter."[114] The same tradition supplied Vizetelly with ideas for his sketches, most obviously in "Contraband of War" (July 1861) and "Night Amusements in the Confederate Camp" (January 1863). In the former illustration, one can spot a number of characters associated with minstrelsy—the carefree Jim Crow, the dandy Zip Coon, and the hapless Uncle Ned. Their features are exaggerated and remind one of illustrations found in Victorian works on physical anthropology. Milling in disorder with their tattered finery, they provide a striking contrast to the stern and elegant Federal sentry who assumes a *contrapposto* like a classical statue. The escaped slaves appear as an exotic Other literally requiring direction from white authority, but would an audience familiar with the subversive nature of minstrelsy have also seen a joke at the expense of the Federal soldier's amour propre? "Night Amusements in the Confederate Camp" (January 1863) must have confirmed to British readers that minstrelsy was an authentic African American folk art. The dancing slave appears in a pose conventionally associated with depictions of Jim Crow. He appears as a carefree Other on exhibit before a sedated-looking and monotonous audience.[115]

In other illustrations, references to minstrel themes in Vizetelly's captions appear at odds with his illustrations. "Negroes at Work on the Fortifications at Savannah" (April 1863) presents a disciplined and efficient workforce operating in ranks. Yet Vizetelly claimed they did "as little for their living as any class of men I ever saw."[116] In "Slaves at Worship on a Plantation in South Carolina" (December 1863), Vizetelly reports that one of the slaves' outstanding characteristics was their "deep, simple fervent piety." Here, a slaveowner, his family, and their slaves listen attentively to the sermon of a black minister. The commendable, Tom-like religiosity of the African Americans, however, is compromised somewhat by Vizetelly's description of the minister, whose extemporaneous sermons were "marred by his predilection for high-sounding phrases and long words (not always appropriate)." This supposed tendency among blacks who gave themselves "airs" (especially in the guise of a minister) was a common theme of minstrel shows.[117]

Vizetelly could dispense with minstrelsy humor to produce a serious statement, yet even in such cases contradictions inevitably arose. In "Domestic Life in South Carolina" (May 1863), "old negro servants" tend to a planter's children. Aside from skin color, there is no real distinction between blacks and whites in this engraving, and there are no caricatured physiognomies as in "Contraband of War." The scene is redolent of bourgeois domesticity for, as the caption informs us, children raised by "negro domestic servants" showed as much affection for these slaves as for their own parents. Vizetelly intended this scene to serve as a defense of slavery, but by portraying slaves as part of a bourgeois family scene, he raised the question of why they should be enslaved at all.[118]

In Vizetelly's work, the ambivalence of minstrelsy became the means by which he attempted to depict what could not be depicted—the paradoxical Other. It seems curious that an intelligent observer with direct experience of a people would subscribe to problematic discourses regarding their nature, but a number of factors pushed visitors like Vizetelly in that direction. Antebellum racist discourses inculcated a "habit of mind," to use Lorimer's phrase, that increasingly led British society to interpret differences between people in racial terms.[119] Clearly, the physical appearance of African Americans contributed to a profound sense of difference that served as a foundation for racism. The significance of these differences is evident in William Howard Russell's account of a slave for auction in Montgomery. A sincere opponent of slavery, the famous correspondent for *The Times* felt compelled to point out that the slave's expression "was by no means disagreeable, in spite of his thick lips, broad nostrils, and high cheek bones," while "on his head was wool instead of hair." The slave's appearance filled Russell with ambivalence about where African Americans stood in relation to whites, for the journalist immediately produced the following ambiguous assessment: "no sophistry . . . could persuade me the man was not a man—he was indeed, by no means my brother, but assuredly he was a fellow-creature."[120] In other words, the slave was human, but not an equal.

Uniquely personal factors also influenced stances on race, as the case of George Augustus Sala, the *Daily Telegraph*'s American correspondent from 1863 to 1864, demonstrates. Peter Blake points out that the rejection of "telescopic philanthropy," protest against "white slavery" at home, and acceptance of scientific racism meant Sala was very much a product of his time, even if the journalist's ideas were "not completely representative" of British opinion. Sala's racism also helped satisfy both professional and personal needs. Blake argues convincingly that Sala sought to "forge his own journalistic identity" by deliberately pushing the traditions of travel literature to their limits and even transgressing them. Sala's bald advocacy of racism and defense of slavery, then, were part of a strategy to create a new public persona closely bound with the sensationalism of his newspaper.[121] At the same time, Sala's work also revealed his need for an Other, an underground self against which he could project his undesirable traits so he could take his place among the respectable. Sala experienced depression, suffered from erratic work habits, drank too much, mismanaged his finances, frequented brothels, and wrote a great deal of pornography.[122] In light of his difficulties, Sala's description of African Americans is most interesting:

> He will always . . . be lazy, indolent, slovenly, good-natured and kind-hearted, but subject to inexplicable fits of caprice, sulkiness, obstinacy, and perversity:—willing and obedient only when he fears the eye or the hand of his master; inconceivably vain, trivial, and puerile, always as lecherous as a

monkey and often as savage as a Gorilla, and finally totally unconscious of or indifferent to the moral laws.[123]

One also cannot discount the influence of white Americans on British visitors, particularly in the South. It would have been difficult for British travelers, many of whom had little previous experience of black people, to avoid succumbing to the ideas of their white American hosts, who claimed superior knowledge on the topic. Indeed, Vizetelly's illustrations reflect some of the traditions at work in the United States during this period.[124] Surely, his work appears to have drawn inspiration from Confederate fantasies about the fatuous yet loyal slave.[125] In some cases, Britons were intimidated or tricked by their hosts.[126] In other cases, British visitors sought congenial company. After spending no more than a few days in New York, Sala fell in with well-known Copperheads.[127]

Finally, American slavery and racism had placed many African Americans in a position where they would undoubtedly fail to impress British visitors already predisposed to judge them harshly. The *British Quarterly Review* freely acknowledged that "slaves *are* inferior" but argued that slavery itself made them inferior. For that reason, "to pretend . . . that because slaves are obviously inferior at present, they are therefore radically and generically inferior, is to reason yet more illogically than shamelessly."[128] But what they saw and what they assumed prepared British observers to reason in such a fashion. In the South, Britons found the slave, on average, uneducated, badly used, and exploited. In January 1861, as it first turned its attention to secession and slavery, the *Westminster Review* quoted Frederick Law Olmsted to the effect that "the field-hand negro is, on an average, a very poor and very bad creature, much worse than I had supposed before I had seen him and grown familiar with his stupidity, indolence, duplicity, and sensuality."[129] It should come as no surprise that British observers would approach slaves in much the same way as Olmsted, who was absolutely hostile to slavery. In the North, British observers found free blacks very frequently shunned, scorned, and condemned to menial occupations. Kemble pointed out that slavery had "debased and degraded" southern blacks, while in the North blacks were "pariahs" who suffered under a regime similar to that of the "Hebrew lepers of old." "Stamped with a badge of infamy of Nature's own devising," they lost their self-respect and became repulsive in the eyes of whites.[130] *The Times* made a similar point in 1862 when it claimed that while southerners could only conceive of the "negro" as a "domestic animal," northerners saw him as "an outcast and pariah for whom no labour is sufficiently vile, for whom no exclusion is sufficiently severe."[131] As Handel Cossham, the colliery owner and Liberal politician, argued: "It is one of the sad . . . evils resulting from slavery that if you degrade a race by oppression, you make them odious in the eyes of their oppressors."[132]

Under these circumstances, when they contemplated the question of whether the slave was degraded because of his condition or his race, British visitors frequently inclined to the latter answer. The encounter with African Americans during the Civil War, then, frequently confirmed what British visitors already believed. These experiences formed part of a self-reinforcing cycle, becoming a cause and a consequence of those "habits of mind" that Lorimer saw as the basis of racism. In June 1864, the *Saturday Review* made a similar argument about how the Civil War had added to the stock of British experience regarding blacks. Now that the conflict had revealed the "peculiar characteristics" of African Americans, "Englishmen have seen [the negro] in three qualities—as a slave in the Southern States; as a freeman, without rights in the Northern States; as a freeman, with all and something more than all the ordinary rights of freedom, in the English colonies." As a slave, the "negro" was "a squalid savage whose sluggish drudgery brought as little profit to himself as to his master." In the North, the "conceited negro," who suffered from the "alternation of slyness and sullenness, of cringing self-abasement and offensive pertness," was "gradually ousted from every decent trade" because he performed "self-complacent half-work." Finally, in the Caribbean, the freeman expressed his "passion for self-indulgence and self-assertion," "doing just as little work as he chooses . . . defiantly jostling his white neighbor in the highways; retaining all the love of finery, all the relish for animal enjoyment, all the delight in mere idleness, which distinguish him both as a savage and as a slave, and glazing over these ineradicable instincts with a superficial mimicry of European habits." Like other British commentators at this time, the author of this piece seemed to recognize that different circumstances produced varying behaviors that stretched from the "squalid savage," to the "conceited negro," and then to the assertive imitator of "European habits." Yet there was no sense that "the prejudices . . . of white rivals" might play a substantial role in influencing black people's behavior or determining their social position. And that was largely because the essay assumed the existence of a universal "negro" who was defined by laziness and immaturity regardless of his environment.[133] Indeed, it is clear from the essay that the author's image of former slaves in the West Indies shaped his conception of black people in North America.

As we have seen, ideas, discourses, and dynamics that initially emerged during the antebellum period grew stronger during the war years and played a large role in bridging the gap between British and American racial attitudes during the Civil War. The conflict, however, did witness one unprecedented development: for the first time, the South mounted a serious effort to influence British opinion. That effort depended largely on Henry Hotze, who introduced many Britons to a racial science with which most of them were unfamiliar.

Hotze is best remembered as a Swiss-born southern propagandist in London who sought to obtain recognition for the Confederacy, founded the *Index,* a pro-Confederate weekly, and surreptitiously extended his influence throughout much of the metropolitan press.[134] Realizing that slavery proved a major obstacle to obtaining British public approval, Hotze concluded that the Confederacy's path to respectability involved making racism and the subordination of inferior races acceptable. In pursuing these ends, Hotze exploited the British taste for social hierarchy and commitment to imperial rule. He also sought to link the Confederate cause with progress by associating it with the new race science. The new field of physical anthropology was central to Hotze's views about race in a way that was not characteristic of British thinking. While living in Alabama before the war, Hotze had produced the first English translation of Arthur de Gobineau's *Essay on the Inequality of the Human Races* (1853–1855), to which he added a one hundred-page introduction.[135] During his stay in London, he became an associate of James Hunt, president of the London Anthropological Society, and sat on the society's council.[136] Hotze was not shy about using Hunt's work to legitimize racism and therefore slavery. Referring to a paper presented by Hunt at the London Anthropological Society that dwelled on blacks' inferior intellect, Hotze presented a typical example of the specious and precious apologias that filled the *Index.* Hotze asserted that, given the "negro's" capacities, it had to be obvious to "the philanthropist and the Christian that the best condition of life in which the negro has until now been placed is that in which he is found in the Confederate States." Hotze hastened to add that he was "not engaged in defending or even in treating slavery in the abstract" and that "it would be illogical for us to assert from the above premise that the peculiar institution of the South is the only system that meets the requirements of the negro." However, Hotze insisted that "for the negro to be happy and useful he must be in immediate subordination to a superior race."[137]

As it became clear that the Confederacy would fail to obtain recognition and also would lose the war, Hotze began to reconceive his mission: the *Index* would serve as a transatlantic mediator in resolving the "negro question." "Emancipation," he asserted, "settles no question," because it did not define African Americans' position in society or explain how they would be cared for. Once political equality had been established, Anglo-Saxons on both sides of the Atlantic would have to discover the "average amount of liberty which can, consistently with social order, attach to the common citizenship of enfranchised Africans and Anglo-American freedmen."[138] Such assertions sound suspiciously close to James Fitzjames Stephen's remark that "slavery is a wretched institution," but it did "solve the fearful problem of getting an inferior and superior race to live together somehow in nearly equal numbers."[139]

Assessing Hotze's significance is difficult partly because he exercised influence behind the scenes among a wide number of politicians and journalists. Without a doubt, this significance was great. His ideas appeared to obtain traction among several British commentators who earnestly began to study the "negro question." However, as a naturalized southerner, Hotze's views on race were considerably harder than those of British partisans of the Confederacy, and they led to his well-known rift with James Spence. For all its flaws, the old abolitionist tradition prevented many Britons from fully embracing the kind of racism that Hotze promoted. Surely, Blackett is correct when he asserts that abolitionism still had "currency."[140] Despite these limitations, Hotze is an important transitional figure whose activities, Robert E. Bonner argues, not only "represented a late episode in the history of New World slavery," but also "anticipated an early chapter of a darker, more modern story" of racialism.[141]

EMPIRE, GREATER BRITAIN, AND THE "NEGRO QUESTION"

The great material interests that help shape discourses largely determined the extent to which racism was both powerful and limited. Britons were reluctant to embrace the full implications of race thinking because it sometimes ran counter to British interests. For instance, the project to separate white Americans into different races (usually along sectional lines) failed to obtain much traction partly because such a project would have promoted Anglo-American disharmony and undermined British influence in North America.[142] For instance, arguing, like John Roebuck, that southerners were Anglo-Saxons and northerners were mongrels would have placed many Americans outside Britain's cultural empire. For all their mixed feelings, Britons preferred to see all white Americans in the same manner as John Bright did—as a "Transatlantic English nation."[143] In fact, by war's end, Britons looked forward to hearty cooperation with America based on a common Anglo-Saxon culture and race. In 1865, William Forster told his constituents in Bradford that despite important wartime differences, he did not "despair of a close alliance and friendship" with the "English-speaking race on the other side of the Atlantic." Such an alliance would serve as a "pattern to the world" and "teach the nations peace by the majesty of its success."[144]

As Forster indicated, a transatlantic reconciliation would help consolidate Anglo-Saxon leadership of other peoples. And indeed, at war's end, Hotze had hoped that the *Index* could find a new role by helping effect that reconciliation. The assumption that blacks required subordination had become widespread, but emancipation had destroyed slavery, the one institution that had "practically" and "temporarily" (to quote Hotze) supplied an answer to the "negro question." By 1865, many Britons had reached a point where, as Charles Dilke put it in *Greater Britain: A Record of Travel in English-Speaking Countries during 1866–1867* (1868), "if it is still impossible . . . to advocate slavery . . . it has . . . become a habit persistently to write down freedom."[145] Yet the precise design of a new social order depended on a knowledge of black capacities, and these remained opaque. Even more so than the white American, the black American remained a mysterious figure in Britain. As *The Times*, which had uncritically embraced Spence's confident assertions about the slave, admitted in 1863, "we have had the Negro so long before us now," but "there is so little agreement as yet upon his intellectual character and capabilities."[146] And for that reason, as *The Times* put it, "the great problem of the African race remains unanswered." The journal continued, "it [the African race] vegetates in Africa; it rises to something better in the Southern States of America; it languishes in the Northern States; it has died out in this country" before surmising that "it may not be well used anywhere."[147]

The same imperial attitudes that sought to subordinate this figure also accounts for his elusiveness. The experiences of Fanny Kemble and her daughter, Fan Butler, illustrate the difficulties associated with this endeavor. Writing from relatively privileged positions, both women found it hard to understand their black subjects. Kemble may have sincerely empathized with the slaves on the Butler estates, but she had the opportunity to represent their thoughts and ambitions (as well as her own)—a power that indicated the extent to which she was not subject to the same regime.[148] In a more obvious and aggressive fashion, Fan Butler frequently interjected herself between blacks and her audience, providing conflicting interpretations of their actions that justified her racist views. Meanwhile, both women asserted a power (unsuccessfully though) that sought to change others while remaining unchanged themselves. Each rejected the southern social order she confronted so she could remake black people according to a different template. Kemble subscribed to a British model that sought to turn slaves into yeoman farmers.[149] Inspired by Lost Cause nostalgia, Fan Butler wanted to produce docile dependents.[150]

These struggles provided both women with the means of defining themselves against blacks who served as surrogate selves. Kemble's attempts to reform her slaves by wiping away filth, ignorance, and laziness served as a means of insulating herself from her own bondage to her husband. Fan's insistence on the superiority of her race permitted her to avoid recognizing that she now shared a common status of freedom with her laborers. In both cases, the widespread miscegenation that had taken place on the Butler estates made blacks there a particularly subversive Other—especially when they claimed privileges on account of their white blood (as they did in Kemble's experience).

As an Other frequently characterized by hybridity, these African Americans inevitably became both known and unknowable. Kemble was confident that blacks would act like whites if provided with similar incentives, but not having been "born among slaves," she admitted she could neither understand them nor accustom herself to slavery.[151] Fan Butler wrote with more ostensible confidence about the nature of the black Americans in her employ. Yet her categorical statements about her black workers were constantly balanced by repeated expressions of surprise at their behavior, revelations that they had misled her, and the admission that her judgments were characterized by contradiction.

Fanny Kemble and Fan Butler differed in many ways, but both women were engaged in similar projects. The very nature of these projects, however, denied them the confidence in their judgment that they sought. Despite their experiences and all they had "learned," like other Britons, they found African Americans inscrutable. As Dicey wrote, they remained "a race apart—a strange people in a strange land."[152]

FIG. 1. "The Civil War in America: 'Contraband of War.'—From a Sketch by Our Special Artist," *Illustrated London News,* 27 July 1861, 83.

Frank Vizetelly served as the *Illustrated London News*'s "Special Artist" for much of the conflict. His representations of African Americans were clearly informed by minstrelsy, which had exerted a great influence in Britain before the war. In this illustration a Federal sentry confronts a motley collection of slaves who have escaped from the Confederacy. The crowd consists of characters whom a British audience would have associated with minstrelsy: carefree Jim Crow, deferential Uncle Ned, and dandy Zip Coon.

FIG. 2. "Night Amusements in the Confederate Camp.—From a Sketch by Our Special Artist," *Illustrated London News*, 10 January 1863, 10.

In the summer of 1862, after witnessing the hostility of Tennesseans to the Federal occupation of Memphis, Vizetelly became a southern sympathizer and smuggled himself into the Confederacy. He completed the original sketch of this scene in the fall of 1862 while accompanying the Army of Northern Virginia. The note on the back of the sketch claimed that whenever Sam Sweeney, the famed banjo player attached to General J.E.B. Stuart's staff, "strikes up one of his quaint old Virginia breakdowns, some nigger is sure to 'wade' in and push his legs through a series of impossible gyrations to the delight of the sympathetic lookers on." (Frank Vizetelly Drawings, 1861–1865 [MS Am 1585], Houghton Library, Harvard University.)

FIG. 3. "The War in America: Negroes at Work on the Fortifications at Savannah—From a Sketch by Our Special Artist," *Illustrated London News,* 18 April 1863, 433.

According to Vizetelly, the slaves compelled to work on Savannah's fortifications dressed in rags for six days a week so that on Sundays they could attire themselves in "a garb of outrageous brilliancy." Indeed, Vizetelly claimed the "very men" in this sketch "have more than once made me feel uncommonly mean and shabby when I have met them . . . and been forced to contrast my own well-worn and somewhat shabby attire with their brilliant costumes." Such a story accorded well with images of the minstrel character Zip Coon, a dandy who wore extravagant clothing.

FIG. 4. "Family Worship in a Plantation in South Carolina," *Illustrated London News*, 5 December 1863, 561.

"A deep, simple, and fervent piety," Vizetelly argued, "characterises a large portion of the slave population." Such a proposition would have seemed natural to a British audience widely exposed to the character of Uncle Tom before the war. While the minister in this engraving possessed "strong good sense and a certain rude native eloquence," his sermons were "sometimes marred by his predilection for high-sounding phrases and long words (not always appropriate)." This latter tendency was a hallmark of minstrel characters who strived to rise above their place.

Fig. 5. "Domestic Life in South Carolina.—From a Sketch by Our Special Artist," *Illustrated London News*, 23 May 1863, 552.

This illustration represented "the old negro servants" of a planter who lived on the banks of the Cumbee River in South Carolina. In what amounted to an apologia for African American bondage, Vizetelly claimed that "however repugnant slavery as an institution must be to the English mind," it was clear that "where the slaves are well treated, many of them grow accustomed to, and happy under, their servitude." A planter's children who grew up among such slaves learned "to regard them with as much affection as they show their own parents."

4

BRITISH VIEWS OF AMERICAN SOCIETY AND POLITICS DURING THE CIVIL WAR

> It is a question of civilisation, and the destiny of free or slave institutions—it is the strife for dominion—not simply of material ascendancy—but dominion of ideas, of a certain system of labour, of a peculiar cast of society, and the forms into which wealth shall run and political power be attained and exercised. The North and the South in many respects are as unalike as ancient Sparta and Athens; and the question is, shall Richmond or Washington—that which each represents—rule?
>
> —*DAILY NEWS*, 1862

> Never before in modern history have the two great political ideas of mankind, aristocracy and democracy, the rule of the many for the benefit of the few, and the rule of the many or the few for the benefit of all, been brought into such direct and visible collision.
>
> —*SPECTATOR*, 1864

SIR JOHN RAMSDEN AND THE BURSTING OF THE GREAT REPUBLICAN BUBBLE

On May 27, 1861, Sir John Ramsden rose in the House of Commons and delivered a speech in which he referred to the American situation, declaring that "we are now witnessing the bursting of that great Republican bubble which had been so often held up to us as the model on which to recast our own English Constitution."[1] Historians have made much of this oration largely because Charles Francis Adams, the American minister in London, along with Benjamin Moran, the assistant secretary at the American legation, made much of this oration themselves in their diaries. Moran, for example, complained that Ramsden's observations were "very warmly cheered by the Tory side and not much disapproved of by the Liberal."[2] Scholars have since debated the significance of Ramsden's words. The traditional interpretation has claimed the speech provides an excellent example of how British opinion "fell into line on American subjects" according to its "already settled attitude on the democratic doctrines of the Manchester School."[3] Revisionists like Duncan Andrew Campbell have stressed that Ramsden's view of the war was not representative of British opinion and that his comments were nothing more than a "calculated insult" aimed at John Bright.[4]

No matter what their point of view, historians have not fully contextualized Ramsden's oration, which means they have not understood its significance. Ramsden's oft-quoted phrase did not appear in a speech about the American Civil War. Instead, it constituted an aside in a discourse concerning the budget of 1861. This was the famous finance bill in which William Gladstone, then chancellor of the exchequer, sought to repeal the paper duty. The main purport of Ramsden's speech was that it was irresponsible to remove this tax when the budget threatened to show a deficit. His digression concerning the United States had been occasioned by his concern that the crisis there would disrupt the cotton supply, lead to unemployment, and depress government revenue. What the speech reflected, then, aside from a widely shared disapproval of Gladstone's finance, was a sensitivity to the way in which the American crisis adversely affected a wide variety of crucial British interests.

Ramsden's famous digression was also very much an aggressive assertion of British national superiority. Like others, he believed that the unfolding crisis on the other side of the Atlantic indicated that the American experiment had gone terribly wrong. He was also not alone in being frustrated with the perceived inadequacies of the Federal government's response to a crisis that damaged British interests. This understanding of the situation accounted for Ramsden's claim that American institutions had clearly shown their inferiority to British political arrangements. As he put it, British statesmen had the "duty of observing, of studying, and of strengthening, that which had hitherto constituted the great distinction between the safe and rational, and tempered liberties of England, and the wild and unreflecting excesses of mob-rule which had too often desecrated freedom and outraged humanity in America."[5] Such a statement was a typical product of the antebellum Anglo-American postcolonial relationship in which American institutions were often represented as a deviation from British benchmarks.

It is an indication of how strained this relationship was in May 1861, though, that Lord John Russell, the foreign secretary, felt compelled to admonish Ramsden. Like many British commentators, Ramsden easily assumed the privilege of passing a severe judgment on American institutions even as he worried about what influence the failure of those institutions would exert on British interests. What Ramsden did not seem to realize was that if it were too often and too aggressively asserted, this privilege would also harm British interests by antagonizing the Americans. Russell, however, sought to neutralize the effect of Ramsden's observations and repair the relationship by referring to the important historical and cultural links between the two states. On May 30, three days after Ramsden's comments, in the midst of a lengthy speech defending the government's budget, Russell objected to Ramsden's "tone" when referring to America. The foreign secretary expressed his sorrow concerning "the events which have lately taken place in America." He believed that the United States, which had been fundamentally shaped by its Anglo-Saxon inheritance, had "been for many years a great and free State" that had afforded "prospects of the progress and improvement of mankind." Neither slavery nor republicanism ought to be held against America, Russell argued: the nature of American society had compelled the founders to erect a republic while Britain ultimately proved responsible for giving America slavery. For these reasons, Russell did not "think it just or seemly that there should be among us anything like exultation at their discord, and still less that we should reproach them with an evil for the origin of which we ourselves are to blame."[6] Russell's speech was of a piece with a statement he had issued just two days before, on May 28, in the Commons while presenting correspondence with the Federal government concerning the blockade. He referred to the United States as a "great and free nation" whose descent into civil war ought to pain "every lover of liberty." He asked that "no words should be used which would either tend to bring the country [Britain] into the conflict or that might create exasperation or bitterness on the one side or the other."[7] For the sake of maintaining good form and avoiding diplomatic difficulties, Russell asked MPs to refrain from expressing their opinions in the Commons regarding the war. On May 30, 1861, in his response to Russell, Ramsden denied exulting over America's misfortune, but persisted in contrasting "the condition of America with that of England, in order to draw from it the lesson that it was our duty to be thankful for and to strengthen those institutions which are the pride and glory of England."[8] Despite this vigorous riposte, MPs muted their criticisms of the United States in the Commons, not so much because they disagreed with Ramsden, but because they saw the wisdom of Russell's request.[9]

If, with greater or lesser degrees of success, MPs bit their tongues inside the House of Commons, the story was different when they visited their constituencies or made public appearances elsewhere. They could not neglect the American crisis for long. Britons had always been fascinated with American politics, but now that the United States showed signs of disintegrating, the subject seemed especially intriguing. What made the American situation all the more interesting was that Britain had been wrestling with parliamentary reform and the democratization of its politics for over a decade; American events spoke to Britons who sought to negotiate the difficulties associated with these changes. Ramsden's statements sounded like an argument against reform. However, the connection between British political change and the American Civil War was not always straightforward. Ramsden was an exemplary figure; his comments about America, his political experiences, and his relationship to parliamentary reform reveal just how twisted that connection actually was.

"THE RULE OF THE MANY . . . FOR THE BENEFIT OF ALL": BRITAIN, REFORM, AND DEMOCRACY

With the exception of Campbell, historians studying British attitudes toward the American Civil War have not sufficiently stressed the degree to which the momentum behind parliamentary reform was strong, particularly in Parliament itself, during the 1850s and 1860s.[10] And until recently, works on the Reform Act of 1867 (which redistributed representation and expanded the electorate) did not see the legislation as fundamentally rooted in the parliamentary maneuvers of the previous fifteen years.[11] In *Democracy and the Vote in British Politics, 1848–1867* (2011), however, Robert Saunders has convincingly reinterpreted the act's genesis. Saunders asserts that reform was an extremely important parliamentary issue throughout the 1850s and 1860s and that, so far as reform politics are concerned, the period ought to be considered a single whole. When reform finally came to a head between 1866 and 1867, the major actors in Parliament were constrained by experiences, convictions, and commitments of the previous fifteen years. In other words, reform was a going concern in Britain well before the Civil War. That the issue remained unresolved for so long had little to do with principled opposition to the expansion of the working-class electorate. Nor was the insincerity of reformers a major factor in holding up the process. As Saunders points out, between 1852 and 1867, seven governments attempted to extend the franchise, and two fell as a result. By 1859, almost every major political figure in both parties was publicly committed to some version of parliamentary reform.[12] The most prominent works on the subject that appeared at the time—Thomas Hare's *Machinery of Representation* (1857), 3rd Earl Grey's *Parliamentary Government Considered with Reference to a Reform of Parliament* (1858), John Stuart Mill's *Thoughts on Parliamentary Reform* (1859), and Walter Bagehot's "Parliamentary Reform"(1859)—clearly assumed reform was imminent.

It was the sheer complexity of the issue that accounted for the delay in passing a reform act. As Saunders writes, throughout these years, both Liberals and Conservatives sought to square a difficult political circle. First, they aimed to extend the franchise to working men without drowning property and intelligence under a sea of unqualified voters or descending into democracy. Second, they hoped to find a "natural resting" place for the franchise—some principle that would limit the potential future expansion of the electorate. Third, they wanted to avoid handing their political opponents an electoral advantage. Achieving all three objectives simultaneously proved difficult, especially when parties in Parliament had become less organized and effective since the repeal of the Corn Laws in 1846.[13] In the twenty years following this political landmark, the Conservatives never enjoyed a majority in the Commons, and the Liberal leadership displayed political maladroitness at key moments, particularly in 1860 and 1866.

Many important features of the reform debate are captured in Ramsden's political experiences of the late 1850s and early 1860s, and his attitudes were typical of mainstream Liberal opinion. Ramsden's position on reform was established well before the American crisis, suggesting that domestic factors played the primary role in determining attitudes toward this issue; the war, then, did not so much change opinion on reform as provide useful arguments to both sides of the debate. In Ramsden's squirmings over reform, we also see the important forces that tugged in different directions and led to conflicted feelings among many politicians as they contemplated the issue. And finally, the choices confronting Ramsden reveal much about the factors that hampered the passage of a reform bill.

Ramsden's background and constituency inspired him with contradictory impulses. Ramsden clearly belonged to that "massive and homogenous landed right wing" (to quote John Vincent) of the Liberal Party.[14] Lord of the Manor of Huddersfield and a broad-acred baronet, he married the daughter of the 12th Duke of Somerset (a notable Whig politician who served as the first lord of the admiralty in Palmerston's second administration). Not surprisingly, then, Ramsden tended toward political moderation. However, his constituency, the West Riding of Yorkshire, was a particularly urban county that surrounded industrial parliamentary boroughs like Bradford, Sheffield, Leeds, and Huddersfield. Nonresident 40s. freeholders in these parliamentary boroughs enjoyed the county franchise in the West Riding. Evidence suggests that such voters accounted for a majority of the county electorate, making the West Riding an unusually popular and radical county politically.[15] That Richard Cobden sat for the West Riding between 1847 and 1857 indicates something about the radical character of this constituency. When Ramsden stood for the West Riding in the general election of 1859, he naturally supported reform, and there is no reason to believe he was insincere.[16]

For personal, partisan, and principled reasons, though, Ramsden was unwilling to support just any reform to Parliament or the franchise, and he clearly believed the issue was a ticklish one. Along with his party, Ramsden opposed the Conservative reform bill of 1859 because its provisions threatened his seat and the Liberals' majority in the House of Commons.[17] However, in 1860, he spoke against Lord John Russell's proposed reform, claiming that since everybody in the Commons viewed it as either "dangerous" or "inadequate," it would not provide a permanent settlement of the question. Rather, he charged, the bill was an "imperfect and unsatisfactory measure" proposed simply to redeem the Palmerston government's pledge to pass some measure of reform.[18] In 1861, he voted against Peter Locke King's bill to extend the borough franchise to the counties as well as Edward Baines's measure to reduce the borough franchise. Ramsden's opposition to these bills was a matter of principle.[19] As he explained to a colleague, he was concerned that these measures would swamp "Property" and "Intelligence" with "numbers":

"This would be a complete transfer of power, the creation of a new governing class and that out of the poorest and least educated class in the community. . . . That is a practical disfranchisement of the class above them . . . and surely the disfranchisement of a higher class, is as unjust and impolitic as the non-enfranchisement of a lower one."[20] When the Armley Reform Association charged Ramsden with breaking his election pledges to support reform, he responded with a letter in *The Times* asserting that his public position had always consisted of supporting reform so long as "property, intelligence, and numbers" were represented "in their proper share and degree" in the Commons and that "no one of them, or no two of them, are entirely swamped by the third."[21] In other words, Ramsden supported expansion of the franchise in general, but felt great unease with the bills brought before him and opposed anything that would lead to democracy. As Kristin Zimmerman points out, this view of the matter was very common among Liberals in the Commons who felt great ambivalence about the reform pledges their leaders had made. In 1861, the *Spectator*, which was generally associated with advanced liberalism, captured this disquiet when it claimed that Liberals had halted "half way between the old and the new regime" while living "discontented with what we have, and dreading what is before us."[22] Ramsden well reflected this general unease. He was only atypical in that he proved so honest and publicly outspoken about his feelings—a trait that ruined his relationship with his radical constituents. In anticipation of the general election of 1865, the West Riding was split into a pair of two-member county divisions, but Ramsden understood that he was unwelcome in both and stood for neither.[23]

The reform debate was not the only source of unease among those who worried about the democratization of politics. Throughout this period it was clear that Britain's political culture was becoming increasingly democratic. Throughout the 1850s and 1860s, Britain's political leaders began courting popular support in novel and highly visible ways.[24] One feature of this transition was that major politicians, particularly Lord Palmerston and William Gladstone, had begun to pursue policies abroad and at home, respectively, in an attempt to obtain legitimacy from public approval. A disciple of George Canning, Palmerston followed what was widely considered a liberal and popular foreign policy.[25] As David Brown, his latest biographer, puts it, Palmerston reconciled *realpolitik* (a "cold assessment of material and strategic self-interest") with *idealpolitik* (support for "liberal, constitutional regimes" abroad). He did so by rationalizing that progressive governments were "the outward expression of a Whiggish notion of 'improvement'" and asserting that they made better international partners due to their stability.[26] Meanwhile, at home, Gladstone transformed himself into "The People's William" through the budgets he introduced as the chancellor of the exchequer. Numerous historians have commented that Gladstone's finance operated within traditions established by Sir Robert Peel: Gladstone balanced budgets, accumulated surpluses, and carefully considered the political, social, and economic consequences of tax policy.[27] But as H.C.G. Matthew asserts, Gladstone was also an executive politician who followed and publicized Peel's fiscal policy for the sake of making budgets a means of renewing the political system's legitimacy.[28] Specifically, Gladstone enhanced that legitimacy by embracing free trade, attempting to reduce overall taxation, and striving to find a balance between indirect and direct taxation (to distribute the burden equitably between the working classes and their betters). Through his well-publicized efforts that appeared to benefit the working classes, Gladstone earned a reputation as a people's tribune. It should come as no surprise that Palmerston applied the adjective "democratic" (as a pejorative) to Gladstone's budgets.[29]

During this period, Palmerston and Gladstone did not merely promote popular policies, they also actively engaged with public opinion in unprecedented ways. Starting in the late 1830s with the *Morning Chronicle,* Palmerston became one of the earliest and most highly skilled politicians to deal with the British press, both to shape and assess opinion. He formed an important relationship with John Thadeus Delane, editor of *The Times,* in the 1850s, just as the abolition of the stamp tax made the penny daily possible and allowed for the rapid expansion of newspaper circulations.[30] For his part, Gladstone cultivated Thornton Hunt, editor of the most successful of these new penny journals, the *Daily Telegraph.* At the same time, in the late 1850s and early 1860s, both statesmen pioneered the practice of touring large urban centers to explain government policy to the nation—an activity that often garnered extensive press coverage. As early as 1856, Palmerston sought out urban audiences in places like Salford, Manchester, and Liverpool, reaffirming the superiority of the British constitution while explaining how it enhanced prosperity and stability.[31] Starting in the early 1860s, Gladstone made similar tours of northern England and the midlands, promoting his budgets and proclaiming the success of free trade. While David Brown does not accept E. D.

Steele's description of Palmerston as a proto-democrat, he does agree that Palmerston initiated a new kind of popular politics on which Gladstone capitalized. Each statesman, to quote *The Times*' obituary of Palmerston, bowed to the "deity" of public opinion, "recognized its power, and used it as he could" in ways that previous statesmen had never imagined.[32]

Difficult questions swirling around extension of the franchise as well as the activities of popular politicians would naturally have led to interest in American democracy. In the years preceding the Civil War, however, no one did more to link the democratization of British politics to American institutions than John Bright, the prominent middle-class Radical. Bright invoked the example of America so frequently in his speeches that he and his political ally, Richard Cobden, were referred to in the Commons as "members for the United States." Although Bright clearly read informed commentary about America, unlike Cobden, he had never traveled across the Atlantic. The United States remained more of an ideal than a real place for him, a location on which he could project images that suited his political needs. Bright's devotion to this American idea and the way he used it to advance his political vision became particularly evident between 1858 and 1859, when he launched a public campaign to pressure the Conservative government into passing a reform bill. Speaking to his constituents at Birmingham in October 1858, for instance, Bright pooh-poohed those who "say we must not on any account 'Americanize' our institutions." In Britain, numbers had not overwhelmed property, and the result had been war, debt, and high taxes. At the same time, in America, with its extensive suffrage, "we find law, order, [and] property secure, and a population in the enjoyment of physical comforts and abundance, such as are not known to the great body of people in this country." Bright could not attribute this difference to the fact that the "English nation in England is a worse nation than the English nation in America." The difference lay, rather, in Britain's political system. He concluded by asserting that "those persons who say that the franchise, the distribution, and the ballot, which operate so well in America would be perilous in England . . . libel the people of this country."[33]

Although he may have won some credit with the working classes in northern towns, Bright's campaign failed.[34] His vision of the postcolonial relationship, which did not assume British superiority, played poorly with a number of commentators. More mainstream politicians worried that reform of the sort that Bright proposed would not only upset the political balance between education, property, and numbers but also lead to class war. Indeed, the widespread perception that he deliberately set class against class prevented him from obtaining a cabinet position when the Liberals took office in 1859.[35] On the eve of secession, then, Bright was a marginal political figure. The leadership of the Liberal coalition did not trust him with executive responsibility, and he could do little in the Commons, which had fallen under the sway of Palmerston (whom the Conservatives had pledged to support should the Radicals push for reform or Gladstone propose a "democratic Budget").[36] Not only that, but Chartists and trades union leaders mistrusted Bright's brand of bourgeois radicalism. Still, upon the outbreak of the secession crisis, the vitriol with which many journals attacked Bright for having used the American example to support reform shows that he had hit a nerve.

THE DISENCHANTING MARCH OF EVENTS AND BRITISH HOSTILITY TO NORTHERN BOURGEOIS DEMOCRACY

It is important to recognize the way in which the timing of these British developments intersected with American events. South Carolina left the Union (December 1860) only six months after Lord John Russell had withdrawn his abortive reform bill at the end of the 1860 parliamentary session. Even more important, South Carolina's secession occurred at the end of a decade in which British politics had been roiled by constant discussion of reform. When the American crisis began, a potentially large and dangerous extension of the franchise seemed imminent. Recently liberated from the "taxes on knowledge," a new, mass-circulation press had begun to cooperate with political leaders. Finally, these political leaders now sought to forge an unmediated connection with the people. These developments appeared to herald the advance of democracy—which, of course, many inevitably associated with America. Surveying the British political and social scene in 1858, Lord Aberdeen, the former Peelite prime minister, lamented to a friend that "we are in a rapid course of *Americanisation*."[37]

Due to the traditions governing depictions of the United States during the antebellum era, British commentators would have implicated democracy in the American crisis no matter how it unfolded. At the same time, their views of that democracy were shaped by important changes in their own domestic politics. Nevertheless, Britain's reaction to the war was not foreordained. If anything, this reaction was initially confused more than anything else. At the beginning of the crisis, the Federal government was the object of British goodwill. It constituted a legitimate authority from which southern states had seemingly seceded for no good reason, and the Union had served British interests for many years. At the same time, many commentators felt little warmth for southerners, who were perceived as a backward, slaveowning people.[38]

Within a few short months, however, British perceptions had changed much to the detriment of the Federal government, the northern people, and their bourgeois democracy. British attitudes transformed and then gelled largely because of what D. P. Crook has referred to as a "disenchanting march of events." Although he used this phrase to describe developments in the spring of 1861, he could just as easily have applied it to the first year of the war. Through a series of missteps, the Federal government relinquished much British sympathy. As one southern state after another left the Union in the winter and spring of 1861, Washington, D.C., seemed incapable of taking effective action to deal with the crisis. Meanwhile, from a British perspective, the adoption of the Morrill Tariff (March 1861) and the imposition of the Federal blockade on southern ports (April 1861) promised to "disrupt the comfortable commercial arrangements of the Atlantic world."[39] The Federal government's angry reaction to the Queen's Neutrality Proclamation (May 1861), which recognized the Confederacy as a belligerent, revealed just how truculent the northern mood had become toward Britain. The Federal defeat at Bull Run (July 1861) indicated that the war, with all its attendant inconveniences for Britain, would continue for some time. The *Trent* affair (November 1861–January 1862) showed what kind of difficulties could issue from the blockade and worsened Anglo-American relations by bringing the two nations to the brink of war. Finally, the Federal defeat in the Seven Days' Battles (June–July 1862) convinced most of British opinion—if it still needed convincing at that point—that the Federal armies could not reconquer the southern states.[40] By the time the Federal government issued the Emancipation Proclamation (September 1862), much of British public opinion was exasperated with the North because it seemed incapable of ending a crisis that threatened or damaged numerous British interests.

Crook is especially adamant that the Federal government's unwillingness to embrace an emancipation policy was not one of the primary reasons British mainstream opinion turned against the North. Indeed, as a number of British journals realized, emancipation presented the Federal government with a Catch-22. For instance, in October 1861 the *Spectator* explained British feelings regarding the North's attitude toward slavery in the following manner: "If you make it a war of emancipation, we shall think you madmen. . . . And if you follow our counsel in holding a tight rein on the Abolitionists, we shall applaud your worldly wisdom . . . but shall deem it our duty to set forth continually that you have forfeited all claim to the popular sympathy of England."[41]

Instead of emancipation, it was the Federal government's inability to either suppress the rebellion or accept secession that most concerned British observers; the longer the crisis lasted, the greater the threat it posed to British interests. Increasing hostility to the North, which began in the spring and summer of 1861, was not fated or permanent; it could easily have been reversed by Federal triumph or concessions that brought the war to an end.[42] Indeed, in the spring of 1862, when the North seemed to be on the verge of suppressing the rebellion, British observers began to take a much more positive view of the Federal government. British hopes were dashed, however, by the failure of McClellan's offensive against Richmond, the northern defeat at the Second Battle of Bull Run, Confederate incursions in Maryland and Kentucky, and the Federal forces' apparent lack of progress in the West.[43] By this point, the British public had long ceased caring about the rights and wrongs of secession; it wanted the war over. As the *Saturday Review* put it, by 1862 Britons admired "the North or South on grounds wholly alien to the original quarrel."[44] The legality of secession and the North's initial response no longer mattered because "the present morality of the war depends wholly on the probability of reconquest, followed by reunion."[45] If the North could not subdue the rebels, so the thinking went, it needed to come to terms, otherwise the war injured the transatlantic world to no good end.

The British public also found the North's demeanor off-putting. For one thing, it had pursued a foreign policy whose tone Britons considered obnoxious. The *Standard* was hardly alone in claiming that the "bluster, insolence, and ferocity" of the Federal government's state papers was "only surpassed by their unparalleled mendacity."[46] The North also suffered from the degree to which it enjoyed a free press and open communication with Britain—both of which allowed British readers to see the unpleasant dissensions that characterized northern politics. *The Times* observed unkindly of the Federals that "democracy has certainly one virtue" in that "it produces a candour of political confession as would be sought for in vain under any other form of government. . . . The Americans dissect and display themselves for the edification of Europe, without caring to put the least gloze upon their designs, or to affect any semblance of political morality."[47] At the same time, lack of intelligence from the South probably worked in the Confederacy's favor. The *Saturday Review* remarked that "the Confederates have probably not suffered in estimation from the mystery which has enveloped then." The ability of this "outnumbered and overmatched" people to defeat their foes allowed the weekly to infer that the southerners were a spirited and united nation.[48] As we shall see, this inference that the southern people constituted a nation confirmed British beliefs that the Federals had embarked on a futile quest.

The North, then, had undertaken a war that it prosecuted badly and apparently could not win. As William Rathbone Greg put it succinctly in a July 1861 essay for the *National Review,* "the Northerners are fighting for what is undesirable and against what is inevitable. They may have right, but they have not reason, on their side."[49] All the while, the North caused untold damage to itself, the South, and Britain. In July 1862, the *Standard* argued that the North had borne a huge material and moral cost for prolonging a futile war: "America is paying . . . an enormous price in wealth, in life, and in political prosperity; she is interrupting progress, imperilling freedom, sacrificing the future—and for what?" The *Standard* concluded that the North's work consisted of nothing more than "national suicide."[50] From the other side of the political spectrum, Cobden observed simply to Bright in October 1862 that "the North will half ruin itself in the process of wholly ruining the South."[51] Rightly or wrongly, then, when British observers looked to the North in the first few years of the war, they saw debility, wrongheadedness, incompetence, and unpleasantness. British commentators reacted vigorously to this unpleasant cocktail for two reasons. First, they worried that it could do immense harm to British interests. Second, since they believed American developments were relevant to Britain, the perceived failures of northern bourgeois democracy became fodder for British domestic politics.

The many critics of northern democracy were inspired by a variety of motives. A number of them, as Campbell argues, simply wanted to use the

American crisis to discredit John Bright. Robert Cecil, whom Campbell uses as a prime example of this phenomenon, was not alone.[52] *The Times* argued that Americans suffered "from the panegyrics of their friends" among the Manchester School in Britain who "would have shaped the course of all British legislation exclusively by the American pattern." Radicals like Bright had made the mistake of eulogizing American government "for the very qualities of which it is now proved to be utterly destitute."[53] In October 1861, during a speech to his constituents, Major William Beresford, Conservative MP for Essex Northern (and formerly the Conservative Party's chief whip), decried the "ultra-Liberal statesmen" who had held up "the institutions of America" before echoing Ramsden in claiming that in America "the bubble of republicanism had burst."[54] The *Saturday Review* accused Bright ("the Birmingham demagogue") of holding up the United States as a model "just at the moment when they were about to exhibit an extreme instance of every vice and weakness with which a political community can be afflicted."[55] Clearly, William Howard Russell was on to something when he complained, as we saw earlier, that American difficulties provided journalists with opportunities to deal "deadly blows at Brightism."[56]

But there was more to the criticism of northern democracy than an attempt to discredit Bright and his schemes for reform—largely because there was more to reform in Britain than Bright. Even Cecil, who was not shy about attacking Bright as an importer of American doctrines, rightfully recognized that before the "breakdown of the American democracy," British "statesmen of all schools" had accepted reform, "so long bowed as to an inevitable necessity."[57] Northern difficulties became an opportunity for commentators to express their unease with reform and the democratization of Britain in general.[58] To name one instance, Sir John Pakington, a progressive Conservative who was a regular in the 14th Earl of Derby's cabinets, made a number of comments expressing this point in October 1861 at the City of Worcester Conservative Association's anniversary dinner in the shire hall. Pakington, who sat for nearby Droitwich, claimed that "we had at this moment before us a warning which ought to bid us beware how we continued to play fast and loose with democratic principles." Using language that was reminiscent of Ramsden's speech, Pakington pointed out that if his audience looked to America, "they would see the sudden and extraordinary collapse of that attempt to promote and increase the happiness and welfare of mankind by governing them on the principles of extreme democracy. (Hear.) That great Republic had fallen to pieces." It would not do to claim that civil war could occur under any form of government, for American institutions had "broken down before that war had begun." Pakington continued by asking his audience a series of questions: "Let them ask any intelligent American citizen what were his views on the subject. Had democracy succeeded? Had extreme democracy contributed to promote the happiness of mankind? What had been the work of American institutions? Had the administration of justice been pure? Had the Government been free of corruption? Was liberty of person secure for the minority?" Pakington had his intelligent American citizen tell the British public: "Take warning from this country [America]. . . . Beware of what you are doing in England. Beware how you copy that democracy which, unhappily, we have adopted. (Cheers.)"[59]

Pakington's comments capture a feature of the postcolonial relationship that also contributed to criticism of northern democracy during the war years. Now that the United States had entered a serious crisis, British national pride insisted on the superiority of British institutions, which were described as normative. While the *Spectator* understood that the denigration of northern democracy had something to do with Bright, it also believed that such criticism was due "to our inordinate national self-esteem."[60] In January 1863, while speaking at an anniversary dinner of the Druids Lodge in his constituency of Oxford, Edward Cardwell (then chancellor of the Duchy of Lancaster in Palmerston's government) provided an excellent example of how national self-esteem contributed to criticisms of American democracy. He recalled "a distinguished American" who had visited the Great Exhibition of 1851 and remarked upon the extent to which the Revolutions of 1848 had almost toppled the various governments of Europe. This same American had also asserted, by way of contrast, that the United States, "though not one of the oldest, was, he verily believed, one of the most firmly established in the world." Years later, now that the United States had experienced a "terrible convulsion" equal to anything witnessed in Europe in 1848, Cardwell implied that the American had been mistaken because a democratic republic was less sound than Britain's mixed constitution. Cardwell mused that "we must . . . be doubly thankful that our lot has been cast under institutions which are at the same time more free than a republic, and more firmly established than the most ancient despotism." Britain's liberty and strength, he argued, arose from an ideal alloy of popular government, a free press, and a respect for the most intelligent portion of the national community—the absence of which in American democracy had presumably led to its failure.[61]

Finally, travel literature in Britain had done so much to make social and political equality the outstanding features of northern society that the influence of democracy became a way of explaining what seemed like otherwise inexplicable northern behavior. Indeed, as they assessed each step in the disenchanting march of events, British commentators frequently saw the effect of democracy at work. To use one example, when the Morrill Tariff was passed, *The Times* laid the blame on the North's "purely Democratic Government," which was irrational enough to "repudiate principles confessedly identified with popular interests." The daily wondered at "the madness of democracy and its utter inability to apprehend and retain the most obvious principles of economical science."[62] Likewise, Bagehot, writing about the tariff in the *Economist,* emphatically stressed the link between democracy and poor judgment:

> The most uncontrolled democracy . . . offers no security whatever to any nation, either for the sagacious perception or for the steady pursuit of its own interests, any more than for respect for the rights and interests of others, or for the simplest principles of morality or justice. The narrowest oligarchy, the most arbitrary autocrat, could scarcely have acted with harder or more unblushing class-selfishness, could scarcely have committed a shallower blunder, could scarcely have displayed greater ignorance and disregard of all economic laws, than have been manifested, in the matter of the new Protective Tariff, by the educated, commercial ochlocratic republic which has been accustomed to hold itself up to the world as an object of supreme envy, admiration, and almost worship.[63]

As the foregoing examples show, a number of motives impelled observers to criticize northern democracy, and it is often difficult to separate these motives from one another. Cecil, Pakington, Cardwell, and Bagehot's statements all overlapped. They shared a faith in the superiority of British institutions, a recognition of the way in which Radicals like Bright used the American example, a concern that America's dangers might become Britain's, and a sense that democracy helped explain the American situation.

Under these circumstances, proposing schemes of reform, let alone highlighting the positive attributes of American democracy, proved extremely difficult. Shortly after the *Trent* affair, in his famous *Fraser's Magazine* essay, "The Contest in America," John Stuart Mill praised the Federal government's willingness to back away from a confrontation with Britain. "That a sense of justice should be the motive which the rulers rely on, to reconcile the public to an unpopular and what might seem a humiliating act," Mill argued, "shows even unlimited democracy to be a better thing than many Englishmen have lately been in the habit of considering it."[64] Yet even journals with advanced liberal inclinations, like the *Spectator,* asserted that Mill was "much too lenient to the temper of the leaders of the North."[65] The North's reputation was badly damaged among radicals, and a number of their journals deliberately sought to uncouple the cause of reform from the American example. *Reynolds's Newspaper,* one of the leading radical, working-class journals in Britain, criticized Bright's defense of the North, asking how long it would take before he learned "that, to defend the inconsistencies, the absurdities, the infatuations, and the iniquities of democrats, is *not* to defend democracy." The newspaper demanded that Bright discriminate "between the idiotic blunders and tyrannical pretensions of Mr. Lincoln and his underlings" and eternal democratic truths.[66] Richard Cobden was appalled by the blundering of the North and argued that Radicals could not afford to be "thrust into the attitude of either partisans or Champions of the Federal party."[67] In this political atmosphere, discussions of reform went into a deep freeze. Sir John Trelawny, a Radical MP for Tavistock, wrote in his diary that "advanced Liberalism is in bad odor" in the Commons because "America has lent false reasoners an appearance of argument or of that which will do as well for the purpose of convincing a large number of persons."[68] As he complained, "Tories will say 'all comes of secret & general suffrage.'"[69] By the fall of 1861, the *Spectator* remarked that the "crisis in American democracy has aided the recoil from the Reform expedient of 1860."[70]

Not until 1864, when William Gladstone, chancellor of the exchequer, made a dramatic public conversion to a sizable extension of the franchise, did the issue of reform suddenly find new life in the Commons. The discussion obtained additional momentum as the general election of 1865 approached; candidates on the hustings, particularly in large, urban boroughs, traditionally made extensive promises regarding reform to their constituents. As we shall see, at the same time, Federal victory went some way—although not all the way—toward softening British attitudes toward the North and its democracy. However, the initial disappointment with the North remained important. As Crook explained with much justice, "the great rallying which accrued to the northern cause in the war's latter years" was less significant than "the doubts and hesitations which beset liberal consciences in the opening phase."[71]

RECKLESS AND LICENTIOUS: CRITIQUES OF NORTHERN DEMOCRACY

In examining the British critique of northern democracy during the Civil War, we ought to keep in mind the postcolonial discourses produced by the antebellum Anglo-American relationship. Although the pressures generated by the conflict would eventually modify several of these discourses, the images used to describe the North were rooted in the prewar years. The disenchanting march of events and the ensuing antipathy toward the North, however, meant that in wartime British observers expressed their ambivalence in much more stinging terms.

At this point, it makes sense to recall the findings of antebellum travel literature and the way that intellectuals like Tocqueville, Mill, and Arnold had distilled these findings for a broader public. According to British travel literature, the North was a bourgeois democracy characterized by great energy, enormous confidence, and tremendous inventiveness. The Yankee, however, also suffered from low ideals that manifested themselves in crass materialism, lack of refinement, and a selfishness that threatened social cohesion. During the war, this collection of antebellum ideas was used to explain Yankee behavior. Now that the war had created an atmosphere that was so much more supercharged than ever before, all of these northern peculiarities and their potential consequences seemed dangerous and destructive to an unprecedented extent. British commentators, then, highlighted unfavorable Yankee traits with much greater frequency than before and turned positive attributes into negative ones (for example, northern confidence contributed to delusion).

In this context, it is worth keeping in mind that some observers, mainly on the Radical side of things, attempted to render northern democracy more palatable by stressing its solid bourgeois virtues: independence, sobriety, intelligence, and self-denial. For example, writing from New York for the *Daily News*, E. L. Godkin described the vast majority of northern voters as respectable proprietors who possessed "more shrewdness, greater quietness, more enterprise, greater love of novelties, or rather less distrust of them," while "reading much more, and speaking better English" than "Englishmen of a similar class."[72] In some cases, we shall see that some observers even added new virtues, such as patriotism, that had not featured prominently in antebellum discussions of the North. Yet even Radicals had generally become exasperated with the North and dwelled on its shortcomings. Harriet Martineau wrote to a friend that "there is abundant cause for disgust with the North" and that she expected little "from a people so profoundly corrupt, and so degenerate in every way." Though in their "blind and foolish way they are now fighting on towards something laudable," their "pride and selfwill . . . is, to my mind, something diabolical."[73]

Not surprisingly, the sense that "low ideals" characterized the Yankee North appeared most strikingly in British discussions of northern motives for fighting. We have already encountered British ambivalence toward the prospect of emancipation becoming a Federal war aim, a feeling that undoubtedly contributed, however unfairly, toward exasperation with northerners. When it finally came, the emancipation policy was often characterized as a cynical war measure that only contributed to the misery and destruction associated with the war. As for the Union, the North's avowed reason for fighting, British commentary was hardly impressed. We will have more to say in chapter 6 about British attitudes toward northern nationalism. For now, it suffices to state that British observers generally underrated the strength of Unionism because they believed it had little moral power. Throughout the war, then, when Union was not incomprehensible, it was often associated with crude, base, or materialistic motives. A number of British writers claimed northerners loved the Union solely for pecuniary reasons or a childishness that mistook sheer hugeness for greatness. The *Standard* was typical in remembering previous wars that had been "carried on in the face of repeated disaster," but these wars "had been for freedom, for honour, for all that good men hold dear." In the North's case, "it was almost inconceivable that the same pertinacity should be displayed in a selfish struggle for empire and commercial supremacy."[74]

British writers distinguished the imperial work of their own country from that of the North not only by stressing the lack of noble ideals among the latter, but also by highlighting the extent to which selfishness and willfulness had replaced those ideals. Some attributed these problems to the middle-class nature of the Yankee.[75] Somewhat more frequently, however, this willfulness was attributed to the political education obtained under a democracy. Americans had been taught, so the argument went, that the people were sovereign. Under these circumstances, everybody felt empowered to do anything, and the privilege had been abused. George Augustus Sala, who served as the *Daily Telegraph*'s northern correspondent between 1863 and 1864, saw the "scheme of pure democracy" as the source of every American's propensity for "doing as he 'dam pleases.'"[76] When there were no barriers to the exercise of popular sovereignty, people naturally confused what was right with their own desires.

From these two broad truths about bourgeois Yankee democracy—a lack of ideals and a terrible "selfwill" (as Martineau described it)—a host of subsidiary problems followed, all made worse by the operation of the American Constitution. The most obvious of these problems to British eyes was the weakness of northern political and military leadership. Writing in late 1863, Sir Henry Holland, the well-known society physician who visited the North during the conflict, noticed a "*want of great men.*" "The 3 years war, & its many emergencies," he explained, "have not raised a single one above the dead level of mediocrity."[77] With almost monotonous frequency, British observers described democracy and mob rule as the cause of this mediocrity. Although he was very discreet about American affairs in public, Lord Palmerston privately described the Federal cabinet as "a Swaggering bullying Set of men. . . .who have no Sense of Honor and who are Swayed by the Passions of irresponsible masses, and by a reckless desire to hold their Positions by all and any means."[78] Even the mild-mannered Lord Lyons agreed, explaining to Earl Russell that the North was not like other places where "a few Statesmen decided what was for the interest of the Community, and guided public opinion by their superior wisdom, talents and authority." Rather, "politicians" were in charge, "men . . . of second rate station and ability who aim at little more than at divining and pandering to the feeling of the Mob of Voters."[79] The *Spectator* put it more humorously when it charged that the Federal cabinet "talk like metropolitan members, and act like the directors of a sinking railway." It was unfortunate that this group fought for "one of the noblest causes confided to men in the tone of a company trying to ruin a rival line."[80] In the midst of a critique of American democracy that appeared in *Blackwood's Edinburgh Magazine,* Edward Bruce Hamley asked, "Are the best Americans willing to accept Mr. Abraham Lincoln and Mr. W. H. Seward as their best men? If not, can they substitute better men? If they cannot, what other proof is needed of the inefficiency of their boasted institutions?"[81]

Lincoln, of course, came in for much criticism. In September 1862, Lord Hartington (later the 8th Duke of Devonshire), who met Lincoln, wrote that the president was "civil" and "well meaning," but "about as fit for his position now as a fire shovel."[82] At about the same time, the *Standard* struggled to be fair to Lincoln, dismissing charges that he was a "self-seeking knave" or a "ferocious half-honest fanatic." The newspaper concluded, however, that the president was a "plain, ignorant, well-intentioned man, thrust by the caprice of fortune and demagogism into a position for which he is totally and laughably incompetent, and anxious to do his duty therein according to the best light afforded by a very limited intellect and a strong but very narrow conscience."[83] Since the North was identified with bourgeois democracy, it should surprise no one that the *Standard* attributed the middle-class qualities of a "limited intellect" and a "strong but very narrow conscience" to Lincoln. British attitudes toward the shortcomings of this bourgeois democracy were evident in sneering about Lincoln's background as a lawyer. For example, the *Economist* argued that Lincoln was "unequal to the situation in which he is placed" because "he has received the training of a rural attorney."[84] In September 1862, even the level-headed Sir George Cornewall Lewis, then secretary of state for war, commented that "the Northerners are now finding out materially what it is to be governed by a village attorney appointed prime minister for 4 years certain."[85]

Leave it to Robert Cecil, writing in the *Quarterly Review,* to articulate a comprehensive view of how democracy produced poor leadership. Cecil argued that democracy had transferred power from the "independent and highly-cultivated classes" to "wire-pullers and caucus-mongers." The latter thus became the media by which the mob elected presidents. American presidential campaigns now resembled the most odious political process Cecil could conceive of—English "metropolitan elections," the closest thing to a popular poll in England and a byword of corruption. The "incompetence of the President," then, was a "direct result" of the process by which he was chosen. Even worse, Americans could not remove their president for at least four years. Thus, they were not governed by the mob; rather, "they are governed by that which is much worse—the irremovable ruler of a mob's choice."[86]

For Radical, working-class weeklies that still took a Chartist view of matters, Abraham Lincoln symbolized the political and social equality of the American republic. The lowly rail-splitter had become an attorney and then president of the United States. In March 1861, *Lloyd's Weekly Newspaper* greeted his inauguration by observing that in Lincoln "we behold . . . a specimen of the Yankee *pur sang*. His fortunes are extraordinary; but they are the natural growth of American institutions. . . . He is the proper child of the vast unmeasured republic."[87] That symbolism, however, did not necessarily prevent these weeklies from criticizing the president and his administration when the going got tough; heavy criticism of Federal leadership came from this quarter as well. In the aftermath of the First Battle of Bull Run, *Reynolds's Newspaper* sadly related that, "as sincere believers in the superiority of democracy—rightly administered—we deeply regret that the defence of a good cause, or the honour of a noble people, should have been entrusted to hands so feeble, heads so contracted, and brains so bemuddled as those of Mr. Lincoln and his subordinates."[88] Later, in the midst of the *Trent* affair, *Reynolds's Newspaper* took Lincoln to task for his first annual message to Congress, declaring that he had a "flabby mind, and therefore a loose, limp, lumbering style of expression." Lincoln's ideas, which were "the very quintessence of driveling imbecility" and announced "in a manner . . . both pompous and ludicrous," reminded the weekly of "the solemnity of a theatrical clown or a funny fool" who "provokes laughter even while [he] inspires disgust."[89]

Below the North's leadership, however, brewed an unstable compound of anarchy and despotism. On this subject, as with so many others, British commentators were rather vague. They did not always use key phrases with sufficient precision, explain the process by which despotism established itself, or confirm anarchy's relationship to despotism. However, as time went on, there was a greater emphasis on the mob's influence over the Federal government as well as the government's sudden accumulation of power.[90] Like the *Spectator*, some observers pooh-poohed this view of matters as "one of the favourite theories of the Conservatives."[91] Robert Ferguson claimed that the Americans "are an eminently practical people, who will submit to whatever the safety of the State demands—and nothing beyond it."[92] Yet for most observers, too much evidence suggested that the North was increasingly despotic. William Howard Russell, for instance, drew attention to "confiscation, martial law, suspension of habeas corpus, coercion of judges, the overthrow of the courts of law, abrogation of trial by jury, paper money, forced contracts, and conscription, and *lettres de cachet*."[93] In the name of sustaining a decaying republic, civil leaders had erected the machinery of tyranny. As early as November 1861, while speaking before the Alford Agricultural Society's anniversary dinner, James Banks Stanhope, Conservative MP for North Lincolnshire, compared the North's domestic policies to those of Russia and Austria before concluding that "when democracy was fairly put to the trial it broke down altogether, and was transformed into an absolute Government and a military nation."[94] By December 1861, *The Times* concluded that "the American Constitution, either by its own intrinsic defects or though the feebleness and violence of its administrators, altogether broke down" and was replaced by a lawless dictatorship.[95] Much commentary suggested that America seemed headed toward military dictatorship. Civilians may have erected the machinery, but it would be generals who would eventually seize control of the system.[96] British observers tended to see democratic republics as particularly vulnerable to military despotism, partly because of their familiarity with the fate of republican Rome along with more recent events, like Louis-Napoleon's destruction of France's Second Republic. Moreover, a number of commentators clearly believed that the civilized world had entered a new era in which traditional, authoritarian governments, such as monarchies and empires, had enjoyed a resurgence due to an unholy and paradoxical alliance with democracy.[97] In 1864, the 4th Earl of Carnarvon, a leading Conservative figure at the time, wrote a long memorandum to himself, entitled "Present State of the Civilised World," in which he argued that in the modern age "not only does Democracy beget Tyranny, but Tyranny when begotten re-engrafts upon herself the democratic principle." Such a phenomenon, he argued, was illustrated by France under Napoleon III as well as by the United States, where "democracy . . . is already merged in the ghastly terrorism of a military monarchy, whilst that terrorism is in turn sustained by the democratic organisation of the country."[98]

From a British perspective, the problem with these regimes—or any undergirded by some form of democracy—was that they were guided by passion rather than reason. Simple appetites or feelings like avarice or vengeance became the motive force behind policy. Writing for the *Spectator* from Boston in June 1862, Edward Dicey marveled at the "self-restraint, the moderation and the patience of the American people in the conduct of this people's war," but in making this claim, he swam against the tide.[99] In April 1862, while writing to Lord John Russell about America, Lord Palmerston articulated a common belief that "republican nations or nations in which the masses Influence or direct the destinies of the Country are swayed much more by Passion than by Interest and for this Plain Reason namely that Passion is a Single Feeling which aims directly at its object, while Interest is a calculation of relative good & Evil . . . moreover Passion Sways the masses, while Interest acts Comparatively on the few."[100] Where Palmerston's statement sounded like a universal law, the *Economist* spoke to the immediate American context while reaching similar conclusions. Neither politicians nor the press, the weekly argued, provided any kind of brake on the American people because they were the supreme power in the land. Americans were "by nature . . . impulsive, and in education they are half-taught; they are especially subject to passions of opinion; they are almost entirely wanting in ballast to resist them." For those reasons, they formed "their judgments easily and change them as easily."[101] Northern emotion, not logic, then, explained the North's otherwise incomprehensible attempt to subjugate the South. In August 1862, the *Illustrated London News* editorialized that the northern people were "impelled by passion and not by reason" since "reason would have allowed the South to go in peace" so soon as it became evident that southerners were unanimous.[102] Likewise, in the same month, the 5th Earl Stanhope wrote to Sir George Cornewall Lewis that northerners' "rancour & resentment seem likely to last much longer than their strength. Still they are so strange a people & so governed by impulse that there is no knowing what new turn any moment may bring."[103] For British diplomats, of course, this unpredictability was frustrating. In a particularly black moment, Lord Lyons wrote to the 3rd Baron Wodehouse, "I wish I saw any signs here that the absolute insanity of any step was a reason to suppose our cousins in their present mood w^{d} not take it."[104] These types of observations were very similar to concerns expressed about democracy at home and show how closely elite Britons could identify northern with British democracy. It does not take much imagination to see how, in this case as in many others, the North served as a kind of Other.

Along with the widespread sense in Britain that Americans were no longer capable of operating their constitution correctly, there was a belief that events in America highlighted the deficiencies of the Constitution itself. British commentators generally admired the Founding Fathers and the complex political machinery they had created, but many could not help concluding that the Constitution had only compounded democracy's shortcomings. For example, a number of observers saw federalism as an important source of American difficulties. As we have already seen, the intimate relationship between democracy and federalism was a source of some confusion.[105] Interestingly, those who clearly distinguished between the two tended to lay the blame for the crisis on one more than the other. If the *Saturday Review* tended to blame democracy, the *Spectator* plumped for federalism. Undoubtedly referring to Cecil, who had claimed democracy was "on its trial" in America, the *Spectator* claimed federal government was "on its trial" and had been condemned by the "voice of Europe." "If a federation be nothing more than [an] intermediate constitution," the weekly charged, "it is . . . doomed to perish alike by success or failure."[106] In the American case, the *Spectator* asserted that federalism had prevented the free play of democracy, which would have actually precluded secession.[107]

Another feature of the Constitution that received much scrutiny in light of the American crisis was the relationship between the people, the legislature, and the executive. Nobody investigated this matter so frequently, perceptively, or coherently as Walter Bagehot in the *Economist.*[108] For Bagehot, America's problems began with the conflict between "pure democracy," which was the "primitive principle" of the Constitution, and the "delicate machinery" implemented by the founders to hobble that democracy. Such a situation contributed to a government where each part suffered from various afflictions, and all parts worked at cross-purposes. The executive's shortcomings made it incapable of responding to a severe crisis. The American political system ensured that it never obtained the best men, the lame-duck period created an awkward four-month vacuum of power, and the president's independence from the legislature made it impossible for him to "share his responsibility with his Parliament."[109] The isolation of the executive from the legislature led to several other difficulties: the two branches could not act in harmony, the legislature could not hold the executive to account, and the executive was cut off from the currents of popular opinion.[110] As Bagehot put it strikingly, "in

America the constitution is an Executive, with a debating society attached." Since the executive was not responsible to the legislature, and the legislature was the main expression of public opinion, the public had become indifferent to politics. This situation created a vicious cycle in which the executive became ever more powerful and isolated as the legislature and the public became increasingly incapable and uninterested in expressing its opinion.[111]

The foregoing discussion about British perceptions of the North's political deficiencies provides some insight into the influence of James Spence's *The American Union* (1861). Since Spence took many of the major criticisms that we have noted and synthesized them in a coherent argument, his work both influenced and reflected British opinion. For these reasons, Blackett argues that *The American Union* was "the most important book published in Britain about the American conflict."[112] Campbell demurs, but we have already seen how even Spence's opponents conceded that his book had given form to British opinion in a way that no other work had.[113] *The American Union* not only asserted that the federal system was bound to fail, but also that the Union had corrupted the political character of the nation.[114] "The vast dimensions of the Union," Spence argued, "filled the national mind with conceptions of size, of amplitude, with the desire to excite astonishment rather than to command respect." In other words, "magnitude had become the standard, in place of worth."[115] Such institutions explained the American tendency toward "exaggeration," "arrogance," "excitability," and "mental intoxication."[116] The rise of mob despotism and the implementation of flawed constitutional arrangements (particularly the separation of the legislature from the executive) had made the Union unworkable.[117] For these reasons, a terrible degeneration had taken place in American public life. Where the Constitution's "marked characteristic" was "moderation," the "prominent characteristic of the people at the present day is excess."[118] Spence concluded his survey of American institutions with a patronizing assertion that was typical of the postcolonial relationship. In America, he argued, "we certainly find much that is at variance with our most cherished ideas of constitutional government." "Either after five hundred years' experience," he continued, "we [in Britain] are ignorant of what representative institutions ought to be, or else these stand in need of very radical reform."[119] Although large portions of the British public would have disagreed with his positions on slavery and recognition of the Confederacy, Spence's survey of the relationship between federalism, the Union, the

Constitution, and democracy provides an excellent summary of mainstream British ideas that influenced attitudes toward the North.

THE SLAVE POWER: BRITISH UNDERSTANDINGS OF SOUTHERN POLITICS AND SOCIETY

Even as *The American Union* was published in September 1861, a riposte of sorts was already in the making. In May 1861, during his last term as Whatley Chair of Political Economy at Trinity College, Dublin, John Elliott Cairnes began delivering a series of lectures on American slavery. Inspired largely by Auguste Comte's philosophy of history, specifically the concept of the "*inévitable consensus universel*," Cairnes assumed that if he could determine the economic relations of a people, he could infer their political and social arrangements as well.[120] The American slave system seemed like an excellent test of this assumption because, as innumerable antebellum observers had stated, the institution appeared to account for almost all of the major differences between the North and South. While writing his lectures, Cairnes relied on John Stuart Mill (his friend and mentor), the works of Tocqueville, British travel literature about the United States, and certain American sources, particularly Frederick Law Olmsted's accounts of the South.[121] During the summer of 1861, as he perceived that British opinion had increasingly turned against the North, Cairnes consulted Mill and eventually decided to write a book.[122] In May 1862, he finally published *The Slave Power: Its Character, Career, and Probable Designs: Being an Attempt to Explain the Real Issues Involved in the American Contest.*

Cairnes defined the "Slave Power" as a "system of interests, industrial, social and political, springing from slavery" that represented "a system of society at once retrograde and aggressive."[123] Not surprisingly, considering Cairnes's starting point, *The Slave Power* demonstrated that slavery's economic needs dictated its political and social tendencies. Slave labor was inefficient, but it thrived in the South because the soil was rich and the crops grown there—cotton, tobacco, sugar, and rice—played to the system's strengths. A number of consequences flowed from these facts. Slavery kept free labor at arm's length because it degraded work. Slavery also contributed to the concentration of capital because big plantations were more efficient than small farms.

All of these circumstances led to the emergence of a primitive three-tiered society. At the top, a wealthy oligarchy led the Slave Power, controlling both politics and society. Below this group was the vast bulk of the white population—a mass of 5 million poor whites (recalculated at 4 million in later editions). Too proud to work and too poor to own slaves, they led a "vagrant and precarious life spent in the desert," "little removed from savage life, eking out a wretched subsistence by hunting, by fishing, by hiring themselves out for occasional jobs, by plunder."[124] Slaves, of course, suffered terribly at the very bottom of this society, providing labor that was "unskillful" and "wanting in versatility."[125]

Such a society was benighted and lacked any kind of culture. Even more important, it was a menace to its neighbors. Because its agriculture was so inefficient, the Slave Power was relentlessly expansionist. For that reason, with great single-mindedness, southern oligarchs steadily pursued their self-interests as they sought to dominate and direct the Federal government. By training, these oligarchs were tyrannical and aggressive. If, according to Spence's reckoning, the United States suffered from an excess of federalism and democracy, from Cairnes's perspective, the pernicious influence of the southern oligarchy suggested that American federalism suffered from an insufficiently democratic character.[126] Cairnes concluded, "The South has been compelled to pursue a policy of aggression towards the North, not because it is less rich or less populous, but because it is different, and all the differences which divide North and South have originated in slavery."[127]

A number of reviewers did not believe that Cairnes's characterization of the South automatically sanctified the North's war effort. As Cairnes himself recognized, "people tell me that I have demonstrated my case as against the South, but that I have not shown that the North is much better."[128] However, the great majority of reviewers found Cairnes's analysis of southern society convincing. The *Spectator,* the *London Review,* the *Economist,* the *National Review,* and *Macmillan's Magazine* all produced encomiums of the work. Harriet Martineau's review of the book in the *Daily News* was full of praise, and she wrote to Cairnes that "I agree so entirely with almost every line in the volume that our way of seeing facts is more like the action of one mind than two."[129] Although he could not assent to Cairnes's discussion of northern motives, Sir Edmund Walker Head in the *Edinburgh Review* observed there could be no disputing "Mr. Cairnes's forcible statement of the evils of slavery, both moral and economical."[130] Or as the reviewer for the *Dublin University Magazine* put it, "If we differ from some of his conclusions, it is not at all because we do not most cordially agree thus far in his premises."[131]

What is most interesting about these reviews is that Cairnes received the most praise in dealing with issues where his analysis proved most faulty. Modern scholars of the American South and the slave economy have questioned many of the fundamental premises that supported Cairnes's argument. For instance, historians have generally concluded that slave labor was not only efficient and versatile, but also extremely profitable. Southern farmers faced no shortage of land and were constantly improving the soils that they tilled. Nonslaveholding whites were hardly an undifferentiated mass of crackers without property; indeed, a fairly high proportion consisted of "plain folk"—peasant proprietors of the sort whom Cairnes praised.[132] Finally, it is clear that southern elites were not unified to the extent portrayed by Cairnes and that slaveowners did not totally dominate southern politics, society, and the economy.[133]

That being the case, how and why did Cairnes's presentation of the South prove so convincing? Much had to do with Cairnes's crisp, logical, and coherent exposition in which each point served as a foundation for succeeding points. The *National Review* rightly remarked upon the "methodical and forcible" nature of the work, and praised the "strong convictions of an ardent thinker . . . expressed in the measured and temperate language of a philosophical historian."[134] At the same time, *The Slave Power* swam very much with the dominant currents of mid-Victorian, classical political economy. Thomas Edward Cliffe Leslie, the professor of jurisprudence and political economy at Queen's College, Belfast, who reviewed *The Slave Power* for *Macmillan's Magazine,* explicitly read the book as an application of Adam Smith's ideas to the dystopian slave economy of the South. "Instead of the theory of wages, profit, and rent, applicable to a free society," Leslie claimed, "he [Cairnes] lays bare the structure of a society which excludes wages . . . in which there is no profit . . . in which there is little or no rent . . . in which fear is substituted for hope . . . and in which wealth exists only in its rudest forms."[135] In Cairnes's work, this classical political economy was seamlessly connected to familiar images of the South associated with widely read antebellum accounts, such as those by Tocqueville, Stirling, and Olmsted.[136] In other words, Cairnes presented a picture of the South that his readers expected to see. Finally, the success of Cairnes's work depended very much on timing. Deprived of information from the South, British readers were thirsty for knowledge about this region so they could understand what course the war might take. In May 1861, *The Times* had asserted that "we are so absolutely cut off from all news of what is passing at the South that we cannot pretend to speak of the popular impulses there, except so far as we may divine them from the well-known character of the Southerners."[137] Cairnes had made such divination possible by delineating the southern character in greater detail than anybody had before. He did not so much establish new ideas as reinforce existing ones that had been developed during the antebellum era: slavery was fundamental, not incidental, to the organization of southern society; the South was dominated by a small clique of oligarchs; and backwardness characterized southern life.

Antebellum stereotypes alone did not fully account for British perceptions of the Confederacy; the events of the war were also highly significant. When the secession crisis first unfolded, Britons initially expressed very little sympathy for the South. Secession launched by a backward region for the sake of slavery seemed to promise pointless anarchy because no one believed the South could win its independence, let alone sustain a worthwhile national life. For example, in April 1861 the *Standard,* which later proved very sympathetic to the Confederacy, declared "the Nemesis of national crimes is fast dogging the heels of the southern states, and the cause of law and religion, of civilisation and of right, forbids a feeling of sympathy for culprits so obstinate and wilful." The newspaper foresaw the extension of slavery throughout the Gulf of Mexico, widespread disorder, and eventual defeat for the Confederacy.[138] *The Times* correctly recollected in July 1862 that in the early months of secession Britons had little reason to embrace slavery, treason, and the disruption of the Union. However, at the time of writing, *The Times* believed "all that is past and gone" because of the South's subsequent achievements.[139] The South's ability to sustain a functioning state under enormous pressure, along with its great military successes, wrought a great transformation of British opinion. If the Confederacy's origin and birth had antagonized Britain, the spirit with which it conducted its struggle, which seemed to make reconstruction of the Union impossible, completely changed the nature of British calculations.[140] The legality of secession and the North's initial response no longer mattered because "the present morality of the war depends wholly on the probability of reconquest, followed by reunion."[141]

British observers needed some way to explain Confederate military success. They did so by referring to what they thought they knew about southern politics, society, and economics. As Cairnes put it unsympathetically, the "Slave Power" was "under the forms of a democracy, an uncontrolled despotism, wielded by a compact oligarchy."[142] Those who viewed the South in a more benign light tended to describe the South as an "aristocracy" rather than an "oligarchy" (although the words appear to have been almost interchangeable). *The Times,* for example, believed southern planters qualified as aristocrats because they were a "class of masters" who enjoyed a fixed position, possessed hereditary rank, exercised authority, and obtained deference.[143] More radical papers agreed with this assessment, with the *Daily News* conceding that the Confederate government was aristocratic because political power was concentrated "in the hands of a very small minority, having a common interest and capable of acting in concert. . . . All the springs of society are in its hands."[144]

Of course, not everybody agreed with such an analysis of southern society. Interestingly enough, in an 1865 *Quarterly Review* article, Spence objected on political grounds, citing the Confederacy's democratic political institutions as proof that the South was not "an aristocratic country."[145] *Lloyd's Weekly Newspaper* protested on cultural grounds, claiming the "southerners are a kind of bastard aristocracy" whose morals, manners, and views were inferior to "the cultivated and highly-educated men of Boston."[146] A number of commentators, however, anticipated such arguments. Lewis, for example, reconciled the South's democratic political institutions with aristocratic domination by asserting that southern democracy resembled "the democracy of the ancients." "It is," he claimed, "a community composed of a privileged class of freemen, but in which all the working classes are slaves"—a situation quite unlike in the North, in "which the working classes form the majority of the votes."[147] Robert Cecil made a similar argument. No society that disenfranchised the "poorest and rudest section of the community . . . because of their colour" could be called a democracy. Not only that, the white remnant of the majority was driven by race prejudice to follow the guidance of the educated, property-owning, white minority. In this manner, "the planters exercise without hindrance the natural influence of wealth, and the levelling tendencies of a democratic form of government are wholly neutralized." For all practical purposes, then, the South was an aristocracy.[148]

Lewis and Cecil's observations make clear that in Britain the southern ruling class's existence was tightly bound to slavery. Tocqueville himself had attributed the South's aristocratic character to slavery.[149] The antebellum debate over whether aristocracy had created slavery or slavery had created aristocracy remained unresolved.[150] In the end, it made little difference: each seemed to reinforce the other. Whatever the case, slavery made it very difficult for Britons to see the Confederacy as a democracy. For these reasons, a visitor to America, like the novelist Anthony Trollope, could state without qualification that "a slave country, which has progressed far in slavery, must be aristocratic in nature,—aristocratic and patriarchal. A large slave-owner from Georgia may call himself a democrat,—may think that he reveres republican institutions, and may talk with American horror of the thrones of Europe; but he must in his heart be an aristocrat."[151]

If the prevailing sense in Britain was that the Confederacy was led by a small group of aristocrats or oligarchs, there was also widespread agreement that this group was especially well suited for political and military leadership. If aristocracy was rule by the best, then the Confederacy enjoyed a great advantage over the North, where social leveling had taken a toll. Robert Cecil argued that in the South aristocracy produced "political ability" because the Confederacy was led by its "strongest" men. "Skill," he argued, "has been more than a match for brute, unintelligent force; and the aristocracy . . . has borne the powerful and braggart democracy to the ground."[152] In September 1861, *The Times* claimed that the South's "social institutions were favourable to military organization, for, though their government was republican in form, it was administered in an aristocratic spirit."[153] For that reason, the southern states produced "the best soldiers, the best Generals, the best Statesmen, the best public functionaries of all kinds . . . and are thereby proved to be the nearest approach to a governing class."[154] In December 1861, the *Spectator*, which likened southern society to that of Sparta, attributed the Confederacy's strong administration and dignified foreign policy to the existence of a "strong oligarchy," perhaps the "strongest, ablest, and most effective, but also the most oppressive and most odious forms of human government."[155] In September 1862, the *Spectator* also argued that the Confederacy had "demonstrated that aristocracy, whatever its other demerits, is the most effective of ruling powers" because "from the very beginning of the contest, the action of the South has been direct, coherent, and singularly able."[156]

According to this view of matters, the southern aristocracy also proved particularly strong because it possessed men habituated to command who could rely on the deference of others. Lieutenant-Colonel Henry Charles Eden Malet (part of the well-connected Malet family that had members in the diplomatic service, the army, and the East India Company) visited the United States in the fall of 1862 and reported that in the Confederacy "good Staff Officers and the Regimental Officers are mostly men of Known families in the districts from whence the regiment was raised." Not only was this aristocracy able, it commanded respect because "the 'mean whites' look up to and obey the sons of the Great Planters."[157] For a Radical paper that had supported the northern cause throughout the war, the *Morning Star* provided a surprisingly sympathetic eulogy of the Army of Northern Virginia after Appomattox, claiming that it possessed a military superiority because "Southern society was formed upon an aristocratic model" with "men accustomed to command as officers."[158] Likewise, the *Spectator* claimed that the "mean white" was "accustomed to look up to the planters as the sole property holders" and "readily obeyed them as officers."[159]

Of course, the existence of an aristocracy presupposes the existence of inferiors, and for Britons, as the previous paragraph suggests, the "mean white" became the character most frequently associated with those inferiors. Not everybody, of course, believed that mean whites constituted the majority of the free population in the South. For instance, in a challenge explicitly aimed at Cairnes, the *Saturday Review* flatly denied the existence of "white trash," claiming that "careless or malevolent observers" had misinterpreted rough, frontier conditions in the South as poverty and backwardness.[160] However, if one accepted that political, social, and economic power was concentrated in a small elite and that slavery degraded labor (as most Britons did), it was hard to escape the conclusion that something like mean whites existed. British attitudes toward this group were often negative. That they made good soldiers did not necessarily compensate for their deficiencies as members of civil society. The *Daily News* claimed that since "poor whites" were not integral to the southern economy, they could be spared as soldiers, a role for which they were well suited since they were "hardy [and] accustomed to out-door life and privations."[161] William Leng, the Scots journalist who later turned the *Sheffield Telegraph* into a provincial newspaper power, presented a far more lurid picture of this class. He argued that "oath-blurting, drink-sodden, knife-carrying, tobacco-squirting [poor] whites," prime specimens of southern "chivalry," inspired by alcohol and employing the arguments of "rifles, revolvers, and bowie knives," willingly served as "missionaries of the Slave Power."[162]

This reference to the Slave Power brings us to the ambivalence that never quite left British attitudes toward the southern leadership. To greater or lesser degrees, many British commentators had difficulty reconciling aristocratic virtue with the practice of slavery. A number of commentators relied on the old abolitionist argument that slavery corrupted the virtue of the slaveowner by undermining his self-restraint. For example, the Reverend G. G. Lawrence visited the United States and reported to his congregation in Huddersfield that "the owner of slaves has constantly the opportunity of giving vent to the worst passions of human nature, almost without control from human laws."[163] The problem with this view was that it was hard to mesh not only with widely accepted views of Jefferson Davis's and Robert E. Lee's characters, but also with the Confederacy's military performance.[164] What these arguments succeeded in conveying, though, was a discomfort with the extent to which British policy as well as opinion often viewed the North and South as moral equivalents. For example, *Lloyd's Weekly Newspaper* expressed frustration with the way in which Britain had sympathized with the slaveowner because he was "so good a gentleman" and "his manners are so much more elegant than those prevalent in the north!" "A man," the weekly complained, "who is morally a monster, is not to be caressed because he has the manners of a Brummell; nor is the honest man to forget his claim to our respect because he eats peas with a knife." The weekly lamented the "dulled consciences" of Britain's public men as well as the "shocking picture" of "Whiggism . . . endeavouring to make John Bull and Legree shake hands."[165]

A few fanatics sought to promote that handshake, believing that Confederate social organization presented some kind of ideal. Francis Lawley, *The Times*' southern correspondent from 1862 to 1865, went so far as to write to a friend that "if England could see the elevating influences which Slavery exercises on the class which draws its wealth from the slave, opinion would be staggered." The "planters or aristocracy . . . are as pure, as intelligent, as soberminded, as thoughtful & conservative a community as can be found anywhere on the earth's surface." To this group belonged Jefferson Davis ("as immaculate & earnest a man, with all his prejudices, as the noblest of England's statesmen") along with the Confederacy's military leadership, from whom the "rank & file of the army take their tone & colouring."[166] Another Confederate sympathizer, the 9th Marquess of Lothian, wrote in a similar vein when he surmised that "if all the stories about cruelty to negroes were as true as most of them are false—if Legree was rather the rule than the exception among the holders of Southern plantations—if non-slaveowning whites of the Confederacy were as brutal and degraded a set as . . . we used to fancy they were,—even then the Confederacy might claim to stand on a pretty high level on the strength of having produced three such contemporaries as Lee, Stuart, and Jackson."[167]

For obvious reasons, however, the South never became a model for Britain. If aristocracy had produced strong leadership, the slavery on which it rested was not only detestable but also the source of backwardness. Early in the secession crisis, the *Daily Telegraph* went so far as to describe the South as "a half-civilized New Guinea, where industry is dishonourable, education rare, freedom a spectre, and domestic comfort entirely dependent upon the manufacturing energy of the North."[168] What a half-civilized New Guinea looked like was rendered in great detail by the *National Review,* which quoted Frederick Law Olmsted at length on the deficiencies of southern culture. Olmsted claimed that between the Mississippi and the James Rivers he found: "No garden, no flowers, no fruit, no tea, no cream, no sugar, no bread . . . no curtains; no lifting windows—three times out of four absolutely no windows; no couch. . . . There was no hay, no straw, no oats . . . no discretion, no care, no honesty. . . . I did not . . . see, except perhaps in one or two towns, a thermometer; nor a book of Shakespeare; nor a pianoforte, or a sheet of music; nor the light of Carcel or other good center-table or reading lamp; nor an engraving, or a copy, of any kind, of a work of art of the slightest merit."[169] The *Economist* provided its readers with a concise explanation of the peculiar institution's flaws: "slavery, as it exists in the Confederate States of America, is a grievous economical error, a blot upon their civilization, a bar to their progress, and (independently of all consideration for the Negro himself) a source of deplorable demoralization to the rich whites who own slaves, and of still worse degradation to the poor whites who do not."[170] The political cost of proposing the South as a model was too high, especially since trade union leaders proved especially sensitive to anything that resembled an attempt to undermine the social or political position of the working class. Not surprisingly, they often saw in the South a regime that was inimical to labor.[171]

Although working-class weeklies often seemed to recognize that events in the United States had some bearing on Britain, aristocracy was not on trial in America. If it was on trial anywhere, it was in Britain, where mass-circulation, working-class, radical weeklies relentlessly employed Chartist rhetoric to attack what they argued was the aristocracy's undue influence. After all, it made less sense to attack a pseudo-aristocracy abroad when there was a real one at home that presented a more immediate political problem. While discussing the Civil War, *Reynolds's Newspaper* reminded its readers of domestic oppression when it described the working men of Britain as "cursed with the rule of a foreign dynasty, a liberty-hating aristocracy, and a fat, bloated, and arrogant Church."[172] Likewise, in 1865, while *Lloyd's Weekly Newspaper* contemplated what it saw as the unwillingness of Parliament to deliver reform, it observed, "We have long existed under the despotism of the small minority; and to this minority, composed of aristocracy and the plutocracy, we are invited to continue our thankful allegiance."[173] Instead of launching an oblique attack on Britain's aristocracy by comparing it to southern planters, these journals took the more direct approach of accusing the British upper class of pro-Confederate sympathies. *Lloyd's Weekly Newspaper* explained that the Confederacy had obtained much sympathy in Britain because "the aristocracy of this country have sung the southerners' praises—seeing in them a race of oligarchs."[174] As the *Bee-Hive* wrote simply, "We are governed by an aristocracy, and the aristocracy *en masse* is on the side of the South."[175]

Instead of becoming a model or an antipode for Britain, the South really served as the antithesis of the North—with each section suffering from its own flaws. Nobody spelled this point out more clearly than James Fitzjames Stephen while writing a review of *The Slave Power* in the October 1863 issue of *Fraser's Magazine*. Stephen judged that "a vague notion prevails in this country that the South are aristocrats and the North democrats; that in some way or other aristocracy and democracy are at issue, and that the triumph either of the South or the North will be the triumph for the principle which the victorious side represents." Although the northerners were wronged first, "the impression they make on the mind is that of an immense number of very commonplace people put by circumstances into an extraordinary position, in which they comprehend nothing distinctly beyond a general notion that they have been very ill used, and ought to set themselves right." On the other hand, southerners, at least initially, "by extreme means asserted an extreme and doubtful right . . . to protect and even to extend a hateful institution." Yet the South—unlike the North—"had produced great men." Stephen continued by arguing that great men like Lee and Jackson "are produced by a special state of society," so it was "no mere accident that nearly all the conspicuous personal ability which this wonderful crisis has produced should have been found on one side."[176] The *Spectator* took advantage of Lincoln's reelection in 1864 to frame a similar argument while manifesting more sympathy for the North. The *Spectator* declared that "never before in modern history have the two great political ideas of mankind, aristocracy and democracy, the rule of the many for the benefit of the few, and the rule of the many or the few for the benefit of all, been brought into such direct and visible collision." In the South, a capable, clear-eyed aristocracy strong in resources and will pursued its objects without restraint—the suppression of "the many in order to give the few broader and freer life." The *Spectator* marveled that "all that adroitness, and valour, and civil energy, and the instinct of governing men can effect for a cause has been accomplished for theirs." The North, on the other hand, enjoyed no such advantages, "save a power of recruiting which springs out of its own attraction for all men like itself." The *Spectator* judged that the North "never had a leader above its own average in capacity, capable of doing more than express its own slowly-forming will, act upon its own slowly-gained convictions." Thus, "the reticent, statesmanlike, selfish aristocracy, the slow, loud-tongued democracy, each left to itself, each guided by its own highest average and no more, has been fighting out foot to foot and face to face, as the Athens and Sparta of the New World, the ancient political battle of mankind." Lincoln's reelection did not guarantee northern victory, the *Spectator* argued, but it did guarantee that the North possessed the moral sense to fight its aristocratic foe to the bitter end.[177]

Even as they apparently clarified the American situation, such arguments obscured the facts. We have already seen how Cairnes's analysis of southern society was flawed. It was unfortunate that this analysis, which was widely prevalent, also rendered the differences between the two sections in especially stark terms. There were important differences between the North and the South, otherwise the Civil War would never have occurred. Yet, by describing these differences as so fundamental, commentators ran the risk of making reunion seem impossible. Indeed, many commentators did believe reunion was impossible, especially since a federal democratic republic depended on the free consent of the governed. They argued that the southern states, which were profoundly different, and which had committed untold blood and treasure to obtain independence, would never willingly reenter the Union.[178] For those in Britain who believed that slavery was at the root of all differences between the two societies, abolition was the key to reconstructing the Union. However, as we have seen and will continue to see, not everyone in Britain saw matters in this light.

THE MOST DIFFICULT PROBLEM OF POLITICS: BRITAIN, THE CIVIL WAR, AND THE REFORM ACT OF 1867

Did Federal victory change British attitudes toward the United States, particularly the North? If so, did this victory play a role in the passage of Britain's Reform Act of 1867? The traditional interpretation of British opinion has answered both questions in the affirmative, although Blackett is too circumspect to respond with a simple yes. Not surprisingly, the revisionists are much more skeptical about the influence of the American example on British reform.

The evidence is difficult to interpret, yet in all likelihood northern victory demonstrated the virtues of democracy—but only to those Britons willing to be convinced.[179] Some journals seemed sincere in arguing that the North had proved the value of democracy. In April 1865, only days before news of Lincoln's assassination reached Britain, the radical *Daily News* asserted that the war "proved that a democratic republic may be as steadfast, as capable of concert, as clear in its aims, and as persevering in its conduct as any nation compacted under the sway of the most sagacious and resolute ruler." In the North, "a high ideal" had "united millions of fellow-citizens" who had displayed neither "fickleness" nor "self-love." The *Daily News* concluded that "the American people have shown themselves to be a nation otherwise than by accident, and to be living under a bond as firm and trustworthy as that of any monarchy, past or present."[180] Other newspapers that had spent four years criticizing the North and insulting Abraham Lincoln had ulterior motives for suddenly changing their editorial policy at war's end. *The Times,* for instance, probably felt compelled to praise the North as well as print a fulsome eulogy of Lincoln for the same reason that it had to sack Charles Mackay as its New York correspondent and propose sending William Howard Russell back to the United

States (see chapter 2); it was necessary to mend ties with America. *Reynolds's Newspaper* was disgusted by this new attitude on the part of its rivals, charging in May 1865 that the "aristocratic and flunkeyish" portion of the press had spent the previous four years "misrepresenting, caricaturing, sneering at, and slandering Abraham Lincoln." Moreover, "with a yell of the most indecent exultation, noble lords and their organs told us, four years ago, that the Republican bubble had burst." Now, however, "the tune is changed." The weekly continued, "The prophets are dumbfounded and shamed. Every one of their predictions has been falsified by events. The Republican bubble has not burst; indeed, it is now seen that there was no bubble in the matter to burst."[181]

Because the war had left behind so many unanswered questions, others were not quite so positive as *Reynolds's Newspaper* that the conflict had proved much of anything. Could a federal democracy reintegrate the seceded states? Could American society find a place for the African American? Could the Federal government pay off its extraordinary war debts? In a January 1865 letter to Charles Sumner, Richard Cobden expressed a certainty that the North would win, but military victory alone would not influence the cause of liberalism in Europe, for the fighting would "have conferred quite as much 'glory,' so far as mere fighting goes, on the South as on the North." "It is in your superiority in other things," Cobden wrote, "that you can alone by your example elevate the old world."[182] By "other things," Cobden meant political and social reconstruction. The *Saturday Review* made a similar point when it conceded that "the great civil war has proved that a democracy is capable of acting with extraordinary vigour," but its "patience in the discharge of less exciting duties will be more severely tested by peace."[183] In other words, the jury was still out on the qualities of American democracy.[184] In 1877, while assessing (and attempting to reinforce) the Anglo-American relationship in the *North American Review,* Gladstone could argue that the United States had surmounted the political, social, and economic challenges of the postwar years. In 1867, however, let alone 1865, this success was not at all clear.[185]

In this context, it is worth remembering a point raised by Gertrude Himmelfarb in relation to the Reform Act of 1867. She wondered whether the Civil War "was more often the occasion for a debater's point than a genuine change of heart toward democracy."[186] Himmelfarb concluded that the war did not convert hearts and minds in Britain so much as it was invoked to support existing beliefs. Evidence from throughout this chapter suggests that she was correct. Such a conclusion seems to jibe with the one point on which both Blackett and Campbell agree: during the Civil War years, many British commentators continued to believe that their nation and system of government were superior to anything the United States could provide.[187] The old postcolonial attitude behind this stance was well captured by Sir Edward Bulwer-Lytton (then an MP for Hertfordshire) in a September 1861 speech to his constituents in Hitchin: "America has more to learn from England than England to learn from America."[188]

So what role, if any, did the Civil War play in reform? For sure, the conflict helped mobilize a popular, radical liberalism that agitated for reform and eventually contributed to the foundation of the Gladstonian Liberal Party. Most recent works on the Reform Act of 1867, however, do not seem to believe that this movement pushed reform through Parliament or determined the specific provisions of that reform.[189] Parliament, these works argue, primarily shaped and passed the reform act. That being the case, the best means of determining the war's impact on the process consists of studying the two party leaders in the Commons who played the leading roles in the reform drama of 1866–1867, William Gladstone and Benjamin Disraeli.

During the war, Gladstone repeatedly insisted to his correspondents that if he could, he would have restored the United States.[190] But restoration was impossible, and for that reason, Gladstone believed the Federal government had "undertaken one of the blindest enterprises on record in human history."[191] For Gladstone, northern persistence in an impossible cause bordered on the immoral, and he found its conduct of the war distasteful.[192] It was for these reasons that he could write to a correspondent in September 1861 that it was not merely the split but "the way the North has behaved itself and its mode and tone in meeting the crisis that have dealt a 'heavy blow and great discouragement' in this country not only to democratic but to all liberal opinions and all that is associated with them."[193] By the end of 1861, Gladstone wrote to Baron Brougham and Vaux that "this has without doubt been a deplorable year for poor 'Democracy' and never has the old woman been at a heavier discount since 1793."[194] Gladstone did not confine these opinions to private correspondence. During the June 1863 Commons debate over John Roebuck's motion concerning recognition of the Confederacy, Gladstone was transparently honest about his opinion concerning the northern effort. He described the conflict as "destructive," "deplorable," and "hopeless."

In so many words, he claimed the war was unjust because its object was "not attainable." He did not believe in emancipation enforced by "coercion" and "bloodshed." Finally, while he stressed the extraordinary material cost of the war, he also pointed to the toll it took on the liberties of Americans. At one point he declared that the war had led to "the discredit to liberty abroad—the discredit, not only to democratic, not only to popular, but I venture to say to all liberal and constitutional principles."[195] Gladstone had much less to say about the war toward its end, so it is difficult to determine if he experienced a change of heart once the North triumphed. However, as late as January 1865, in a letter to the Duke of Argyll, he broached the question of British mediation in the conflict, a step indicating that he saw the war as futile as ever.[196] This evidence seems to match with the widespread belief among Gladstone biographers that his public conversion to reform, which took place in 1864 during the Commons debate on Edward Baines's bill to lower the borough franchise, had little to do with the war.[197]

Against these arguments, one could point to Gladstone's April 1866 speech at Liverpool, in which he used the American experience to support the Liberals' reform bill. In America during the war, he argued, "a largely extended franchise" had given "forcible expression to the national will" and allowed their governments to execute that will in unprecedented fashion. Under this system, Gladstone declared, Americans had "developed an amount of heroism, a power of self-sacrifice, an energy, a perseverance, a forgetfulness of every personal interest, and have marshalled an amount of actual force, and expended an amount of treasure, in support of their chosen rulers on the one side and on the other, such as I know not where to seek for in the annals of the history of the world."[198] The Commons reacted very badly to this speech, for it seemed as if Gladstone sought to overawe that body by setting himself up as the leader of "the people."[199] More important for our purposes, Gladstone hedged in his assertions about American democracy with a variety of qualifications that limited its application to Britain. He told his audience that he was not interested in the "comparative merits of English and American institutions" and that he did not prefer American institutions to his own. Moreover, the image of democracy that he presented to his auditors was colored in moderate hues as a "progressive extension to each man in his own sphere of every privilege and of every franchise he can exercise with advantage to himself and with safety to the State." Finally, Gladstone's notion of Britain limited the relevance of American democracy. Gladstone described his country as standing between the feudalism of Europe and the pure equality of America while partaking in both. For this reason, although Gladstone believed Britain possessed democratic elements, it was a "country aristocratic in feeling" that ought to cherish its inheritance.[200] The subtext was that the balance Britain had achieved made it different and probably better than America. This speech, considered so radical at the time, seems to indicate that the American experience did not convert Gladstone—rather, he used it as a debating point, and a rather tentative one at that.

Disraeli's case is somewhat different. Robert Blake asserts that Disraeli welcomed secession as it portended the division of the United States and "a blow in favour of aristocracy."[201] Disraeli's correspondence, however, does not provide much evidence supporting this conclusion. As the leader of the opposition in the Commons during the war, he did not have to engage with American questions or help construct a foreign policy in the same way that Gladstone did. Yet he and the Conservative leadership did watch the war closely to see if it presented an opportunity to overthrow Palmerston's administration. For instance, in 1863 the Conservatives' "shadow" cabinet met to figure out how it could somehow exploit Roebuck's infamous motion on recognition of the Confederacy and push the Liberals out of office.[202] In 1863 and 1864, Disraeli also responded to the queen's Speech from the Throne by pointing out inconsistencies or deficiencies in the government's response to the American conflict.[203]

On several occasions Disraeli provided sweeping analyses of the American situation that were both more discreet yet oracular than anything Gladstone produced.[204] As articulated in various speeches, Disraeli's public view of the Civil War was consistent. He described it as an enormous, violent conflict proceeding from great causes—"the emancipation of a race, the creation or defence of national independence, or the maintenance of a great empire"—that had gestated for a long period of time.[205] The war was an event akin in significance to the French Revolution of 1789.[206] It was also a necessary war.[207] Wars that proceeded from such causes, especially civil wars, Disraeli claimed, took many years to finish. And as we saw in chapter 2, Disraeli believed that when the war ended, a very different America would emerge. This divided America would no longer be postcolonial. Rather it would resemble Europe in its strength, turbulence, and imperialism.[208]

The preceding observations appear to suggest that Disraeli did not think the war was quite so futile as Gladstone did. When it came to American democracy, however, Disraeli appeared to be in step with most of his countrymen. In September 1862, at a speech in the Buckingham town hall, delivered before the annual dinner of the "North-West Bucks and the adjoining portions of Oxfordshire and Northamptonshire Agricultural Association," Disraeli was forthright about the superiority of British institutions. He conceded that the war had "certainly increased our confidence in the energy of human nature." History, however, had taught that more was required to sustain a "powerful and enduring community." Disraeli reminded his audience that Englishmen had achieved as much as Americans, but in so doing, had better preserved order. Because Britons had established their "state and society on sounder and truer principles," they had "solved the most difficult problem of politics" by combining "not only freedom with order, but progress with tradition." It would not do to proclaim such truths to Americans during this difficult time, Disraeli concluded, but Englishmen could be proud of their society and "wisdom of the principles on which it is established."[209] Clearly, Disraeli believed that democracy, dynamic though it was, could not constitute a lasting foundation for an ordered society; Britain rather than America had found the appropriate political balance.

The war, then, had little influence on Disraeli's attitude toward reform. His party chief, the Earl of Derby, had committed to reform in 1858 for purely domestic reasons and renewed this commitment (somewhat against Disraeli's will according to Angus Hawkins) in 1866.[210] During the reform debates in the Commons, Disraeli mentioned the United States in only one speech. Among other things, this wide-ranging oration, which he delivered in April 1866, took Gladstone to task for the Liverpool performance three weeks earlier. Disraeli's speech clearly sought to dismiss the American experience as irrelevant to British politics. In America, one found "a great body of educated men in possession of a vast expanse of cultivated land," and even the landless could obtain access to such property. The vote could be conferred upon a democracy dominated by such a bourgeoisie, and this kind of society could be represented by a "House of the People." American institutions, thus, were adapted for American bourgeois democracy. In Britain, however, replacing the House of Commons as it was then constituted with an American-style House of the People would lead to the representation of a "mere indiscriminate multitude" and mob rule. Intelligence and property, Disraeli implied, would be submerged. Britain would degenerate from a "first-rate Kingdom" to a "third-rate Republic." Disraeli, of course, preferred approaching reform in the "spirit of the English Constitution" rather than "in the spirit of the American Constitution." Gladstone's Liverpool speech, Disraeli charged somewhat unfairly, indicated an inclination to follow "American principles."[211] Such language does not suggest that the Civil War influenced any of Disraeli's thinking about reform. Rather, Anglo-centric political considerations appeared to have pushed Disraeli in that direction. If, in 1867, Disraeli would steer a much more radical bill through the Commons than the one Gladstone introduced in 1866, this development was the product of British parliamentary circumstances that no one could have foreseen (Saunders refers to it as an "accidental revolution").[212]

Gladstone's and Disraeli's understandings of the Civil War differed in important ways. Most important, Disraeli saw the conflict as much more purposeful. What is surprising, though, is the degree to which their views on the conflict and American democracy coincided. During the war, both argued that Britain's political system was superior. In the course of the reform debates after the war, they both asserted that the American experiment was not really relevant to the British situation. What is perhaps more intriguing is that such an attitude was not so distant (although more diplomatically expressed) from the sentiments voiced by Ramsden at the beginning of the war.

Ramsden himself changed his tune somewhat as the war dragged on. Harassed by his constituents for ostensibly breaking a public commitment to reform and chastised by Lord John Russell for his comments about America, Ramsden sounded a bit jaded when he spoke in September 1862 at the Master Cutler's Feast in Sheffield. *The Times* reported Ramsden as "deprecating the civil war, setting little value on the Union, for the sake of which such torrents of blood are shed, disclaiming the slightest wish to mediate or to intervene, and speaking with proper regret for the awful catastrophe which we are compelled to witness." *The Times* observed, not entirely without reason, that Ramsden "gave . . . fair expression to the feelings generally entertained throughout the country."[213] These were the words of a politician who, like Gladstone and Disraeli, did not believe the United States offered much of a political model to Britain and who was only willing to democratize British politics if it did not mean embracing democracy.

5

BRITAIN AND THE CIVIL WAR'S MILITARY SIGNIFICANCE

> Whatever may have been the case in former times, war springs now less from the caprice of rulers than from the madness of the people.
>
> —*THE TIMES*, 1861

> It is a war of giants! The armies are hosts, the field of battle a continent, the movements journeys and voyages, and the slaughter, unhappily, hecatombs.
>
> —*DAILY TELEGRAPH*, 1862

> Nobody can deny that going to war has its disadvantages; on the other hand, it is also a rich mine of experience. America has been for the last four years making a very expensive experiment for the benefit, as Mr. LINCOLN says, of "whom it may concern;" and, as nobody is exempt from the possibility of going to war, America may be said to have been laboring for the benefit of the whole human race.
>
> —*THE TIMES*, 1864

HENRY CHARLES FLETCHER AND THE *HISTORY OF THE AMERICAN WAR*

For a man of generally commonplace abilities, Lieutenant-Colonel Henry Charles Fletcher possessed several striking attributes: numerous connections, a knack for making a good impression, and some intellectual ambition. These qualities enabled him to create or exploit a series of opportunities that eventually led him to earn two distinctions. First, Fletcher was the only British officer (and one of very few British subjects) who obtained Federal permission to visit the Confederacy. Second, Fletcher wrote the first complete history of the American Civil War ever published in Britain.

Fletcher's American odyssey began in mid-December 1861, when the War Office sent him along with the 2nd Battalion, Scots Fusilier Guards, to Canada to reinforce the British garrison there during the *Trent* affair. Like many British officers stationed in Montreal, Fletcher was intrigued by the great civil war roiling south of the border. After the *Trent* affair was resolved, he made his way to the Federal capital. Fletcher enjoyed very high status; the twenty-nine-year-old Crimean War veteran, who was the son of a major-general and a baron's daughter, belonged to one of the British army's most prestigious infantry regiments. It is likely that Fletcher was among the soldiers who visited the world-weary and asocial Lord Lyons, who complained about being "overrun by Officers from Canada" who did not stay "long enough to be much more than trouble."[1] Fletcher eventually ingratiated himself with General George B. McClellan (then commander of the Army of the Potomac), for whom he conceived a lasting admiration. The result of the ensuing friendship was that he and a brother officer from the Scots Fusilier Guards, Lieutenant-Colonel Edward Neville (William Gladstone's cousin), secured an invitation to accompany McClellan's forces as they moved southward against Richmond. In winning this privilege, Fletcher was terribly lucky. William Howard Russell, who was supposed to have accompanied them, was unable to obtain the necessary passes to join the army, mainly due the influence of Edwin Stanton, the secretary of war.

Fletcher and Neville, who were accompanied by H. Percy Anderson, the head of the Chancery at the British legation, witnessed all the major events of the Peninsula Campaign, from the siege of Yorktown to the end of the Seven Days' Battles.[2] They left the Army of the Potomac's headquarters on July 1, the day the Battle of Malvern Hill took place, which effectively marked the end of the Peninsula Campaign. Fletcher and Neville immediately reported to William Stuart, the secretary of the legation, who was, in Lyons's absence, the chargé d'affaires. The rank, status, and connections of the two officers helped ensure that their impressions received wide circulation among major British military and political figures.[3] Fletcher's and Neville's accounts could not have disposed recipients favorably toward the North. According to the two British officers, in the wake of the Seven Days' Battles, the Army of the Potomac was "completely disorganized—the Generals having with very few exceptions lost their heads," while the men showed "no enthusiasm whatsoever for their cause." In fact, Fletcher and Neville apparently heard several officers "openly saying the Confederacy must now be recognized" and placing the whole blame for the Federal defeat on "the Washington Politicians."[4] These observations certainly played a part in convincing official opinion that Federal military and political objectives were impossible. Further northern defeats in the eastern theater only reinforced this view and pushed the cabinet toward considering mediation later in the year.

Fletcher next appears in the historical record steaming down the Mississippi River from St. Louis to Memphis in October 1862, hoping to enter the Confederacy. Why he applied openly to the irascible Major General William Sherman, then the military governor of Memphis, for a pass to head into the Confederacy is a mystery. Why Sherman granted Fletcher a pass to enter Confederate territory is also a puzzle.[5] Over the next two months, Fletcher took the well-trodden tour of the South in reverse, minus the usual visit to New Orleans, which was under Federal occupation. Like many British travelers before him, Fletcher spent a great deal of time on trains and in hotels, both of which were dirty, uncomfortable, and crowded. He passed from northern Mississippi to Jackson, then Vicksburg, and then to Mobile. From Mobile, he made his way to Charleston, where he met General P.G.T. Beauregard, and then journeyed north to Richmond.[6] While staying in the Confederate capital, Fletcher appears to have encountered Francis Lawley, *The Times*' southern correspondent, who had entered the Confederacy only two months before.[7] A Confederate officer helped Fletcher make arrangements to leave Richmond on the condition that Fletcher escort a woman and her two grandchildren to Alexandria. The party left Richmond just as the Battle of Fredericksburg began. Making their way through a Virginian landscape devastated by fighting as well as by the march of armies, Fletcher and his small group were picked up by a Union cavalry patrol near the old Bull Run battlefield. He was eventually permitted to move on to Alexandria, where he caught a steamer to Washington, D.C.

Fletcher was inspired to write an account of his southern travels in *Cornhill Magazine*. In many ways, this article reveals more about Fletcher than it does about the South. If his narrative indicates that he was friendly, generous, good-humored, and willing to rough it when necessary, it also shows that he was not particularly self-aware or insightful—deficiencies that were probably of a piece with his guilelessness. Moreover, a number of months in the United States had not stripped Fletcher of his aristocratic mien. To give one small example, after he and his luggage were deposited at the train station in Coldwater, Mississippi, Fletcher vainly waited for someone to put his bags in a carriage until a guard called out, "Well, I guess if you want that luggage put in, you'd better be smart about it, and hand it up." Fletcher was mortified at learning that "if a man does not wait on himself, no one else will do it for him."[8] This aristocratic vantage point was on display throughout the article as he described relations with equals and inferiors. For example, a "lady" demonstrated to Fletcher the tyranny of Major General Benjamin Butler's rule in New Orleans by recounting how a northern officer had confiscated her horses "for the use of the army." Since these horses included "a small pony" that was dear to her little grandson (who was crying) and too small for military service, the lady protested to the officer. The northerner replied, "*One of the causes of this war is the manner in which you Southerners have pampered your children, therefore I shall remove the pony.*"[9] The anecdote is laughable and, as evidence of northern villainy, leaves something to be desired. Clearly, Fletcher was affected because a "lady" was involved. Fletcher's sympathy, however, did not extend to ostensible inferiors like slaves. He characterized African Americans as "a most ridiculous" and "unaccountable race of beings." As evidence of their inexplicable nature, Fletcher produced the following story: "I remember once seeing a lot of niggers sitting round a house which was being shelled, and on my remarking to their master, who was looking very mournful, that he was being shot at, they went into fits of laughter."[10] That these fits of laughter might have been warranted by his comment never seems to have occurred to Fletcher. Of course, it also never seems to have crossed his mind that something more than a favorite pony had been taken from these slaves.

Publishing an article with *Cornhill Magazine*, one of Britain's leading literary journals (it was then edited by William Makepeace Thackeray), must have whetted Fletcher's ambitions as an author, for he soon began work on *History of the American War.* The first volume of this triple-decker was published in 1865, while the last appeared in 1866. One is compelled to admire Fletcher's industriousness. The three volumes add up to around fifteen hundred pages. Not only that, but in a short period of time Fletcher gathered a great number of sources, including official military reports, government publications, published speeches, newspapers from both sides of the Mason-Dixon Line, correspondence in *The Times,* communications from northern and southern officers, a variety of secondary sources from both sides of the Atlantic, and his own recollections of his visit. *History of the American War,* however, is not a great work of scholarship or literature. It was perhaps folly to start writing the history of an event before it had concluded. Moreover, long stretches of the book discuss military movements in the driest manner. In a generally negative review, the *Spectator* complained that his work was "cold and superficial, and in short dull."[11] In the preface, Fletcher claimed that he tried his best to write an unbiased work, but he suffered from the same predicament as many antebellum travel writers; since it was still considered extremely bad form to criticize one's hosts, Fletcher generally avoided condemning the American officers whom he had accompanied.[12] Although this tendency gave his work an appearance of evenhandedness, his predilections were fairly clear.[13] While he grudgingly respected the Federals, who had finally mastered the tools necessary for fighting a massive conflict, Fletcher's heart was drawn to the southern people, whom he believed had displayed great virtue. *The Times* described *History of the American War* as "impartial," but the newspaper's subsequent observations revealed as much about Fletcher's biases as they did about the daily's: "His [Fletcher's] admiration as a soldier may be given to the soldierly qualities of the Southern leaders and of their armies, but he is not blind to their faults. . . . He inclines apparently to the belief that the South had the right to secede, and has no good words for Mr. Lincoln and his advisers, or for the cruel and furious fanaticism of the North, but no Federal would find in his pages the smallest ground for offence."[14] This pro-southern and aristocratic bias was evident in Fletcher's thesis. It had taken the North a long time to deploy its full power during the first years of the conflict, he argued, because its democracy was ill-suited to wage war: fatuous politicians meddled in military affairs, incompetent generals made a hash of operations, and an immature public opinion fomented unrealistic demands. At the same time, Federal leaders, particularly McClellan, had deliberately sought to fight a limited war that targeted the Confederate armies rather than the southern people. This strategy failed, in part, because the South displayed a high order of political and military leadership backed by a patriotic people. Fletcher intimated that the South's aristocratic spirit accounted for its military superiority over the North's bourgeois democracy. However, frustration with repeated Federal military failures led the northern people to accept the expansion of the central government's powers to the point of tyranny. These expanded powers increasingly permitted the Federals to employ their enormous resources more effectively and ramp up their efforts. Stubborn and relentless men like Grant and Sherman became the representative figures of a new war that grew in size and intensity. Bound by an inflexible classically republican constitutionalism, the Confederacy failed to counter these efforts by enhancing its government's war-making powers. Fletcher intimated, then, that the South was "too good" to win. The saintly Lee, gentleman and true republican to the end, became the archetypal southerner—a man whose virtues made it impossible for him to impose the dictatorship that was necessary to save the Confederacy.

With some allowance for his idiosyncrasies, Fletcher's narrative represented the conventional British wisdom about the war's military dimension. It was only on the subject of the Emancipation Proclamation that Fletcher's understanding of the conflict departed substantially from those of his contemporaries. Where most British observers believed this initiative heralded a new, harder policy in which the Federal government made war on the southern nation, Fletcher did not seem to think the proclamation was particularly significant.[15] Fletcher, however, agreed with his fellow observers that northern policy took a turn for the harsher during this period. Much of what the British wrote at this time about northern "hard war" corresponds with the old Lost Cause argument about northern depredations. Scholars like Mark Grimsely have explained why the myth of northern atrocities persisted for so long in the South, but this explanation is not fully applicable to British observers.[16] Why did they see the war in this light?

Yet again, we are brought face to face with the fact that British discourses about America were not entirely self-referential. Fletcher, like other British visitors, relied heavily on American sources. These included not only written works, but correspondence with Americans, particularly southerners, as well.[17] In this particular case, Fletcher was undoubtedly impressed by the complaints of southerners and the rhetoric of hard war espoused by northerners.[18] Like many brother officers who were associated with the upper classes, Fletcher (who was somewhat naive) proved susceptible to the appeal of southern aristocratic pretensions and tended to sympathize with Confederate testimony.

Of course, Fletcher also perceived the American situation through a lens ground by British discourses about the United States that were, in turn, shaped by British interests. We have already encountered many of these discourses in previous chapters. Mid-Victorian Britons generally believed that big, destructive wars among civilized powers threatened the moral and material progress of mankind. The increasing scope of the American war made them especially nervous. For sentimental reasons, many Britons hoped the bloodletting within the English-speaking family—of which they stood at the head—could be kept to a minimum. A number of British commentators also worried that as the war grew larger it would eventually extinguish Anglo-Saxon liberty in North America and reduce the small number of free societies in the world still further. Finally, and perhaps most important of all, many British observers feared that an increasingly destructive war would present a greater threat to the political and economic ties that bound the transatlantic relationship.

For these reasons, British observers hoped the American conflict would remain a war of armies rather than of nations. This preference partly explains the widespread appreciation in Britain of General George B. McClellan (an appreciation Fletcher shared), who was associated with limited war. Confederate arms also became associated with this type of war—a test of soldiers' skill, courage, and motivation, not a battle involving brute force, material, and the spoliation of civilians. The vain hope that the war would remain contained accounts for the British reaction to the North's adoption of hard war. Although, as we shall see, a number of British commentators proposed a revolutionary conflict as the only tool that could destroy slavery and restore the Union, most journalists and public figures found such a prospect appalling. A war large in scope would prove destructive, wasteful, and indiscriminate. Not only that, but as we have already seen, many Britons believed the northern effort was futile. They were convinced the Federal government's objectives were simply unattainable and that a large conflict simply meant more useless destruction than a smaller one.

During the war, Fletcher agreed with most of these judgments. However, he completed the last volume of his history after the North's victory had confounded such views. The shock of this reversal is captured in an observation that appeared at the very end of the third volume in Fletcher's history: "Hitherto almost every prophecy rashly hazarded at the commencement, during the continuance, and at the termination of the war, has proved false." Fletcher excused Britain's poor record of predicting the course of American events by claiming that "few in Europe understand American feelings or politics—it may even be doubted whether they are understood in America itself." Having conceded the impossibility of forecasting America's future, Fletcher proceeded to make a prediction anyway (Fletcher's statements here are a classic example of the hybridity of the American who was simultaneously known and unknown). Reconstruction, he argued, could turn out very well for the United States. America's confidence, wealth, and good sense, he asserted, would allow it to surmount its great difficulties.[19] The sudden shift in Fletcher's assessment of America's future occasioned by the Federal government's unexpected victory was mirrored by changes in the way commentators judged the military performance of the North and the South. For sure, the Confederacy's conduct of the war continued to receive praise in the postbellum era, but in 1865 the northern armed forces began to earn more credit—a new development captured in embryo by Fletcher's work, which needed to find some way of explaining an unforeseen Federal victory.

BRITISH PERCEPTIONS OF THE NORTHERN AND SOUTHERN ARMIES

In late 1864, *The Times* mused, "From first to last the campaigns are nothing but rifles and earthworks, just as the armies are nothing but Volunteers. . . . Perhaps it would be curious to inquire whether the men suggested the tactics, or the tactics were made necessary by the men—whether this Volunteer system, in short, created or adopted this method of warfare."[20] In this particular leader, *The Times* eventually decided that the rifle dictated tactics and strategy. *The Times* was in good company. By the late 1850s, many thinking British officers believed that various technological advances, particularly the widespread adoption of rifled small arms and artillery, would make the tactical offensive more difficult to assume. The new arms of precision would probably inflict many more casualties, but the officer corps did not seem to think they presented an insurmountable obstacle to decisive victory. Employing offensive tactics that emphasized speed along with firepower, a new breed of intelligent, versatile, and independent soldiers could triumph against a well-armed, entrenched enemy.[21] In other words, the armies of the future would require more skill than ever before to overcome the advantages that had accrued to the defensive.

The American war appeared to confirm certain expectations among military theorists—rifled artillery reduced masonry fortifications at fantastic ranges, rifled small arms inflicted terrible casualties, and soldiers resorted frequently to entrenchments.[22] Yet many of the war's features looked unfamiliar and puzzling. Despite the massive loss of life, few major battles proved decisive.[23] Infantry rarely "closed" with the enemy, and cavalry played only a minor role. Observers believed that both the new firearms and the broken nature of American terrain partially accounted for the inconclusive battles that characterized the war.[24] Yet another explanation dwelled on the shortcomings of volunteers, the *Daily News* pointing out that citizen-soldiers "are entitled to, as well as demand, a somewhat different treatment" from regulars.[25] Volunteers expected better conditions of service and bridled at the hard discipline of the professional soldier, making them less effective in combat.[26]

Attempts to explain the character of the war most often revolved around the very different social constitutions of the two belligerents. Northerners, most observers agreed, did not display a natural aptitude for war because of their democratic and commercial instincts. The more hierarchical southerners, on the other hand, enjoyed a military advantage because they produced capable leaders as well as men who knew how to obey. The *Saturday Review* claimed "the unwarlike democracy of the [North] never encouraged the ablest of its sons" to join the army, "which was held in little honour, and held out few chances of rewards worth having." Conversely, "the South, aristocratic by temper and by social constitution, however democratic in politics, had the military spirit which always distinguishes an aristocracy."[27] This contrast helped explain why battles were constantly drawn. The Federals had the quantity, but the Confederates had the quality. Or as Lord Lyons put it, pithily, the two sides were evenly balanced because the Federals had "larger numbers and better material—and the Confederates, better Generals and more desperation."[28] Such statements should not surprise us. In chapter 4 we saw a great many British commentators across the political spectrum claim that a democratic regime's spirit proved incapable of providing decent leadership or an orderly society. Not surprisingly, these observers deployed a very similar argument in the realm of military affairs. This argument did much to shape British commentary about the course of the war.

British observers saw much to admire in the rank and file of the Federal armies. In 1861, as he reviewed Federal troops outside Washington, D.C.,

Frank Vizetelly, no small man himself, was impressed by the number of "huge, brawny fellows, six feet three and four in height . . . in whose hands a musket and bayonet is no more than a toasting fork."[29] Likewise, before the Battle of Fredericksburg, Lieutenant-Colonel Henry Charles Eden Malet remarked that the northern ranks were filled with "fine healthy boys born of well fed parents," not the "miserable undersized half-Slave creatures that we are glad in times of pressure to take to recruit our armies with."[30] Edward Dicey concluded that "as far as the average raw material of the rank and file is concerned, the American army is the finest."[31] Not only that, but northern soldiers seemed more intelligent, versatile, and energetic than their European counterparts.[32] For instance, George Augustus Sala, who was not exactly sympathetic to the northern cause, nonetheless believed that northern soldiers understood their orders with "considerable quickness of appreciation," even if they were "little troubled with rules or regulations."[33]

The problem with Federal soldiers had little to do with their physique or intelligence. Rather it was their egalitarian attitudes that blunted their effectiveness. These attitudes militated against the imposition of discipline and made the exercise of authority almost impossible. Countless observers referred to this phenomenon. The *Standard* argued that the North's military ineffectiveness was due "first to the ill-discipline of their armies, and, secondly, to that demoralization wrought by democratic institutions and democratic habits of thought which has made military discipline impossible to them."[34] *Colburn's United Service Magazine* noted in the northern armies "the want of discipline among men who will not brook a superior, and cannot have any confidence in their officers."[35] These were not merely the views of armchair analysts safely ensconced in Britain; visitor after visitor in America made the same remarks. Russell complained of the "principle of equality intruding itself in military duty, confounding civil rights with the relations between superior and inferior, between officer and rank and file."[36] Russell recounted the following incident to show how the democratic habits of civil society made the exercise of command difficult: "'Sergeant, will you come and look at this man's pass,' called out a sentry at the Long-bridge [next to Washington, D.C.] the other day; 'do you think I'm going to shout myself hoarse for you?' And when the sergeant did arrive the sentry, who had been sitting down when I came up, used bad language and threatened to report him!"[37]

George Alfred Lawrence saw much the same thing in the North, for "all the antecedents of the Federal recruit" interfered with his training as a soldier. Throughout their lives, northerners had been "taught to contemn all such old-world ideas as respect for persons," and the result was that "the volunteer carries with him into the ranks, an ostentatious spirit of self-assertion and independence." Consequently, he went into action "fully prepared to criticize the orders of his superiors" because "he has no intention of abating one iota of his franchise, or one privilege of an enlightened citizen."[38] After spending some time with a pair of Federal regiments, Samuel Phillips Day, correspondent for the *Morning Herald*, wrote that the "the troops acted as though they were released from all manner of restraint." "They addressed their officers," he continued, "with whom they appeared on an equal footing, and on terms of the closest intimacy—in the most off-hand way, in which respect for their position was entirely ignored." Day concluded by stating that the attitude of the soldiers and officers alike accounted for this situation: "*Tel maître, tel valet*."[39] Other observers came to similar conclusions about the confidence and assertiveness of Federal officers. Dicey observed that the officers were the weak point of the Federal armies because "they have not the military air, the self-possession which long habit of command alone can give; while the footing of equality on which they inevitably stand with the volunteer privates, deprives them of the *esprit de corps* belonging to a ruling class."[40] Even the military mission Britain sent in 1864 noticed these problems, its report noting that the Federal army's defects could "be traced to inferior discipline, which it may be said is mainly due to the want of proper regimental officers and good non-commissioned officers."[41] Russell understood that northern generals had come from "the bar, the railroad board, the bench, the church, the counting-house, [and] the surgery," while officers had been found at "the desk, the shopman's corner, and the indigence of the bourgeoisie." Under these circumstances, he marveled that the northern army was as well led as it was.[42]

A strong clique among British visitors also believed that the North, like most commercial societies, had lost its warlike instincts and patriotism.[43] Men served for pay, they asserted, not from love of country. Lawrence claimed the Yankee "looked at his duty in a hard, practical, business-like way; he is disposed to give his country its money's worth."[44] According to these observers, since most Yankees did not see much profit in soldiering, the Federal government employed huge bounties to recruit enormous numbers of Irish and German "mercenaries."[45] This assertion, which became one of the most enduring British myths about the northern army, emerged very early in the conflict. As early as 1861, Sir James Fergusson, who had served with the Grenadier Guards, represented Ayrshire as an MP during the war, and visited both the North and the South, reported that the best part of the Union army consisted of Germans and Irish who "are just such troops as high pay will attract to any service in the world."[46]

Although the Confederates had organized their forces in much the same manner as the Federals, a more aristocratic ethos prevailed, or so the argument went, and the army benefited accordingly. According to British observers, everyone knew his place, with predictable consequences for discipline. John Worden wrote that southern society was divided into a "wealthy oligarchy and a needy populace," which meant that "a select and special class had thus been provided to act as the military commanders and officers of ready-made soldiers." "How naturally," he observed, "they have fallen into their places."[47] *The Times* put the matter succinctly when it argued that the South's "social institutions were favourable to military organization" because "although their Government was republican in form, it was administered in an aristocratic spirit, and some classes were habituated to command while others were not unwilling to obey."[48] William Howard Russell explained how this deference operated within a nominally democratic system: "The Southern armies contain a larger proportion of men who have been accustomed to command and to obey than the Northern armies. They are under better discipline, because . . . they have been more habituated to military life. The social distinctions which exist in the South between rich and poor, between landed proprietors and their dependents, extend their influence to the field. No Southern company would . . . elect a mere *bourgeois,* a shopkeeper, or the keeper of a house of ill fame, to be an officer."[49] Captain Charles Cornwallis Chesney, who taught at Sandhurst and wrote some of the earliest and most influential studies of the American war, claimed, "the South had enjoyed the special advantage, derived from her aristocratically composed society, of a class of men accustomed to command and lead others," thus providing "officers whom the privates could respect."[50] In other words, the Confederates possessed gentlemen who automatically commanded deference and authority. Russell, whose correspondence exerted enormous influence on a British public that otherwise obtained little information about the Confederacy, also wrote of southerners:

> It may readily be imagined how these young gentlemen, full of warm blood and pride, despising labour and all base mechanical arts, lorded it over the hard-working plodding offspring of [Northern] manufacturers, commercial men, and traders who were studying by their sides [in college or at West Point]. Cradled among slaves, growing up in exercise of command, engaging in the sports of the field early in boyhood, they became imperious, self-reliant, and haughty, and entered upon manhood bold horsemen, good shots, quick-eyed and strong-nerved, amid the youth of the Northern cities, who were their fellow students without being their equals, or even their associates.[51]

Although this description sounds fairly similar to what a pro-southern propagandist like Lawley might have written, we can absolve Russell of such partisanship since he tried very hard to be fair and was well aware of southern deficiencies.

One can overstate these distinctions that British observers drew between the northern and southern armies. Commentators who looked seriously at Confederate discipline found it far short of perfect, while many agreed that the Federals learned the military virtues as the war went on.[52] Nevertheless, British commentators generally assumed that a democratic as well as commercial ethos interfered with the efficiency of the Federal army far more than with the Confederates. An army commanded by gentlemen, so the argument went, would always perform better than one officered by "electioneers, stump-orators, tradesmen, and attorney's clerks."[53] Although such an opinion may have had some basis in fact, it is hard to escape the conclusion that when it came to the Confederate army, fantasy often took the place of real knowledge. As we have already seen, once the war started, the Confederacy was less closely studied or understood than the North. Antebellum assumptions about the South's aristocratic composition became the foundation for hypotheses and speculations about the source of its military success. Moreover, the observers who found their way South, especially once the war started in earnest, were much more well-disposed to the Confederacy than otherwise. These men often tended to view southerners less than critically.

At the same time, it is important to recognize that not everybody distinguished between the two armies in this way. Among the radical press in particular, there was a belief that democracy possessed a variety of military strengths. As the product of an egalitarian society, the Federal citizen-soldier had become habituated not to following leaders, but to acting in conjunction with his fellows. Although seemingly "disorganized," the Federal army resembled a "polypus" that proved exceedingly difficult to destroy.[54] E. L. Godkin, who was the *Daily News*'s New York correspondent, described how this strength manifested itself on the battlefield: "They [the Federals] may be routed and disorganized and lose their officers; but as neither the organisation nor the officers were ever of much consequence to them, they rally in the first wood they reach and return to the charge without the slightest suspicion that anything fatally disastrous has occurred." In such a manner, Godkin explained why the routs at Shiloh, the Seven Days' Battles, and Murfreesboro did not prove fatal to the Federal army.[55] Indeed, such incidents seemed to confirm claims that the Federal armies made up for poor leadership through the order, self-restraint, discipline, intelligence, and sobriety of a middle-class rank and file.[56] Some radical newspapers refused to admit that the North's democracy or republicanism accounted for any inferiority whatsoever. Throughout the war, *Reynolds's Newspaper* insisted that both the northerners and southerners were republicans and therefore great military powers. Indeed, if there was any difference that accounted for the Confederacy's military superiority, it was that southerners were *more* republican than northerners.[57] What *Reynolds's Newspaper* apparently meant by this observation was that southerners were more patriotic, selfless, practical, and honest than their northern counterparts.

Reynolds's Newspaper, however, was working against the grain of British opinion. British commentary generally made a clear distinction between the military effectiveness of a southern aristocracy and a northern bourgeois democracy. Observers generally assumed that the former would be better behaved than the latter, with important consequences for civilians. Fletcher was not alone in noting the extent to which southern officers as well as soldiers, despite great temptation and provocation, behaved in an exemplary manner toward noncombatants. During the Maryland campaign, Fletcher pointed out that the "ragged and shoeless legions" of the Confederacy had maintained their discipline. "Men who had long fed on nothing but the roughest and most scanty fair" had refrained "not only from pillage, but from the harshness common to soldiers." Northerners "beheld the gentlemen of the South . . . as poorly clothed as their men, yet retaining their courtesy and refinement, and combining deep-seated hatred to the Northern nation with kindness and forbearance toward individuals composing it."[58] This representation of the southern armies, written by a soldier who had been to America, compared favorably with a lurid description of the Federal forces that appeared in the *Army and Navy Gazette* (which was then edited by William Howard Russell). According to this latter account, which appeared only a couple of months after the Maryland campaign's conclusion, the northern armies consisted of a "horde of infamous mercenaries, and the wild desperate ruffianhood of the cities and Western States. . . . The most rascally scum that ever followed lansknecht [*sic*], or the vilest band of condottieri that ever plundered Italy, were Bayards and Sidneys compared to such gangs of desperadoes."[59] Although these two accounts exaggerate the perceived distance between the behavior of the southern and northern armies, British observers clearly saw a distance. Commentary generally presumed that an army where gentlemen commanded their deferential social inferiors would refrain from molesting civilians. A force of immigrants and militant egalitarians who served for pay and who were led by bourgeois officers would resemble a disorderly mob and treat noncombatants accordingly.

These differences were personalized in comparisons between southern and northern military leaders. Against the pure Lee, whose admirers insisted on describing him as a "splendid specimen of an English gentleman" and even "a perfect gentleman," the northern cad par excellence was Benjamin Butler.[60] Among a great many Britons, Butler's occupation regime in New Orleans became a byword for tyranny, corruption, and theft. Butler, of course, became infamous in Britain due to his General Order No. 28, more commonly known as the "Woman's Order," which was widely understood in Britain as encouraging Federal troops to rape the ladies of New Orleans. The order almost caused an international incident, with Palmerston writing an angry private letter to Charles Francis Adams, the American minister, and Earl Russell instructing William Stuart, the chargé d'affaires at the British legation, to issue a formal protest to William Seward.[61] The *Saturday Review*'s analysis of the order was typical of British public opinion.[62] Generals and officers, it argued, had a code of honor that led them to restrain the "ferocities of war" and dictated that they shrink from the "maltreatment of women." Unfortunately, the Federal army had drawn its leaders from the "Methodist parson, the German adventurer, and the New York pettifogger," who tended to be "more barbarous and unmanly than the private soldiers." A man like Butler, who had not imbibed of the officer's code and therefore had no sense of war's limits, acted out of passion; he hated the ladies of New Orleans and subjected them to dishonor by allowing "men of a degraded class" to handle them roughly. "Being only a New York attorney," the *Saturday Review* asserted (wrongly—Butler was born in New Hampshire and politically active in Massachusetts), "he acts after his kind." A moral of Butler's regime in New Orleans was that if nations insisted on obtaining their generals from "some low civilian occupation," war would become much more atrocious.[63] It is worth noting, however, that Butler had his defenders, who seemed to indicate that his worst crimes consisted of ruling occupied New Orleans sternly and making southerners understand their powerlessness.[64]

If in Britain Butler was widely considered the prototypical Yankee general, George B. McClellan served as the great northern exception and antidote. A professional soldier, McClellan was often referred to as a "gentleman."[65] Everyone in Britain understood that, as a Democrat, he opposed emancipation.[66] Finally, he received credit for disciplining the Army of the Potomac.[67] For these reasons, he seemed like the northern general most capable of containing the war's violence and limiting its revolutionary impact.[68] Until the later years of the war, he also seemed like the most capable of the northern generals who had tried their hands at beating Lee in Virginia. In *Blackwood's Edinburgh Review*, as the 1864 election approached, Edward Bruce Hamley (a colonel and professor at the Staff College, then at Sandhurst) summarized the attitude toward McClellan that prevailed among a great many British commentators. Hamley asserted that McClellan was the "one man who stands out in honourable distinction from the other public men of the North, remarkable alike for his consistency, his moderation, his singleness of purpose, his eminently respectable personal character, and his abstinence from the practice of those low arts to which men so commonly resort when they wish to gain the suffrages of a democracy." When considering the general's "fighting quality," Hamley could "not estimate it very highly." McClellan was "eminently a prudent and safe general" who "suffered from slowness and overcaution." Nonetheless, he was "by far the best leader" the Federal armies had found. Not only that, there was "one aspect in which McClellan shines with absolute lustre when compared with the other generals of the North": he made war in a "human and honourable" spirit, refraining from devastation while engaging in a "civilised contest."[69] As a regular officer, a gentleman, a conservative, and a capable soldier, then, McClellan had no desire to expand the war beyond the limits imposed by modern civilization. For that reason, a number of commentators respected him because they feared that the intensification of the war would threaten British interests and submit the Anglo-American relationship to even greater pressures.

In November 1862, when Lincoln removed McClellan from command of the Army of the Potomac, the *Spectator* suspected that many of the general's "English panegyrists" admired him not so much because he was a good man or an able soldier, but because they supported the Confederacy and expected he would fail to defeat it. The *Spectator* was being unfair (the admiration of "English Southerners" for McClellan was indeed sincere), but the weekly had a point; it believed McClellan and the northern forces would fail because he *was* conservative.[70] A group of British radicals and abolitionists claimed that, so far from being too bellicose, the northern war effort was insufficiently zealous, and McClellan was part of the problem. According to the *Spectator*, McClellan had "no idea of revolutionary war, no conception of the moral effect of incessant attack and victory."[71] What the North needed, such commentators argued, was a principled cause that would improve as well as inspire it while providing the Federal government with the necessary energy to put down the rebellion. For most, that cause was emancipation. In other words, radicals called for the North to confront the revolutionary act of secession with the revolutionary act of emancipation. From early 1862 onward, the *Spectator* proved one of the most persistent advocates of this policy in the metropolitan press. Only "a crusade for emancipation" would provide the North with the "revolutionary energy" to crush the rebellion.[72] The North could no longer face "revolution" without adopting "revolutionary principles" itself.[73] When the Emancipation Proclamation eventually did arrive, the *Spectator* summarized its position by claiming that John Brown was the only man who could counter Stonewall Jackson.[74] According to the *Spectator*, emancipation was a good in itself, but it would obviously lead to a much more energetic prosecution of the war.[75]

While this interpretation of the conflict was an important one among radicals and abolitionists of various stripes, it was not at all a majority view. We have already noted on repeated occasions that much British commentary was ambivalent about emancipation. In this particular context, many observers did not look forward to an intensification of the war that emancipation promised—especially since they believed that northern objectives were unattainable. However, while many northerners showed no enthusiasm for emancipation, the logic of the war inevitably pulled the Federal government in that direction.

The ideas about the opposing armies that emerged early in the war—many of which owed something to images developed during the antebellum period—would exercise an important influence on how British observers perceived various military developments as the conflict dragged on. Democratic indiscipline, or so the argument went, hobbled the Federal armies on the battlefield and contributed to drawn battles.[76] The *Saturday Review* complained that the predilection of northern troops for entrenching and refusing to close with the enemy resulted from their desire to fight on the principle of "making an omelette without breaking eggs," a method that led to a protracted, costly, and indecisive war.[77] The better-led Confederates, who seemed to possess all of the military virtues, were apparently too capable to lose, but not numerous enough to win.[78] At the same time, the egalitarian spirit and indiscipline of the Federal armies contributed to the mistreatment of southern civilians through vandalism, theft, and violence (the lone, shining example of McClellan notwithstanding). As Lawley put it pithily, northern forces committed atrocities because "we are contemplating an army which is at once republican and undisciplined."[79] British beliefs that the Federal armies were incompetent and tended to mistreat southern civilians helped set the stage for the way observers understood the emergence of northern hard war.

BRITISH VIEWS OF THE NORTH'S HARD WAR

The year 1862 proved an important turning point in British conversations about the Civil War's military dimension. In the spring, it looked to many observers like the North might very well win the war that year. The victories at Fort Henry and Fort Donelson, the capture of Island No. 10, the occupation of New Orleans, the triumph at Corinth, and the commencement of the Peninsula Campaign all seemed to herald imminent Confederate defeat.[80] We have already noted that northern success in bringing the war to a close at this point would have done much to dissipate British exasperation with the Federal government; the dangers that a protracted war posed to British interests would have disappeared. Had the war wound up in this manner, Britons would have ceased referring to northern military inferiority as a way to explain the American situation. However, not only did the Confederacy turn back Federal advances in several key areas, but southern forces also launched offensives of their own. British hopes that the war would soon come to an end were transformed into deep disappointment with the performance of the Federal armies.[81] The South's military reputation obtained a luster that it would not lose for the rest of the war, with men like Lee, Jackson, and others becoming household names in Britain. The events of the summer and fall weighed heavily on the North's stature as a military power. Repeated Federal defeats convinced British commentators that northern victory was absolutely impossible. It mattered little that southern incursions into Kentucky and Maryland were turned back. So long as the Confederacy held on to most of its territory and kept forces in the field, the restoration of the old Union remained unlikely. In other words, stalemate was identified with northern military failure. It was under these circumstances that the Federal government issued the Emancipation Proclamation.

We have already seen that British reactions to emancipation—as with many other things American—was ambivalent. Some greeted Lincoln's announcement more or less joyfully. The *Daily News,* for instance, observed that Lincoln's "great mistake from the first has been not to perceive that revolution could only be met with revolution," but with the proclamation, the Federals had finally realized "the true ground of the solemn revolution which has been forced on the Republic."[82] Yet many others described the proclamation as illegal, inconsistent, ill-timed, and hypocritical. Much commentary saw the proclamation primarily as a war measure (and a cynical one at that) that sought to harm the Confederacy rather than help the slaves. It was widely described as the Federal government's "last card," an attempt to destroy an aristocratic society by igniting a servile insurrection.[83]

To many observers, the Emancipation Proclamation also seemed like an admission of failure. Having met with reverses on the battlefield, Federal armies had redoubled their efforts and apparently embraced a new strategy of making war on the southern home front. In other words, the proclamation signaled a Federal intent to expand the scope of the war. An amoral democratic government and its ill-disciplined soldiery, which had already displayed a tendency to abuse civilians, would now be joined by a mob of vindictive slaves in tearing down the southern people. According to Robert Hogarth Patterson in *Blackwood's Edinburgh Magazine,* "the President has at length owned the impossibility of success in fair warfare, and seeks to paralyse the victorious armies of the South by letting loose upon their hearths and homes the lust and savagery of four million negroes."[84] The *Standard* charged: "Beaten in fair fight, [Lincoln] has resorted in desperation to a method of warfare which . . . is likely to produce the most frightful and murderous contest that the civilised and Christian nations have yet seen. . . . Its aim is the excitement of servile war . . . the subornation of murder, arson, outrages of every kind describable and indescribable. . . . It desires vengeance, bloody, terrible, and above all, *safe*. . . . The Southerners, who have hitherto made war like civilised soldiers, will take awful vengeance for this last unpardonable outrage. No quarter will be given to the accomplices and instigators of slave revolts."[85] Many observers agreed with the *Standard* that the proclamation's main purpose consisted of escalating the war. Unlike the British, they argued, who had sought to minimize social disruption by carefully providing both gradual and compensated emancipation in 1833, the Federals had done neither.[86] Instead, as a costly war raged, Lincoln had given the slaves license to liberate themselves. Once freed under these dangerous circumstances, so the argument went, the slave would express his true bestial nature by embarking upon horrible sprees of killing and destruction.[87] The war would enter a new, more violent phase. As early as July 1861, the *Economist* had described a slave insurrection cooperating with northern arms as a "desperate expedient," "an enormous crime," and "the most enormous sin ever laid upon a human conscience" because "the barbarism of savage life and the barbarism of civilized life would be let loose upon each other."[88] Early the next year, Earl Russell, the foreign secretary, feared that a "war of emancipation" would mean "a war of greater destruction than has been seen since the revival of letters."[89] Once emancipation had become an established fact, a number of journals did not hesitate to agree with Russell. Southern whites would visit their wrath on the Federal soldier who served as the "propagator of the most infamous and sanguinary doctrines, as an apostle of servile war, murder and outrage, as a confiscator and a robber."[90] A "war to the knife" would ensue, and "all traces of civilization would disappear over great regions of the South," turning it into a "wilderness of bloodshed and misery."[91] The *Daily Telegraph* argued that since it would unleash "the worst of all horrors, a servile rising," the proclamation would contribute to the "embittering and prolonging of the sanguinary war."[92]

Emancipation failed to fulfill these dire predictions, and such comments revealed more about their authors than they did about events in America. Whatever the case, emancipation looked like a clear turning point in the war to many observers. First, it seemed to signify a new earnestness among the Federals. Even journalists and newspapers that tended to sympathize with the Confederacy increasingly noticed a stern resolution among northern forces throughout 1863. The *Standard* grudgingly admitted that eighty years of degradation under democracy had not extinguished among northerners "all the stubborn manhood of their race" and that they still showed "many of the qualities of a great nation." Remarking upon the North's "unbroken obstinacy," the newspaper conceded that "there is something heroic in their perseverance."[93] By late 1863, even Francis Lawley, *The Times*' southern correspondent, sensed that something had changed. Two and a half years of war had not shaken northerners' faith in their cause, and he granted that "there is something sublime in this shadowy earnestness and misty magnificence of Northern faith and self-reliance."[94] Second, although black slaves did not engage in an orgy of rapine, many British commentators believed the Emancipation Proclamation was an important step in erasing the traditional distinction between civilians and soldiers, no matter what the moral or material cost. If black slaves had failed to make war on the Confederate home front, it seemed undisciplined Federal troops would have to do so alone. Many commentators found this policy revolting, for they agreed that in a Christian, civilized, and progressive age, armies increasingly ought to wage war on opposing armies but not peoples.[95] The *Saturday Review*, for instance, observed that barbarians had seen war as a "contest to extremity" in which no one was spared. As mankind discovered that waging armed conflicts in such a manner "cost humanity too dear," it began to spare noncombatants and extend "immunity to their property as well." Over time, the conventions that curbed armed conflict served "to mitigate the sufferings of war and diminish the bitterness of the passions which it rouses." After citing the trespasses of various Federal commanders, the *Saturday Review* commented that the precedents they had established pointed "in a retrograde direction" toward a "very cruel and pitiless world." "To injure for the sake of injuring—to use the apparatus of war directly for the purpose of gratifying vindictive feelings against a hostile population," as the Federals had, the weekly concluded, "is not civilized war, but Vandalism."[96]

Federal armies, which consisted of the mob in uniform, so the argument went, had obtained permission to act according to their true nature, which meant systematic robbing, destroying, and killing. The emergence of this strategy merely reflected the unethical nature of northern democracy, which could indulge its vengeance and perhaps make a profit by victimizing southern civilians. Such activities would supply the Federal commissary and demoralize the Confederate home front. In the *Quarterly Review,* while exaggerating the barbarity of the conflict, Robert Cecil sardonically analyzed the northern logic that justified this kind of war: "It is easier to burn barns than to take strong cities; it is safer to wage war against small farmers, and to punish the Confederacy by the ruin of its women and children, than to discomfit the armies of Beauregard and Lee. . . . Ruining non-combatants is ruining the enemy's tax-payers; devastating vast regions is emptying the enemy's exchequer. Killing women and children is removing those who will ultimately furnish recruits to the enemy's conscription. . . . All the restraints which humanity has placed upon the ferocity of war are logically indefensible."[97] Those like Cecil, who overstated the crimes committed against southern civilians, saw the northern way of war as deliberate, consistent, and cruel. The *Saturday Review* charged that Federal behavior in the South "is not the vagary of any solitary commander. It is part of the system on which they all act."[98] In such a manner, "the hordes of the North, the scum of the great towns, the refuse of the Old World, are let loose upon the cities and plains of the South, to burn, pillage, and destroy."[99] Specifically, British observers pointed to the stone fleet sunk outside Charleston harbor, Benjamin Butler's rule in New Orleans, John Pope's general orders concerning the treatment of southern civilians, Ambrose Burnside's bombardment and sack of Fredericksburg, Ulysses S. Grant's destruction of Jackson, Mississippi, Federal incursions along the Confederacy's Atlantic seaboard, Quincy Gillmore's shelling of Charleston with Greek fire, William T. Sherman's march to the sea, Philip Sheridan's destructive course through the Shenandoah Valley, and the depredations committed by irregulars in the border states.[100] When Chesney surveyed the American scene, he lamented that "the horrors of the Thirty Years' War have been revived to the disgrace of the boasted civilization of the age."[101]

Those most inclined to support the North (or at least the cause of abolitionism for which the Federals fought) displayed mixed feelings as they contemplated hard war. We have already seen how some radicals called upon the North to wage a revolutionary conflict, and it appears that the more clear-eyed among them fully understood the consequences of such a war. In his famous *Fraser's Magazine* article of February 1862, John Stuart Mill had seen the war as a test of wills in which the North would have to attrite the southern spirit. As he put it, the Federals would succeed by "wearing them [southerners] out, exhausting their resources, depriving them of the comforts of life, encouraging their slaves to desert, and excluding them from communication with foreign countries." Only a "succession of humiliations" could subjugate the Confederates because "they are in no mood to learn from anything but disaster."[102] Mill intimated that the North should not be too fastidious in dealing with an immoral regime, and other journals made a similar case. While discussing Sherman's destructive march through South Carolina, the *Daily News* conceded that it had destroyed "the beauty and gaiety of plantation life," but such had been necessary to destroy the state's "monstrous pride" as well as the "curses and woes" of slave society. And yet many had terrible reservations about the war's size and destructiveness. In an 1863 letter to Charles Sumner, Richard Cobden remembered that he had told John C. Frémont some two years before that "the total abolition of slavery . . . was the only issue which could justify the war to the civilized world." Looking back to that conversation, Cobden marveled, "But at what a price is the negro to be emancipated!" He continued by remarking that, "I confess that if *then* I had been the arbiter of his fate I should have refused him freedom at the cost of so much white men's blood & women's tears."[103]

The volume of white men's blood and women's tears that would be shed only rose as time went on. As the war entered 1864, British observers increasingly remarked on a democratic complement of the hard war strategy the North had apparently embraced: attrition. Commentators had begun discussing this strategy as early as 1863 in an attempt to explain why the North continued fighting even though it lost battles with monotonous frequency. Unable to muster the military skill necessary to beat the Confederacy on the battlefield, so the speculation went, the North would gladly trade casualties, even at a discount, to reduce the South to exhaustion. It was a kind of majority rule on the battlefield. In January 1863, the *Army and Navy Gazette* predicted that, from the North's perspective, "exhaustion, produced by want of money, men, and faith . . . seem to us the old agencies to be relied on—in default of the smallest military genius—to procure the termination of this most deplorable contest."[104] According to the *Saturday Review,* the North calculated that with its superior population and immigration, it could afford to keep losing battles while bleeding the South to death: "At this game of exchanging pieces, if the North loses three men to every one lost by the South, the North wins in the long run."[105]

This idea became especially prevalent in the spring of 1864 during Ulysses S. Grant's Overland Campaign, in which he made a bid to destroy the Army of Northern Virginia before Richmond. Very few commentators understood Grant's vision or intentions; a simple and deliberate strategy of attrition seemed to many British observers the only possible explanation for the Army of the Potomac's willingness to take such horrendous casualties.[106] The British press was both awed and appalled by the nature of the fighting in Virginia, in which the Federals had reportedly suffered forty thousand casualties in less than a week.[107] Referring to the contests in the Wilderness and around Spotsylvania Court House, *Reynolds's Newspaper* claimed it was "the plain literal truth . . . that the blood of the brave has been poured out like water, and that the soil of Virginia, for miles upon miles has been manured with the corpses of the slain. Such a prodigal waste of human life has seldom if ever been seen, even in the Old World itself."[108] Of the same battles, *The Times* declared, "It would not be impossible to match the results of any one day's battle with stories from the wars of the Old World; but never, we should think, in the history of man, were five such battles as these compressed into six successive days."[109]

Focusing on casualty lists to the exclusion of all else, most commentators concluded Grant had simply chosen to purchase Confederate casualties at any price in blood, trusting to the North's limitless supply of men to see him through.[110] *The Times* described it as "an auction of men,—two Federals, five Federals, ten Federals for a single Confederate life."[111] The *Standard* claimed that Grant's "only idea of the science of war is that primitive one of overpowering an enemy by force of superior numbers."[112] Even Lord Lyons, who should have known better, remarked that Grant's plan simply consisted of "crushing Lee by force of numbers."[113] Cecil likened the principle underlying Grant's campaign to those of some chess players, who, "when they have by any contrivance obtained the advantage of a piece or a pawn over their adversaries, clear the board by exchanging pieces, and remain masters of the game with that simple piece."[114] The North could afford such profligacy because it paid in debased coinage: "German and Irish soldiers, as they are expended, leave few regrets in the philosophic American mind."[115]

As almost everybody recognized, a war of attrition required a novel set of talents, qualities, and values. Lee had won plaudits for characteristics traditionally associated with gentility: skill, daring, leadership, and purity of motives. As we have already seen, Lee was described as a gentleman. The much-admired Stonewall Jackson was a somewhat more problematic figure because British observers found his flair as a general difficult to reconcile with his austere Presbyterianism. The *Spectator* was not alone in turning over the relationship between "Jackson's Puritan style of piety and a cause which we are probably in the habit of identifying with the manly, loose *enjoying* aristocracy of an old cavalier state."[116] Yet Grant, who was widely seen as the architect of attrition, was something altogether different. British observers could use existing language and images to portray Lee as a gentleman or Jackson as an incongruous mix of Cavalier and Roundhead. But for Grant, initially, they had to employ words not normally associated with generalship. The plebeian qualities of "tenacity," "determination," "stubbornness," "fortitude," "resolution," "persistence," "thoroughness," and "inflexibility" were the types of adjectives affixed to the Federal commander.[117] *The Times* provided a fairly typical assessment of Grant when it claimed that he had "bid for [success] more desperately . . . than any of his predecessors," and in so doing, had "fully justified his reputation for dogged and unconquerable tenacity." No one in the North "thought him a military genius, but they believed him to be a most determined man—a man who would bring everything to the immediate issue of hard fighting, and who might either beat or be beaten, but who would never be hesitating or inactive." Grant fully justified the northern people's assessment of his character, for "he has fought unceasingly, and has clung like a bulldog to his work."[118] There is something inhumanly relentless in this description as well as something simultaneously horrifying and impressive.

British commentary makes it clear that discomfort with Grant's strategy stemmed from several sources. For one thing, a number of papers clearly believed that Grant's efforts and the resulting casualty lists would be for naught. After the Battle of Cold Harbor, *The Times* conceded that Grant's force had "displayed very high military qualities" (although Lee's Army of Northern Virginia was "a still more admirable instrument"), but that the Army of the Potomac's enormous "fortitude" fed on the "miserable delusion" that the North could win the war.[119] In other words, the Federal army's peculiar strength fed on a fantasy that would lead nowhere except a futile hecatomb. Even if this way of war culminated in victory, there was an evident reluctance to embrace it in Britain. Such a war was extremely destructive, and a number of observers protested that it threatened the progress of civilization.[120] In this destruction, which involved the annihilation of traditional institutions, relationships, and usages, several commentators detected the specter of revolution.[121] Indeed, the Federal way of war threatened to change the fundamental nature of armed conflict in such a way that Britain would be placed at a disadvantage in the future; the size and scope of land warfare threatened to expand beyond Britain's capacities. The *Spectator* implied this point when it commented on northern reports that the Army of the Potomac had lost forty thousand casualties at the Wilderness and Spotsylvania: "It is difficult to realise the full extent of such an admission—the army of WELLINGTON in the Peninsula, the British in the Crimea, the sum total of our countrymen who fought at Waterloo, lost in a week."[122] At the same time, this sort of democratic warfare in which numbers overwhelmed quality would potentially lead to the extinction of the British army as it was then constituted. Back in early 1863, the *Saturday Review* had insisted that the "old traditions of war have been borne out" by the American conflict, partly because "armies of inferior numbers, led by gentlemen, and trusting to themselves and not to *matériel,* have won victories over much larger forces."[123] Grant's strategy, however, threatened such presumptions. For that reason, there was a strong desire to dismiss Grant's generalship. Something of this attitude inspired *The Times* when it made the following comment about the Overland Campaign: "It is hard to withhold a certain admiration from such stubborn and invincible resolution, but though it is wonderful, it is not war. War is not made in this fashion by skillful generals."[124]

Although they recognized the brutality of Grant's style, those who were better disposed to the cause for which the North fought put a somewhat more positive construction on his activities.[125] For example, Grant was the energetic, revolutionary leader the *Spectator* had been waiting for. In the aftermath of the struggles at the Wilderness and Spotsylvania (battles it described as greater than anything since Borodino, then a byword for Napoleonic slaughter), the *Spectator* pointed out that Grant, not Lee, possessed the initiative. The Federal general had obtained the upper hand because he was a "man who whether or not a great strategist or great organizer, can give the most effective use to the special qualities of the force under his command." This "democratic force" lacked traditional European-style discipline, but it compensated for this shortcoming with numbers, gallantry, and ardor. Grant fought as "revolutionary generals should fight" and as the revolutionary military leaders of France's National Convention had fought in the 1790s—with enormous energy and a disregard for casualties. This strategy was perhaps "mere pommeling," the *Spectator* admitted, but the weekly claimed such a style of fighting was distinctly English and thus all but admitted Grant to the pantheon of Anglo-Saxon military heroes. Was the great slaughter immoral? The *Spectator* had less qualms here than *The Times*. The *Spectator* answered that the "swiftest war is the most merciful war, and with the means at his disposal . . . General Grant is . . . securing the swiftest war."[126] In other words, Grant was the ideal leader for an effective democratic army and an honorary Englishman to boot.

Generally, British opinion concerning Grant's methods seemed located between *The Times* and the *Spectator*, hovering like a compass needle between horrified dismissal and uncomfortable admiration. A similar ambivalence characterized attitudes toward Sherman and his march through Georgia and the Carolinas. Sherman seemed a strange combination of military genius and preeminent purveyor of hard war against southern civilians. Most observers rated Sherman very highly as a general and even thought he was more capable than Grant. Once Sherman had maneuvered his way to Atlanta, *The Times* praised him for "his economy of life and his employment of strategy instead of force," features of his campaign that compared favorably with Grant's bloody venture before Richmond.[127] The *Spectator* asserted that his Atlanta Campaign was "as yet the most brilliant and the most solid achievement in the war" while also marveling at the ingenuity of his march to the sea.[128] *Reynolds's Newspaper* described him as "the most daring, if not the greatest, of the Federal generals."[129] The *Illustrated London News* claimed Sherman's reputation was "second to none in the military service of the Federal Government."[130] Even the military men who became the earliest British historians of the war gave Sherman high marks. Hamley may have thought that Sherman was overrated ("no commander ever obtained a reputation equal to Sherman's with so little actual fighting, and with such odds in his favour"), but others were impressed. Fletcher believed the Atlanta Campaign showed that Sherman possessed a special aptitude for war.[131] In a lecture at the Royal Staff College, Sandhurst, the influential Chesney labeled Sherman a "man of original genius" for defying the traditional principles of war and maintaining an army in enemy country without any "regular line of communication at all."[132] Yet, Sherman also fell under much criticism for the behavior of his troops during their march through Georgia and the Carolinas. *The Times* understood that the "laws of war" justified the plundering of civilians for the sake of feeding the army, but it believed Sherman had "carried military usages to an excess the world has not heard of since the ravages of NAPOLEON'S legions" and therefore stamped the American war "as one of the most barbarous in history."[133] Moreover, the same soldier-historians who often praised his military acumen were disturbed by the destruction his army left in its wake. For Hamley, who was not impressed with Sherman to begin with, a "grisly fanaticism" had inspired the Federal general to lay waste to the South as a form of sacrifice to the "extinct Union." From this perspective, Sherman's behavior was somewhat akin to Butler's in bringing misery to the South through "peculation, corruption, and tyranny," all in the name of the "political Moloch" of democracy.[134] In criticizing Sherman's transgressions, Chesney confined his observations to grounds of expedience. Extensive plunder and destruction, which were initially limited, eventually extended to "everything within reach." This behavior demoralized Sherman's army, antagonized southern civilians, and thereby made the process of reconstruction much more difficult.[135] Even though he believed Sherman's army had transgressed the rules of war, Fletcher struggled mightily to be fair to his former host. Eventually he decided that the behavior of Sherman's soldiers toward southern civilians was inexcusable, for it erected the "the most vile system of plunder, devastation, and crime which ever disgraced the advance of a conquering army." "His army became an awful scourge," and Sherman did not care "so long as its excesses did not interfere with its efficiency in the field." By way of mitigation, Fletcher claimed Sherman did not hate the South; instead, he was so focused on the war effort that he spared no thought for its impact on southern civilians.[136]

Some observers sought to justify the behavior of Sherman's men. Referring to Sherman's march through Georgia, the *Bee-Hive* expressed sympathy for the Confederate civilians who had suffered but argued that the state had paid "the penalty—a terrible one, no doubt—of her unjustifiable and unwarrantable rebellion."[137] E. L. Godkin, the *Daily News*'s New York correspondent, along with the paper's editorials, argued that Sherman's men would make southern civilians more eager to end the war and less likely to start another one in the future.[138] However, most commentators found Sherman's activities especially troubling because they assumed that the devastation would not bring the North any closer to victory; the loss of property was utterly futile.[139] Yet by April 1865 it was clear that the Confederacy was finished militarily, and this unforeseen development, which seemed sudden to many British observers, led to a rapid reevaluation of the war.

"HITHERTO ALMOST EVERY PROPHECY . . . HAS PROVED FALSE": FEDERAL VICTORY AND THE REVERSALS OF BRITISH OPINION

In Britain, as 1864 turned into 1865, there was a sense that all was not well with the Confederacy's military situation, but the collapse of southern fortunes in April 1865 caught observers by surprise. Some accommodated this unforeseen development by sustaining the same narrative they had pursued for much of the war. The *Standard*'s elegy for the Confederacy lamented that "after a series of brilliant victories gained under unequalled disadvantages—courage and skill and devotion have succumbed to brute force." "By sheer power of numbers," the *Standard* continued, "a race inferior in every quality of soldiership and manhood have prevailed over the bravest and most united people that ever drew the sword in defence of civil rights and national independence."[140] The *Saturday Review* also met the Federal victory with an ill grace, admitting that democratic institutions "favour the vigorous prosecution of great enterprises" such as wars. Still, the weekly charged, the North had yet to prove that "the triumph of the Federal arms is not an unmixed misfortune for mankind."[141] Most observers, however, felt that the Federal victory warranted reassessment of the northern armies.

This reassessment ran the gamut from grudging praise to more wholehearted recognition of the Federal army's qualities. Only days before news of Richmond and Petersburg's surrenders made its way to Britain, *The Times* observed the four-year anniversary of the war's commencement by remarking that many of the conflict's events had been "so unexpected and . . . so unforeseen."[142] For *The Times*, the collapse of the Confederacy was just such an event. Critical of the Federal government for much of the war and convinced that the North could not win, the newspaper suddenly fell into confusion. On the one hand, it feared the social revolution unleashed by the Federal government during the war while hoping that northerners were not disposed to solve all of the nation's problems by force.[143] On the other, it recognized the "great achievement" of the Federal armies, whose discipline and leadership helped them prevail. "If the North has not gained in this struggle that reputation for desperate valour which has been achieved by the Confederates," *The Times* judged, "they have shown a patience, a fortitude, and an energy which entitle them to rank among the very first of military nations." The bid to create an independent southern state had failed "when opposed to almost equal genius and courage backed by superior numbers."[144] Such an assessment of the North's efforts was far different from what the newspaper had published for most of the war.

Praise from other quarters tended to dwell more on the qualities of the northern people than on the abilities of northern leadership. The *Daily News* protested against this view of events. Not only did it complain about how the "noble youth of New England" had been described in the British press "as mercenary hirelings," but it also denounced the way in which Grant had been labeled a "butcher" whose sole qualities were "'pertinacity' or 'obstinacy.'" It feared that there would "be few hearty recognitions of his military genius" in Britain.[145] The *Spectator* was one of the few journals that recognized the sterling qualities of the North's generals. Although it gave due weight to the North's superior numbers and paid the usual tribute to Grant's "superb tenacity," the weekly also marveled at the way in which the Federal armies coordinated their efforts through the last year of the war, effectively rendering all operations throughout the South "one campaign." The North may have owed much to "numbers and resources," but the "chief cause of their success is to be found in the skill of their leaders."[146]

Interestingly enough, once the North had finally won a war widely considered unwinnable in Britain, commentary about the American military experience witnessed an attempt to reclaim northerners as Englishmen. The *Daily Telegraph* paid tribute to the armies of both North and South, expressing pride in their "ingenuity" and "valour." "In this feeling," the newspaper claimed, "we English have a certain share; for it can never be indifferent to any mother-nation to see its children vigorous and brave."[147] In the *Economist,* Bagehot conferred even greater honors on the North, claiming that "every Englishman at least will feel a kind of personal sympathy with the victory of the Federals" because "they have won, as an Englishman would have won, by obstinacy." "They would not admit the possibility of real defeat," and "though they seemed to be beaten they were not." Reworking a phrase from Edward Gibbon's *History of Rome* ("one of the greatest specimens of English narrative" written by a "great English historian"), Bagehot continued, "panic did not for a moment unnerve the iron courage of the American democracy, and their resolute will striving beyond its present power created, as is the law of our nature, the power which it required."[148] Such statements are striking when compared with earlier attempts to distance Britain from the United States during the mid-war years. Of course, these judgments did not issue forth solely in recognition of the Federal triumph. For the same reason that British assessments of Lincoln suddenly turned upon his death, there was an attempt here to repair the Anglo-American relationship by admitting northerners to the status of Englishmen in recognition of their fighting prowess.

This praise for the Federal armies that emerged immediately upon the war's conclusion did not necessarily lead to a lasting appreciation of the North's military accomplishment. The Franco-Prussian War soon eclipsed the Civil War as the preeminent subject of study among British soldiers, but by the mid-1880s there was a resurgence of interest in the American conflict. By this point, however, it was Lee and Jackson who attracted the most attention. This curious phenomenon warrants an explanation. For one thing, much of the primary source material from which later British officers drew was highly critical of the northern effort. In this particular case, one can draw an analogy between the attitudes of British commentators toward politics and military affairs. We have already seen D. P. Crook observe with regard to American politics that "the great rallying which accrued to the northern cause in the war's latter years" was less significant than the "doubts and hesitations" that characterized the first half of the conflict.[149] The same could be said about military matters. The North's initial military failures (especially in Virginia) and the criticisms they elicited created memories that eventual Federal victory could not obliterate. In retrospect, this victory did not seem so very impressive when compared to the resistance put up by the outnumbered and outgunned Confederates who had produced a number of capable military leaders. This impression emerged in part because the British officers who had visited the South, commented most extensively about the war's military dimension, and in later years wrote studies of the American conflict tended to sympathize with the Confederacy. We can attribute much of this attitude to the conservatism of these British officers as well as their social background. The British officer corps was fairly homogenous, with the great majority consisting of gentry who came from small rural communities in the conservative counties—just the sort of areas that proved most sympathetic to the South.[150] Because they came from such a background, they were inclined to fight according to the "old traditions of war" (as we have seen the *Saturday Review* put it), where small, professional armies "led by gentlemen" trusted to their special qualities rather than to superior material resources.[151] In other words, they tended to embrace what they saw as the Confederate way of war. G.F.R. Henderson, Britain's leading military thinker in the late nineteenth century, who wrote extensively on the Civil War, foresaw that Britain might fight a future conflict with a large volunteer army over a vast area.[152] Yet neither he nor anybody else showed much taste for a protracted, destructive war of nations fought on a continental scale.[153] Rather, Henderson preferred, as he put it in his famous biography of Stonewall Jackson, a war in which the "big brains" beat the "big battalions."[154] Jackson's genius, Henderson claimed, stemmed from a recognition that the "moral is to the physical . . . three to one" and that "war is a struggle between two intellects rather than the conflict of masses."[155]

For these reasons, Henderson's understanding of the war resembled Fletcher's to a remarkable degree. Fletcher had visited the United States during the war and started writing about the conflict before the guns had fallen silent. Henderson, on the other hand, possessed the superior intellect and started writing about the conflict some twenty years later. Yet both, like most British officers, displayed a predilection for the Confederacy. This predilection was extremely important because over the years officers became the most important custodians of the Civil War's military lessons. At the end of his massive history of the war, Fletcher delivered the following eulogy, describing southerners as "a gallant people who . . . fought against overwhelming odds, and with a courage the world has seldom previously witnessed. . . . Gallantly did those who boast to be descended from the best blood of England maintain their asserted rights in the battle-field, courageously have they supported individually and collectively their misfortunes and their fall."[156] Henderson displayed a similar admiration, claiming that "the armies of the Confederacy, allied by the 'crimson thread of kinship' to those of Wellington, of Raglan, of Clyde, owed much of their enduring fortitude to 'the rock whence they were hewn.'"[157] Instead of the journalists who had sought to take ownership of the Federal victory in 1865 and make it their own by designating northerners as Englishmen, these officers chose to confer the honor of English descent on the South. This inclination led to an emphasis on southern achievements at the expense of Federal triumphs, something that would color British attitudes toward the conflict until after World War I, when a new generation of military historians took up the study of the Civil War.

6

BRITISH UNDERSTANDINGS OF AMERICAN NATIONALISMS DURING THE CIVIL WAR

It is strange that Englishmen should find difficulty in understanding that the United States is a nation among the nations of the earth.
—JOHN LOTHROP MOTLEY, 1861

The whole question turns on the point whether the Southerners are now a distinct people from the Northerners.
—*ARMY AND NAVY GAZETTE*, 1862

England has withheld recognition, not because the South maintains negro slavery, but because it has not definitively succeeded in establishing its independence.
—*SATURDAY REVIEW*, 1865

A MISTAKE OF INCREDIBLE GROSSNESS: GLADSTONE'S NEWCASTLE SPEECH

In October 1862, William Gladstone, then chancellor of the exchequer, headed to northern England on a tour of several industrial cities that included Newcastle. He intended to celebrate the Liberal government's recent achievements, particularly his budgets, which had heralded the final victory of free trade by bringing an end to almost all protective tariffs. Gladstone had lately earned much popularity among the working class (along with its press) for repealing the paper duty—the last of the "taxes on knowledge" that had inflated the price of newspapers—and he was prepared to capitalize on that popularity. Gladstone's tour was part of a new development noted in chapter 4, in which major political figures increasingly spoke before large urban audiences as a means of forging a direct connection with the people and obtaining popular legitimacy for the government.

Gladstone's trip also occurred as the British cabinet seriously began to consider intervening in the American Civil War. Over the summer of 1862, various ministers exchanged correspondence on the topic. Lord Lyons, head of the British legation in Washington, D.C., who arrived in Britain on vacation early in the season, was consulted repeatedly. The Commons debated a resolution on mediation in mid-July, and although it was withdrawn, the cabinet discussed the issue before Parliament adjourned in August. Earl Russell, the foreign secretary, exchanged thoughts with the French and Russian governments about intervening in the American war. Throughout the summer, the British press relentlessly speculated about what the government would do. Events in America, especially the Battle of Antietam (widely perceived as indecisive in Britain), the Emancipation Proclamation (which many thought would precipitate a humanitarian disaster), and later the congressional elections (where the Democrats made great gains), seemed to increase the likelihood of British action.

Whatever the shortcomings of Gladstone's attitude toward the war, inconsistency was not one of them. Almost from the very beginning of the crisis he thought the war was "without cause, and a war without cause is a foolish and wicked war."[1] It had nothing to do with abolition, he argued, and even it if it did, the Federal government had no right to destroy slavery through force. At the same time, Gladstone did not see how the North could coerce the South back into a democratic federation whose foundation was goodwill. Although he repeatedly claimed that the continuation of the old Union would have suited Britain's interests better than anything else, he could not help wondering if America had grown too big for such an arrangement to continue. From this perspective, secession represented "a vindication of the natural order, a disentanglement rather than a divorce."[2] In April 1862, Gladstone publicly expressed several of these ideas at a speech in Manchester, where he anticipated a number of themes that would be articulated more fully during his visit to Newcastle. Among other things, he counseled sympathy for Americans and suggested that a people with its heart set on separation could not be denied.[3] In September 1862, Palmerston, Russell, and Gladstone agreed that the time had come to take some action with regard to the American conflict. Gladstone believed in the propitiousness of the moment for two reasons.

First, if the string of Confederate triumphs continued, the South would be less inclined to make peace along lines the North could accept. Second, if the war ground on, disorder might ensue in Lancashire due to the cotton famine. In that case, Gladstone thought, "we might *then* seem to be interfering [in the American war], with loss of dignity, on the ground of our immediate interests" rather than "representing the general interests of humanity and peace." Having exchanged views with Palmerston on this matter, Gladstone assured the prime minister that "with respect to the Dinner at Newcastle, and the speech it will require, I have no difficulty, known to myself, in giving you satisfaction."[4] A concern for British interests (conflated as always with global progress) mingled with postcolonial hubris, however, would compel Gladstone to imply that he knew northerners' business better than they did.

And so, on the evening of October 7, Gladstone appeared at the Newcastle town hall for a dinner banquet, the first of several festive events associated with his visit (the next day, with a variety of local worthies, he would sail down the Tyne from Gateshead to Tynemouth to see improvements in navigation and acquire "from personal observation some conception of the magnitude and variety of the trade and commerce carried on upon its banks").[5] Some five hundred people attended the banquet, including MPs, local mayors, and prominent businessmen. Gladstone started his discourse on the American crisis by stating that Britain had no interest in the disintegration of the Union. He continued by defending the government's policy of neutrality. He then pleaded with the British public to show some patience with the North. Because northerners had enjoyed "a course of prosperity and advancement without example and without a single break," they had "never drunk the bitter cup of misfortune, disappointment, and mortification." They therefore found it difficult to accept their military reverses. For that reason, Gladstone counseled his fellow Britons, "let us be very cautious about indulging in adverse criticisms upon them [northerners] on this side of the water." "They are our kin," he added, before tastelessly joking (no doubt moved by the character of his audience), "they were, if they are not now, our customers, and we hope they will be customers again." Gladstone then uttered the most famous words of this speech in the context of Britain needing to show some sensitivity to northern feelings: "We know quite well that the people of the Northern States have not yet drunk of the cup—they are still trying to hold it far from their lips—the cup which all the rest of the world see they nevertheless must drink of. We may have our own opinions about slavery; we may be for or against the South; but there is no doubt that Jefferson Davis and other leaders of the South have made an army; they are making, it appears, a navy; and they have made what is more than either—they have made a nation. (Loud cheers.)" Several sentences later, Gladstone openly stated what he had hitherto implied about the war's outcome: "We may anticipate with certainty the success of the Southern States so far as regards their separation from the North. (Hear, hear.) I cannot but believe that that event is as certain as any event yet future and contingent can be. (Hear, hear.)" The time would come when Europe might have to arbitrate between the North and the South, and the task would be easier if northerners' minds were "not embittered by the recollection that unkind things have been said and done towards them in Europe, and, above all, in England, the country which, however they may find fault with it from time to time, has we know the highest place in their admiration and esteem."[6]

Twenty years later, Catherine Gladstone, the chancellor of the exchequer's wife, reminisced to a reporter, "Oh, I shall never forget that day! It was the first time, you know, that he was received as he deserved to be."[7] In other words, the visit to Newcastle completed Gladstone's apotheosis as a popular politician, "The People's William." Most others, however, remembered the day for quite different reasons. The newspapers raised a sensation as they assumed—with greater or lesser degrees of enthusiasm—that Gladstone's speech heralded the cabinet's recognition of the Confederacy.[8] The cabinet, of course, had agreed to no such thing, and Gladstone would soon suffer serious embarrassment.

Upon learning about Gladstone's speech, Sir George Cornewall Lewis, then the secretary of state for war as well as one of the most able and prominent members of the cabinet, determined to counter the impression that his colleague had made. Lewis wrote to the 4th Earl of Clarendon (his brother-in-law) that so long as the North sustained its colossal efforts to subjugate the Confederacy, "it is impossible to say that the South have de facto established their independence."[9] On October 14, at the annual meeting of the Herefordshire Agricultural Association, Lewis told his audience much the same thing: while the South undoubtedly qualified for belligerent rights, it could not be recognized as independent because "the war must be admitted to be undecided."[10] Lewis's statement revealed to the public that the cabinet was divided, the Confederacy was not about to obtain recognition, and Gladstone had spoken without authorization from his colleagues. Subsequent discussion of the Newcastle speech in the press dwelled as much on Gladstone's mistakes as it did on the American crisis. For example, the *Saturday Review* charged that Gladstone's "panegyric upon President DAVIS and the Southern Confederacy would have been in place if it had been uttered in Cabinet as an argument in favour of recognition," but "as part of an after-dinner speech addressed to the citizens of a second-rate borough, by a member of a Government which still declines to recognize the South, it was an extraordinary indiscretion."[11]

Criticisms of Gladstone in the press mirrored criticisms of Gladstone within the cabinet. Palmerston and Russell were both dissatisfied with Gladstone for having attempted to predict the future and making such an important statement without cabinet sanction.[12] Nonetheless, it took Gladstone some time to recognize his blunder.[13] With some reluctance, he eventually came to realize that his "mode of speech must have been faulty" and that a public speaker "ought to know besides his own meaning the meaning which others will attach to his words."[14] Thirty years later, Gladstone was convinced that his speech was a special error of "incredible grossness," the "most singular and palpable, I may add the least excusable of them all." His opinion had been "founded upon a false estimate of the facts," and coming from a cabinet minister whose nation was "allied in blood and language, and bound to loyal neutrality," it was terribly inappropriate. All he could say in his defense was that he has been moved by a friendship for the North that sought to avoid "future bloodshed and greater calamity."[15] It would appear that in his own ham-fisted way, Gladstone had acted according to what he saw as the terms of the postcolonial relationship; for the sake of preserving the arrangements that had traditionally characterized the Anglo-Saxon transatlantic world, he was permitted to give what amounted to extremely unpalatable advice to northerners that would destroy their nation.

More than thirty years on, Gladstone could take the long view and dwell on how the episode at Newcastle had harmed the Anglo-American relationship. At the time, though, he must have been aware that the speech had undermined his ability to advocate on behalf of mediation within the cabinet. On October 13, Russell sent out a memorandum explaining why the time was right for British mediation. This effort inspired various cabinet members to lobby one another. Several days later, Lewis responded to Russell with a memorandum of his own. An October 23 cabinet meeting was postponed, but at an informal gathering of ministers that day Russell failed to obtain much support for his initiative, except from Gladstone, who wrote a memorandum supporting Russell's position (October 24). At the end of the month, Russell learned that Napoleon III intended to share a proposed armistice plan with Britain and Russia that would lead to mediation of the American crisis. A week later, on November 7, Lewis produced a much longer memorandum. This later work, Howard Jones has pointed out, concentrated on the "toughest single problem in the recognition crisis: deciding when a people in revolt had achieved independence."[16] In other words, Lewis problematized one of Gladstone's most important assumptions. There was something of an anticlimax when the cabinet met on November 11 to consider Napoleon III's plan. Lewis appeared to have rallied much of the cabinet against this initiative. Reporting to the 4th Earl of Clarendon, Lewis doubted that Palmerston's "support [for the measure] was very sincere—it certainly was not hearty." Once the proposal "was thrown before the Cabinet," various members "proceeded to pick it to pieces." "Every body present threw a stone at it, of greater or lesser size," a delighted Lewis reported, "except Gladstone, who supported it, & the Chancellor [1st Baron Westbury] & [Edward] Cardwell [chancellor of the Duchy of Lancaster], who expressed no opinion."[17] The cabinet agreed to decline the French offer. Gladstone was extremely frustrated with his colleagues and unhappy with the result.[18] Then again, he was partly responsible for this outcome with his ill-timed and ill-judged speech. As Jones puts it, Gladstone's Newcastle oration had inspired his cabinet colleagues to scrutinize the "complexities in the American war, and in doing so, mobilized more Englishmen against intervention."[19]

This story has been related many times before, mostly in the context of transatlantic Civil War diplomacy. In the retelling, however, most scholars have missed the degree to which Gladstone's "misjudgment of the case" (as he described it) reflected public opinion and that of his cabinet colleagues.[20] Many agreed that the Confederacy was a nation. For instance, *The Times,* normally no great friend of Gladstone's, claimed he had "only made a statement considerably within the truth." He had concluded "very reasonably that the Confederates who are a nation will remain so, and that their nationality will not be absorbed back into the Union."[21] At the same time, Palmerston admitted to Russell that "Gladstone was not far wrong" in anticipating the independence of the South.[22] Evidence suggests that Russell agreed.[23] Even more interesting, Lewis, who had taken the lead role in challenging the Newcastle speech and countering Russell's influence in the cabinet, actually agreed with Gladstone's assessment of the American situation. The *Spectator* speculated that Gladstone and Lewis did "not feel very differently concerning the American struggle, at least as regards the North," and the weekly was correct.[24] Upon reading the Newcastle speech for the first time, Lewis wrote, "I agree in the view taken by Gladstone, & on the whole I am not sorry he said what he did, though perhaps it was not discreet." It was Gladstone's prescription of mediation that Lewis—and most of the cabinet—found faulty.[25]

A FRIENDLY, LIBERAL, AND PACIFIC DIRECTION: BRITISH ATTITUDES TOWARD NATIONS AND NATIONALITY

That Gladstone's colleagues agreed with him in his assessment of Confederate nationality should not surprise us. As a whole, the Newcastle oration very much reflected British liberal mid-Victorian ideas about nations and nationality. Unfortunately, scholars studying the address have focused so intently on Gladstone's observations concerning the United States that they have not recognized the degree to which the rest of the speech contextualizes those observations.

That Gladstone referred to the Italian question at the end of the Newcastle speech reminds us that the statesmen of the post-1848 period believed they lived in a new Atlantic world characterized by the emergence of nations and nationalism. Gladstone's reference to Italy also suggested, however, the degree to which British Liberals were not unconditional supporters of all nationalisms. Only nations prepared to govern themselves through moderate, liberal, constitutional regimes warranted wholehearted approval. At Newcastle, Gladstone hoped that a united Italy would prove "that constitutional freedom, administered in the spirit of freedom, relished and apprehended by the people, rooted in their hearts and enlightening their understandings, is the best security that human wisdom can devise, not only for the maintenance of the privileges which are due to man as a free agent, but likewise for the increase of loyalty and the maintenance of order and of the law." In particular, the recent battle at Aspromonte, where the Italian army had prevented Giuseppe Garibaldi from marching on Rome (then ruled by Pope Pius IX), annexing it to Italy, and causing a European crisis, had convinced Gladstone that the Italians were mature enough for self-government.[26] Gladstone's conditional approval of nationalism was entirely characteristic of British liberal thinking. In an 1864 essay, Walter Bagehot remarked that the "principle of nationalities is not a good in itself . . . but a means to an end, to be applied rationally and discriminately towards that end."[27] Scholars often portray John Stuart Mill and Lord Acton, the two intellectual giants who wrote the most influential considerations of nationality during this period, as antagonists, but on this subject, as in many others, they both agreed with Bagehot. Nationalities, they believed, ought to be judged on a case-by-case basis by the good that they could accomplish.[28] And that good usually had something to do with freedom, constitutional government, and the rule of law. This attitude was reflected not merely in Gladstone's speech or the scribblings of public intellectuals. It also appeared in the British government's policies toward the nationalities that emerged in the period stretching from the Revolutions of 1848 to the Risorgimento and German unification. In most cases, the British government and public preferred moderate, liberal, constitutional monarchies as the best guarantee of peace and freedom in other states.[29] As we shall see, this type of thinking had a big impact on British perceptions of northern and southern nationalism.

At the same time, in approving of a new, emerging nation in Italy, Liberals such as Gladstone did not wish to see the increasing fragmentation of the civilized world; their conception of nationalism was not tribal, insular, or parochial. Rather, they were cosmopolitan in that they saw nations as building blocks for international cooperation and possibly larger political units. As Bagehot put it, nations formed in his time because modern, civilized men possessed a "taste for union," a sentiment with which Mill agreed.[30] In October 1862, Richard Cobden told his constituents at Rochdale much the same thing when he asserted that the great tendency of his day was "not a desire to separate, but to agglomerate, to bring together in greater concentration different races."[31] This attitude was captured by Gladstone's reference to the Cobden-Chevalier Treaty (the free trade agreement signed between Britain and France in 1860) during his Newcastle speech. He stressed that "the augmentation of mere wealth and material strength" was not the "exclusive object" of the treaty. Indeed, the "highest part of all its work is to knit more closely the ties of goodwill first between England and France (loud cheers), and then between the various nations of the world." The treaty would give "to the minds of men a friendly, liberal, and pacific direction" as they all worked together.[32] This Liberal sentiment went hand in hand with what we might find a surprising respect for existing multi-national states, so long as they preserved the freedoms of all. Only through a mingling of diverse people under one government, so the argument went, could progress take place. As Acton asserted, it was only within a multinational state "that the fusion takes place by which the vigour, the knowledge, and the capacity of one portion of mankind may be communicated to another."[33] Mill agreed: having referred to the benefits enjoyed by Basques in France or Welshmen in Britain, he argued that "whatever really tends to the admixture of nationalities, and the blending of their attributes and peculiarities in a common union, is a benefit to the human race."[34] During the Civil War, Gladstone reflected this attitude when he claimed repeatedly that he preferred the maintenance of the "old Union" in North America to any other arrangement; it had the best potential for knitting much of the North American continent together in a liberal, peaceful way.[35]

Gladstone's Newcastle speech is also helpful in understanding British attitudes toward nationality because it implied a specific vision of that country's own national mission. (Like many other statesmen at the time, Gladstone used "England" throughout the speech as a synonym for "Britain.") According to the oration, England would serve as a model for the world. With the operation of its government, it would show Italy how to reconcile order and progress through constitutional monarchy. By pursuing free trade, it would teach France to set aside an aggressive and militaristic foreign policy in favor of commerce and harmony. And as the head of the English-speaking world, it would instruct the Americans (in this case northerners) on their duties to themselves and to the rest of the globe. Such a conception of England's role corresponds well with what present-day scholars have written about nineteenth-century English nationalism. Peter Mandler, for instance, has recently argued that, taking their cue from the Enlightenment, the English adapted a universalist perspective: all the world's peoples were ranged on different rungs of the same ladder and capable of traveling toward civilization at the top—a position occupied by England.[36] In other words, England was a model for others. While the Revolutions of 1848 undermined the faith of Englishmen that the civilization they had achieved was accessible to all peoples, the events of that year also inspired "a heightened sense of global responsibility on the part of liberal Englishmen who lent their support to nationalities on the Continent struggling towards the common goals of liberty and order."[37] Such a thesis is not difficult to reconcile with Krishan Kumar's contention that England's "missionary identity" was characterized by an "outwardness" whereby the "English saw themselves in the mirror of the larger enterprises in which they were engaged for most of their history."[38] Although Kumar identifies these larger enterprises primarily with the construction of Great Britain and the British Empire, he suggests that these projects formed part of an endeavor to remake the entire world in England's own image.[39]

The "outwardness" of English identity and its desire to remake the world in its own image brings us to the United States, which figured prominently in this project. As we have already pointed out repeatedly, the British Empire still claimed Americans as subjects and saw their work as contributing to the larger endeavor of Anglo-Saxon progress. And yet, as we have also seen, there was much confusion and ambivalence about the American nation. Recent work on nineteenth-century American nationalism helps explain why it was difficult for British observers to understand and accept. For one thing, this scholarship has not reached consensus on fundamental questions, such as the strength of American nationalism, its basic elements, its relationship to the understanding of Union, and the degree to which it resembled its European analogues.[40] If scholars do not agree on such matters today, it is easy to see why British observers in the mid-nineteenth century had difficulty in making heads or tails of the same issues. The sectional crisis only added to the confusion as the South and the North developed competing visions of what the Union meant and what the Founding Fathers intended. Where the South eventually inclined toward independence as a means of preserving what it saw as the ideals of 1776, the North increasingly conceived of the Union not so much as an end in itself, but as a means to a freer and more moral community—one that had to include the entire United States.[41] Historians today recognize, of course, that the federal or national element of American government at this time was decentralized, and well might British commentators have wondered what would hold the American community together.[42]

As always, the influential Tocqueville's thoughts illustrate the way in which many British writers approached these issues. Although Tocqueville believed there were fundamental variations among Americans, he still represented them as nothing more than Englishmen living under different social conditions.[43] Tocqueville conceded that the Americans had erected a distinct civilization, but he also asserted that their English antecedents had fundamentally shaped that civilization.[44] Much more difficult for Tocqueville to dissect were the federal system, the Union, and the nationalism that made the Americans unique. Tocqueville conceived of the United States as neither national nor federal but somewhere in between. It was, he reasoned, an "incomplete national government."[45] While the United States was more national than any previous federal government, he believed that American patriotism was "directed to the State, and . . . not excited by the Union" because Americans had "much more to hope and to fear from the States than from the Union."[46] Not only that, but Tocqueville questioned the strength of American nationalism, which he described as civic and self-interested.[47] As he put it, "I do not rely upon that calculating patriotism which is founded upon interest" because a change of interests could undermine that patriotism. We should take note here of how a calculating patriotism founded on interest—one devoid of high principle or ideals—seemed like the natural expression of a bourgeois society. Far more durable, Tocqueville claimed, was a nationalism based on instinct and feeling.[48] In any event, Tocqueville suggested that America's "calculating patriotism" was particularly vulnerable to the sectionalism that had arisen due to the confinement of slavery to one half of the nation. The Union, he argued, had made American interests and points of view increasingly similar over time.[49] However, slavery had conferred upon the South an aristocratic nature, while freedom had led the North to assume middle-class habits.[50] These differences in character, Tocqueville implied, would assume greater importance as northerners inevitably grew much more prosperous and numerous than southerners.[51] The frictions that would arise from these developments would only increase with time and, when coupled with what Tocqueville perceived as the increasing debility of the national government, they would eventually undermine the union.[52]

Tocqueville's *Democracy in America* helped guide a generation of British travel writers. As a Frenchman, however, his work was obviously not as sensitive to the needs of the Anglo-American postcolonial relationship as the books of English authors were. Not surprisingly, this relationship colored British perceptions of American identity and accounted for much friction. Americans considered themselves exceptional and unique, and while some British observers were willing to concede this point, many were not. A number of British visitors insisted that Americans were nothing more than Britons living under different circumstances and that American institutions were the offspring of a British heritage. This insistence was a product of increasing insecurity that America's membership in the Anglo-Saxon tribe was imperiled by democracy, immigration, materialism, and a host of other evils. Only so long as they cultivated their Englishness could Americans carry on with the Anglo-Saxon civilizing mission, reconcile progress with order, and achieve their potential. For that reason, the assertion among Americans that they were the best of all potential nations with ambitions of their own was bound to create friction. Britons who believed that they belonged to the best of all actual nations found such notions pretentious and worried that the United States would work at cross-purposes with Britain by promoting a competing but faulty version of progress. The important distinction that most British visitors willingly granted to Americans was that they were a middle-class people. Such a distinction, of course, was a dubious one, since the bourgeoisie was widely seen as materialistic and incapable of holding high ideals.

The foregoing antebellum thoughts about nationality, the Americans, and their Union helped prepare the British response to the Civil War. The bonds of union seemed weak, questionable, and obscure. Meanwhile, there was some skepticism that the Yankee bourgeois values sweeping the country formed a solid basis for a true national feeling in the North, let alone the entire United States. This "calculating patriotism" seemed especially menaced by the increasing intensity and prevalence of sectional feeling. Under these circumstances, secession did not come as a total surprise in Britain. As we shall see, many Britons presumed in favor of a Confederate nation due to the South's size, prosperity, unity, and ability to erect a functioning state. Southerners, however, were also perceived as particularly suited for responsible self-government. Their English heritage and peculiar cast of society (in which conservative, aristocratic elements balanced more democratic ones) made it seem likely that they could rule themselves in a moderate fashion. The disagreement in Britain over Confederate nationality had little to do with whether southerners formed a distinct people; most commentators agreed with Gladstone that the Confederacy was indeed a nation. The issue had much more to do with whether or not Confederate nationality was worth supporting. In other words, how was the principle of nationality to be "applied rationally and discriminately" in the Confederate case? Another important question concerned the degree to which the Confederacy had fulfilled the legal criteria of nationhood. Because they saw Britain as the leader of the Anglo-Saxon world, British politicians and commentators believed they had a special role to play in determining the Confederacy's status. As they argued over the degree to which each section had retained its Englishness, they also pursued rhetorical strategies that ensured that neither was lost to Greater Britain.

THEY HAVE MADE A NATION: BRITISH PERCEPTIONS OF THE CONFEDERATE NATION

An older tradition in the historiography of the Civil War South was interested in determining if the Confederacy was a nation and how strong that nationality was. Scholars eventually left this question behind for the sake of assessing, to use Paul Quigley's words, southern nationalism's "character, evolution, and diverse meanings."[53] Mid-Victorian British observers were interested in exploring both sets of questions. Although they reached a degree of consensus in each case, they expressed greater unanimity in discussing the strength of Confederate national feeling than in characterizing it.

British discussions concerning the character of Confederate nationality revolved around its Englishness, the Cavalier inheritance, conservative republicanism, and the influence of slavery in shaping the South. Possibly taking their cue from Confederate propaganda, British partisans of the South often stressed that section's English character, primarily as a means of distinguishing it from a North that had experienced a great deal of immigration in the previous fifteen years.[54] The erratic and undiplomatic John Roebuck put it most baldly when he spoke at Sheffield in the Master Cutler's Hall in August 1862 with Lord Palmerston in attendance: "The North will never be our friends. (Cheers.) Of the South you can make friends. They are Englishmen; they are not the scum and refuse of Europe. [The Mayor of Manchester.—"Don't say that; don't say that."] (Cheers and disapprobation.) I know what I am saying. They are Englishmen, and we must make them our friends."[55] A.J.B. Beresford Hope, the founder-owner of the *Saturday Review* as well as a staunch Confederate supporter (he was then in between stints as MP for Maidstone and Stoke-on-Trent) expressed similar sentiments repeatedly, and even went so far as to depict the South as a collection of "communities of Englishmen still living in the 18th century" while the North had completely lost its English character.[56] For his part, Francis Lawley, *The Times*' southern correspondent, never lost an opportunity to explain that the South was superior to the North by virtue of the former's Anglo-Saxon blood.[57] This way of viewing southerners was a means of reaffirming their postcolonial status, which in turn promised magnificent opportunities for Britain. There was, of course, cotton, but the crisis fired ambitions grander than merely turning a pound sterling through free trade.[58] Several commentators saw a chance to renew British influence in the South, ostensibly for the sake of progress and civilization. Beresford Hope believed that unlike the North, which was as "clay that had been moulded and baked, and had come out a showy but coarse and inferior article," the South was like "clay in the potter's hands." It was up to Britain and Europe to "take in hand its rude semi-civilization, bring its own refinement and cultivation to bear on it, and endeavor to raise and purify its character." With a Confederate victory and British guidance, Beresford Hope saw "glimmering in the distance, freedom for the slave, something like a Liberal-Conservative constitution growing up out of unbridled democracy, free trade with a boundless expanse of the richest soil, from which English mills and vessels might reap a golden harvest, and the high civilization of Europe pervading a people prepared for its influence."[59] Not everybody, however, willingly recognized the South's Englishness. Abolitionism was so central to British identity that there was a tendency in some quarters to describe slavery and therefore the South as "un-English."[60] Rather, it was the industrial North, which honored labor and commerce, which more closely resembled Britain. At the same time, the antebellum habit of looking at all Americans as varieties of Englishmen was hard to break. Moreover, there was such faith in the capacity of the North's English culture to absorb other peoples that the great waves of immigration to the free states had not really changed that section. For example, Edward Dicey dwelled on the degree to which a flexible Anglo-Saxon civilization in the United States had modified itself according to local conditions while assimilating German and Irish immigrants.[61]

If, however, southerners and northerners were both Englishmen, what accounted for the war? Many commentators claimed the American conflict was merely a continuation of England's seventeenth-century Civil War. Cavaliers and Roundheads (or Puritans), so the argument went, had founded incompatible civilizations in America that now renewed their old battle in the New

World. Southerners were nothing more than nineteenth-century descendants of Cavaliers, with all the characteristics of that group. A number of Confederate sympathizers liked employing this interpretation because it made the war look like it had nothing to do with slavery.[62] Such an explanation had a long antebellum pedigree, but it was problematic, for it suggested a profound division within the Anglo-Saxon community that threatened to tear it apart.[63] A number of observers suggested that references to the Cavalier-Puritan struggle were a made-up pedigree for what was simply a class conflict. In *Letters from the Slave States* (1857), James Stirling used the narrative of the Cavalier-Puritan struggle to explain the American crisis. At the same time, however, he seemed to imply that this story was nothing more than a convenient myth of origin that explained what was simply a collision between southern aristocracy and northern democracy.[64] Toward the end of the war, Goldwin Smith, then the Regius Professor of History at Oxford, told a Boston audience that they need not be distracted by talk of Puritans and Cavaliers: "The soldiers of the Union are not Puritans, neither are the planters Cavaliers." "But the present civil war," he asserted, "is a vast episode in the same irrepressible conflict between Aristocracy and Democracy; and the heirs of the Cavalier in England sympathise with your enemies, the heirs of the Puritan with you."[65] In other words, "Cavalier" really meant nothing more than "aristocrat" while "Puritan" merely signified "democrat."

If the Confederacy was not a Cavalier society, most Britons agreed that it was an aristocratic one. Pro-southern Britons tended to emphasize how this quality fostered a unique, conservative Confederate republicanism. The Confederacy possessed an aristocracy, so the argument went, that contributed to the formation of a hierarchical society where deference and paternalism bound southerners together in a national community. Although politically the South was a democracy, the social conditions within which that democracy operated contributed to moderation and the safeguarding of individual liberty. In such a state of things, the 9th Marquess of Lothian wrote, the Confederates "have just about as much aristocracy and as much democracy in their composition as is good for them."[66] Appearing in works by a variety of Confederate sympathizers, these arguments were well calculated to appeal to a British audience. They provided a reassurance that the Confederacy, even more so than, say, Italy, would promote moderate, constitutional government inspired by traditional English values.[67] Such arguments were a staple of Confederate propaganda, with Henry Hotze explaining in the *Index* that the Confederacy was fighting "the great moral and political battle of this generation": "The battle of established right against popular will; of liberty against democracy; of law against numbers. She is the representative of all conservatism, vested right, traditional institutions, solemn constitutional compromises, against the 'giant strength of an awakened people,' determined to respect no precedent and be bound by no pledges." From this perspective, states' rights were "to America what the Crown, the Church, the Peerage, the diversity of constituencies, the limitation of the franchise, are to England—the checks by which liberty is protected against the populace, and the few secured against the uncontrolled and unlimited tyranny on the part of the many."[68] Admiration for the apparent efficacy of the Confederate government and the strengths of its leadership led many in Britain to find such assertions plausible. Of course, where some saw equilibrium, others discerned a tyranny that sought to suppress profound social discord. One has only to recall John Elliott Cairnes's *The Slave Power* (1862) to understand that many commentators believed the southern aristocracy (or oligarchy) held large numbers of whites and blacks in its thrall. Beneath this repressive regime, many British observers detected instability and significant dissension. The "radical opposition of local rights and interests to the central authority in a matter so important as war" proved to the *Daily News* that "whatever else Mr. DAVIS may have done, he has *not* yet made the South a 'nation.'"[69] Francis Newman, Cardinal John Henry Newman's brother and a professor of Latin at University College, London, claimed a "rotten tyranny is like a cone poised on its sharp end" and that "of all tyrannies the most rotten is that of an oligarchical slave-power." Aside from having "no past history, no noble memories to kindle it," the Confederacy also had "no cohesion of orders, no middle class." A society of "a few slaveholding families . . . with a great mass of despised poor whites, and by their side the three million slaves" was bound to collapse under a conflict of interests.[70]

Slavery's centrality to Confederate identity was one thing that almost all British commentators could agree on. As we have already noted in chapter 1, antebellum travel writers had repeatedly dwelled on the degree to which slavery molded southern economic, political, and social life. Cairnes's very well-received *Slave Power* was predicated on this very notion. Not only that, but slavery was an interest that, no matter how perverse and noxious, bound the southern people together. Sir George Grey, the home secretary, claimed simply that unlike the North, the South was united "on one Principle, if it be a detestable one, Slavery."[71] Very few British commentators could elide the fact that the Confederate state represented a society fundamentally rooted in slavery. Even James Spence admitted that "in the Union, slavery as a system identifies the Southerner with his own land. Remove it, and you obliterate the line of demarcation. Right or wrong, it is essential to his national existence."[72] Spence's observation expressed one of the greatest weaknesses of Confederate nationality when he implied that the destruction of slavery would lead to the end of a discrete South—something that many British abolitionists were not slow to understand. Dicey pointed out that "there is no difference in race, or language, or religion, or geographical position to keep the two divisions of the Union apart." If an immoral institution like slavery was the only barrier to reunion, it had to be destroyed.[73] From this perspective, emancipation was the necessary prelude to a sustainable Union.[74] As we have already seen, though, the problem was that many British commentators quailed before emancipation, finding it a far too radical and potentially dangerous step.

If British commentators could and did argue about the character of Confederate nationality, they did not dispute the existence of a Confederate nation. Three factors indicated to them the existence of such a nation. First, there was the alacrity with which the seceding states formed a functioning federation that appeared to command the respect of its citizens. Second, the new Confederate state easily passed the "threshold principle" (to use historian Eric Hobsbawm's phrase): it was large, culturally united, and economically viable.[75] Third, the enormous sacrifices that southerners made during a protracted war to protect their new state indicated a high level of commitment to their national community.

Paul Quigley has recently pointed out that in 1861 "southern nationalists demanded international acceptance of an independence they claimed to have already achieved." To obtain this acceptance, in fact, to attain legitimacy, southern leaders realized they had to erect a stable, functioning government.[76] While they failed to obtain formal recognition from the British government, they did succeed in convincing most of the British public that they had indeed created a working state. In October 1861, Lord Lyons, the British minister in Washington, D.C., reported that the Confederate state was "obeyed without question and exercises all the functions of Government with the most perfect regularity."[77] The British press agreed. To take one example, in the wake of McClellan's failure to take Richmond in 1862, the *Standard* asserted that the Confederate government "has maintained order and enforced law with remarkable vigour and success. It has a perfect organization and it received from its subjects a cordial and thorough-going support. . . . The thorough loyalty of the people is shown by the thorough confidence reposed in them by the Administration."[78] In his November 7, 1862, memorandum concerning recognition of the Confederacy, Sir George Cornewall Lewis accepted that the existence of a Confederate state that "received the general obedience of the Southern population" was "indisputable."[79] For a pro-southern propagandist like Spence, this argument was the biggest arrow in his quiver. The Confederacy's character and origins, he argued, did not matter. As he put it, Britons "have no more right to inquire why it [the Confederacy] has come into existence than to question of a man what right he had to be born."[80] All that did matter was that the southern states formed "a distinct community, and have over them a government approved by themselves, and reasonably executing the functions of administration."[81] Indeed, the existence of such a government proved that the southerners were a "separate people."[82] Regardless of what one thought of its institutions, the Confederate nation, Spence argued, was a fact, and facts, by virtue of being facts, had to be recognized.

Moreover, this new Confederate state represented what was widely considered a viable nation. When the Confederacy's first commissioners to Europe—Ambrose Dudley Mann, Pierre Rost, and William Yancey—first made their case in writing to Earl Russell, they attempted to justify secession and explain away the role of slavery in the war. But the commissioners also stressed the degree to which the Confederacy was large and prosperous enough to constitute a nation. They dwelled on "the great extent of fertile country over which the Confederate States exercised jurisdiction, producing in ample quantity every variety of cereal necessary to the support of their inhabitants; the great value of products of cotton and tobacco grown by them; [and] the number and character of their people." Using figures from the census of 1850, they also asserted that the "Confederate States possess the elements of a great and powerful nation, capable not only of clothing, feeding, and defending themselves, but also of clothing all the nations of Europe under the benign influence of peace and free trade."[83] The veiled reference to King Cotton diplomacy was not effective, and these arguments did not inspire Russell to recognize formally the Confederacy. Nonetheless, claims about the Confederacy's size did tell with the British public. For instance, in July 1862, when William Schaw Lindsay, a pro-Confederate MP representing Sunderland, introduced a motion in the Commons recommending that it ought to mediate the American conflict and recognize the Confederacy, he returned repeatedly to the size of the South's population, the region's territorial extent, and the vigor of its economy.[84] Even *Reynolds's Newspaper*, which was not terribly enamored of the Confederacy, argued that its "nationality and independence" were "indubitable" because "They occupy a territory larger than the half of all Europe. Their resources, naval, military, fiscal, agricultural, and commercial are equal to many a European Power. They have a population of ten millions of human beings. . . . They have large and populous cities—magnificent harbours—flourishing manufacturers—inexhaustible mineral and vegetable wealth."[85] As *The Times* put it somewhat crudely in November 1861, "numbers make right as well as might." "When ten millions of men occupying a vast territory declare political independence," the newspaper argued, "it is superfluous to discuss the arguments by which they justify their purpose."[86] Not everyone, however, bought this argument. With his usual perspicacity, Mill pointed out that it was "rather cool in English writers who talk so glibly of the ten millions (I believe there are only eight) to pass over the very existence" of four million slaves—"human beings entitled to human rights"—who had not been consulted about secession and in all likelihood did not support the southern cause.[87] In other words, to the legitimacy of numbers, Mill opposed the illegitimacy of slavery. Unfortunately, this argument did not stick; while many British commentators recognized the slave as a potential source of social strife or as an Uncle Tom-like victim, they did not see him as part of the national calculus.

Although the sheer size and populousness of the South told in favor of a Confederate nation, these features alone did not necessarily a nation make. We have already seen in chapter 4 that Federal victories in the spring of 1862 undermined British faith in southerners' commitment to the Confederate cause. Starting with the Seven Days' Battles, it was the Confederate victories in the Eastern theater and the energy with which the South sustained a struggle against a very powerful foe that convinced British observers the southern people had truly formed a nation. In November 1862, the *Daily Telegraph* marveled that "a people which is led as the Confederates are; which can go to war with its soldiers hungry and in rags; which can manufacture its own arms, literally out of its domestic furniture; which can forego pay if the exigencies of the State demand it; which is all of one mind, and is prepared to sacrifice present comfort, family property, life itself, in order to keep the country independent, its soil inviolable—such a people is one to sustain the contest indefinitely, by the strength of motives with which we Englishmen cannot fail to sympathise."[88] The widespread assumption in Britain seemed to be that such a nation could not be defeated, let alone destroyed.[89] William Corsan, who headed a Sheffield firm that manufactured cutlery for the American market, visited the Confederacy in the fall of 1862 and observed in relation to the South: "Nations, no matter how small and unmeritorious, *cannot* be annihilated." Such an assumption might seem questionable in light of what had recently happened in Europe—emerging nations had either required assistance from outside powers to obtain independence (Greece from 1827 to 1832, Belgium from 1830 to 1832, and Italy in 1859) or been defeated (Hungary in 1848–1849 and, later, Poland in 1863). But British commentators saw the Confederate situation as different in two vital ways. First, many believed that as Anglo-Saxons, southerners possessed a special genius for governing and fighting. As Corsan himself wrote, it was "vain" to think that "twelve to thirteen millions of human beings, two-thirds of them Anglo-Saxons" could be subjugated.[90] Second, the peculiar nature of the Federal Union—which depended on the consent of the governed—made it unlikely that hostile southerners could ever be reassimilated within the framework of a democratic republican constitution. It was one thing for a tyranny like Russia or Austria (or even a monarchy like Britain) to restore authority over rebellious subjects. It was quite another for a democracy to compel an unwilling population to rejoin a free association. The Confederates were a separate people, so it seemed, and the hard feelings engendered by the war rendered reunion all but impossible. As the *Daily Telegraph* put it, "if, morally, the two confederacies were divided before the election of President LINCOLN, how much more widely must they be estranged since they have undergone actual bloodshed, and sustained such fearful injuries at each other's hands?"[91] Responding to the queen's Speech from the Throne in 1863, the 14th Earl of Derby, leader of the Conservatives, ruminated that the North's difficulties would only start once it had conquered the South. "It was out of the question that where such mutual animosity existed, and such injuries had been inflicted on one side and on the other," he surmised, that "any cordial reconcilement or union could take place between them." Lengthening casualty lists would lead to "increasing bitterness of feeling" and "aggravating atrocities on both sides." "Under the circumstances," he declared, "there is no possibility of re-establishing the Union between the North and the South."[92] The big question of course was how the conquered states could be administered within a federal democratic republic. *The Times* wondered "what becomes of the theory that Government derives its powers from the consent of the governed, if the population of seven or eight great States . . . are now to be . . . kept down by a standing army in the name of Republican freedom?"[93]

In this context, it is instructive to note that until very late in the day, even a number of those who were utterly hostile to the South did not believe the North could achieve anything more than containing the Confederacy and reducing it to a rump territory. From an early date, John Bright had been convinced that the Union would be restored and the slaves freed, but he was exceptional in that respect.[94] Cairnes's attitude was much more typical. Rule of a conquered South by some sort of military government, he believed, would deal a grievous blow to America's free institutions. Far better, he thought, that the Confederacy should be shorn of the Border States (which included Virginia) as well as the far West (Texas, Arkansas, and Louisiana) and find itself confined by the Alleghenies, the Mississippi River, and the ocean (otherwise referred to as the "Mississippi Compromise" by Joseph Hernon).[95] Despite his publicly stated view that governing a subjugated South "as free and equal commonwealths" presented very little difficultly, John Stuart Mill privately agreed with Cairnes.[96]

Most British observers presumed, then, that a version of the Confederacy would survive for some time. Discussions about this state's future often revealed sharp disagreements about its essential character. For some, the Confederacy, by its very nature, presented a powerful and aggressive challenge to civilization and regional stability. In addition to the inefficiency of slave labor, the rapid exhaustion of lands under cotton cultivation, and the natural belligerence of southern oligarchs, a new self-confidence in their social system born of military victory would inspire southerners to conquer yet more new lands. A slave domain stretching down to Central America and the Caribbean would result, and the Confederacy would reopen the slave trade.[97] As Cairnes described it, Confederate victory would create "a slave empire, commanding the resources of half a continent, fired with an ardent ambition, and cherishing vast designs of aggression and conquest."[98] Mill foresaw the new nation, "professing the principles of Attila and Genghis Khan" propagating its "national faith at the rifle's mouth through Mexico and Central America," while "Cuba, Porto Rico, and Hayti and Liberia" would be "conquered and brought back into slavery."[99] Such things would come to pass unless the Federal government could contain the Confederacy, shut it out of the western territories, and prevent it from expanding southward. Other commentators, who entertained a divergent assessment of the Confederacy's character, predicted that it would chart a far different course with regard to slavery. In this telling of the future, the new Confederacy would be deprived of the Union's protection, leaving southerners alone to face their slaves. If they no longer had the full force of the Federal government to rely on in confronting their chattels, they would at least be free from the meddling of northern abolitionists (who, so the argument went, needlessly antagonized southerners and turned slavery into a charged, political question). Not only that, but as an independent state reliant on foreign goods, the South would be increasingly subject to pressure from "world" opinion, by which most proponents of this argument meant British influence. That the Confederacy would be receptive to this influence was self-evident; southerners were Englishmen living under a conservative republic that respected individual liberty as well as the rights of property. Under these circumstances, the Confederacy would become progressively inclined to abolish slavery while falling increasingly into the British orbit.[100] Peddled most aggressively by British partisans of the South, this understanding of the Confederacy's destiny exercised an influence well beyond this clique, partly because the argument relied somewhat on Tocqueville.[101] Gladstone, for instance, believed that emancipation would come more quickly with southern independence than from Federal victory.[102] This understanding of the Confederacy's destiny, however, brought adherents in collision with Confederate officials like Hotze, who refused to countenance future emancipation.[103]

Regardless of what they wrote concerning the future of an independent South, most British commentators saw the Confederacy as a nation, but one marred by slavery (although the degree to which slavery disfigured the nation was a matter of dispute). For that reason, if most Britons believed that they would eventually have to come to terms with the fact of Confederate nationality, a great many were not at all enthusiastic about the prospect. That being the case, it is tempting to claim that slavery prevented British statesmen from officially recognizing what they themselves saw as the fact of Confederate nationhood. Such, however, was clearly not the case. Bright may have claimed that the Confederacy was uniquely a pariah state because it was exclusively founded to further the principle of slavery, but he did not sit in the British cabinet.[104] As Earl Russell, who did sit in the cabinet as foreign secretary, made clear in his September 1863 speech at Blairgowrie, slavery was no bar to recognition of the South.[105] So why did the Confederacy, which was widely considered a nation in Britain, never obtain official recognition? In this case, it is helpful to recall the distinction between sentiment and policy that appeared in chapter 2. British opinion might have seen the Confederacy as a nation, but British policy, which was guided partly by interests and partly by the precedents associated with international law, could not.

The best place to start studying this question is with William Vernon Harcourt. In November 1862, Harcourt, then a young lawyer (later appointed Whewell Professor of International Law at the University of Cambridge), collaborated with his wife's stepfather, Sir George Cornewall Lewis, to counter Gladstone's arguments in favor of recognition. At the same time that he assisted Lewis in writing his November 7 cabinet memorandum, Harcourt sent a pair of letters to *The Times* publicizing the reasons for avoiding both recognition and mediation. Writing under the pseudonym "Historicus" in these letters, Harcourt made a clear distinction between recognition, which was a matter of law, and intervention, which he associated with policy. In the former case, so far as law was concerned, every state was bound to respect the sovereignty of every other state. No state could recognize the independence of a rebellious people so long as they were "still capable of being regarded in any sense" subjects of a government that they had renounced. In other words, rebels needed to have attained de facto independence before obtaining recognition. While the law was clear, its application was not, for establishing whether rebels had achieved de facto independence was difficult. Referring to the precedent of the South American revolutions, Harcourt determined that rebels could attain this status by establishing their freedom "beyond the probability or almost the possibility of reverse." Such a situation usually occurred, he argued, when their former sovereign had "virtually and substantially abandoned the struggle for supremacy." So long as the outcome of the struggle remained in doubt, however, no other state had the right to recognize the insurgents. Harcourt's thesis rested largely on precedents associated with the American Revolution and the independence struggles of the South American republics.[106] The examples of Greece and Belgium, however, fell into the category of intervention. Intervention was an act of policy: "its essence is illegality, and its justification is its success." These two states, Harcourt asserted, were not recognized after having achieved de facto independence; rather, they were created through the machinations and armed force of the European great powers. While Harcourt conceded that intervention "may be wise, may be right,—nay, sometimes may even be necessary," the main point he developed in referring to the Greek and Belgian precedents was that it was never "short, simple, or peaceable." Using these premises and precedents, Harcourt argued that the Confederacy had not achieved de facto independence, and that intervention in the American conflict was a risky venture.[107] These two main points formed the basis of Lewis's November 7 cabinet memorandum, "Recognition of the Independence of the Southern States of the North American Union."[108] The only significant difference between Harcourt's letters and Lewis's memorandum is that the latter went into much greater detail concerning the historical precedents relevant to the Confederate situation.

We have already seen that on November 11 these arguments carried the day in the cabinet. There were a number of reasons for Lewis's triumph. For one thing, his memorandum and Harcourt's letters were incisive. The latter in particular were models of concision. A number of experts in the field, including Montague Bernard, then Chichele Professor of International Law and Diplomacy at Oxford, agreed entirely with Harcourt and Lewis's position.[109] By contrast, the arguments of Confederate agents and diplomats, as well as those of their British sympathizers, seemed fumbling, irrelevant, or unsound.[110] While Spence's *American Union* (1861) had been a tour de force, his grasp of the precedents that underpinned international law, as evidenced by his pamphlets such as *On the Recognition of the Southern Confederation* (1862), was feeble.[111] For his part, Hotze seemed more focused on showing that southerners constituted a distinct nationality than on proving that their state had fulfilled the criteria for recognition.[112] James Mason, the Confederate commissioner to Britain, proved no more adept. When he claimed in a letter to *The Times* that the Confederacy had achieved de facto independence but that recognition would dissuade the Federal government from continuing its efforts to recover the South, Lewis quickly pointed out the contradiction: if the Confederacy was truly independent and "the contest was really decided," he asked, why was it necessary to discourage the Federals from continuing the fight?[113] Perhaps most important of all, Lewis and Harcourt's arguments gave a majority of the cabinet legal justification for doing what it was already inclined to do, which was nothing. The idea that intervention might entangle Britain in all manner of difficulties and lead to the damage of important British interests influenced this group.[114] On this occasion, as on others, when some combination of Palmerston, Russell, and Gladstone contemplated an adventurous foreign policy initiative, the cabinet sought to keep them in check (although by the fall of 1862 Palmerston had come around to the view that intervention in the American situation was unwise—something that accounted for his "feeble and half-hearted" support of Russell during the cabinet debate of November 11).[115] The rivalry between Lewis and Gladstone, men of very different temperaments, also played a role. Both had clashed in the past, and both were seen as potential successors to Palmerston, but MPs as well as cabinet members tended to like Lewis and respect his judgment more.[116] As the *Spectator* put it, where Gladstone's specialty consisted of stoking public enthusiasm, Lewis's tendency was to dampen it.[117] The cabinet seemed more in tune with Lewis than "The People's William"; so long as the North sustained its enormous efforts to defeat the Confederacy, recognition and mediation seemed dangerous. Finally, the cabinet must have taken heart from the fact that a great many MPs along with much of public opinion hoped Britain would steer clear of the American crisis.[118]

As time went on, the South's military fortunes declined and so did any interest in recognition. Asked in September 1863 by Russell about recognition, Palmerston responded, "As to the Southern States of America, it would not be very logical to acknowledge Their Independence when they are less prosperous in their war than they have been for Some Time."[119] And so, at the end of the day, while the British public recognized the Confederate people, law and self-interest prevented the British government from recognizing the Confederacy.

CONTENDING FOR EMPIRE OR FOR OUR COUNTRY?: THE YANKEE NATION

International law may have presumed in favor of the old Union, but much of British public opinion did not. The mere fact of secession seemed to indicate that something was profoundly deficient in American national feeling. That such a large, well-organized territory wanted to leave the federation suggested that the Union must have suffered from terrible flaws during the antebellum period. In late 1861, the *Daily Telegraph* surmised that "before the war the total disunion between North and South as a matter of feeling was such as amounted practically to a severance. . . . The two communities were as much divided as husband and wife who live apart, who have grown strangers to each other, who have ceased to know each other's way of life, but who have simply deferred the formalities of the Divorce Court."[120] Likewise, *The Times* concluded, "if a nation is to be defined as a community which desires to live under one Government, then the United States before secession were certainly not a nation."[121] The Federal government's initial, dilatory response to secession also implied that the state was not well suited to bind the nation when a crisis hit.[122]

Doubts about the strength of American nationality that had circulated throughout the antebellum period prepared many British commentators to give up very quickly on the Union. As early as January 1861, Lord John Russell concluded that the Union was finished, writing to Lord Lyons that "I do not see how the United States can be cobbled together again by any compromise. I cannot see any mode of reconcil[g] such parties as these."[123] That sense would grow only stronger over the next couple of years, as the Confederacy seemed willing to sacrifice a great volume of blood for the sake of securing independence. The longer the Confederacy remained independent and the harder it fought, the less like a nation the United States appeared.

At the same time, brutal party politics in the North seemed to form a striking contrast with the Confederacy's "anti-party ideology," which stressed "both political unity and social harmony" (to use George Rable's words).[124] Very early in the crisis, Newman noticed that where Lincoln's speeches expressed the difficulties of a man who had to patch the North together, Davis spoke with the "fluent decision of a man who knows that every word is backed up by unanimous zeal."[125] The Confederacy's unity was more apparent than real—as we have seen, the difficulty of getting news out of the South allowed British observers to imagine that a coherent society there explained repeated battlefield victories. The free flow of information from the North, largely in the form of its newspapers, however, seemed to reveal a society that was on the verge of further disintegration. Throughout the war years, Democrats and Republicans threatened to tear the North apart as they argued over the Federal government's violations of civil liberties, slavery, and the war itself.

At almost every important moment during the conflict, British authorities both outside and inside the United States believed civil war was imminent in the North. Shortly before the Emancipation Proclamation was issued, Edward Archibald, the British consul in New York, predicted that "we are in not a little danger of a subordinate war of factions in the North."[126] As the 1862 congressional elections approached, Edmund Hammond (under-secretary of state for foreign affairs) believed the resultant strife would lead to "civil war within civil war."[127] Even in the wake of Gettysburg and Vicksburg, he sensed "the cohesion between the Federal States is weakening daily," and expected the "break up of the Northern federation."[128] Writing to his superiors after the Emancipation Proclamation had taken effect, Lord Lyons claimed "party strife seems to grow more intense" and that "there is no longer a semblance of unanimity in the North."[129] He nervously foresaw "a break up" in the northern states.[130] Such statements were not confined to British officials. To take only one example, shortly before the presidential election of 1864, the *Daily Telegraph* predicted that the political contest would precipitate a civil war in the North.[131]

Many of these criticisms stemmed from a nationalism that sought to deny American exceptionalism and superiority for the sake of sustaining a British sense of preeminence. Where northerners and a number of British Radicals saw a unique experiment of worldwide significance—the last best hope of mankind—many British commentators did not. For those more skeptical of America's uniqueness and importance, like the *Saturday Review*, "Americans are little else than second-rate Englishmen put in a first-rate position." "If we want to understand how they feel and think and act," the weekly continued, "we have only to ask how the well-meaning, half-educated people of a large provincial town in England would act and feel if they were suddenly called upon to govern an empire."[132] The war, so the argument went, had brought American deficiencies to a crisis point, revealed their nature with stark clarity, and made northern delusions untenable. By asserting American inferiority, British commentators could continue to claim the right to counsel and guide. In other words, they could sustain the postcolonial relationship.

Postcolonial considerations alone, however, do not explain why British observers tended to underrate and belittle the strength as well as the idealism of Union feeling. For one thing, many Britons could not identify with a Federal government that initially showed no interest whatsoever in an idealistic antislavery policy. As the *Economist* put it, "if 'Union' meant Negro emancipation as surely as 'Secession' means Negro servitude,—then, indeed, we should be called upon to take a very different view of the subject."[133] With slavery removed from consideration, many observers could not love the Union for its own sake. Even the *Spectator*, which often showed greater empathy for the North than other journals, saw no reason to lament the Union's demise. The *Spectator* understood "Union feeling," but "sincere as this feeling is, we certainly could never be expected as a nation to indulge in any profound grief over the break-down of a democratic constitution which we never affected to admire." For that reason, the *Spectator* could "pretend to no national emotion, and were not the cause of the struggle [slavery] one of far deeper principle, we should probably watch with equanimity" the political crisis in America. Northern claims that the Union was formed for "the whole family of man" was "simply American rodomantade [*sic*]."[134] As F. D. Maurice, the prominent public theologian and Christian Socialist, wrote, "The North may be well excused for loving the Union often more than they love any other cause. But *we* cannot. It makes no appeal to our consciences; it cannot mean freedom to *us*."[135]

Whatever the case, many reasons were adduced to explain the apparent collapse of American nationalism. To cite one example, a *Fraser's Magazine* article from August 1861 presented five factors: rapid growth and prosperity contributed to a lack of virtue; the Americans had detached the liberating spirt of English institutions from their ballast (an established church); the Constitution was inflexible and popular sovereignty was false; the Federal legislature was absurd; and once the political organization collapsed, there was no social cohesion that could glue the Americans together.[136] Out of various lists of this sort that different journalists and politicians compiled, the following three major themes emerged: the United States was too big to remain under one government; the political framework erected by America's federal democratic republic was too flimsy; and American national sentiment, enfeebled by democracy and bourgeois attitudes, was weak.

If the Confederacy was big enough to pass the threshold test of nationality, many British commentators thought the United States was too big. Its very size meant that it included too many divergent interests and diverse peoples. For instance, the *British Quarterly Review* called attention to the wide varieties of climate and geography in the United States, wondering if such a massive territory could "long remain under a single government." The journal went on to ask:

> Is it not certain that the inhabitants of a land stretching from the perpetual summer of Florida to the five months' winter of Maine, and from the Atlantic to the Pacific in the unbroken continuity of a line that would reach from Bantry Bay to Nova Scotia; which, with its 10,000 miles of sea and river coast, offers to some parts of its population every facility for wealthy fisheries, for maritime enterprise and foreign commerce; which, with its near three millions of square miles of soil, offers prairies of virgin earth to the plough, illimitable pastures for cattle, and capacity to become the very granary of the world—is it not, we ask, morally certain beforehand that a people possessing such a country would present, independently of domestic institutions, some marked diversity of character and habit?[137]

To use another example, writing in the *Edinburgh Review,* Henry Reeve (the first English translator of *Democracy in America* and then the review's editor) believed the United States had literally outgrown the Constitution, asking if it could be "extended to embrace purchased and conquered territories, the slave-holding States of the South, and the semi-civilised States of the Far West, nay, even to include the mongrel population of California and the priest-ridden polygamists of Utah?"[138] As we shall soon see, this kind of argument lent credence to the idea that the United States was an empire, but one destined to fail. The large-scale German and Irish immigration that began in the late 1840s only exacerbated these difficulties because it had introduced a foreign and backward culture not easily assimilated by English-style political institutions. George Augustus Sala put the matter in as bigoted a light as possible when he argued that the Founding Fathers had never dreamed that the suffrage they had granted to "respectable gentlemen, farmers, and mechanics of a whilome British colony, would come in eighty years' time to be enjoyed by bogtrotters from Connemara and boors from Westphalia."[139] While an authoritarian government might hold together such a miscellaneous population, there was much doubt that a free state could thrive without a homogenous people.[140]

Reeve's observation, like those of many others, suggested that the American political system was also to blame for the collapse of the Union. Democracy was widely understood as a fundamentally unstable foundation on which to build a national community. Toqueville had argued that "aristocracy has made a chain of all the members of the community . . . democracy breaks that chain, and severs every link of it."[141] Democracy left individuals bereft of a figure or institution to which they could direct their loyalty, and an absence of public feeling was the result. *The Times* declared that "a democracy has no bond of loyalty such as that we own, and no sense of honour or fealty to a Sovereign Power."[142] Since Andrew Jackson's presidency, *The Times* argued, "the doctrine of the sovereignty of the people came to mean the sovereignty of any section of them, and half-a-dozen ruffians thought themselves entitled to hang a man on the ground that supreme power was vested in themselves."[143] Since equality undermined all authority, there were no barriers to the exercise of this popular sovereignty. People raised under such a state of affairs naturally confused what was right with their own interests.[144] Imagining that this attitude was prevalent, many British observers believed that democracy exacerbated conflicts of interest instead of reconciling them. Writing in *Blackwood's Edinburgh Magazine,* Edward Bruce Hamley asserted that democracy was "principally responsible as the cause of that marked and hostile separation of interests."[145]

At the same time, the federal system was not the kind of mechanism that could bind together such an individualistic society. Founded in recognition of heterogeneity, federalism only perpetuated diversity and contributed to the disintegration of the American nation. Many intellectuals assumed that federalism could not be a permanent state of affairs; it was either a step toward fragmentation or further centralization. As we have seen, Tocqueville described American federalism as an incomplete form of national government and suggested that the Union would either be completed one day or, more likely, fall apart. This argument made sense to observers who surveyed the wreckage of the Union during the secession crisis. In an April 1861 article on Lincoln's election and the sources of the American disruption, Lewis cited Tocqueville to the effect that the Federal government was "inferior" to the state governments in a number of areas, that Washington, D.C., would find it impossible to prevent the independence of states, and that "the doctrine of the perpetuity of the Union, except in as far as it is based on the consent and common interests of the States, is a manifest absurdity."[146] In short, the federal system militated against the centralization necessary to keep the Union together. To use another example, the *National Review* also referred to Tocqueville's opinions regarding federalism when arguing in July 1861 that the disintegration of the Union was "always natural and inevitable, and has long been imminent."[147]

According to many British commentators, though, the most important problem of all was the nature of American nationalism, which was materialistic rather than idealistic. Such an argument dovetailed nicely with Tocqueville's argument that American patriotism was calculating. It also fit with Matthew Arnold's assertion that the main weakness of a bourgeois democracy was its low ideals. According to the *Standard,* the Federal government waged neither a "patriotic war" nor a "philanthropic war." Instead, the North fought for "empire, for trade, for the lust of conquest, to gratify vindictive feeling, and to glut their revenge."[148] Thomas Colley Grattan simply described the bonds of Union as "a common craving for money, a common swagger about the prodigious power of the stars and stripes, and a common love of trickery in diplomacy."[149] Robert Hogarth Patterson, the prominent Conservative journalist, writing for *Blackwood's Edinburgh Magazine,* reduced the North's struggle for the Union to a matter of commerce and finance because northerners were not "patriots" but rather "worshippers of the 'almighty dollar.'"[150] These arguments complemented the common view that the Yankee bourgeoisie's naturally thrusting nature made it unsuited for any kind of real community. An anonymous essayist in *Fraser's Magazine* complained about the "obliteration of social ties" in the North which was mainly due to the "gain-getting that was ground into the Federal nature by generations of stern necessity." If England "has been called a nation of shopkeepers," the "Federal States are a nation of traders" who robbed one another relentlessly.[151]

The most common and important charge brought against northern patriotism, however, was that it was enamored of empire for its own sake—a shallow concern with nothing more than territorial grandeur.[152] Accusations along these lines were legion. For example, Robert Cecil did not believe the North fought for a "sentimental cause" or "higher civilization." Rather, it was inspired by "an ancient and vulgar object" that spurred Russia in Poland or Austria in Italy: empire.[153] Sala wrote essentially the same thing in his own inimitable way: "May I ask, calmly and dispassionately, whether patriotism, according to the American acceptation of the term, is not a potent, arrogant, insatiate desire that the United States of North America should be a republic so vast in her territory, so powerful by her population, her wealth, and her industry, as to command the respect and fear of the rest of the world; and whether patriotism of this kind is not, after all, only so much collective selfishness and corporate vanity?"[154] The *Saturday Review* proved especially critical, arguing that northerners equated greatness with control of the entire North American continent, blustering declarations about their power, and unfounded affirmations about democracy. Yet, the weekly charged, northerners mistook the nature of greatness, which was "a moral, not a material quality." America's "big, burly, hectoring frame," the *Saturday Review* concluded, "turns out not to be tenanted by a big soul."[155] Such views were not confined to irresponsible journalists—they were also articulated by British statesmen. In an April 1862 dispatch to Earl Russell, Lord Lyons expressed the conviction that the North sought nothing more than to restore its "extensive Territory." More than two years later Lyons reiterated this charge: "The 'Union' and the 'Constitution' are mere words—what the people really want is the territory—what they cannot bring their minds to submit to is a diminution of the territorial greatness of the Nation."[156]

In October 1861, these views about northern imperialism appeared to obtain semi-official approval of sorts when Earl Russell delivered a speech in Newcastle where he was initially reported as saying: "we now see two parties contending together, not upon the question of slavery—though that, I believe, is the original cause of the conflict . . . but contending as so many States of the Old World have contended, the one side for empire and the other for power."[157] Thanks to *The Times*, "independence" was somehow substituted for "power" in a subsequent and fuller report of the speech, and it was this formulation that the British public remembered.[158] Looking at just these words to the exclusion of all else, many critics jumped on Russell for ignoring slavery (even though earlier in the speech he had clearly referred to its role in causing the war) and accused him of rejoicing at the Union's discomfiture (which the speech did not). These critics were correct, however, in sensing that the manner in which Russell framed the issue—as one of empire versus independence or power—seemed to array the Federal government on the side of oppression and imperialism.

Russell's remarks, which were quoted repeatedly throughout the war, reaffirmed the concerns of those who found something fearsome in America's hugeness and potential for further growth. For instance, in December 1861, during a speech to his constituents at Stroud, Edward Horsman, a well-known independent Liberal MP, quoted Russell and claimed the foreign secretary had "told the truth clearly and forcibly." "The Northerners," he charged, "have been swelling almost to bursting with the contemplation of the future grandeur of the great American republic, embracing one whole continent, with a population so vast and so compact in its structure that it would give the law to all the other nations of the world." Horsman had never met an American "who could give any assignable limit" to "the future grandeur" of the United States. Indeed, Americans saw their country as the "future Government and guide of the whole world."[159] In other words, an independent and newly assertive Yankee civilization would throw off the postcolonial relationship and make a bid to replace the mother country as *the* global power. Some were especially concerned with the ideological component of this challenge. *The Times* in particular seemed consumed with this problem—probably because its southern correspondent, Francis Lawley, was preoccupied with the global objectives of "Yankeedom." Lawley was convinced that Britain was confronted by dual and complementary threats: at home, a party would work to make Britain "more conformed to the American type," while abroad, the Americans would make war on Britain to destroy its position in the world.[160] In correspondence for *The Times* written shortly after the Federal defeat at Fredericksburg, Lawley charged that the Union was not the "best hope for mankind," but rather "a great and overmastering nationality, the terror and scourge of all other nations."[161] Lawley and others, then, foresaw an unscrupulous Yankee global dominion without ideas beyond money and power. In a January 1864 leader, *The Times* emphasized the revolutionary destructiveness of this worldview when it stated that the Federals would eviscerate everything that could possibly limit their will. The Federals represented:

> a new world disclaiming all affinity and sympathy with the old; a new bond of union that was to destroy all other unions, and absorb their materials. . . . Where, by inevitable chance, the new creation came in contact with the old, the old feelings, old rights, old habits, old opinions, there was no compromise, no joining of the broken bones, no healing of the sore, but simply, life, health, and universal extension to the new, and defiance, destruction, confusion, abolition, extermination, death to the old. . . . Their territorial maxims had no other reason than the will of the tyrant. Their future was terrible, gigantic, universal, crushing, and overwhelming, till the vision itself became an incubus, and thoughtful men began to see that if this was the American future, America had no future.

In this future, a "universal organization" would dominate "in which the sovereign will of a majority should override all Constitutions, all international law, all institutions, every right and interest that stood in its way."[162] *The Times* described this ideology as a "Caesarean" imperialism. "Start with a dream of universal unity," *The Times* suggested to its readers, "tolerate no barrier, refuse all compromise, recognize no will but your own, and habitually deal with your fellow-creatures as if they lay at your feet awaiting your clemency or dependent on your kindness." Such a means of proceeding would create difficulties only an emperor could solve.[163]

Against this hostile reading of America's imperial future, however, a number of commentators sympathized with northern nationalism and saw it as analogous to British national feeling. William Howard Russell recognized that the Union had been responsible for "a wonderful prosperity and great social happiness." He also conceded that "the idea of the Union is . . . the idea of one sole dominant Power in the whole Continent of North America." With his characteristic empathy, however, he forthrightly admitted that if he were a northerner, he "would fight for that idea."[164] Writing in *Fraser's Magazine,* James Fitzjames Stephen, who was neither a northern supporter nor a friend to democracy, stressed that the North fought "to support the credit and glory of the nation" and that "if ever a nation in this world sacrificed itself deliberately and manfully to an idea, this has been the case with the Americans." Such "intense and earnest sincerity, and their singleminded devotion . . . ought to have excited the admiration, instead of the sneers, of their kindred."[165] Others were more explicit in their defense of the northern vision of empire. In *Macmillan's Magazine,* Charles Bowen, later a prominent judge, admitted that though the North was not fighting for emancipation, "it is contending for a noble and sacred stake." "If love of country means anything at all," he argued, "if national honour is a cause for which war is lawful, if the existence of a great empire is worth preserving, if the patriotic traditions of strength and unity have a right to touch the hearts of its citizens, the North may claim our sympathies."[166]

It was the ever-insightful Edward Dicey, however, who presented the most articulate defense of northern nationalism. His language harkened back to antebellum conceptions of Americans as a fellow Anglo-Saxon people whose continental imperialism resembled Britain's in civilizing the backward parts of the world. From the perspective of northerners, Dicey argued, the Federal government had been a good one that had allowed a united people to enjoy "freedom, order, and happiness" as they promoted progress across an entire continent. The North fought, then, to preserve the principle of rule by the majority which made Union possible (by putting down the secession of the minority), the dignity of the government (which could not submit "placidly to its own dismemberment"), and the spectacular future that the Union promised (a "vast continent . . . occupied by a hundred states, each ruling itself as it thought best, and all living under one common free government"). Dicey thought this vision was no more "absurd" than that "the little island of England should rule over India and Australia and Canada." Much like an Englishman who admired his own empire, the American "feels that his pride and sense of dignity are involved" in the North American imperial project. Certainly, Dicey stressed, "it is not for an Englishman to ridicule the idea."[167] Writing for the *Spectator,* Dicey also presented perhaps the most affecting view of what this nationalism looked like at ground level. On a train to Boston he encountered a woman with a sick child. Her husband and brother had perished in the Seven Days' Battles. Across from her sat a soldier, "dreadfully worn and ill," who had lost his health in the Chickahominy swamps and received a discharge, yet had never obtained his bounty money. Dicey wrote, "they told each other their sorrows and finally the man consoled the woman with: 'Well, after all, it's for our country, and we were bound to do it.' The woman answered him, 'Yes, that's so;' and though the words might be vulgar, it seemed to me that about them there was something of true heroism."[168] Eventually, northerners who felt the same way as this widow and this broken-down soldier would bring down the Confederacy.

KIN BEYOND THE SEA: GLADSTONE AND AMERICA AFTER THE WAR

In 1876, Gladstone wrote a long essay for the *North American Review* entitled "Kin Beyond the Sea." The date is significant. By this point, Reconstruction had almost concluded, and whatever scholars today might think, British commentators generally judged it a success. The southern states had been reincorporated into the Union in what appeared to be a sustainable manner, and the American nation had decisively surmounted the secession crisis. At the same time, international arbitration had settled the *Alabama* claims (1872), redressing American grievances and restoring to transatlantic relations the goodwill that had been absent since the Civil War. Gladstone, who was prime minister between 1868 and 1874, played a key role in sending the case to international arbitration. His past, however, rendered his position somewhat awkward, since American diplomats supported their claims by using the infamous Newcastle speech as "proof of the unfriendly feeling of members of the British Cabinet."[169] Gladstone took great pains to defend himself against this allegation and wrote a lengthy apologia to Robert Schenck, the American minister in London, that appeared in *Harper's New Monthly Magazine* several years later. In the words of H.C.G. Matthew, one of Gladstone's preeminent biographers, this missive represented "the start of that assiduous cultivation of American liberal opinion which was to be so marked a characteristic of the rest of his life."[170]

"Kin Beyond the Sea" was part of this assiduous cultivation. It reads somewhat like a long, rambling after-dinner speech, but it reveals the crucial ways in which Gladstone's attitudes toward the United States had changed between 1862 and the mid-1870s.[171] Much of this essay confirms Duncan Bell's assertion that as the years passed in Britain, the Civil War was often "dismissed as a minor blip in an otherwise linear march of [American] progress."[172] Gladstone's main purpose in this piece consisted of comparing the British and

American political systems to see how they would influence the destinies of the two states.

Gladstone relied on several well-established tropes throughout this essay. For instance, he used the traditional language of Britain as a mother and the United States as her daughter. Moreover, he stressed the family resemblance between the two: both valued self-government, freedom of expression, practical policies, self-reliance, decentralization, and so on.[173] Yet "Kin Beyond the Sea" was more notable for the way in which it represented important shifts in how Britons thought about America. Gladstone clearly conceded that the day when America surpassed Britain as the strongest nation on earth could not long be deferred. And despite the family metaphors, Gladstone did not believe that America could or should be judged by British standards. The British were an island people among whom "inequality lies embedded in the very base of the social structure."[174] By contrast, the Americans who had taken possession of a continent had "equality combined with liberty" as "the groundwork of their social creed." For good reason, neither nation preferred the institutions of the other because each was suited for its particular mission.[175] As Gladstone put it, the United States had "a marvelous and unexampled adaptation for its peculiar vocation" and "it must be judged, not in the abstract, but under the fore-ordained laws of its existence."[176]

At the same time, in "Kin Beyond the Sea" Gladstone implicitly renounced several of the positions that he had assumed during the war. Gone was the belief that the Confederacy was a nation. The North "gave to the country as a whole its political and moral atmosphere," while the "New England Puritan" supplied "the type and form of manhood for America."[177] Meanwhile, the doctrine of states' rights had become nothing more than "an archaeological relic, a piece of historical antiquarianism."[178] And gone was the sense that the behavior of the North during the war discredited representative institutions. Indeed, if anything, according to Gladstone, the war experience confirmed the virtues of the American people and the soundness of their institutions. In fact, Gladstone went out of his way to praise the North for the skill with which it had resolved difficult social and political questions (for example, freeing the slaves *and* preserving the liberties of the southern states), the self-restraint it had displayed by avoiding military dictatorship, and the honor it had maintained by making great progress in paying off its war debt.[179] Indeed, he closed the essay by remarking on the "great acts and the great forebearances, which immediately followed the close of the civil war," and which proceeded "from the free choice and conviction of the people" who had "rendered a splendid service to the general cause of popular government throughout the world."[180] The United States was by no means perfect, and Gladstone was perhaps flattering his readers, but the Anglo-American relationship had clearly begun to enter a new phase.

NOTES

INTRODUCTION

Epigraph note: Martineau, *Society in America,* 1:v. Martineau introduced her book with this quote borrowed from Thomas Carlyle. See [Thomas Carlyle], "State of German Literature," *Edinburgh Review* 46 (June–October 1827), 310. Also see Elizabeth J. Deis and Lowell T. Frye, "British Travelers and the 'Condition-of-America Question': Defining America in the 1830s," in DeVine, ed., *Nineteenth-Century British Travelers,* 144–145.

Epigraph note: Mackay, *Western World,* 1:219, 224.

1. Russell to Delane, 1861, J. T. Delane Correspondence 10, News International plc.

2. The phrase is Duncan Andrew Campbell's. Jay Sexton draws some important distinctions between books that he sees as classic expressions of the "traditional interpretation" (those that rely on a sociological approach) and R. J. M. Blackett's work. Sexton, however, concedes that Blackett's *Divided Hearts* is "a revised and nuanced variation of the traditional view." See Campbell, *English Public Opinion,* 2; Jay Sexton, review of Duncan Andrew Campbell, *English Public Opinion and the American Civil War,* in H-CivWar, H-Net Reviews, January 2005, http://www.h-net.org/reviews/showrev.php?id=10157.

3. Cobban, *Social Interpretation of the French Revolution.* See particularly chapter 3, "The Problem of Social History," 15–24.

4. This formulation appeared in Jordan and Pratt, *Europe and the American Civil War,* 48.

5. Blackett, *Divided Hearts,* 35, 119–120. Campbell's description of the traditional interpretation divides British opinion into two camps with "a pro-northern one consisting of the working class, radicals and liberals and a pro-southern one containing the aristocracy, reactionaries and conservatives. The first, admiring American democracy and loathing slavery, supported the Union while the second, despising American republicanism and tolerating slavery, championed the Confederacy." Campbell, *Unlikely Allies,* 143.

6. Again, this is Duncan Andrew Campbell's phrase. See Campbell, *English Public Opinion,* 6.

7. Crook, *The North, the South, and the Powers,* 14. See also Crook, "Portents of War," 163–179.

8. Campbell, *English Public Opinion,* 2.

9. Leventhal and Quinault, *Anglo-American Attitudes,* 1.

10. Campbell refers to this problem. Campbell, *English Public Opinion,* 12. For Crawford's work, see Crawford, "British Travellers," 203–219; Crawford, "Anglo-American Crisis of the Early 1860's," 406–423; Crawford, *Anglo-American Crisis of the Mid-Nineteenth Century.*

11. *Saturday Review,* 26 April 1862, 474.

12. See Tamarkin, *Anglophilia*; Hynes, *Unfinished Revolution*; Yokota, *Unbecoming British*; Hanlon, *America's England.* Other works seem to recognize the nature of this relationship without resorting explicitly to the language of postcolonial analysis. Frank Prochaska, for instance, argues that while Americans sometimes claimed that they had invented a new political and social order, many British commentators "continued to see the United States as the wayward offspring of the mother country." For that reason, he asserts, "Where Americans saw differences, they [the British] saw resemblances." Christine DeVine argues, though, that "travel writing about the post-independence United States has been neglected to some extent, in part because of its lack of appeal to post-colonial theorists and its want of that sense of the truly exotic. European Americans were seen in many respects as close cousins to the British and therefore not 'other' in the same way as inhabitants of many faraway places." As we shall see repeatedly throughout this book, however, Britons frequently saw Americans as an Other. The affinity between the two peoples only complicated relations and made the Americans look like the ultimate "mimic men" (to use Homi Bhabha's concept). Prochaska, *Eminent Victorians,* 16; Christine DeVine, "Introduction: Seeing America," in DeVine, ed., *Nineteenth-Century British Travelers,* 2.

13. Hulme, "Including America," 120, 122.

14. Armitage et al., "Interchange," 460.

15. *The Times,* 20 October 1859, 6.

16. Ibid., 14 January 1863, 5.

17. It is hard to describe what exactly unites this area of study, and D. A. Washbrook has observed that it does not "constitute a coherent body of theory itself." Washbrook, "Orients and Occidents," 598.

18. Bush, *Imperialism and Postcolonialism,* 123.

19. Mulvey, *Transatlantic Manners,* 3. Harriet Martineau noted that Americans' "veneration for England" was excessive. See Prochaska, *Eminent Victorians,* 20, 35–36.

20. In this context, a comparison of Fanny Trollope's *Domestic Manners of the Americans* (1832) and Harriet Martineau's *Society in America* (1837) is instructive. Both criticized the United States—but from radically different positions. Trollope was a middle-class housewife whose husband was a failing barrister, while Martineau was a successful single woman who earned her living as a professional writer. Trollope analyzed the domestic manners of America, while Martineau sought to write as a social scientist. Trollope was a conservative who unabashedly employed British standards of bourgeois propriety to judge American society and manners, hoping her description of American deficiencies would inspire readers to uphold the unreformed constitution at home. Martineau subjected the United States to an immanent critique that reproved Americans because their treatment of women and blacks did not conform to the ideals of 1776. Yet both, as women, found themselves walking a fine line. As Christine DeVine argues, "women had to negotiate between appealing to audiences with their adventures or their detailed accounts of the difficulties of travel, while appearing to remain respectable English women who had certain standards of dress and behavior and displayed an aura of domesticity." DeVine, "Introduction: Seeing America," in DeVine, ed., *Nineteenth-Century British Travelers,* 9. Martineau recognized this fine line by attempting to write as a "scientific enquirer" in *Society in America* (1837) and producing a more conventional

(and feminine) travel narrative in *Retrospect of Western Travel* (1838). Kendall A. McClellan, "National Adolescence and Imaginative Freedom: The Traveling Desires of Martineau and Bird," in DeVine, ed., *Nineteenth-Century British Travelers,* 91–92. Unfortunately, women travelers often were criticized for commenting on the public sphere (not their place) or making observations about the private sphere (too intrusive). For an example of these types of criticisms, see Frederick Marryat's complaints about the way British female visitors wrote about American domestic matters. Marryat, *Life and Letters of Captain Marryat,* 2:55–64.

21. DeVine, "Introduction: Seeing America," in DeVine, ed., *Nineteenth-Century British Travelers,* 13.

22. To name one example, Fanny Trollope's *Domestic Manners of the Americans* (1832) was largely inspired by Basil Hall's *Travels in North America in the Years 1827 and 1828* (1829). Hall played an indispensable role in getting Trollope's book published, not only reading Trollope's manuscript for Whittaker and Treacher and offering her a variety of suggestions to improve it, but also helping her negotiate a contract with the publisher. Finally, Hall ensured favorable notice of Trollope's work when he praised *Domestic Manners of the Americans* in the *Quarterly Review.* Heineman, *Three Victorians,* 15–17; Ransom, *Fanny Trollope,* 74; Neville-Sington, *Fanny Trollope,* 163, 168. See also DeVine, "Introduction: Seeing America," in DeVine, ed., *Nineteenth-Century British Travelers,* 7–8.

23. See Nathalie Vanfasse, "Intertexuality in Charles Dickens's *American Notes* and Basil Hall's *Travels in North America,*" in DeVine, ed., *Nineteenth-Century British Travelers,* 169.

24. As Basil Hall recognized, each British visitor to America only took "correct notice of a small part . . . of the objects presented to his view" and these suggested "images in his mind, suitable to his own particular character, and of course essentially modified by the peculiar circumstances of his past life." Hall, *Travels in North America,* 1:184.

25. For just one example, see Nathalie Vanfasse, "Intertexuality in Charles Dickens's *American Notes* and Basil Hall's *Travels in North America,*" in DeVine, ed., *Nineteenth-Century British Travelers,* 170–182.

26. For example, Thomas Colley Grattan's *Civilized America* (1859) devoted an entire chapter to an interview with John C. Calhoun, who argued that "slavery is a necessity for the purposes of civilization." Grattan, *Civilized America,* 1:182.

27. For instance, James Silk Buckingham represented Americans participating in the Second Great Awakening as foreign, alien, marginal, deviant, exotic, irrational, and inexplicable when he compared behavior at a Methodist camp meeting to the rituals of "backward" and "superstitious" faiths from throughout the world: "I had seen the Howling Dervishes in Turkey, the Faqueers and Pilgrims in India and Arabia, the Santons in Egypt and Syria, the Ranters and Jumpers in England, and the Shakers in America; but among them all, I never witnessed more of convulsive excitement, and religious frenzy, than at this Methodist Revival in Carlisle." Such language rendered the Americans as an Other who required the salutary benefits of British guidance and civilization. Buckingham, *Eastern and Western States,* 1:514.

28. DeVine, "Introduction: Seeing America," in DeVine, ed., *Nineteenth-Century British Travelers,* 3.

29. Bhabha, *Location of Culture,* 121–131, 145–174.

30. For a scholarly treatment of this episode, see Coulter, "Great Georgia Railway Disaster Hoax," 25–50.

31. *The Times,* 15 October 1856, 9.

32. Ibid., 16 October 1859, 6

33. Ibid.

34. Crawford, "The Great Georgia Railway Disaster Hoax Revisited," 331–339.

35. For an example, see Charles Dickens's description of an American passenger car. Dickens, *American Notes,* 62.

36. Dickens, *American Notes,* 63. For democratic sociability, see Tocqueville, *Democracy in America,* 2:183. For the surprising way in which a lack of privacy could play out on American public conveyances, see Buckingham, *Slave States of America,* 1:469.

37. Dickens, *Letters of Charles Dickens,* ed. Dexter, 1:395.

38. See, for example, Alexander Mackay's anecdote in Mackay, *Western World,* 1:33.

39. Buckingham, *Eastern and Western States,* 3:39.

40. Coulter, "Great Georgia Railway Disaster Hoax," 30–48. No one could establish definitively whether Arrowsmith "was the victim of a hoax or a dreamer of dreams" (44).

41. For Tattnall's specific comments, see Beeching, *Chinese Opium Wars,* 270; Holt, *Opium Wars in China,* 245.

42. For English-language accounts of the events leading up to the battle and the battle itself, see Holt, *Opium Wars in China,* 224–245; Beeching, *Chinese Opium Wars,* 258–272; Hurd, *Arrow War,* 180–185. For Sir James Hope's account of the fight and his losses, see Bonner-Smith and Lumby, eds., *Second China War,* 393–400. See also Langdon, "Josiah Tattnall," 156–158; Curtis, "Blood Is Thicker Than Water," 157–176. For a more recent recounting of these events, see Platt, *Autumn in the Heavenly Kingdom,* 46–48. For Tattnall's own report from 4 July 1859, see Karras, *Commodore Josiah Tattnall,* 515–519, and Jones, *Life and Services of Commodore Josiah Tattnall,* 94–103.

43. For an excellent account, see Jones, *American Problem.*

44. Reid, "Power, Sovereignty, and the Great Republic," 53.

45. Allen, *Great Britain and the United States,* 413.

46. [Sherard Osborn], "The Fight for the Peiho," *Blackwood's Edinburgh Magazine* 86 (December 1859), 664; *The Times,* 3 December 1859, 6.

47. Crawford, "British Travellers," 213.

48. [David Brewster], "Sir Charles Lyell's *Travels in North America,*" *North British Review* 14 (1851), 541–542.

49. *The Times,* 2 November 1859, 8.

50. *Spectator,* 18 March 1865, 290.

1. ANTEBELLUM AMERICA IN THE BRITISH IMAGINATION

Epigraph note: Bird, *Englishwoman in America,* 321.

1. Nightingale, *Letters from Egypt,* 73–74.

2. [Edward Dicey], "The Outlook for the War," *Macmillan's Magazine* 6 (September 1862), 411.

3. Mulvey, *Transatlantic Manners*, 3.

4. Trollope, *North America*, vi. See Kinser, *American Civil War in the Shaping of British Democracy*, 9. For the widespread nature of this idea among notable British public intellectuals, see Prochaska, *Eminent Victorians*, 21.

5. Tocqueville, *Democracy in America*, 1:227.

6. For a recent analysis of Mill's reaction to *Democracy in America*, particularly in the matters of democracy and constitutionalism, see Prochaska, *Eminent Victorians*, 25–32.

7. [John Stuart Mill], "*Democracy in America*," *Edinburgh Review* 72 (October 1840), 13–14, 40. Prochaska, *Eminent Victorians*, 34.

8. Crook, *American Democracy in English Politics*, 179.

9. For a more extensive summary of Mill's attitudes toward antebellum America, see Prochaska, *Eminent Victorians*, 23–46.

10. Arnold, *Democratic Education*, 16, 18, 23–25.

11. John Brewer, "The Binding of the Free: Creating Great Britain and Its Other," review of *Britons: Forging the Nation, 1707–1837*, by Linda Colley, *Times Literary Supplement* (October 16, 1992), 6.

12. Berger, *British Traveller in America*, 32.

13. Mackay, *Western World*, 2:205.

14. [Henry Hart Milman], "Lyell's Second Visit to the United States," *Quarterly Review* 85 (1849), 190.

15. Colley, *Britons*, 134.

16. Elizabeth J. Deis and Lowell T. Frye, "British Travelers and the 'Condition-of-America Question': Defining America in the 1830s," in DeVine, ed., *Nineteenth-Century British Travelers*, 123.

17. Derby, *Journal of a Tour*, 1. See Prochaska, *Eminent Victorians*, 12, 19.

18. Crawford, "British Travellers," 204–205.

19. *The Times*, 10 April 1858, 7.

20. Tocqueville, *Democracy in America*, 1:14, 400

21. Grattan, *Civilized America*, 1:vii.

22. Tocqueville, *Democracy in America*, 2:230–231.

23. Ibid., 1:12, 15, 27.

24. Ibid., 1:40–42.

25. See Hamilton, *Men and Manners*, 1:299; Combe, *Notes on the United States*, 1:163; Marryat, *Diary in America*, 464; Featherstonhaugh, *Excursion through the Slave States*, 35–36, 167; Hall, *Travels in North America*, 3:394; Grattan, *Civilized America*, 1:114; Lyell, *Second Visit*, 1:53–54; Martineau, *Society in America*, 3:38.

26. Bell, *Soldier's Glory*, 2:315.

27. Combe, *Notes on the United States*, 1:147.

28. Martineau, *Society in America*, 3:29.

29. Trollope, *Domestic Manners*, 2:137.

30. Dickens, *American Notes*, 245.

31. Buckingham, *Eastern and Western States*, 3:39.

32. Kemble, *Journal,* 37–38; Martineau, *Society in America,* 3:14

33. Dickens, *American Notes,* 158.

34. Grattan, *Civilized America,* 1:25.

35. Hamilton, *Men and Manners,* 2:139.

36. Marryat, *Diary in America,* 416.

37. Tocqueville, *Democracy in America,* 1:258–259.

38. Allen, *Great Britain and the United States,* 148. See [Sydney Smith], "America," *Edinburgh Review* 33 (January–May 1820), 78–80. This criticism was echoed by Thomas Carlyle thirty years later in "The Present Time" (1850). After paying due tribute to the prosperity of America (which he could not "worship"), Carlyle asked, "What great human soul, what great thought, what great noble thing that one could worship, or loyally admire, has yet been produced there?" "None," he answered: "the American cousins have yet done none of these things." Kinser, *American Civil War in the Shaping of British Democracy,* 17.

39. Hall, *Travels in North America,* 2:19.

40. [Arnout O'Donnell], "Democracy in America," *Blackwood's Edinburgh Magazine* 37 (May 1835), 766.

41. Dickens, *American Notes,* 248.

42. Mackay, *Western World,* 1:212.

43. Martineau, *Society in America,* 3:206.

44. Grattan, *Civilized America,* 2:373, 375.

45. Lyell, *Second Visit,* 1:159.

46. Hamilton, *Men and Manners,* 1:368.

47. Acton, *Acton in America,* 55–56.

48. Hall, *Travels in North America,* 2:171.

49. Martineau, *Society in America,* 3:283.

50. Lyell, *Second Visit,* 1:48.

51. Ibid., 1:79.

52. Buckingham, *Eastern and Western States,* 1:515; Lyell, *Second Visit,* 1:74.

53. Trollope, *Domestic Manners,* 2:295.

54. Tocqueville, *Democracy in America,* 2:231.

55. Dickens, *Letters of Charles Dickens,* eds. House, Storey, and Tillotson, 3:151.

56. Martineau, *Society in America,* 3:14.

57. Buckingham, *Slave States of America,* 1:470.

58. Ibid., 1:469.

59. Hamilton, *Men and Manners,* 1:122.

60. Billington, *Land of Savagery, Land of Promise,* 195–196.

61. Mackay, *Western World,* 3:36.

62. Featherstonhaugh, *Excursion through the Slave States,* 2:137–139.

63. Ibid., 1:337–338.

64. Ibid., 2:42–43.

65. Ibid., 2:66.

66. Ibid., 2:176.

67. Martineau, *Society in America,* 3:21.

68. Alexander, *Transatlantic Sketches,* 2:85.

69. Featherstonhaugh, *Excursion through the Slave States,* 2:68.

70. Alexander, *Transatlantic Sketches,* 2:63.

71. Martineau, *Society in America,* 1:108.

72. Only a rare few defended slavery outright. Amelia Murray argued that slavery served as a means of Christianizing blacks who were incapable of self-government because God had made them barbarians. Real philanthropy, she asserted, consisted of assisting slaveowners in improving the conditions of slaves as much as possible, not promoting abolition. Fanny Trollope also claimed slavery was "far less injurious to the manners and morals of the people than the fallacious ideas of equality." Although she had left Britain "strongly opposed to slavery," her American experience apparently changed her mind. Murray, *Letters from the United States,* 197, 219, 305, 361; Trollope, *Domestic Manners,* 1:10, 261.

73. Foner, *Free Soil,* 40.

74. Tocqueville, *Democracy in America,* 1:14, 357.

75. For southern views of this interpretation, see Osterweis, *Romanticism and Nationalism*; William P. Taylor, *Cavalier and Yankee.*

76. Stirling, *Letters from the Slave States,* 63–64.

77. Buckingham, *Slave States of America,* 1:557.

78. Stirling, *Letters from the Slave States,* 271.

79. Martineau, *Society in America,* 2:343.

80. Mackay, *Western World,* 2:136.

81. Dickens, *American Notes,* 236.

82. Buckingham, *Eastern and Western States,* 3:32–33.

83. One of the only major works to detail such interactions was Fanny Kemble's *Journal of a Residence on a Georgian Plantation in 1838–1839* (1863). Kemble's situation, however, was unique. She was married to one of Georgia's greatest slaveowners, a position that allowed her full and intimate access to slaves. Nevertheless, Kemble waited for almost twenty-five years to publish her journal because, although she had divorced her husband in 1849, he had retained custody of their two daughters, and she wished to hold on to her visiting rights. See Clinton, *Fanny Kemble's Civil Wars,* 131–132, 178–179.

84. Kemble, *Journal of a Residence,* 304.

85. Hall, *Travels in North America,* 3:39.

86. Grattan, *Civilized America,* 2:181.

87. Martineau, *Society in America,* 2:302.

88. Kemble, *Journal of a Residence,* 249.

89. Buckingham, *Slave States of America,* 2:198–199.

90. Kemble, *Journal of a Residence,* 111, 182.

91. Stirling, *Letters from the Slave States,* 221–222.

92. Buckingham, *Slave States of America,* 1:210; Hall, *Travels in North America,* 3:355.

93. See H. B. Hackler, "'Condemned of Nature': British Travelers on the Landscape of the Antebellum American South," in DeVine, ed., *Nineteenth-Century British Travelers,* 191–193.

94. Tocqueville, *Democracy in America,* 1:354.

95. Buckingham, *Slave States of America,* 2:395; Buckingham, *Eastern and Western States,* 2:446, 494.

96. Stirling, *Letters from the Slave States,* 204–205.

97. Dickens, *American Notes,* 134.

98. Mackay, *Western World,* 2:67–69.

99. Stirling, *Letters from the Slave States,* 221.

100. Tocqueville, *Democracy in America,* 1:389.

101. Stirling, *Letters from the Slave States,* 45, 63–64.

102. Grattan, *Civilized America,* 1:203.

103. Lyell, *Second Visit,* 1:245.

104. Buckingham, *Slave States of America,* 1:123.

105. Hamilton, *Men and Manners,* 2:283.

106. Mackay, *Western World,* 2:80, 133.

107. Kemble, *Journal of a Residence,* 305.

108. Stirling, *Letters from the Slave States,* 343–344.

109. Ibid., 52, 59, 235–236, 245, 298, 301.

110. Mackay, *Western World,* 3:348.

111. Ibid., 2:140.

112. Tocqueville, *Democracy in America,* 1:372, 375.

113. Albert Hourani, review of *Orientalism,* by Edward Said, *New York Review of Books* 26 (8 March 1979), 29.

114. Martineau, *Society in America,* 1:v. DeVine writes that British visitors merely used their American experience to reinforce existing stereotypes and confirm what they had already learned by reading the travel literature of previous visitors. DeVine, "Introduction: Seeing America," in DeVine, ed., *Nineteenth-Century British Travelers,* 8. Elizabeth J. Deis and Lowell T. Frye stress how the political nature of much travel literature made it "almost formulaic in its predictable shrillness." See Elizabeth J. Deis and Lowell T. Frye, "British Travelers and the 'Condition-of-America Question': Defining America in the 1830s," in DeVine, ed., *Nineteenth-Century British Travelers,* 148.

115. [John Barrow], "Duke Bernard of Saxe-Weimar and Captain Hall: Travels in North America," *Quarterly Review* 41 (1829), 417.

116. [Thomas Hood], "Boz in America," *New Monthly Magazine and Humorist* 66 (1842), 397. Still later, on the eve of the Civil War, Thomas Colley Grattan admitted, "No one who writes about the United States of America should be considered an oracle." Grattan, *Civilized America* 1:v.

117. [William Empson], "Captain Marryat's *Diary in America,*" *Edinburgh Review* 70 (October 1839), 125.

118. In the midst of the Civil War, the Reverend Samuel Marcus Dill, former Moderator of the General Assembly of the Presbyterian Church in Ireland, claimed that most Irishmen believed they could farm "by a sort of instinct, without learning the business at all." "A similar pleasing conviction rests upon most minds," he argued, "respecting the American problem, which every one can solve without study." Dill, *The American Conflict,* 7.

119. Kendall A. McClellan, "National Adolescence and Imaginative Freedom: The Traveling Desires of Martineau and Bird," in DeVine, ed., *Nineteenth-Century British Travelers,* 91.

120. Logan, *The Hour and the Woman,* 78–79, 81, 88–89.

121. In any event, both contemporaries and present-day scholars have generally found her work inferior to Tocqueville's, especially when it came to developing "a theory of US society." See Prochaska, *Eminent Victorians,* 21.

122. Kinser, *American Civil War in the Shaping of British Democracy,* 4; Prochaska, *Eminent Victorians,* 21. See also Elizabeth J. Deis and Lowell T. Frye, "British Travelers and the 'Condition-of-America Question': Defining America in the 1830s," in DeVine, ed., *Nineteenth-Century British Travelers,* 149–150.

123. [Robert Lawley], "The Prospects of the Confederates," *Quarterly Review* 115 (April 1864), 292. Circumstantial evidence indicates that Francis Lawley either wrote this article or supplied much of the information that went into it.

124. [Basil Hall], "Tocqueville on the State of America," *Quarterly Review* 57 (September 1836), 134–135.

125. Crook, *American Democracy in English Politics,* 187–188.

126. See Fish, *Is There a Text in This Class?*

127. Reeve himself agreed, writing that *Democracy in America* was "hailed with equal satisfaction by the ardent friends of democracy and by those who dread the exclusively predominance of democratic power." [Henry Reeve], "Remains of Alexis de Tocqueville," *Edinburgh Review* 113 (April 1861), 430, 432.

128. Grattan, *Civilized America,* 2:166–167.

2. THE FORMATION OF BRITISH ATTITUDES TOWARD THE CIVIL WAR

Epigraph note: *Daily Telegraph,* 26 November 1864, 4.

1. Some weeks later, the 5th Duke of Newcastle, the former secretary for war in Aberdeen's cabinet, conceded to Russell, "It was you who turned out the government." Hankinson, *Man of Wars,* 88.

2. *The Times,* 10 September 1861, 6.

3. Russell, *My Diary North and South,* 5.

4. As Sir James Fergusson, who visited America at this time, claimed, if Russell's "exposure of pretensions and fallacies" in both the North and South "gained for his statements a degree of reliance" in Britain, they also "rendered him unpopular with both parties engaged." [Sir James Fergusson], "Some Account of Both Sides of the American War," *Blackwood's Edinburgh Magazine* 90 (December 1861), 768.

5. *The Times,* 6 August 1861, 7–8.

6. "If you could see what I have to bear in railway trains & in the streets," Russell wrote to Mowbrey Morris, *The Times*' manager, "you would at least give me the credit of no common duration & endurance." Russell to Morris, 16 February 1862, Russell Papers 1, News International plc.

7. Russell, *My Diary North and South,* 501.

8. Ibid., 497.

9. On 27 December 1861, toward the end of the *Trent* crisis, the Federal government informed Lord Lyons, the British minister in Washington, D.C., that it would release James Mason and John Slidell. Lyons relayed this information to Edmund Monson, then a secretary at the legation, who then conveyed it to Russell. Later that day, when Russell received a note from Samuel Ward lamenting that the United States and Britain might go to war, Russell sent Ward the following message: "Act as if you heard some very good news for yourself. Dine as soon as you get this." Since Ward was a well-known speculator and lobbyist who was not above shady dealings, it appeared that Russell had given him important political information that would undoubtedly affect the stock market. The management at *The Times* believed this indiscretion was so serious that it considered removing Russell from his post. Mowbray Morris, *The Times*' manager, wrote to Delane, "Russell has committed a grave offence which would be quite enough to entail instant dismissal upon any other man." Delane expressed his "extreme mortification" to Russell as well. Morris and *The Times,* however, did not recall Russell for fear of appearing to credit the *New York Herald*'s accusations. See Atkins, *Life of Sir William Howard Russell,* 2:100–101, 112.; Morris to Delane, n.d., J. T. Delane Correspondence 10, News International plc; Delane to Russell, 14 April 1862, J. T. Delane Correspondence 25, News International plc.

10. Russell to Delane, 13 September 1861, Russell Papers 1, News International plc.

11. Bell, *Soldier's Glory,* 2:309.

12. For example, see Russell to Delane, 14 October 1861, Russell Papers 1, News International plc.

13. Russell to Delane, 13 September 1861, Russell Papers 1, News International plc.

14. Morris to Delane, n.d., J. T. Delane Correspondence 10, News International plc.

15. Morris to Russell, 6 March 1862, Morris Letterbooks, News International plc.

16. Russell to Delane, 16 October 1861, Russell Papers 1, News International plc.; Russell to Morris, 4 April 1862, Russell Papers 1, News International plc.

17. *The Times,* 6 August 1861, 8.

18. Bigelow, *Retrospections of an Active Life,* 1:605.

19. Russell, *William Howard Russell's Civil War,* 100.

20. Russell, *My Diary North and South,* 39.

21. When accused by a Cincinnati paper that he had erred in claiming that President Andrew Jackson had created the spoils system, Russell responded in one column that he was "glad to find M. de Tocqueville, who was in America at the time, labored under the same impression, and he [Russell] is forced to maintain the accuracy of his assertion." *The Times,* 30 May 1861, 10.

22. Indeed, Crawford has asserted that Russell's reporting in 1861, particularly his tour of the South, was the preeminent force that shaped British perceptions of the secession crisis. Crawford, *Anglo-American Crisis of the Mid-Nineteenth Century,* 116–117.

23. *The Times,* 6 December 1861, 6.

24. Ibid., 22 October 1861, 6.

25. As Russell explained to Charles Sumner, the senator from Massachusetts, *The Times* was determined to use the opportunity presented by the war to discredit parliamentary radicalism in Britain: "The troubles in America afford our politicians & writers easy means of dealing deadly blows at Brightism which is often attacked under the guise of war & the trouble in America. The

most irritating articles are often meant for home opinion and Washington is often attacked that Manchester may be beaten to the dust." Russell, *William Howard Russell's Civil War,* 155.

26. Russell, *William Howard Russell's Civil War,* xli. The phrase "*de haut en bas*" (or "*dehaut en bas*" as Summer spelled it) means, literally, "from high to low" or "condescendingly." See also *The Times,* 22 October 1861, 6. To an American correspondent, Russell conceded that, in "dealing blows at Cobden & Bright & Chartism under the shield of the U.S.," the British press was "exciting much ill feeling here [in America]." Russell, *William Howard Russell's Civil War,* 142.

27. Russell to Delane, 16 February 1862, Russell Papers 1, News International plc.

28. Russell to Delane, 27 January 1862, Russell Papers 1, News International plc.

29. Russell, *My Diary North and South,* 5.

30. *The Times,* 22 October 1861, 6.

31. Monson to Baron Monson, 8 July 1861, Monson Papers, MON 25/12/2/23/34, Lincolnshire Record Office.

32. Russell, *My Diary North and South,* 5, 529; Russell, *William Howard Russell's Civil War,* 138, 165; *The Times,* 16 April 1861, 5; *The Times,* 24 September 1861, 8; *The Times,* 22 October 1861, 6; *The Times,* 26 November 1861, 9; *The Times,* 10 December 1861, 9; and *The Times,* 22 February 1862, 9.

33. Russell, *My Diary North and South,* 244, 299, 320; *The Times,* 19 June 1861, 9; *The Times,* 10 July 1861, 5.

34. *The Times,* 12 July 1861, 12.

35. Russell, *My Diary North and South,* 512.

36. Admittedly, Russell stated, "I would rather the North shd. be the victor than the South," but his private and public correspondence is so mixed on this issue that he could not have felt this sentiment wholeheartedy. Russell, *William Howard Russell's Civil War,* 117.

37. Conboy, *Journalism: A Critical History,* 116, 125; Hampton, *Visions of the Press,* 35; Lee, *Origins of the Popular Press,* 55–65.

38. Koss, *Rise and Fall of the Political Press,* 1; Hampton, *Visions of the Press,* 26; Brown, *Victorian News and Newspapers,* 54.

39. Gilzean-Reid and MacDonnell, "The Press," 276.

40. Hampton, *Visions of the Press,* 33–34; Koss, *Rise and Fall of the Political Press,* 1, 93.

41. Lee, *Origins of the Popular Press,* 47–48.

42. Chalaby, *Invention of Journalism,* 35; Hampton, *Visions of the Press,* 35; Brown, *Victorian News and Newspapers,* 30–32.

43. [Charles Bowen], "Passing Events—Retrospect of the American Difficulty," *Macmillan's Magazine* 5 (February 1862), 354.

44. Conboy, *Journalism: A Critical History,* 127, 165; Hampton, *Visions of the Press,* 8, 30.

45. *The Times,* 4 November 1862, 9.

46. [Francis Lawley], "The Prospects of the Confederates," *Quarterly Review* 115 (April 1864), 289, 291–292.

47. Hampton, *Visions of the Press,* 28.

48. [Eneas Sweetland Dallas], "Popular Literature—The Periodical Press," *Blackwood's Edinburgh Magazine* 85 (January 1859), 101–102.

49. [James Fitzjames Stephen], "Journalism," *Cornhill Magazine* 6 (July 1862), 54, 56.

50. Ibid., 54, 55.

51. Writing to Richard Monckton Milnes, the MP and literary figure, Harriet Martineau declared that she sought to "disclaim & denounce the brutality of the *Times* to America," for "if a war between us & the U.S. were possible (which I am confident is it not) it wd be a duty & a necessity to remember & publish how far the *Times* is answerable for it." Likewise, *Reynolds's Newspaper* argued that through its "incessant and malignant misrepresentations," *The Times* had "engendered an immense amount of ill will between" the United States and Britain. In 1863, the *Morning Star* charged that nothing could be more "surprising," "gross," and "monstrous" than "the astounding audacity" with which *The Times* had tried to "gull the public." Referring to *The Times*' readers, the *Morning Star* continued: "we can really have no pity for such credulous and easy dupes, and can wish them no better fate than still to be 'led tenderly by the nose'—as asses are." Toward the end of the conflict, John Elliott Cairnes, the classical economist and protégé of John Stuart Mill, wrote to an American correspondent, "The *Times* blundered and blundered and will continue to blunder to the end of the chapter, all this while as one illusion after another is dissipated, straining hard to assume an air of complacent and self-satisfied wisdom, as if each new event were a fresh testimony to its sagacity." During a debate in the Commons regarding the defense of Canada, John Bright claimed *The Times*' editorial policy was inspired by "a wish to cover its own confusion" and that "four years' uninterrupted publication of lies with regard to America" ought to have destroyed the paper's "influence on foreign questions for ever." Martineau, *Collected Letters of Harriet Martineau*, 4:356; *Reynolds's Newspaper*, 25 October 1863, 1; *Morning Star*, 21 July 1863, 4; Cairnes to Shaw, 14 January 1865, Cairnes Papers, MS 4993, National Library of Ireland; *Hansard* (Commons), 177:1618 (13 March 1865).

52. *Bee-Hive*, 24 January 1863, 4; *Bee-Hive*, 11 April 1863, 4.

53. Stephen, *The "Times" on the American War*, 4–5.

54. Stephen's accusations were echoed by journals that were closer to *The Times* politically. The *Saturday Review* claimed, "If the *Times* is inconsistent, it is so very frequently in order to make itself correspond to a view which it had either failed to anticipate or had misinterpreted. Powerful as that organ is, it follows as much as it is followed." Some issues later, the *Saturday Review* also charged, "There is a certain dash and vigour about the *Times* which is quite without a parallel. The *Times* does everything in 'the grand style,' and it blunders in the grand style also." *Saturday Review*, 26 January 1861, 96; *Saturday Review*, 25 May 1861, 524. See also Leng, *The American War*, 31–32.

55. Webb, *Harriet Martineau*, 315; *The Times*, *The History of* The Times, 2:130–131.

56. Sala, *Life and Adventures*, 2:19.

57. [James Fitzjames Stephen], "England and America," *Fraser's Magazine* 68 (October 1863), 423.

58. Morris to Mackay, 21 April 1865, Morris Letterbooks, News International plc.

59. Beloff, "Great Britain and the American Civil War," 47–48.

60. See the comparison between Gladstone and Palmerston in Steele, *Palmerston and Liberalism*, 23–42

61. Palmerston to Lyons, 10 November 1863, Lyons Papers, 1/26 D3/123, West Sussex Record Office.

62. [James Fitzjames Stephen], "England and America," *Fraser's Magazine* 68 (October 1863), 419.

63. Ibid., 420.

64. [Charles Bowen], "Passing Events—Retrospect of the American Difficulty," *Macmillan's Magazine* 5 (February 1862), 554.

65. *The Times,* 9 October 1862, 7–8.

66. See for instance Russell to Palmerston, 18 October 1862, Palmerston Papers, GC/RU/734/1-2, Hartley Library, University of Southampton.

67. *Saturday Review,* 25 October 1862, 494.

68. Belmont to N.M.R. & Sons, 24 October 1862, Belmont Papers, RA XI/62/108, Rothschild Archive.

69. See the United States of America, *Case of the United States,* 41. For Gladstone's response, see William E. Gladstone, "Letter of Mr. Gladstone," *Harper's New Monthly Magazine* 54 (December 1876), 105–111.

70. Gladstone, "Record of Special Errors," 7 November 1896, Gladstone Papers, British Library, Add. Mss., 44,791; Gladstone, "Some of My Errors," 1894, Gladstone Papers, British Library, Add. Mss., 44,790.

71. Bell, *Soldier's Glory,* 2:306; Sala, *My Diary in America,* 1:289. For a typical, dismissive British screed about the American press, see "The Periodical Press of the United States of America," *Fraser's Magazine* 68 (September 1863), 325–334.

72. *Saturday Review,* 27 February 1864, 248.

73. *The Times,* 21 August 1862, 8.

74. Fremantle, *Three Months in the Southern States,* 5–6.

75. *The Times,* 4 November 1862, 8. There was a widespread belief that northern newspapers were subject to severe Federal censorship, leading the *Army and Navy Gazette* to spoof the report of a northern war correspondent in the following manner: "If something which I am not at liberty to mention takes place, a result which I cannot particularly specify will follow, and if that to which I dare not specially allude should not occur, then the consequence I am forbidden to mention will not ensue." *Army and Navy Gazette,* 6 June 1863, 353.

76. Hotze wrote, "One writer usually writes for several publications, and I have thus the opportunity of multiplying myself, so to speak, to an almost unlimited extent. . . . The establishment of the Index enabled me on occasion to assume the position of employer of the pens of some of these gentlemen. . . . At least half the articles in the Index are written by Englishmen, who, only a few months ago, had but imperfect knowledge of and little active sympathy with the South. It is my object and hope, by this means to found a school of writers whose service in the moral battles we still have to fight will, from their positions, be more valuable than those of the ablest pens of our own country." Hotze to Benjamin, 26 September 1862, *Official Records of the Union and Confederate Navies,* 3:535.

77. *Spectator,* 29 March 1862, 352. It would also appear that British readers preferred British authors, the Duchess of Argyll opining to Charles Sumner that "no American has written better (perhaps not so well) as Cairnes and Mill" on the war. Weinberg, *John Elliott Cairnes,* 75.

78. Brown, *Victorian News and Newspapers,* 213.

79. See letters from Russell to Lyons, Lyons Papers, 1/26 F1/197, West Sussex Record Office.

80. Palmerston to Hammond, 20 April 1861, FO 391/7, National Archives.

81. Palmerston to Newcastle, 1 September 1862, Palmerston Papers, GC/NE/98/1-2, Hartley Library, University of Southampton.

82. Brian Jenkins would probably beg to differ with this assessment of Washington, D.C. He quotes Sir Edward Malet to the effect that the British legation in that city was "the most important mission next to the Embassies." Jenkins, *Lord Lyons,* 213.

83. For an excellent defense of Lyons's record, see Jenkins, *Lord Lyons.*

84. Newton, *Lord Lyons,* 13. Lyons accompanied the Prince of Wales on a tour of the United States in 1860, but aside from that, he spent only four days away from the capital between 1859 and 1862. In the latter year, he took a summer vacation to Britain and made brief visits to Canada (via New York) in 1863 as well as 1864. See Jenkins, *Lord Lyons,* 196.

85. Russell to Delane, 20 December 1861, J. T. Delane Correspondence 10, News International plc.

86. In a positive assessment of Lyons's career as a diplomat, Brian Jenkins describes the minister's approach to collecting intelligence as "professional." As Jenkins puts it, "He placed before his superiors the material with which to formulate policy and then implemented it without reference to his personal opinion." While Lyons was scrupulously honest and fair in detailing his interactions with the Federal government, his representations of northern public opinion were often characterized by glib and unsympathetic stereotypes. Jenkins's positive view of Lyons as a diplomat, however, is otherwise very much on the mark. See Jenkins, *Lord Lyons,* 7, 111.

87. See Jenkins, *Lord Lyons,* 163.

88. See Stuart to Lyons, 10 August 1862, Lyons Papers, 1/26 F2/201, West Sussex Record Office; Stuart to Lyons, 24 August 1862, Lyons Papers, 1/26 F2/201, West Sussex Record Office; Monson to Baron Monson, 31 December 1861, Monson Papers, MON 25/12/2/23/73, Lincolnshire Record Office. See also Newton, *Lord Lyons,* 87.

89. Monson to Baron Monson, 23–27 April 1861, Monson Papers, MON 25/12/2/23/22, Lincolnshire Record Office.

90. Stuart to Lyons, 29 July 1862, Lyons Papers, 1/26 F2/201, West Sussex Record Office.

91. Jenkins, *Lord Lyons,* 120.

92. Russell to Dascent, 15 September 1861, Delane Correspondence 10, News International plc.

93. Lyons to Russell, 29 September 1863, Russell Papers, PRO 30/22/27, National Archives; Trollope, *North America,* 195; Lothian, *The Confederate Secession,* 109–110.

94. The letter is no longer extant. Extracts from the letter remain in only two places: Williams to Monck, 29 November 1861, enclosed in Monck to Newcastle, 30 November 1861, CO 42/628, National Archives, and "Extract from a private letter from Colonel J. Eardley-Wilmot . . . ," Lewis Papers, 2931, National Library of Wales.

95. Williams to Layard, 10 September 1861, Layard Papers, British Library, Add. Mss., 38,987.

96. This report has no title. See WO 33/11, National Archives.

97. Lyons to Russell, 3 November 1863, FO 5/896, National Archives.

98. Lieutenant-Colonel T. L. Gallwey, R.E., and Captain H. J. Alderson, R.E., Report upon the Military Affairs of the United States of America, 2 August 1864, WO 33/14, National Archives.

99. Gallwey to Lyons, 27 May 1864, enclosed in Lyons to Russell, 4 July 1864, FO 5/954, National Archives.

100. Palmerston's note, 3 May 1864, in Lyons to Russell, 19 April 1864, Russell Papers, PRO 30/22/38, National Archives. On the same date, de Grey wrote on the same sheet, "I will have the officers now in America written to in this sense."

101. Borcke, *Memoirs of the Confederate War,* 2:178.

102. *Illustrated London News,* 6 July 1861, 22.

103. Lawley to Gregory, 26 March 1863, Gregory Family Papers, Mss. 624, Box 24, Folder 3, Emory University Library Special Collections.

104. *Reynolds's Newspaper,* 2 June 1861, 1.

105. Blackwood to Spence, 11 December 1862, Blackwood Papers, MS 30360, National Library of Scotland; Blackwood to Bourke, 6 August 1862, Blackwood Papers, MS 30360, National Library of Scotland.

106. See, for instance, Fremantle to Blackwood, 3 October 1862, Blackwood Papers, MS 4180, National Library of Scotland.

107. *The Times,* 12 August 1861, 6.

108. *Saturday Review,* 4 March 1865, 265.

109. *Spectator,* 14 December 1861, 1362.

110. *Economist,* 26 April 1862, 451.

111. *The Times,* 16 October 1863, 7.

112. Ibid., 16 September 1862, 6. The *Saturday Review* reached similar conclusions in much the same manner: "One of the strangest things about the American civil war has been the almost total absence of authentic news from the South. . . . The Confederates have probably not suffered in estimation from the mystery which has enveloped them. . . . The substance of what is known about the South is, that with a comparatively small population and with no military resources except such as they could improvise during the struggle, they have often outnumbered and greatly overmatched the forces which the reckless prodigality of Mr. Lincoln's Cabinet has been able to bring into the field. From this we may safely enough infer the spirit with which the battle of independence is being fought." *Saturday Review,* 6 September 1862, 267.

113. *The Times,* 9 October 1862, 8. For a different explanation of the same phenomenon, see *Bee-Hive,* 28 February 1863, 1.

114. Churchman, "Walter Bagehot and the American Civil War," 378–379, 382–388.

115. Steele, *Palmerston and Liberalism,* 40. See also C. Collyer's assessment of Gladstone's opinion, which he claimed was influenced by "political principle, humanitarian feeling, considerations of policy, and the military situation in America." Collyer, "Gladstone and the American Civil War," 590.

116. Stephen Meardon, "Richard Cobden's American Quandary: Negotiating Peace, Free Trade, and Anti-Slavery," in Howe and Morgan, eds., *Rethinking Nineteenth-Century Liberalism,* 223, 225.

117. Lord Lyons is yet another example of a figure who balanced a number of considerations as he struggled to determine his position on the American question. Brian Jenkins argues that upon the outbreak of the conflict, Lyons believed that while the North would probably win the war, the fighting would be extremely destructive, the crisis would inflict "irreparable damage" on Britain's textile industry, and reconstruction would present the Federal government with insoluble problems. At the same time, "his private sympathies were with the Union and were generated by a

loathing of slavery, a respect for law, and a greater social affinity for the North than for the South." Jenkins, *Lord Lyons,* 7.

118. Campbell asserts that "it would probably not be too much to claim that the litmus test of whether or not one opposed the South depended almost entirely upon one's views about slavery." Campbell, *English Public Opinion,* 18.

119. For example, in October 1862, as the cabinet contemplated intervention in the war, Sir George Grey, the home secretary, wrote to Russell that once the Federal government had given up trying to subdue the rebellious southerners, "we may then well recognize them without any regard to the question of Slavery." Grey to Russell, 27 October 1862, Russell Papers, PRO 30/22/25, National Archives.

120. *The Times,* 28 September 1863, 7.

121. William Schaw Lindsay, "Lecture of Mr. W. S. Lindsay, MP on America and the Americans at the North Shields Mechanic's Institute," 1861, Lindsay Papers, LND/7, National Maritime Museum.

122. Crook, *The North, the South, and the Powers,* 39–40.

123. See *Reynolds's Newspaper,* 27 July 1862, 1; *Colburn's United Service Magazine* (May 1862), 96.

124. See *Illustrated London News,* 26 July 1862, 111, and [Frank Vizetelly], "Underground to Richmond," *All the Year Around* 17 (16 February 1867), 172–178.

125. Gregory, draft of letter, July 1862, Gregory Family Papers, Mss. 624, Emory University Library Special Collections.

126. *The Times,* 27 May 1863, 9.

127. [Edward Bruce Hamley], "Our Rancorous 'Cousins,'" *Blackwood's Edinburgh Magazine* 94 (November 1863), 638.

128. R.J.M. Blackett, who has presented the most recent and most nuanced work in this tradition, has reiterated this point, albeit with a number of qualifications. Blackett, *Divided Hearts,* 17, 119–121.

129. *Lloyd's Weekly Newspaper,* 8 February 1863, 1. See also the *Bee-Hive,* 11 April 1863, 4.

130. *Economist,* 31 October 1863, 1209.

131. Harrison, "British Labour and the Confederacy," 92–95; Harrison, "British Labour and American Slavery," 304–308.

132. *Reynolds's Newspaper* ran front-page leaders every week from 29 September 1861 to 8 December 1861 giving reasons why the Federal blockade should be broken. For the quote about the United States as a working-class haven, see *Reynolds's Newspaper,* 25 October 1863, 1.

133. See Frederick Peel's speech to his constituents in Bury in *The Times,* 15 January 1864, 9. See also Sir Roundell Palmer's oration in Richmond (England) in *The Times,* 16 October 1863, 7, and W. E. Forster's speech in Leeds, which appears in Forster and Smith, *Speech of Mr. W. E. Forster,* 6–7.

134. Colonel Edward Bruce Hamley, who frequently wrote about America in *Blackwood's Edinburgh Magazine,* got to the heart of the matter when he asked whether a policy dictated by self-interest or one of "sentiment" would guide Britain with regard to the American quarrel. (He clearly

favored the former.) [Edward Bruce Hamley], "Our Rancorous 'Cousins,'" *Blackwood's Edinburgh Magazine* 94 (November 1863), 651.

135. *Spectator*, 18 May 1861, 324.

136. John Stuart Mill, "The Contest in America," *Fraser's Magazine* 65 (February 1862), 259.

137. *Economist*, 31 October 1863, 1482.

138. *The Times*, 10 January 1865, 8.

139. *Spectator*, 1 June 1861, 580. Examples of this distinction abound. For one example among many, in speeches to his constituents in Essex, Major William Beresford, the former Conservative chief whip, staunchly supported the government's policy of nonintervention even as he proudly avowed his southern "proclivities." At the other end of the political spectrum, John Elliott Cairnes, the protégé of John Stuart Mill and the classical economist who wrote the influential work *The Slave Power: Its Character, Career, and Probable Designs* (1862), supported neutrality even as he argued vehemently that not only were northerners fighting the good fight, but that they were also impelled by good motives. "The duty of neutrality," he asserted, "is not incompatible with the rendering of moral support." Likewise, in a December 1861 dinner speech at Rochdale, John Bright counseled against "mingling in the strife," but believed that staying out of the war did not dictate neutrality in "opinion or sympathy." For Beresford's speeches to his constituents (he was an MP for the northern division of Essex), see *The Times*, 21 October 1861, 9; *The Times*, 25 October 1862, 9; *The Times*, 19 October 1863, 10–11; Cairnes, *Slave Power*, 24–28; 299–303; Bright, *Speeches of John Bright*, 28.

140. Lawley to Gregory, 26 March 1861, Gregory Family Papers, Mss. 624, Box 24, Folder 3, Emory University Library Special Collections.

141. Lawley to Gregory, 26 March 1863, Gregory Family Papers, Mss. 624, Box 24, Folder 3, Emory University Library Special Collections.

142. Ross, *Cities and Camps*, 42.

143. [Edward Bruce Hamley], "The Convulsions of America," *Blackwood's Edinburgh Magazine* 91 (January 1862), 118–119.

144. Palmerston to Russell, 28 October 1862, Russell Papers, PRO 30/22/14D, National Archives.

145. *The Times*, 23 November 1861, 7.

146. Ibid., 10 December 1862, 8.

147. *New York Times*, 27 July 1862, 4.

148. Stevenson, *Thirteen Months*, 8 (italics in the original).

149. Field to Gladstone, 2 December 1862, Gladstone Papers, British Library, Add. Mss., 44,399.

150. Gladstone to Field, 27 November 1862, Gladstone Papers, British Library, Add. Mss., 44,399.

151. Lewis to Gladstone, 11 January 1863, Gladstone Papers, British Library, Add. Mss., 44,236.

152. Derby, *Disraeli, Derby and the Conservative Party*, 219.

153. [Edward Bruce Hamley], "The Convulsions in America," *Blackwood's Edinburgh Magazine* 91 (January 1862), 118.

154. Griffiths, *Plant Here* The Standard, 105.

155. *Standard,* 14 August 1861, 4; *Standard,* 4 December 1861, 5; *Standard,* 22 August 1862, 5; *Saturday Review,* 23 May 1863, 652.

156. For an example of such a disclaimer, see *Standard,* 22 August 1862, 5.

157. Mill to Cairnes, 15 June 1862, Mill-Taylor Papers, vol. 55, London School of Economics Archive and Special Collections; Cairnes to Mill, 8 July 1862, Mill-Taylor Papers, vol. 56, no. 1, London School of Economics Archive and Special Collections.

158. *The Times,* 11 December 1861, 8.

159. *Spectator,* 18 March 1865, 290.

160. Ibid., 30 May 1863, 2052.

161. *The Times,* 6 February 1863, 7; Monypenny and Buckle, *Life of Benjamin Disraeli,* 4:333.

162. See *Proceedings at the Public Breakfast,* 31–33.

163. Sir George Cornewall Lewis, Recognition of the Independence of the Southern States of the North American Union, 7 November 1862, WO 33/12, National Archives. Only three days earlier, *The Times* had declared, "Everyone feels that this struggle is the most remarkable event in our time. Since the first French Revolution, nothing to be compared with in tragic interest, has been before the world." *The Times,* 4 November 1862, 8.

164. Delane to Russell, 24 April 1865, J. T. Delane Correspondence 25, News International plc.

165. Russell to Morris, 10 May 1865, Russell Papers 1, News International plc.

166. Russell to Delane, 16 October 1861, Russell Papers 1, News International plc.

3. BRITAIN, THE CIVIL WAR, AND RACE

Epigraph note: Cairnes, *Revolution in America,* 16.

Epigraph note: *The Times,* 5 September 1863, 8.

1. Jenkins, *Fanny Kemble,* 441–442.

2. Kemble, *Journal of a Residence,* 15–16.

3. Ibid., 441–442.

4. Kemble, *Journal of a Residence,* 11–12.

5. Deirdre David follows Christopher Mulvey in claiming that Kemble was "unusual in the force of her rejection of Southern claims to civilisation . . . but she was not unusual in her acceptance of certain attitudes, beliefs, and responses that would be identified as racist in the twentieth century." While twentieth-century Americans might find some of her descriptions and metaphors offensive, Kemble's oft-repeated conviction that the deficiencies of black slaves had everything to do with their circumstances as slaves rather than their blackness is a striking assertion that does not place her at all in the same category as Bird, Murray, Thackeray, and Trollope, all of whom subscribed much more clearly and ardently to racial typologies. See David, *Fanny Kemble,* 162–163, 310.

6. Kemble, *Journal of a Residence,* 263.

7. Ibid., 23–24, 255–256.

8. Ibid., 73.

9. Ibid., 183.

10. Armstrong, *Fanny Kemble,* 448–450; David, *Fanny Kemble,* 171.

11. Butler, *Mr. Butler's Statement,* 12–13.

12. Leigh, *Ten Years on a Georgia Plantation,* 70–71, 228.

13. Ibid., 83, 148.

14. Ibid., 147.

15. Clinton, *Fanny Kemble's Civil Wars,* 255.

16. Although David insists that Fan Butler identified herself primarily as an American, the fact that she married an English clergyman and moved to Britain rather than remain in the United States—let alone the old Butler estates—speaks to her fundamentally transatlantic nature. See David, *Fanny Kemble,* 247.

17. Bolt, *Victorian Attitudes to Race,* 46.

18. Adams, *Great Britain and the American Civil War,* 1:32.

19. Blackett, *Divided Hearts,* 36–47. See also Blackett, *Building an Antislavery Wall,* 155.

20. Blackett, *Divided Hearts,* 3–5, 88.

21. Campbell, *English Public Opinion,* 126–127.

22. Lorimer, "Reconstructing Victorian Racial Discourse," in Gerzina, ed., *Black Victorians/ Black Victoriana,* 187.

23. For a recent argument that Britain was an "anti-slavery nation," see Huzzey, *Freedom Burning,* 19.

24. Beasley, *Victorian Reinvention of Race,* 159.

25. Colley, *Britons,* 354–359.

26. Mandler, "'Race' and 'Nation' in Mid-Victorian Thought," in Collini et al., eds., *History, Religion, and Culture,* 226–227.

27. Stocking, *Victorian Anthropology,* 49–53. See also Augstein, *James Cowles Prichard's Anthropology.*

28. Fredrickson, *Comparative Imagination,* 77–87; Fredrickson, *Racism: A Short History,* 1.

29. James Hunt, "Introductory Address on the Study of Anthropology," *Anthropological Review* 1 (May 1863): 5, 13. As J. W. Barrow has pointed out, "the diversity of interests," "the loose terms of reference," and the "fluid state of scientific opinion in many fields" meant that the Anthropological Society was often the "stamping-ground of cranks and exhibitionists of every description." J. W. Barrow, "Evolution and Anthropology," 147. See also Beasley, *Victorian Reinvention of Race,* 9–11.

30. See Hall, *Civilising Subjects,* passim.

31. Banton, *Racial Theories,* xiii–xiv; Beasley, *Victorian Reinvention of Race,* 14, 69–70.

32. Hall, *Civilising Subjects,* 214.

33. Thomas, *Thackeray and Slavery,* 4–16.

34. Trollope, *West Indies and the Spanish Main,* 63, 61, 60, 56.

35. *Saturday Review,* 18 January 1862, 62. For a similar recognition, see *The Times,* 1 March 1861, 9.

36. Lorimer, *Colour, Class and the Victorians,* 33–37.

37. Utrinque, "Concerning Free British Negros," *Fraser's Magazine* 47 (January 1853), 121.

38. Lynn, "British Policy, Trade, and Informal Empire," 3:107, 109; Porter, "Trusteeship, Anti-Slavery, and Humanitarianism," 3:213–214.

39. Lorimer, *Colour, Class, and the Victorians,* 109–114, 200.

40. Hall, *Civilising Subjects,* 427, 432–433.

41. Beasley, *Victorian Reinvention of Race,* 15, 157–158. See also Wood, *Blind Memory, 143–181.* Of particular interest is Wood's discussion of George Cruikshank's illustrations for John Cassell's edition of *Uncle Tom's Cabin*—probably Britain's most elegant pirated edition of the work.

42. Allen, *Great Britain and the United States,* 148; [Sydney Smith], "America," *Edinburgh Review* 33 (January–May 1820), 78–80.

43. Lorimer believes minstrelsy "reinforced rather than caused" the "growth of English racial conceit." The growth of racism, he believes, can "best be explained by the social changes and stresses within English society itself." See Lorimer, "Bibles, Banjoes, and Bones," 45.

44. Pickering recognizes, however, that "imperialist discourse" was not "monolithic" and that there was nothing "fixed or rigid" about it. At the same time, he also admits that "minstrelsy was not simply or wholly subsumed by racial and imperialist discourse." See Pickering, "Mock Blacks and Racial Mockery," 185, 188–196, 208.

45. See for instance, Pickering, "White Skin, Black Masks," 76; Rehin, "Harlequin Jim Crow," 682–701; Rehin, "Blackface Street Minstrels," 19–38. See also Bratton, "English Ethiopians," 138.

46. Pickering, "White Skin, Black Masks," 88.

47. Lott, *Love and Theft,* 20.

48. Ibid., 234. Richard Huzzey's interpretation of minstrelsy's impact on Britain does not stress this multivalence. He argues "minstrel shows must be counted as anti-slavery entertainment." See Huzzey, *Freedom Burning,* 17.

49. Huzzey's understanding of how *Uncle Tom's Cabin* influenced British opinion is of a piece with his analysis of minstrelsy. Huzzey appears to argue that Stowe's book was read simply as an anti-slavery work. Huzzey, *Freedom Burning,* 18, 21–22.

50. Meer, *Uncle Tom Mania,* 44.

51. Ibid., 7.

52. Ibid., 157.

53. Douglass, *Frederick Douglass Papers,* 3:335–336.

54. Kemble, *Journal of a Residence,* 304.

55. Hall, *Travels in North America,* 3:39. In her study of the way British artists represented American slavery, Susan Casteras argues that they "had little taste for extremes." Instead, "silence, concealment, suppression, avoidance or restraint from expressing emotion often prevail. . . . The inhumanity of the abusers is downplayed, with the white males more indifferently observed than vilified; similarly, the separation of black families is implied but not portrayed as acutely felt or excruciating to those suffering this harsh fate." In many renderings, slaves "endure stoically, accepting the dehumanization, trauma, and the violence leveled against them." Casteras thinks these "visual prejudices" helped mute "deep emotions and powerful themes." Susan P. Casteras, "'Too Abhorrent to Englishmen to Render a Representation of it . . . Acceptable': Slavery as Seen by British Artists Traveling in America," in DeVine, ed., *Nineteenth-Century British Travelers,* 249–250.

56. Grattan, *Civilized America,* 2:181.

57. Lorimer, *Colour, Class, and the Victorians,* 17.

58. Blackett, *Building an Antislavery Wall,* 169, 195, 155, 157, 159, 188, 190, 160. See also Huzzey, *Freedom Burning,* 33–34.

59. Drescher, "Servile Insurrection," 506, 509, 513–515.

60. *The Times,* 19 December 1859, 8.

61. For an interesting discussion of what *The Times* was willing to countenance and why, see *The Times,* 28 December 1859, 6.

62. Lorimer, *Colour, Class, and the Victorians,* 166.

63. Ibid., 90.

64. Lhamon, *Raising Cain,* 138.

65. Dicey, *Spectator of America,* 52.

66. Ludlow, *American Slavery,* 1–3.

67. *The Times,* 30 January 1861, 6; Seebohm, *Crisis of Emancipation,* 40.

68. Huzzey, *Freedom Burning,* 33.

69. [Bernard Cracroft], "The American War," *National Review* 14 (April 1862), 507.

70. *Lloyd's Weekly Newspaper,* 10 February 1861, 6.

71. For an example of how British commentators worried about how sudden changes in the status of the South or of slaves would affect commercial opportunities, see the *Economist,* 26 January 1861, 88. See also *The Times,* 16 January 1861, 8.

72. "Our Relations with America," *British Quarterly Review* 34 (October 1861), 490.

73. [Sir George Cornewall Lewis], "Election of President Lincoln and Its Consequences," *Edinburgh Review* 113 (April 1861), 566, 584–585.

74. For General Orders 23, see 3 February 1864, *The War of the Rebellion: A Compilation of the Official Records of the Union and Confederate Armies,* ser. 1, vol. 34, 227–231.

75. Ripley, *Slaves and Freedmen,* 57.

76. Tunnell, *Crucible of Reconstruction,* 84; Ripley, *Slaves and Freedmen,* 58. See also Dawson, *Army Generals and Reconstruction,* 14–23; Gerteis, *From Contraband to Freedom,* 75–77.

77. *Spectator,* 5 March 1864, 258.

78. *Economist,* 5 March 1864, 287.

79. *Saturday Review,* 18 June 1864, 749; *Saturday Review,* 5 November 1864, 552.

80. *The Times,* 3 March 1863, 8.

81. Ibid., 26 April 1863, 8.

82. *Daily News,* 25 December 1861, 4; *Economist,* 6 July 1861, 732; Dicey, *Six Months in the Federal States,* 1:66–67.

83. *Saturday Review,* 11 October 1862, 436.

84. See Doyle, *The Cause of All Nations,* 211–216; Huzzey, *Freedom Burning,* 24.

85. Worden, *The Plain English of American Affairs,* 20.

86. See *The Times,* 9 September 1861, 8.

87. *Lloyd's Weekly Newspaper,* 18 September 1864, 6.

88. It was for this reason that Francis William Newman accused the Southern Independence

Association of "want of frankness" and dared it to defend slavery with the brazenness that the Confederate leadership displayed. *Spectator,* 21 June 1862, 691; Newman, *Character of the Southern States,* 11–12.

89. *Saturday Review,* 2 February 1861, 106.

90. The *Saturday Review*'s founder and owner, A.J.B. Beresford Hope, was a member of the London Southern Independence Association.

91. *Spectator,* 12 October 1861, 1123.

92. *Saturday Review,* 2 November 1861, 460.

93. Ibid., 16 February 1861, 160

94. [Harriet Martineau], "The Negro Race in America," *Edinburgh Review* 19 (January 1864), 204; *Saturday Review,* 20 February 1864, 221.

95. Lorimer, *Colour, Class, and the Victorians,* 164–165, 166.

96. Blackett, *Divided Hearts,* 62, 140.

97. Spence, *The American Union,* 121, 129.

98. Ibid., 125.

99. Ibid., 122.

100. Ibid., 126.

101. Ibid., 127.

102. Ibid., 129.

103. *Economist,* 21 June 1862, 680.

104. Earl Russell's 1862 mediation plan was premised on the fear that the proclamation would "excite the passions of the slave" and culminate in "acts of plunder, of incendiarism, and of revenge." Bourne and Watt, eds., *British Documents on Foreign Affairs—Reports and Papers from the Foreign Office Confidential Print., Part 1, From the Mid-Nineteenth Century to the First World War, Series C, North America, 1837–1914,* vol. 6, *The Civil War Years, 1862–1865,* 95. Richard Huzzey stresses the degree to which British commentators feared that emancipation would spark a race war with all sorts of terrible atrocities. Huzzey, *Freedom Burning,* 24.

105. The *Standard* claimed the slaves were not ready for immediate emancipation because they still lived in a "semi-savage state, unaccustomed to provide for themselves or one another," and remained "strangers to the restraint of lust and passion." An insurrection waged by such people would include "murder, arson, [and] outrages of every kind describable and indescribable." The origins of their "semi-savage state" remained unclear in this explanation. *Standard,* 7 October 1862, 4; *Standard,* 8 October 1862, 4.

106. *Reynolds's Newspaper,* October 19, 1862, 1. Few journals viewed a slave insurrection with as much equanimity as *Reynolds's Newspaper* when it argued "we should hail a successful servile insurrection as one of the greatest blessings that could befall mankind. . . . We have no pity for the slave-master; all our sympathies are enlisted with the slave." *Reynolds's Newspaper,* 18 January 1863, 4.

107. Cobden to Bright, 7 January 1862, Cobden Papers, British Library, Add. Mss., 43,652; *Standard,* 8 October 1862, 4.

108. Tocqueville, *Democracy in America,* 1:372–375.

109. *Army and Navy Gazette,* 14 February 1863, 97; *Economist,* 25 October 1862, 1178.

110. *Morning Star,* 1 January 1863, 1.

111. *Saturday Review,* 2 February 1861, 106.

112. Lawrence, *Border and Bastille,* 297. For other examples of the same phenomenon, see *The Times,* 9 October 1862, 9; *Saturday Review,* 11 October 1862, 437; *Economist,* 25 October 1862, 1178.

113. *Illustrated London News,* 26 July 1862, 111; [Frank Vizetelly], "Underground to Richmond," *All the Year Around* 17 (16 February 1867), 172–178.

114. [Frank Vizetelly], "Charleston Under Fire," *Cornhill Magazine* 10 (July 1864), 100–101.

115. *Illustrated London News,* 10 January 1863, 44.

116. Vizetelly's reference in the caption to their song "I Don't Like the Lowland Gal" (whose lyrics look much like those associated with minstrelsy) is particularly interesting. Some years after the war, while writing an essay about smuggling himself into the Confederacy, Vizetelly had a crew of six African Americans rowing him across the Patuxent River in Maryland while singing "I Don't Like the Lowland Gal." Apparently, from Vizetelly's perspective, all African American songs had a kind of generic quality that made them interchangeable. *Illustrated London News,* 18 April 1863, 432; [Frank Vizetelly], "Underground to Richmond," *All the Year Around* 17 (16 February 1867), 175.

117. *Illustrated London News,* 5 December 1863, 561.

118. Ibid., 23 May 1863, 552.

119. Lorimer, *Colour, Class, and the Victorians,* 210–211.

120. *The Times,* 30 May 1861, 10.

121. Evidence suggests that Edward Lawson, the owner, and Thornton Hunt, the editor, had a good understanding of what kind of correspondence Sala would supply to the *Daily Telegraph.* According to Sala, "frequent and protracted were the conferences between the proprietors of the *Daily Telegraph* and myself as to how my mission to America in the midst of war was to be carried out. They knew perfectly well that as the son of a West Indian lady and the grandson of a West Indian slave-owner, my sympathies were on the side of the South." Sala, *Life and Adventures,* 2:19.

122. Straus, *Sala,* 138, 140.

123. Sala, *My Diary in America,* 1:39.

124. Fahs, *The Imagined Civil War,* 13–14, 152–153.

125. Ibid., 181–189.

126. See Lawley to Gregory, 26 March 1863, Gregory Family Papers, Mss. 624, Box 24, Folder 3, Emory University Library Special Collections. On the basis of incidents he related in *Down South; or, An Englishman's Experience at the Seat of the American War,* the *Economist* was certain that Samuel Phillips Day, southern correspondent for the *Morning Herald,* had been fooled by his hosts. See Day, *Down South,* 2:167–168; *Economist,* 19 April 1862, 1–2.

127. Sala, *Things I Have Seen,* 1:218.

128. "Moral Aspects of the American Struggle," *British Quarterly Review* 38 (July 1863), 226–227.

129. [Thomas Ellison], "American Slavery: The Impending Crisis," *Westminster Review* 75/19 (January 1861), 87.

130. Kemble, *Journal of a Residence,* 10–13.

131. *The Times,* 26 April 1862, 8.

132. Cossham, *The American War,* 22.

133. *Saturday Review,* 18 June 1864, 748–749.

134. The most significant recent work linking the Civil War to the development of racist attitudes in Britain consists of essays focusing on the activities of Hotze. See Robert J. C. Young, "Egypt in America, the Confederacy in London," in *Colonial Desire*; Bonner, "Slavery, Confederate Diplomacy, and the Racialist Mission of Henry Hotze," 288–316.

135. Hotze, *Henry Hotze,* 3–5.

136. Bonner, "Slavery, Confederate Diplomacy, and the Racialist Mission of Henry Hotze," 289–290, 295, 303, 305.

137. *Index,* 10 December 1863, 523.

138. Hotze to Benjamin, 29 July 1864, Hotze Papers, Library of Congress; *Index,* 27 April 1865, 264.

139. [James Fitzjames Stephen], "England and America," *Fraser's Magazine* 68 (October 1863), 437.

140. Blackett, *Divided Hearts,* 87. See also Huzzey, *Freedom Burning,* 31.

141. Bonner, "Slavery, Confederate Diplomacy, and the Racialist Mission of Henry Hotze," 316.

142. This failure was also partly due to the tremendous problems inherent in such a project and the fact that the Britons and Americans who promoted these ideas subscribed to very different racial mythologies. See Bonner, "Roundheaded Cavaliers," 34–59; Dawson, "The Puritan and the Cavalier," 597–614.

143. See Bright's 4 December 1861 dinner speech at Rochdale in Bright, *Speeches of John Bright,* 11. See also Bolt, *The Anti-Slavery Movement,* 141–146.

144. *The Times,* 13 January 1865, 7.

145. Dilke, *Greater Britain,* 1:25.

146. *The Times,* 5 September 1863, 8.

147. Ibid., 26 March 1863, 10.

148. Kristianne Kalata Vaccaro, "Telling 'A Still More Dismal Story': Cultural Role-Playing and Surrogate Narration in Kemble's *Georgian* Journal," in DeVine, ed., *Nineteenth-Century British Travelers,* 263–266.

149. Indeed, Pierce Butler complained that Kemble "constantly indulged" in a "spirit of unwise comparison . . . between my country and her own." "Almost every thing which she found different from what she was accustomed to," he wrote, "was pronounced inferior and wrong." Butler, *Mr. Butler's Statement,* 21–22.

150. Kristianne Kalata Vaccaro quotes Jenny Sharpe to the effect that female British abolitionists suffered from "double-positioning," where they oscillated "between a dominant position of race and a subordinate one of gender" and thereby enjoyed "restricted access to colonial authority." A woman in such a position tended to "make the analogy between [her] own subordinate place in the antislavery movement and that of the slaves on whose behalf [she] speaks." This positioning is evident in Kemble's tendency to argue that she and the slaves on Butler Island and Hampton Point

were subject to the same master—Pierce Butler. Kristianne Kalata Vaccaro, "Telling 'A Still More Dismal Story': Cultural Role-Playing and Surrogate Narration in Kemble's *Georgian* Journal," in DeVine, ed., *Nineteenth-Century British Travelers*, 259–259.

151. Kemble, *Journal of a Residence*, 171.

152. [Edward Dicey], "Notes of a Tour through the Border States," *Macmillan's Magazine* 6 (June 1862), 139.

4. British Views of American Society and Politics during the Civil War

Epigraph note: *Daily News*, 18 November 1862, 5.

Epigraph note: *Spectator*, 26 November 1864, 1346.

1. *Hansard* (Commons), 163:134 (27 May 1861).

2. Campbell, *English Public Opinion*, 142. See Moran, *Journal of Benjamin Moran*, 2:820.

3. Jordan and Pratt, *Europe and the American Civil War*, 57.

4. Campbell, *English Public Opinion*, 142–144.

5. For the entire speech, see *Hansard* (Commons), 163:131–136 (27 May 1861).

6. Ibid., 163:276–278 (30 May 1861).

7. Ibid., 163:195 (28 May 1861).

8. Ibid., 163:278 (30 May 1861).

9. In October 1861, at the South-West Middlesex Agricultural Society's annual show, George Byng, Viscount Enfield (Liberal MP for Middlesex), revealed to his constituents that the House of Commons had considered discussing the American crisis repeatedly during the previous session. However, "that House expressed an unanimous opinion that that delicate and painful subject should not be debated." In 1862, even the notoriously choleric and independent-minded Sir John Roebuck chose to express his controversial opinions about the war in his constituency of Sheffield rather than in parliament. As he told *The Times*, "if he were to say in the House of Commons what he has now said at Sheffield, the House would be held partially responsible for the opinions he expressed, whereas he wished that responsibility to be wholly his own." As we shall see, while MPs made few observations in the Commons regarding America, like Roebuck, they were far less restrained when they visited their constituencies. William Schaw Lindsay did constitute an exception. In July 1862, Lindsay, a Confederate sympathizer and a Liberal MP for Sunderland, brought forward a motion to recognize the Confederacy. Lindsay acknowledged Russell's request that the Commons refrain from using words that "might exasperate the Northern States" and stated that "he would endeavor as far as possible to avoid all subjects likely to cause irritation." For that reason, Lindsay continued, he would refrain from mentioning the sinking of the stone fleet in Charleston harbor or General Benjamin Butler's activities in New Orleans. It is hard to determine whether Lindsay, who had a reputation as a poor speaker, was being obtuse or deliberately provocative. At one point in the discussion, Palmerston plainly expressed "regret that the debate had been brought on" because "things have been said in the warmth of debate which must tend to irritate and wound

the feelings of both" the North and the South. Palmerston later wrote to Queen Victoria that he "regretted the discussion because many violent things had been said against both belligerents." *The Times*, 10 October 1861, 7; *The Times*, 2 August 1862, 8; *Hansard* (Commons), 168:511, 570 (18 July 1862); Krein, *The Last Palmerston Government*, 65.

10. Campbell, *English Public Opinion*, 141.

11. Cowling, *1867: Disraeli, Gladstone and Revolution*, 2, 80; Smith, *Making of the Second Reform Bill*, 28, 45, 50; Hall, McClelland, and Rendall, *Defining the Victorian Nation*, 9, 83. For criticisms of all three works, see Saunders, *Democracy and the Vote*. See also Saunders's response to Henry Miller's review: Henry Miller, review of *Democracy and the Vote in British Politics, 1848–1867: The Making of the Second Reform Act*, by Robert Saunders, "Reviews in History," January 2011, http://www.history.ac.uk/reviews/review/1131 (accessed May 3, 2013).

12. In November 1863, even the radical working-class *Bee-Hive* declared, "There is but a handful of men in the House of Commons at present who are opposed to Reform in *every* shape and to *any* extent. Even the Derbyites have committed themselves to a Reform policy. The difficulty, however, is that there is considerable division in the Liberal camp on this subject." *Bee-Hive*, 21 November 1863, 4.

13. Saunders, *Democracy and the Vote*, 8–9.

14. Vincent, *Formation of the British Liberal Party*, 4.

15. For an explanation of how borough freeholders participated in county elections, see Saunders, *Democracy and the Vote*, 111, 114.

16. Campbell, *English Public Opinion*, 143.

17. The Conservatives sought to lower the county franchise to £10 (a move that would have resulted in more Liberal votes) but also proposed barring borough freeholders from voting in county elections (a change that probably would have transformed the West Riding into a Conservative stronghold). At the same time, the Conservatives planned to create a boundary commission that would cut the suburbs of towns out of the counties and place them in parliamentary boroughs (another move that would have resulted in Conservative dominance of the counties). Campbell, *English Public Opinion*, 143; Saunders, *Democracy and the Vote*, 111.

18. *Hansard* (Commons), 163:605–609 (3 May 1860).

19. At the time, qualifications for voting in the counties were higher than in the boroughs.

20. Zimmerman, "Liberal Speech," 1180.

21. *The Times*, 6 July 1861, 12.

22. *Spectator*, 3 August 1861, 832.

23. Zimmerman, "Liberal Speech," 1184–1185. Throughout 1861, there was obviously a great deal of dissatisfaction with Ramsden in his constituency, most of which had to do with his position on parliamentary reform and the repeal of the paper duties. See *The Times*, 23 August 1861, 9; *The Times*, 29 August 1861, 6.

24. Hawkins, *British Party Politics*, 1–13.

25. Brown, *Palmerston*, 312.

26. Ibid., 299–300.

27. Biagini, *Gladstone*, 33.

28. Matthew, *Gladstone*, 114.

29. Feuchtwanger, *Gladstone*, 114.

30. Laurence Fenton claims that "the true moment of rapprochement" between Palmerston and *The Times* took place in August 1855, toward the beginning of Palmerston's first administration, when he appointed Robert Lowe vice-president of the Board of Trade. Lowe, who was a leader writer for *The Times*, had been John Thadeus Delane's tutor at Oxford. Other developments that contributed to this rapprochement included the repeal of the Stamp Act (July 1855) and Henry Reeve's departure from *The Times* (also in July 1855) to assume the editorship of the *Edinburgh Review*. Fenton, *Palmerston and* The Times, 136–138.

31. Steele, *Palmerston and Liberalism*, 25.

32. Ibid., 24. See also *The Times*, 20 October 1864, 6.

33. *The Times*, 28 October 1858, 7.

34. Edsall, *Richard Cobden*, 329.

35. Robbins, *John Bright*, 147.

36. Hawkins, *The Forgotten Prime Minister*, 2:241, 245, 249, 253.

37. Maxwell, *Life and Letters of the Fourth Earl of Clarendon*, 2:167. For more evidence of such fears, see Shain, "English Novelists," 402.

38. See, for example, *Standard*, 19 January 1861, 4; *Standard*, 2 April 1861, 4; *Daily Telegraph*, 4 February 1861, 4.

39. Crook, *The North, the South, and the Powers*, 39–40.

40. Ibid., 206.

41. *Spectator*, 5 October 1861, 1084. The *Economist* laid out some of the most important considerations influencing this conflicted discussion about emancipation. Assessing the North's situation, it was clear now that "there were achievements which even *its* power could not compass, and deeds which even *its* cause could never sanction." In other words, the Federals were faced with a bad choice: either continue their ineffective prosecution of the war (and lose) or embrace emancipation. If the Federals chose "to adopt a decided and energetic policy on the emancipation question," such a tack would divide the North and produce a war of a "more desperate character"—a prospect that hardly enthused the *Economist*. *Economist*, 23 August 1862, 925–926. See also Huzzey, *Freedom Burning*, 24–25.

42. For commentary on the change in British opinion during this period, see *Standard*, 2 April 1861, 4; *The Times*, 9 October 1861, 6.

43. For instance, after McCellan's defeat during the Seven Days' Battles, *Reynolds's Newspaper* proclaimed, "The great Federal windbag has collapsed. The blatant boastings of the Yankees have fructified the disaster. The grand army of the Potomac has been beaten, driven, routed, and reduced to the condition of the fag end of a mob." *Reynolds's Newspaper*, 27 July 1862, 1

44. *Saturday Review*, 27 December 1862, 765.

45. Ibid., 26 November 1864, 646.

46. *Standard*, 5 September 1862, 4.

47. *The Times*, 6 January 1862, 8. While the *Spectator* commented on how little was known about the South, it observed that "in the North every detail pleasant and unpleasant is instantly

given to the world." In his famous *Fraser's Magazine* article of February 1862, a sympathetic John Stuart Mill admitted that "a democratic Government always shows worst where other Governments generally show best, on its outside." *Spectator,* 25 May 1861, 552; John Stuart Mill, "The Contest in America," *Fraser's Magazine* 65 (February 1862), 259.

48. *Saturday Review,* 6 September 1862, 267. For similar remarks from the other side of the political spectrum, see the *Morning Star,* 8 September 1862, 4.

49. [William Rathbone Greg], "The Civil War in America," *National Review* 13 (July 1861), 167.

50. *Standard,* 16 July 1862, 4.

51. Cobden to Bright, 6 October 1862, Cobden Papers, British Library, Add. Mss., 43,652.

52. [Robert Cecil], "Democracy on Its Trial," *Quarterly Review* 111 (July 1861), 285.

53. *The Times,* 12 August 1861, 6.

54. Ibid., 21 October 1861, 9. On the same page, see the speech of Charles Du Cane, the other Conservative MP for Essex Northern. For a similar statement, see the speech by the Honorable Frederick Lygon, then Conservative MP for Tewksbury, later the 6th Earl Beauchamp, in *The Times,* 1 November 1861, 9, and the speech by Lord John Manners (Conservative MP for North Leicestershire and later the 7th Duke of Rutland) in *The Times,* 24 October 1861, 8.

55. *Saturday Review,* 1 February 1862, 118

56. Russell, *William Howard Russell's Civil War,* 155.

57. [Robert Cecil], "Democracy on Its Trial," *Quarterly Review* 111 (July 1861), 286.

58. Not surprisingly, Charles Neate, the Liberal MP for Oxford (as well as a fellow at Oriel College), detected a tendency among British journalists to make American democracy serve the same purpose as drunken helots had in Sparta—as an example to be shunned. As Neate claimed, "It now seemed to be the practice of a large portion of the English press to place all the defects of the American institutions before the English people with a view of warning them against the errors of democracy, and he could not help thinking that this was done chiefly for the purpose of decrying popular institutions in this country." *The Times,* 2 January 1862, 10.

59. *The Times,* 1 November 1861, 9.

60. *Spectator,* 10 January 1863, 1492.

61. *The Times,* 2 January 1863, 7.

62. Ibid., 5 March 1861, 9; ibid., 12 March 1861, 9.

63. *Economist,* 16 March 1861, 283.

64. John Stuart Mill, "The Contest in America," *Fraser's Magazine* 65 (February 1862), 260.

65. *Spectator,* 1 February 1862, 126.

66. *Reynolds's Newspaper,* 23 February 1862, 1.

67. Cobden to Bright, 29 December 1862, Cobden Papers, British Library, Add. Mss., 43,652.

68. See entry for 30 March 1862 in Trelawny, *Parliamentary Diaries,* 195.

69. See entry for 7 August 1862 in ibid., 220.

70. *Spectator,* 26 October 1861, 1167.

71. Crook, *The North, the South, and the Powers,* 380.

72. *Daily News,* 11 April 1865, 5.

73. Martineau, *Harriet Martineau's Letters to Fanny Wedgwood,* 232. Richard Cobden shared the same misgivings. He wrote to Bright, "I can't help looking with dismay at the imbecility of the

government at Washington. . . . There seems to be an utter want of central force to direct, control, or correct. . . . This deplorable incapacity is reflecting injuriously on popular interests & damaging every where democratic principles." Cobden to Bright, 10 July 1863, Cobden Papers, British Library, Add. Mss., 43,652.

74. *Standard,* 30 December 1862, 4.

75. "The Periodical Press of the United States of America," *Fraser's Magazine* 68 (September 1863), 331–332.

76. Sala, *My Diary in America,* 2:81.

77. Holland to Russell, 18 November 1863, Russell Papers, PRO 30/22/39, National Archives.

78. Palmerston to Newcastle, 1 September 1861, GC/NE/98/1-2, Palmerston Papers, Hartley Library, University of Southampton. Palmerston also wrote, "The History of the world in all Times and Countries shows that Power in the Hands of the Masses throws the Scum of the Community to the Surface and that Truth and Justice are Soon banished from the Land—we Should all fare in the Same way under the Sway of Bright and his associates." Palmerston to Russell, 28 October 1862, Russell Papers, PRO 30/22/14D, National Archives.

79. Lyons to Russell, 21 October 1861, FO 5/772, National Archives.

80. *Spectator,* 12 October 1861, 1114.

81. [Edward Bruce Hamley], "The Convulsions of America," *Blackwood's Edinburgh Magazine* 91 (January 1862), 121.

82. Hartington to Devonshire, 29 September 1862, Devonshire Collection, 340.180.

83. *Standard,* 9 September 1862, 4.

84. *Economist,* 14 December 1861, 1373.

85. Lewis to DeGrey, 27 September 1862, Ripon Papers, Add. Mss., 43,533, British Library.

86. [Robert Cecil], "The Confederate Struggle and Recognition," *Quarterly Review* 112 (October 1862), 549–559, 562.

87. *Lloyd's Weekly Newspaper,* 3 March 1861, 6.

88. *Reynolds's Newspaper,* 11 August 1861, 1.

89. Ibid., 22 December 1861, 1. When Lincoln issued the Emancipation Proclamation, however, much was forgiven. See, for instance, *Reynolds's Newspaper,* 18 January 1863, 4.

90. *The Times,* 26 August 1861, 6.

91. *Spectator,* 12 October 1861, 1114

92. Ferguson, *America during and after the War,* 120. See also Dicey, *Six Months in the Federal States,* 1:291.

93. *Army and Navy Gazette,* 9 August 1862, 501. Russell expressed something similar when he wrote to John Bigelow in August 1861: "When you left America last, you left also

A free Press—Prosperity—A Constitution

Habeas Corpus

Peace

I hope you may come back and find them. There is now—

No freedom of the Press—A passport system—Domiciliary visits

Police surveillance—Fort Lafayette—a bastille

No freedom of the person—

War calamity and distress—

Irresponsible Govt.—"

See Bigelow, *Retrospections of an Active Life,* 1:370; Lyons to Russell, 6 September 1861, Russell Papers, PRO 30/22/35.

94. *The Times,* 19 November 1861, 6.

95. Ibid., 31 December 1861, 7. Such arguments became a staple of Charles Mackay's correspondence from New York. See *The Times,* 4 August 1862, 9; *The Times,* 16 September 1862, 7; and *The Times,* 13 July 1863, 2. See also Sala, *My Diary in America,* 1:15; *Lloyd's Weekly Newspaper,* 31 May 1863, 1

96. *The Times,* 22 November 1864, 6.

97. Ibid., 18 March 1862, 9.

98. 4th Earl of Carnarvon, "Present State of the Civilised World" (1864?), Carnarvon Papers, British Library, Add. Mss., 60,959.

99. *Spectator,* 5 July 1862, 744.

100. Palmerston to Russell, 25 April 1862, Russell Papers, PRO 30/22/22, National Archives.

101. *Economist,* 4 January 1862, 1.

102. *Illustrated London News,* 30 August 1862, 221.

103. Stanhope to Lewis, 14 August 1862, Lewis Papers, Harpton Court Mss., C/2441, National Library of Wales.

104. Lyons to Wodehouse, 16 July 1861, Lyons Papers, 1/26 C5/106, West Sussex Record Office.

105. *Saturday Review,* 18 January 1861, 67. See also the *Saturday Review,* 8 February 1862, 151.

106. *Spectator,* 28 February 1863, 1688, 1699.

107. Ibid., 28 February 1863, 1700.

108. For a good summary of Bagehot's thoughts on these matters, see Prochaska, *Eminent Victorians,* 47–71. Bagehot's earliest extended treatment of the American Constitution appeared in [Walter Bagehot], "The American Constitution at the Present Crisis," *National Review* 13 (October 1861), 465–493.

109. *Economist,* 20 April 1861, 424–425; *Economist,* 1 June 1861, 591–593.

110. Ibid., 14 January 1865, 35; ibid., 21 December 1861, 1401–1402.

111. Ibid., 9 August 1862, 872; ibid., 10 January 1863, 30. For an extensive discussion of Bagehot's views of American democracy, see Kinser, *American Civil War in the Shaping of British Democracy,* 91–126.

112. Blackett, *Divided Hearts,* 63.

113. *Economist,* 21 June 1862, 680. See chapter 3.

114. Spence, *The American Union,* 6–15.

115. Ibid., 27.

116. Ibid., 47.

117. Ibid., 42–44, 65–66, 72–73.

118. Ibid., 21, 23.

119. Ibid., 44.

120. For a discussion of these ideas, see Weinberg, *John Elliott Cairnes,* 16–18. See also Cairnes, *The Slave Power,* 69–70.

121. For a precise discussion of Cairnes's sources, see Miller, "J. E. Cairnes on the Economics of American Negro Slavery," 335.

122. Mill to Cairnes, 18 August 1861, Mill-Taylor Papers, vol. 55; Mill to Cairnes, 25 November 1861, Mill-Taylor Papers, vol. 55; Cairnes to Mill, 25 August 1861, Mill-Taylor Papers, vol. 56, no. 1; Mill to Cairnes, 18 August 1861, Mill-Taylor Papers, vol. 55; Mill to Cairnes, 25 November 1861, Mill-Taylor Papers, vol. 55; Cairnes to Mill, 21 November 1861, Mill-Taylor Papers, vol. 56, no. 1, all in London School of Economics Archive and Special Collections.

123. Cairnes to Mill, 25 August 1861, Mill-Taylor Papers, vol. 56, no. 1, London School of Economics Archive and Special Collections; Cairnes, *The Slave Power,* lxii, 18.

124. Cairnes, *The Slave Power,* 81.

125. Ibid., 43–44.

126. Ibid., 96.

127. Ibid., 259.

128. Cairnes to Mill, 8 July 1862, Mill-Taylor Papers, vol. 56, no. 1, London School of Economics Archive and Special Collections; Cairnes to Shaw, 15 July 1862, Cairnes Papers, MS 4493, National Library of Ireland.

129. Martineau to Cairnes, 6 June 1862, Cairnes Papers, MS 8957, National Library of Ireland.

130. [Sir Edmund Walker Head], "The American Revolution," *Edinburgh Review* 116 (October 1862), 558.

131. "Slavery and Secession," *Dublin University Magazine* 61 (May 1863), 605.

132. For a discussion of how Frank Owsley's thesis related to *The Slave Power,* see Woodman's introduction to Cairnes, *The Slave Power,* xliv–xlvii.

133. For modern works that dispute Cairnes's findings, see the following: Owsley, *Plain Folk of the Old South*; Wade, *Slavery in the Cities*; Fogel and Engerman, *Time on the Cross*; Thornton, *Politics and Power in a Slave Society*; Wright, *The Political Economy of the Cotton South*; Ransom, *Conflict and Compromise*; Oakes, *Slavery and Freedom*; Bolton, *Poor Whites of the Antebellum South*; Bond, *Political Culture in the Nineteenth-Century South*; and Oakes, *The Ruling Race.*

134. [Bernard Cracroft], "The Slave Power and the Secession War," *National Review* 29 (July 1862), 168–169.

135. [Thomas Edward Cliffe Leslie], "The Wealth of Nations and the Slave Power," *Macmillan's Magazine* 40 (February 1863), 271–273.

136. James Stirling had explicitly described the South as a "downright Oligarchy." See Stirling, *Letters from the Slave States,* 60.

137. *The Times,* 10 May 1861, 8.

138. See *Standard,* 10 January 1861, 4; *Standard,* 19 January 1861, 4; *Standard,* 29 January 1861, 4; and *Standard,* 20 April 1861, 4.

139. *The Times,* 5 July 1862, 11.

140. *Saturday Review,* 27 December 1862, 765.

141. Ibid., 26 November 1864, 646.

142. Cairnes, *The Slave Power,* 103. Mill also referred to the South as a "white oligarchy." See John Stuart Mill, "The Contest in America," *Fraser's Magazine* 65 (February 1862), 263.

143. *The Times,* 15 April 1863, 9.

144. *Daily News,* 27 September 1862, 4.

145. [James Spence], "The Close of the American War," *Quarterly Review* 118 (July 1865), 119. See also *Saturday Review,* 7 March 1863, 302.

146. *Lloyd's Weekly Newspaper,* 27 April 1862, 6.

147. [Sir George Cornewall Lewis], "Election of President Lincoln and Its Consequences," *Edinburgh Review* 113 (April 1861), 585.

148. [Robert Cecil], "The Confederate Struggle and Recognition," *Quarterly Review* 112 (October 1862), 554–555.

149. Tocqueville, *Democracy in America,* 1:389.

150. See chapter 2.

151. Trollope, *North America,* 356.

152. [Robert Cecil], "The Confederate Struggle and Recognition," *Quarterly Review* 112 (October 1862), 555–556.

153. *The Times,* 17 September 1861, 6.

154. Ibid., 9 July 1863, 8.

155. *Spectator,* 14 December 1861, 1360.

156. Ibid., 20 September 1862, 1040. See also ibid., 14 December 1861, 1360.

157. Malet to Layard, 27 December 1862, Layard Papers, British Library, Add. Mss., 39,104.

158. *Morning Star,* 24 April 1865, 4.

159. *Spectator,* 20 September 1862, 1040. See also *Spectator,* 4 May 1861, 468.

160. *Saturday Review,* 4 October 1862, 405–407.

161. *Daily News,* 27 September 1862, 4.

162. Leng, *The American War,* 11.

163. Lawrence, *Three Months in America,* 51.

164. See [Garnet Wolseley], "A Month's Visit to the Confederate Headquarters," *Blackwood's Edinburgh Magazine* 93 (January 1863), 18; Fremantle, *Three Months in the Southern States,* 248. In discussing whether southern leaders were "gentlemen" who expressed the virtues of "chivalry," John Elliott Cairnes granted that they possessed "in a high degree those qualities which the principle of caste tends to engender—pride, courage, loyalty to the interests of their order, capacity for government, perseverance in a fixed course of policy." He even went so far as to concede that southern leaders possessed gentility and chivalry. But he reminded his readers that the "chivalry and gentility of the South is not incompatible with the systematic appropriation of the fruits of another's labour, with laying the whip on the shoulders of a woman . . . ; with turning one's own flesh and blood to pecuniary profit; or . . . with such atrocities as that committed by a Southern gentleman on the person of Mr. Sumner." Cairnes, *The Revolution in America,* 19.

165. *Lloyd's Weekly Magazine,* 27 July 1862, 6

166. Lawley to Gregory, 25 March 1863, Gregory Family Papers, Mss. 624, Emory University Library Special Collections.

167. Lothian, *The Confederate Secession,* 165.

168. *Daily Telegraph,* 4 February 1861, 4.

169. [Richard Holt Hutton], "The Slave States and the American Union," *National Review* 12 (January 1861), 256.

170. *Economist*, 15 February 1862, 170–171.

171. For a typical example, see the *Bee-Hive*, 5 November 1864, 4.

172. *Reynolds's Newspaper*, 11 December 1864, 1.

173. *Lloyd's Weekly Newspaper*, 8 January 1865, 6.

174. Ibid., 20 November 1864, 6.

175. *Bee-Hive*, 14 February 1863, 4.

176. [James Fitzjames Stephen], "England and America," *Fraser's Magazine* 68 (October 1863), 424, 435–436.

177. *Spectator*, 26 November 1864, 1346. For similar observations, see *Spectator*, 2 May 1863, 1940, and *Spectator*, 10 September 1864, 1034. See also Smith, *England and America*, 10.

178. For an early articulation of what became a very common argument, see *The Times*, 25 September 1861, 6.

179. Brent Kinser argues that during the Civil War, Victorian public intellectuals (or "literary politicians," to use Woodrow Wilson's term) such as Thomas Carlyle, Anthony Trollope, Walter Bagehot, and John Stuart Mill expressed so many reservations and so much ambivalence about American democracy that they succeeded in slowing the "progress of democratization" in Britain. Kinser, *American Civil War in the Shaping of British Democracy*, 9.

180. *Daily News*, 21 April 1865, 4.

181. *Reynolds's Newspaper*, 7 May 1865, 1.

182. Cobden to Sumner, 11 January 1865, Cobden Papers, British Library, Add. Mss., 43,676.

183. *Saturday Review*, 6 May 1865, 521.

184. Indeed, debates about the success of the United States continued throughout the Reconstruction period, with the battle lines very much resembling those that had existed during the war. See Bolt, "British Attitudes to Reconstruction," 43.

185. Saunders, *Democracy and the Vote*, 156.

186. Himmelfarb, *Victorian Minds*, 339.

187. Campbell, *English Public Opinion*, 246; Blackett, *Divided Hearts*, 35.

188. *The Times*, 26 September 1861, 7. In early 1865, *The Times* implied much the same thing when it stated, "The events in America, the prosperity which peace and free trade have brought upon the country, the conviction that, whatever may be the theoretical faults of our constitution, we are the best governed country in the world, have all tended, as it would seem, to reconcile opinion to the Conservative party." See also *The Times*, 2 February 1865, 8.

189. Some scholars have argued that this new force was responsible for the passage of reform in 1867. But did the agitation associated with this movement (via the Reform League, the Reform Union, the London Working Men's Association, and the London Trades Council) push through reform or shape its specific provisions? This question has been the subject of much discussion, and the conclusion of most classic accounts is a qualified "no." Cowling admits that reform was passed "in a context of a public agitation" while a dialogue took place between Parliament and the people. However, he also asserts that Parliament was not afraid of public demonstrations and that its actions were not determined by them; the explanation of reform is best found in Parliament. For his part, Smith concedes that the Hyde Park riots, coupled with widespread agitation, convinced the Commons that the working class wanted the vote and that reform was thus an urgent ques-

tion. However, he sees no radical influence at work in the specific provisions of either the Liberal bill of 1866 or the Conservative bill of 1867. Saunders falls, perhaps, between Cowling and Smith. "Agitation forced Parliament to take reform seriously," he argues, but it "did not . . . compel MPs to act against their principles, nor did it determine the shape of legislation." In explaining Derby's decision to push for a bill, Saunders writes, "there were compelling *parliamentary* arguments for dealing with reform." Biagini, *Liberty, Retrenchment and Reform*, 69–81, 371–376; Cowling, *1867: Disraeli, Gladstone and Revolution*, 3; Smith, *Making of the Second Reform Bill*, 127, 132–133, 230; Saunders, *Democracy and the Vote*, 230.

190. Gladstone to Smith, 17 June 1862, British Library, Add. Mss., 44,532; Gladstone to Field, 27 November 1862, British Library, Add. Mss., 44,399.

191. Gladstone to Sinclair, 19 December 1861, British Library, Add. Mss., 44,532. It appears that Gladstone maintained this position very late into the war. See Gladstone to Harris, 31 August 1864, British Library, Add. Mss., 44,534.

192. See Gladstone to Sutherland, 29 May 1861, British Library, Add. Mss., 44,531; Gladstone to Argyll, 15 July 1861, British Library, Add. Mss., 44,531; Gladstone to Argyll, 26 August 1861, British Library, Add. Mss., 44,532.

193. Gladstone to Phillimore, 4 September 1861, British Library, Add. Mss., 44,532.

194. Gladstone to Brougham, 27 December 1861, British Library, Add. Mss., 44,532.

195. *Hansard* (Commons), 171:1806–1808 (30 June 1863).

196. Gladstone to Argyll, 3 January 1865, British Library, Add. Mss., 44,534.

197. Gladstone's famous budgets of the 1850s had sought to forge a connection between voting and paying income taxes. Such a connection, he believed, would guarantee cheap government. However, in the first half of the 1860s his experience of the House of Commons and the Palmerston administration led him to conclude that such an arrangement would not keep taxes low. As Gladstone's speech on Baines's bill indicated, he believed the most skilled portion of the working class was capable of exercising the franchise responsibly. Moreover, he saw this articulate portion of the working class as susceptible to his guidance and leadership. Gladstone justified extending the franchise to this group because it paid a large portion of government revenue through indirect taxation. Most important of all, though, he believed that bringing these respectable artisans into the electorate would make the Commons more frugal. Matthew, *Gladstone*, 120–128; St. John, *Gladstone and the Logic of Victorian Politics*, 111–116; Feuchtwanger, *Gladstone*, 114–119.

198. Gladstone, *Speeches on Parliamentary Reform*, 84.

199. St. John, *Gladstone and the Logic of Victorian Politics*, 125–127; Matthew, *Gladstone*, 133–134.

200. Gladstone, *Speeches on Parliamentary Reform*, 84–87.

201. Blake, *Disraeli*, 413.

202. Hawkins, *The Forgotten Prime Minister*, 2:279. See also Lord Stanley Diary, 9 July 1863, Stanley Family Papers, 920 DER (15), Liverpool Record Office.

203. *Hansard* (Commons), 169:81–84 (5 February 1863).

204. Blake, *Disraeli*, 413.

205. *The Times*, 22 September 1864, 9.

206. *Hansard* (Commons), 169:81–84 (5 February 1863). See also *The Times,* 6 February 1863, 7; Monypenny and Buckle, *Life of Benjamin Disraeli,* 4:333.

207. *The Times,* 22 September 1864, 9.

208. Ibid., 6 February 1863, 7.

209. Ibid., 18 September 1862, 7.

210. See Hawkins, *The Forgotten Prime Minister,* 2:319–320, 335.

211. *Hansard* (Commons), 183:103–104, 110–111 (27 April 1866).

212. Saunders, *Democracy and the Vote,* 225.

213. *The Times,* September 8, 1862, 8. Brent Kinser's description of Thomas Carlyle's attitude toward the war is not so different: "While many in Britain viewed the American War as the ultimate test of democracy, Carlyle professed continually that he did not understand it [the war], and he did not need the war to teach him whether or not American democracy would work in Britain." Kinser, *American Civil War in the Shaping of British Democracy,* 37.

5. BRITAIN AND THE CIVIL WAR'S MILITARY SIGNIFICANCE

Epigraph note: *The Times,* 30 April 1861, 9.

Epigraph note: *Daily Telegraph,* 21 July 1862, 4.

Epigraph note: *The Times,* 17 September 1864, 8.

1. Lyons to Minna, 6 May 1862, Lyons Papers, 1/26 J2/299, West Sussex Record Office. See also letters from 11 April 1862 and 28 April 1862. Fletcher was good friends with Lieutenant-Colonel Henry Charles Eden Malet, whose brother, Edward Malet, was then second secretary at the British legation in Washington, D.C.

2. Anderson to Lyons, 29 April 1862, Lyons Papers, 1/26 D2/122, West Sussex Record Office.

3. Throughout the spring of 1862, in one way or another, their observations were shared among a group of highly placed personages, including Lord Lyons (head of the British legation), Earl Russell (the Foreign Secretary), Major-General Lord Frederick Paulet (commander of the Brigade of Guards then stationed in Canada), William Gladstone (chancellor of the exchequer), the Duke of Cambridge (commander in chief of the British army), Austin Henry Layard (under-secretary of state for foreign affairs), Major-General Sir William Fenwick Williams (commander of British forces in North America), and the Earl of Ripon (under-secretary of state for war). Gladstone to Neville, 23 July 1862, Gladstone Papers, British Library, Add. Mss., 44,532; Gladstone to Cambridge, 10 June 1862, Gladstone Papers, British Library, Add. Mss., 44,532; Williams to Layard, 11 July 1862, Layard Papers, British Library, Add. Mss., 38,988; Paulet to de Grey, 11 April 1862, Ripon Papers, British Library, Add. Mss., 43,621.

4. Stuart to Russell, 4 July 1862, Russell Papers, PRO 30/22/36, National Archives.

5. As Fletcher himself related in his account of this trip, later published in *Cornhill Magazine,* he sought Sherman's assistance with "some scruples" since "such a favor was never granted at Washington." Because the Federal government regularly refused such passes, the majority of British visitors to the South had themselves smuggled across the lines with the assistance of guides or

southern sympathizers. Nevertheless, the irrepressible Fletcher reported that he "was most kindly received by General Sherman, an officer of the old regular army, and like all those officers, most ready to assist in any way an English officer. . . . Directly he had heard my request, he said there was no difficulty." [Henry Charles Fletcher], "A Run through the Southern States," *Cornhill Magazine* 7 (April 1863), 496.

6. Beauregard impressed Fletcher as a "remarkably nice person and good officer." Ibid., 509.

7. Morris to Lawley, 19 March 1863, Morris Letter Books 12, New International plc.

8. [Henry Charles Fletcher], "A Run through the Southern States," *Cornhill Magazine* 7 (April 1863), 500.

9. Ibid., 503.

10. Ibid., 508, 512.

11. *Spectator,* 8 March 1865, 304. More recently, the military historian Jay Luvaas labeled Fletcher's work "disappointing." "For all practical purposes," Luvaas argued, the book "must be regarded as a secondary source" and not an "eyewitness account" because Fletcher "wrote about battles he did not see and leaned heavily upon the published works of others." Luvaas, *Military Legacy of the Civil War,* 18.

12. The *Saturday Review* implied this point when it surmised that Fletcher "has enjoyed the hospitality of both parties, and would be on good terms with both." *Saturday Review,* 11 February 1865, 177.

13. Fletcher used Spence's *American Union* as a source to discuss the origins of the American Civil War. Most reviewers saw Fletcher's survey of the war's origins as the weakest part of the book, and the *Spectator* objected to the use of Spence as a source. See Fletcher, *History of the American War,* 1:8, 11, 12; *Spectator,* 8 March 1865, 304.

14. *The Times,* 15 April 1865, 7.

15. Fletcher, *History of the American War,* 2:234.

16. Grimsley, *The Hard Hand of War,* 208–212; Fletcher, *History of the American War,* 3:389. For a more recent work arguing that the Federal way of war was limited, see Neely, *The Civil War and the Limits of Destruction.*

17. See, for example, his sources for Sherman's campaign in Georgia; Fletcher, *History of the American War,* 3:328.

18. See Royster, *The Destructive War,* 39

19. Fletcher, *History of the American War,* 3:548.

20. *The Times,* 22 September 1864, 7.

21. Discussions about the influence of rifled small arms and artillery on warfare filled the professional journals of the army before and during the American Civil War. The following articles give a good idea of how seriously various officers studied the question: Lieutenant-Colonel Dixon, R.A., "The Rifle—Its Probable Influence on Modern Warfare," *Journal of the Royal United Service Institution* 1 (1858): 95–120; Lieutenant-Colonel Wilford, "On the Rifle; Showing the Necessity for Its Introduction as a Universal Infantry Weapon," *Journal of the Royal United Service Institution* 1 (1858): 238–253; Captain Tyler, R.E., "The Effect of the Modern Rifle Upon Siege Operations, and the Means Required for Counteracting It," *Journal of the Royal United Service Institution* 2 (1859): 225–253; Captain Tyler, R.E., "The Rifle and the Spade, or the Future of Field Operations,"

Journal of the Royal United Service Institution 3 (1860): 170–194; Sir John Fox Burgoyne, "Memorandum on the Increased Power of Breaching to Be Obtained by the Use of Rifled Ordnance," *Papers on Subjects Connected with the Duties of the Corps of Royal Engineers* 10 (1861): 1–7; Captain Tyler, R.E., "The Rifle and the Rampart; or, the Future of Defence," *Journal of the Royal United Service Institution* 4 (1861): 331–375; Major Talbot Harvey, "The Progressive and Possible Development of Infantry Drill and Manoeuvres," *Journal of the Royal United Service Institution* 8 (1865): 292–301; MacDougall, *Modern Warfare.*

22. MacDougall, *Modern Warfare,* 4; Hamley, *The Operations of War,* 389–390.

23. *Standard,* 26 December 1862, 4; *The Times,* 7 June 1864, 11.

24. For observations on these issues, see Fletcher, *History of the American War,* 2:439–440; *Standard,* 8 October 1864, 5; *The Times,* 7 March 1865, 5; Sala, *My Diary in America,* 1:390; Ross, *Cities and Camps,* 33; Borcke, *Memoirs of the Confederate War,* 107; [Garnet Wolseley], "A Month's Visit to the Confederate Headquarters," *Blackwood's Edinburgh Magazine* 93 (January 1863), 27.

25. *Daily News,* 8 January 1862, 5.

26. The *Spectator* pointed out, however, that while a volunteer could not be disciplined to the same standard as a regular, the volunteer system had a peculiar strength. For "as long as a volunteer war is carried on, the mere continuance of the struggle is a proof that the heart of the army is in the contest." A volunteer army in a democratic society, like the Federal force, was "to a great extent identical with the people," and if such an army remained in the field, that was a good sign the people supported the war. *Spectator,* 11 April 1863, 1861.

27. *Saturday Review,* 20 September 1862, 338.

28. Lyons to Russell, 5 January 1863, Russell Papers, PRO 30/22/37, National Archives. For similar remarks, see *Illustrated London News,* 27 June 1863, 702; *Saturday Review,* 30 May 1863, 396.

29. *Illustrated London News,* 3 August 1861, 121.

30. Malet to Layard, 27 December 1862, Layard Papers, British Library, Add. Mss., 39,104.

31. Dicey, *Six Months in the Federal States,* 2:7.

32. See Burn, *Three Years among the Working-Classes,* 229; *The Times,* 9 December 1861, 7; Campbell, *A Short American Tramp,* 355.

33. Sala, *My Diary in America,* 1:285.

34. *Standard,* 11 September 1862, 4. See also *Standard,* 31 March 1863, 5; *Standard,* 23 August 1864, 5.

35. "Soldiering in the United States," *Colburn's United Service Magazine* (September 1861), 41.

36. *The Times,* 22 February 1862, 9.

37. Ibid., 21 August 1861, 7.

38. Lawrence, *Border and Bastille,* 242–243.

39. Day, *Down South,* 2:283–284. "*Tel maître, tel valet*" translates as "like master, like servant."

40. Dicey, *Six Months in the Federal States,* 2:7.

41. Lieutenant-Colonel T. L. Gallwey, R.E., and Captain H. J. Alderson, R.E., Report upon the Military Affairs of the United States of America, 2 August 1864, WO 33/14, National Archives. See also *Saturday Review,* 17 January 1863, 76; *Saturday Review,* 17 August 1861, 157; *Saturday Review,* 5 July 1862, 9; *Saturday Review,* 26 July 1862, 92; Chesney, *A Military View,* 1:60.

42. *The Times*, 19 October 1861, 8.

43. See Fletcher, *History of the American War*, 1:109.

44. Lawrence, *Border and Bastille*, 248–249.

45. See Day, *Down South*, 2:275, and Francis Lawley in *The Times*, 17 June 1863, 9; *Standard*, 11 September 1862, 4. For echoes of these accusations years later, see Henderson, *Stonewall Jackson*, 599.

46. [Sir James Fergusson], "Some Account of Both Sides of the American War," *Blackwood's Edinburgh Review* 90 (December 1861), 770. See also Fergusson to Derby [in Palmerston's hand], 11 November 1861, GC/DE/71/Enclosure 1-6, Palmerston Papers, Hartley Library, University of Southampton.

47. Worden, *The Plain English of American Affairs*, 54.

48. *The Times*, 17 September 1861, 6. Later in the war, *The Times* fantasized that "the Confederate army more resembles the forces by which the Wars of the Roses and the Civil War of the 17th century were fought in this country, when the great landowners assembled their retainers in the form of militia and yeomanry." *The Times*, 15 April 1863, 6.

49. *The Times*, 10 September 1861, 8.

50. At the time, Chesney served as professor of military history at the Staff College at Camberley. Chesney, *A Military View*, 1:17. See also *Saturday Review*, 20 September 1862, 338; Lothian, *The Confederate Secession*, 113–115.

51. *The Times*, 1 November 1861, 7.

52. For comments on Confederate indiscipline, see the otherwise sympathetic Fremantle, *Three Months in the Southern States*, 122–123. On improvements in the Federal army, see Fletcher, *History of the American War*, 2:437; Chesney, *A Military View*, 1:203, 233.

53. *Standard*, 11 September 1862, 4.

54. *Spectator*, 12 December 1863, 2844.

55. Godkin, *Life and Letters*, 1:206–207.

56. See Dicey, *Six Months in the Federal States*, 2:9, 243; *Daily News*, 11 April 1865, 5; *Spectator*, 14 June 1862, 659.

57. *Reynolds's Newspaper*, 11 August 1861, 1; *Reynolds's Newspaper*, 14 September 1862, 4.

58. Fletcher, *History of the American War*, 2:161. For similar such comments, see [Robert Bourke], "A Month with 'the Rebels," *Blackwood's Edinburg Magazine* 90 (December 1861), 764; Chesney, *A Military View*, 1:146.

59. *Army and Navy Gazette*, 20 December 1862, 805.

60. Garnet Wolseley, "A Month's Visit to the Confederate Headquarters," *Blackwood's Edinburgh Magazine* 93 (January 1863), 18; Fremantle, *Three Months in the Southern States*, 248.

61. Jones, *Union in Peril*, 126; Palmerston to Russell, 14 June 1862, GC/RU/1141/1-2, Palmerston Papers, Hartley Library; Stuart to Russell, 10 July 1862, FO 5/833, National Archives.

62. See also *The Times*, which claimed that "the present condition of New Orleans gives us an opportunity of judging what the fate of the whole South would be under the dominion of a victorious Northern Democracy." *The Times*, 14 October 1862, 6.

63. *Saturday Review*, 5 July 1862, 9.

64. The *Spectator* understood that Butler had been smeared as the "flower of all that was evil

in Yankee training, Yankee manners, and Yankee disposition towards its foes." However, in reviewing a biography of Butler, the weekly concluded that he was, "A stern, efficient, straightforward tyrant, without the smallest disposition to cruelty, but with an inflexible determination to make his own cause succeed, upright as a politician, and personally kind, but with a certain coarseness of fibre in his moral composition offensive to men of more refined or softer habits of thought." William Corsan, a British businessman who visited New Orleans during Butler's rule, suggested that widespread hatred of the general stemmed from shame at the "discreditable defence" mounted by Confederate forces on behalf of the city and amazement "at the cool manner in which step by step General Butler had disarmed them [the people], and placed them at his mercy." *Spectator,* 13 February 1864, 185; Corsan, *Two Months in the Confederate States,* 16.

65. See, for example, Lyons to Russell, 2 August 1861, FO 5/758, National Archives.

66. Stuart to Russell, 10 November 1862, FO 5/838, National Archives. See also Chesney, *A Military View,* 1:154; *Spectator,* 4 October 1862, 1096.

67. See Russell's praise for McClellan in this respect in *The Times,* 20 August 1861, 7; *The Times,* 10 September 1862, 8; *The Times,* 27 March 1862, 9. See also Sala, *My Diary in America,* 1:284; Day, *Down South*; 2:297; *Illustrated London News,* 22 March 1862, 296; Fletcher, *History of the American War,* 1:341.

68. Stuart to Russell, 21 July 1862, FO 5/834, National Archives; Stuart to Russell, 14 August 1862, FO 5/835, National Archives. See also *Spectator,* 4 October 1862, 1096.

69. [Edward Bruce Hamley], "General McClellan," *Blackwood's Edinburgh Review* 96 (November 1864), 619, 637, 640, 642–643.

70. William Gregory, the pro-Confederate MP sitting for Galway, actually hoped the Republicans would drive McClellan from the army because "they will deprive it of a gentleman, a gallant soldier, and an able general and place it in the hands of such men as Fremont or Pope." Gregory to Mason, 5 November 1862, Gregory Family Papers, Mss. 624, Box 31, Folder 4, Emory University Library Special Collections. For the *Spectator*'s claims, see *Spectator,* 29 November 1862, 1321.

71. *Spectator,* 2 August 1862, 846.

72. Ibid., 11 January 1862, 39.

73. Ibid., 26 April 1862, 455.

74. Ibid., 11 October 1862, 1125.

75. Ibid., 1 February 1862, 122.

76. For various comments to this effect, see Lyons to Russell, 5 January 1863, Russell Papers, PRO 30/22/37, National Archives; Stuart to Russell, 22 September 1863, Russell Papers, PRO 30/22/37, National Archives; *The Times,* 7 June 1864, 11; *Standard,* 26 December 1862, 4.

77. *Saturday Review,* 17 January 1863, 77.

78. See *Illustrated London News,* 27 June 1863, 702. See also Lyons to Russell, 5 January 1863, Russell Papers, PRO 30/22/37, National Archives; *Saturday Review,* 30 May 1863, 680.

79. *The Times,* 4 August 1864, 9.

80. For British hopes that Federal victories in the spring of 1862 heralded the end of the war, see *Saturday Review,* 15 March 1862, 285; *Reynolds's Newspaper,* 1 June 1862, 1; *Spectator,* 14 June 1862, 650; *The Times,* 16 May 1862, 8; [Bernard Cracroft], "The American War," *National Review* 14 (April 1862), 492–493, 499; *Lloyd's Weekly Newspaper,* 1 June 1862, 6. Perhaps even

more important, Earl Russell at the Foreign Office wrote, "The news from Yorktown, New Orleans, & Corinth seem to portend the conquest of the South," and Lord Lyons, surveying American affairs from the British legation, expressed similar opinions. Russell to Lyons, 17 May 1862, Russell Papers, PRO 30/22/96, National Archives; Lyons to Russell, 31 March 1862, Russell Papers, PRO 30/22/36, National Archives.

81. *Reynolds's Newspaper,* 27 July 1862, 1.

82. *Daily News,* 7 October 1862, 4.

83. See Jones, *Union in Peril,* 179–180. Both William Gladstone and *The Times* used this expression. See Gladstone's marginalia on Sir George Cornewall Lewis, Memorandum on the American Question, 17 October 1862, Gladstone Papers, British Library, Add. Mss., 44,595, and *The Times,* 7 October 1862, 8. For negative reactions to the Emancipation Proclamation, see *Daily Telegraph,* 6 October 1862, 4; *Daily Telegraph,* 7 October 1862, 4; *Standard,* 7 October 1862, 4; *Standard,* 8 October 1862, 4; *Standard,* 21 September 1864, 4; *The Times,* 2 January 1863, 9; *The Times,* 24 September 1863, 6; [Sir Edmund Walker Head], "The American Revolution," *Edinburgh Review* 116 (October 1862), 556; [Robert Cecil], "The Confederate Struggle and Recognition," *Quarterly Review* 112 (October 1862), 536–537.

84. [Robert Hogarth Patterson], "The Crisis of the American War," *Blackwood's Edinburgh Magazine* 92 (November 1862), 636.

85. *Standard,* 8 October 1862, 4.

86. See, for instance, Earl Russell's comments in his famous 13 October 1862 memorandum on intervention, in the Gladstone Papers, British Library, Add. Mss., 44,595. Huzzey emphasizes the extent to which British commentators objected to sudden and violent emancipation because they were very much influenced by a "cross-party tradition deriving from Whiggish conceptions of gradual reform." Huzzey, *Freedom Burning,* 26.

87. See, for instance, Lawrence, *Border and Bastille,* 279.

88. *Economist,* 6 July 1861, 731. See also *Economist,* 21 September 1861, 1041.

89. Russell to Gladstone, 26 January 1862, Gladstone Papers, British Library, Add. Mss., 44,292.

90. *Army and Navy Gazette,* 17 January 1863, 33.

91. *Daily Telegraph,* 6 October 1862, 4; *The Times,* 19 September 1862, 6; [Robert Hogarth Patterson], "The Crisis of the American War," *Blackwood's Edinburgh Magazine* 92 (November 1862), 636.

92. *Daily Telegraph,* 6 October 1862, 4. See also *Standard,* 8 October 1862, 4.

93. *Standard,* 22 July 1863, 4.

94. *The Times,* 15 December 1863, 12.

95. Many British observers praised General George McClellan's conduct of war for this very reason. See Fletcher, *History of the American War,* 2:120, 3:192; [Edward Bruce Hamley], "General McClellan," *Blackwood's Edinburgh Magazine* 96 (November 1864), 642–643.

96. *Saturday Review,* 12 September 1863, 356. See also the *Economist*'s discussion of this issue in relation to the blockade in *Economist,* 25 January 1862, 88.

97. [Robert Cecil], "The United States as an Example," *Quarterly Review* 117 (January 1865), 273–274.

98. *Saturday Review,* 11 July 1863, 41.

99. *Standard,* 31 December 1862, 4.

100. See (stone fleet) [Edward Bruce Hamley], "The Convulsions of America," *Blackwood's Edinburgh Magazine* 91 (January 1862), 124; (Pope's orders) Fletcher, *History of the American War,* 2:120, and *The Times,* 11 August 1862, 9; (Burnside's bombardment) Chesney, *A Military View,* 1:164; (Grierson's raid) *Standard,* 4 July 1863, 5; (Grant's sacking of Jackson, Mississippi) Fletcher, *History of the American War,* 2:357, and Walker to Russell, 27 May 1863, FO 5/906, National Archives; (Federal depredations along the Confederate coast) Fletcher, *History of the American War,* 2:232, and Walker to Russell, 5 June 1863, FO 5/906, National Archives; (Gillmore's bombardment) *Illustrated London News,* 5 December 1863, 574; Ross, *Cities and Camps,* 107–108; Stuart to Russell, 14 September 1863, Russell Papers, PRO 30/22/37, National Archives; Walker to Russell, 18 October 1863, FO 5/907, National Archives; (Sheridan's campaign) *The Times,* 26 October 1864, 8; and (the border states) Bunch to Russell, 14 August 1862, FO 5/844, National Archives.

101. Chesney, *A Military View,* 1:36.

102. John Stuart Mill, "The Contest in America," *Fraser's Magazine* 65 (February 1862), 266.

103. Cobden to Sumner, 13 February 1863, Cobden Papers, British Library, Add. Mss., 43,676.

104. *Army and Navy Gazette,* 10 January 1863, 17.

105. *Saturday Review,* 11 July 1863, 41.

106. One of the few exceptions appeared to be the *Bee-Hive,* which remarked, "The operations against Richmond have been conducted upon a comprehensive, and we admit complicated plan, but in so skilful a manner that they can fail only by the incapacity of some of the generals entrusted to carry them out." *Bee-Hive,* 28 May 1864, 4.

107. For example, see *Standard,* 24 May 1864, 4.

108. *Reynolds's Weekly Newspaper,* 29 May 1864, 1.

109. *The Times,* 25 May 1864, 8.

110. Most journals seemed to think that Grant's objective was Richmond, and they repeatedly compared his progress to that of McClellan's in 1862, noting that McClellan had gotten closer to Richmond with fewer casualties. Only a couple of journals realized that Grant's objective was Lee's army. For instance, the *Morning Star* pointed out that Grant's operations against Petersburg sought to interfere with Lee's communications and bring the Army of Northern Virginia into the open field. Grant "is manoeuvring to compel [Lee] to come out and fight a battle in the open field away from his prepared fortifications and entrenchments, a result which LEE is wisely striving to avoid." *Morning Star,* 2 July 1864, 4.

111. *The Times,* 7 November 1864, 6. See also *The Times,* 25 May 1864, 8: "The strategy of GRANT consists simply in pushing forward his whole force, hurling it against the Southern positions, and inflicting loss on the enemy by submitting to a loss which is greater on his own side."

112. *Standard,* 24 May 1864, 4.

113. Lyons to Russell, 23 May 1864, Russell Papers, PRO 30/22/38, National Archives.

114. [Robert Cecil], "The United States as an Example," *Quarterly Review* 117 (January 1865), 257.

115. *Saturday Review,* 6 June 1863, 715.

116. *Spectator,* 30 May 1863, 2056. For more contemporary comment concerning the Puritan

and Cavalier sides of Jackson's personality, see Cullop, "English Reaction to Stonewall Jackson's Death," 1–5.

117. See *Daily News,* 21 May 1864, 5; *The Times,* 24 May 1864, 10; *The Times,* 4 August 1864, 9; *The Times,* 17 April 1865, 8; *Daily Telegraph,* 24 April 1865, 6; *Daily Telegraph,* 25 May 1865, 4.

118. *The Times,* 24 May 1864, 10.

119. Ibid., 20 June 1864, 8.

120. *Saturday Review,* 5 July 1862, 9; *Saturday Review,* 12 September 1863, 355.

121. Britons as disparate as Benjamin Disraeli, Henry Reeve, and William Forster all insisted on describing the Civil War as a revolution. See *Hansard* (Commons), 169:81 (5 February 1863); [Henry Reeve], "The Disunion of America," *Edinburgh Review* 114 (October 1861), 580; *Hansard* (Commons), 171:1817 (30 June 1863).

122. *Standard,* 24 May 1864, 4

123. *Saturday Review,* 31 January 1863, 145.

124. *The Times,* 2 July 1864, 11.

125. For instance, *Reynolds's Newspaper* asserted that in Grant the North had found "a leader of unsurpassed pertinacity of purpose, combined with a strategic skill of the highest order." *Reynolds's Newspaper,* 25 September 1864, 1.

126. *Spectator,* 28 May 1864, 610.

127. *The Times,* 20 September 1864, 8.

128. *Spectator,* 24 September 1864, 1096; *Spectator,* 10 December 1864, 1406. For an analysis of how Sherman and Grant worked together as a team at the strategic level, see *Spectator,* 31 December 1864, 1491. See also the *Bee-Hive*'s analysis of the march: "Its chief merit, next to the boldness of its conception, is the way in which it has been performed, showing a perfectness of organization, combined with certainty and plainness." *Bee-Hive,* 7 January 1865, 4.

129. *Reynolds's Newspaper,* 11 December 1864, 1.

130. *Illustrated London News,* 21 January 1865, 65.

131. Fletcher, *History of the American War,* 3:364–365.

132. Captain C. C. Chesney, R. E., "Sherman's Campaign in Georgia," *Journal of the Royal United Service Institution* 9 (1865): 205, 206.

133. *The Times,* 30 March 1865, 8–9.

134. [Edward Bruce Hamley], "General McClellan," *Blackwood's Edinburgh Magazine* 96 (November 1864), 642, 643.

135. Captain C. C. Chesney, R. E., "Sherman's Campaign in Georgia," *Journal of the Royal United Service Institution* 9 (1865), 218, 219.

136. Fletcher, *History of the American War,* 3:365, 366, 370.

137. *Bee-Hive,* 31 December 1864, 4.

138. *Daily News,* 12 November 1864, 5; *Daily News,* 3 April 1865, 5; *Daily News,* 11 April 1865, 4; *Daily News,* 24 April 1865, 4.

139. See for instance *Reynolds's Newspaper,* 11 December 1864, 1.

140. *Standard,* 25 April 1865, 4.

141. *Saturday Review,* 22 April 1865, 458.

142. *The Times,* 12 April 1865, 8.

143. Ibid., 18 April 1865, 6.

144. Ibid., 24 April 1865, 8.

145. *Morning Star,* 24 April 1865, 4.

146. *The Spectator,* 22 April 1865, 437. The *Spectator* was also impressed with Grant and Sherman's ability to "operate on a plan of unprecedented magnitude, to knit together the effect of operations hundreds of miles apart" and "build up their successes even when divided by the greatest breadths of country." *Spectator,* 31 December 1864, 1491.

147. *Daily Telegraph,* 24 April 1865, 6.

148. *Economist,* 22 April 1865, 461.

149. Crook, *The North, the South, and the Powers,* 380.

150. Spiers, *The Late Victorian Army,* 95–97; Blackett, *Divided Hearts,* 101.

151. *Saturday Review,* 31 January 1863, 145.

152. Henderson, *The Science of War,* 190, 310.

153. See Dubrulle, "A Military Legacy of the Civil War," 178.

154. Henderson, *Stonewall Jackson,* 310.

155. Ibid., 493, 638, 691.

156. Fletcher, *History of the American War,* 3:548.

157. Henderson, *Stonewall Jackson,* 610.

6. BRITISH UNDERSTANDINGS OF AMERICAN NATIONALISMS DURING THE CIVIL WAR

Epigraph note: Adams, *Great Britain and the American Civil War,* 1:175.

Epigraph note: *Army and Navy Gazette,* 31 May 1862, 341. The journal continued, "If they [the South] constitute a different nationality, then the task of the Federals, who will probably be rent in twain, or divided into more than two factions respecting the best means of governing what they have conquered, will become one of a very great difficulty."

Epigraph note: *Saturday Review,* 28 January 1865, 103.

1. Gladstone to Duchess of Sutherland, 29 May 1861, Gladstone Papers, British Library, Add. Mss., 44,531.

2. Gladstone to Coke, 5 June 1861, Gladstone Papers, British Library, Add. Mss., 44,396.

3. At Manchester, Gladstone declared that "there never was an occasion in which the civilized nations of the world in general bore, and were content to bear, so much real misery resulting from a civil and municipal quarrel in another State, without interference as there has been on the present occasion." *The Times,* 25 April 1862, 7.

4. Gladstone to Palmerston, 25 September 1862, Palmerston Papers, GC/GL/94/1-2, Hartley Library, University of Southampton.

5. *The Times,* 10 October 1862, 7.

6. Ibid., 9 October 1862, 7–8.

7. Feuchtwanger, *Gladstone*, 116.

8. *Spectator*, 11 October 1862, 1124; *The Times*, 9 October 1862, 8; *Reynolds's Newspaper*, 12 October 1862, 4; *Saturday Review*, 11 October 1862, 427–428.

9. Lewis to Clarendon, 10 October 1862, Clarendon Papers, Mss. Clar. dep. c. 531, Bodleian Library.

10. *The Times*, 17 October 1862, 5.

11. *Saturday Review*, 25 October 1862, 494. For a gentler version of the same criticisms, see the *Economist*, 18 October 1862, 1149.

12. Russell added that he found Lewis's speech "almost as imprudent." Palmerston to Russell, 17 October 1862, Russell Papers, PRO 30/22/14D, National Archives; Russell to Palmerston, 18 October 1862, Palmerston Papers, GC/RU/734/1-2, Hartley Library, University of Southampton; Russell to Gladstone, 20 October 1862, Gladstone Papers, British Library, Add. Mss., 44,292.

13. While he quickly realized that "some words I have used at Newcastle respecting America bear a wider sense than I intended," he naively explained to Russell that James Spence, the pro-Confederate propagandist, whom Gladstone had met in Liverpool shortly after the speech, "did not appear to have put any such construction on my words as that they signified any intention of the Government." Gladstone to Russell, 17 October 1862, Gladstone Papers, British Library, Add. Mss., 44,292. See also Ryan to Egan, 1862, Russell Papers, PRO 30/22/19, National Archives.

14. Gladstone to Russell, 20 October 1862, Gladstone Papers, British Library, Add. Mss., 44,533.

15. Gladstone, "Some of My Errors," 1894, Gladstone Papers, British Library, Add. Mss. 44,790; Gladstone, "Record of Special Errors," 1896, Gladstone Papers, British Library, Add. Mss., 44,791.

16. Jones, *Union in Peril*, 214.

17. Lewis to Clarendon, 11 November 1862, Clarendon Papers, Mss. Clar. dep. c. 531, Bodleian Library.

18. Morley, *The Life of William Ewart Gladstone*, 2:85.

19. Jones, *Union in Peril*, 196. For a good summary of these events with an emphasis on Lord Lyons's role in them, see Jenkins, *Lord Lyons*, 198–215.

20. Gladstone, "Some of My Errors," 1894, Gladstone Papers, British Library, Add. Mss., 44,790.

21. *The Times*, 9 October 1862, 8. *Lloyd's Weekly Newspaper*, which, as a working-class, radical journal, sat on the other end of the political spectrum, expressed very much the same opinion, arguing that Gladstone had simply stated the truth. See *Lloyd's Weekly Newspaper*, 12 October 182, 2.

22. Palmerston to Russell, 12 October 1862, Russell Papers, PRO 30/22/22, National Archives.

23. Russell to Palmerston, 18 October 1862, Palmerston Papers, GC/RU/734/1-2, Hartley Library, University of Southampton.

24. *Spectator*, 18 October 1862, 1152.

25. Lewis to Clarendon, 10 October 1862, Clarendon Papers, Mss. Clar. dep. c. 531, Bodleian Library.

26. *The Times*, 9 October 1862, 8.

27. Bagehot, *The Collected Works of Walter Bagehot*, 8:151–152.

28. Varouxakis, *Mill on Nationality*, 8.

29. Parry, *The Politics of Patriotism,* 4, 7, 15, 59, 148–150, 221, 231. See also Beales, *England and Italy 1859–60,* 28; Miller, *Britain and the German Question,* 1, 208.

30. Varouxakis, *Mill on Nationality,* 4; Hobsbawm, *Nations and Nationalism,* 38; Parry, *The Politics of Patriotism,* 21–22.

31. *The Times,* 30 October 1862, 5.

32. Ibid., 9 October 1862, 7.

33. Acton, "Nationality," in McNeill, ed., *Essays in the Liberal Interpretation of History,* 150–151.

34. Mill, *On Liberty and Considerations on Representative Government,* 295.

35. Gladstone to Field, 27 November 1862, Gladstone, British Library, Add. Mss., 44,399; Gladstone to Sumner, 1 February 1864, Gladstone Papers, British Library, Add. Mss., 44,534.

36. Mandler, *The English National Character,* 18, 21, 32.

37. Ibid., 60.

38. Kumar, *The Making of English National Identity,* ix.

39. Ibid., 189–191.

40. See, for example, Nagel, *One Nation Indivisible*; Nagel, *This Sacred Trust*; O'Leary, *To Die For*; Grant, *North Over South*; Kersh, *Dreams of a More Perfect Union*; Lawson, *Patriot Fires*; Parish, *The North and the Nation.*

41. See Nagel, *This Sacred Trust,* 129–145, and Kersh, *Dreams of a More Perfect Union,* 153–197, for arguments to the effect that the North increasingly saw Union as a means of securing moral values. For arguments about how northern and southern nationalism diverged and how the northern vision "hijacked" American identity, see Parish, *The North and the Nation,* xviii, 130.

42. Bender, *A Nation among Nations,* 135.

43. At one point, he described Americans as "that portion of the English people which is commissioned to explore the wilds of the New World," an expression that well captures their English and imperial character. Tocqueville, *Democracy in America,* 2:36.

44. For an example of a later author making a similar and striking version of this argument, see Alexander Mackay's *Western World.* At the conclusion of this work, when he summarized the true position of Americans, Mackay described the United States as part of a far-flung collection of Anglo-Saxon settlements on "the continent of North America, on many points on the coast of South America, at the southern extremity of Africa, throughout wide Australia, in New Zealand, in Van Diemen's land, and the Indian archipelago." Clearly, Mackay conceived of the United States as part of nothing less than Greater Britain (although the term would not pass into common usage until Charles Dilke's book of the same name was published in 1869). Mackay, *The Western World,* 3:359.

45. Tocqueville, *Democracy in America,* 1:144.

46. Ibid., 1:379–380.

47. Ibid., 1:232–233.

48. Ibid., 1:386.

49. Ibid., 1:386–388.

50. Ibid., 1:388–390.

51. Ibid., 1:393–398

52. Ibid., 1:402, 410.

53. Paul Quigley, review of Lesley J. Gordon and John C. Inscoe, eds., *Inside the Confederate Nation: Essays in Honor of Emory M. Thomas*, H-Nationalism, H-Net Reviews. January 2008, http://www.h-net.org/reviews/showrev.php?id=14024. Historians have realized the extent to which southerners possessed multiple identities and expressed their nationalism in different ways. As a result, recent scholarship has more fully explored the tensions that characterized Confederate nationalism, recognizing in particular the degree to which slavery was a central yet problematic element of this identity. In so doing, this research has come to understand the extent to which southerners appreciated that developing a national identity was a problem to be solved and self-consciously attempted to solve it. This more nuanced approach to the qualities of Confederate nationalism has revealed that it was contingent, responded to events, and thus changed over time. At the same time, historians have tended to place Confederate nationalism within a much broader context—in both time and place—than ever before. On the one hand, the ways in which antebellum southern experiences within the Union helped inform Confederate identity have become much better understood. On the other, historians have increasingly compared the Confederate experience to that of other national movements, studied the ways in which foreign events such as the Revolutions of 1848 influenced the development of southern identity, and attempted to describe the Civil War as part of a global phenomenon that witnessed nation-building in a wide variety of areas. While this thoughtful scholarship has produced a number of provocative ideas, it has not necessarily led to consensus. For example, there is some disagreement over whether the Confederate experience of nationalism was revolutionary or not. Although they have ceased to discuss the prevalence and depth of Confederate nationalism among the southern people during the war, historians continue to stress the movement's problems, contradictions, and immaturity. In other words, they tend to depict the Confederacy as a potential nation that needed to work out a number of difficulties.

For scholarly discussions of Confederate nationalism, see Potter, "The Historian's Use of Nationalism and Vice Versa," 924–950; Escott, *After Secession*; McCardell, *The Idea of a Southern Nation*; Channing, "Slavery and Confederate Nationalism"; Stampp, "The Southern Road to Appomattox," in *The Imperiled Union*; Beringer et al., *Why the South Lost*; Faust, *The Creation of Confederate Nationalism*; Fehrenbacher, *Constitutions and Constitutionalism in the Slaveholding South*; Thomas, *The Confederacy as a Revolutionary Experience*; McPherson, "American Victory, American Defeat," in Boritt, ed., *Why the Confederacy Lost*; Rable, *The Confederate Republic*; Davis, "Lost Will, Lost Causes," in *The Cause Lost*; Gallagher, *The Confederate War*; Davis, *Look Away!*; Gordon and Inscoe, eds., *Inside the Confederate Nation*; Rubin, *A Shattered Nation*; Sheehan-Dean, *Why Confederates Fought*; Bonner, *Mastering America*; Bernath, *Confederate Minds*; Hutchinson, *Apples and Ashes*; Quigley, *Shifting Grounds*; Binnington, *Confederate Visions.*

54. Pro-southern sympathizers may have taken their cue from Henry Hotze, the Confederate agent who published the *Index* in London. Very early in the *Index*'s life, he wrote that "the South, for generations back, has been proud of its closer affinity of blood to the British parent stock, than the North, with its mongrel population of all the world, could boast of." *Index*, 15 May 1862, 40.

55. *The Times*, 11 August 1862, 6.

56. Beresford Hope, *Social and Political Bearings*, 38.

57. See *The Times*, 4 November 1862, 9; *The Times*, 16 June 1863, 12; *The Times*, 25 September 1863, 7; and *The Times*, 15 November 1864, 9.

58. It was for this reason that William Gregory, among a number of others, foresaw that when secession occurred, "all our commercial sympathies [would be] with free trade and the South." Gregory to Gregory, 14 December 1859, Gregory Family Papers, Mss. 624, Box 31, Folder 3, Emory University Library Special Collections.

59. *The Times*, 17 January 1862, 7.

60. See *Lloyd's Weekly Newspaper*, 17 August 1862, 6; Gibbs, *Recognition*, 46.

61. Dicey, *Six Months in the Federal States*, 1:295, 1:308–309, 2:56, 2:168, 2:179.

62. For an archetypal expression of this idea and its application, see Day, *Down South*, 1:172–173.

63. See the beginning of the last section in chapter 3.

64. According to Stirling, the "bona-fide Democracy in the North" was descended from the Puritan character, while the "downright Oligarchy" of the South was an inheritance of the Cavaliers. Stirling, *Letters from the Slave States*, 60. In the *National Review*, Thomas Ellison wrote pretty much the same thing, arguing that the settlement of New England was "entirely Puritain" while the South was settled by a mix of "noble and gentle families" along with "middle class commercial adventurers, and lower class labourers and convicts." This original settlement accounted for why the North was "from the first essentially democratic and republican" while the South was "aristocratic and plebeian." [Thomas Ellison], "The Rival American Confederacies," *Westminster Review* 76/20 (October 1861), 487–488.

65. Smith, *England and America*, 10.

66. Lothian, *The Confederate Secession*, 174–175.

67. Beresford Hope, *Social and Political Bearings*, 5.

68. *Index*, 23 March 1865, 186.

69. *Daily News*, 4 November 1862, 4.

70. Newman, *The Good Cause of President Lincoln*, 22. In April 1865, the *Bee-Hive* made a similar argument when it attributed Confederate defeat to the fact that southern society was divided into three orders: "'the equestrian, plebeian, and servile classes;' or, in plain terms, 'gentlemen,' 'mean whites,' and 'niggers,' for so they call them 'down South.'" "Was it to be expected," the *Bee-Hive* asked, "that the three classes of the South, each pulling in a different direction, according to its separate interests," could assert a single nationality and win the war? *Bee-Hive*, 22 April 1865, 4.

71. Grey to Russell, 26 August 1862, Russell Papers, PRO 30/22/25, National Archives. For an interesting analysis of the extent to which southerners were wedded to slavery not merely as an economic system but a social one as well, see the *Economist*, 29 October 1864, 1231–1232.

72. Spence, *On the Recognition of the Southern Confederation*, 22.

73. Dicey, *Six Months in the Federal States*, 2:91.

74. For examples of this very common view, see *Spectator*, 21 June 1862, 679; *Daily News*, 5 September 1862, 5; E[dward] D[icey], "The Outlook of the War," *Macmillan's Magazine* 6 (September 1862), 417–418; [John Stuart Mill], "The Slave Power," *Westminster Review* 78/22 (October 1862), 509; Lawrence, *Three Months in America*, 59; Thomas Milner Gibson's speech in *The Times*, 13 January 1864.

75. Hobsbawm, *Nations and Nationalism*, 31–32.

76. Quigley, *Shifting Grounds*, 132–133.

77. Lyons to Russell, 28 October 1861, Russell Papers, PRO 230/22/35, National Archives.

78. *Standard,* 1 July 1862, 4.

79. Sir George Cornewall Lewis, Recognition of the Independence of the Southern States of the North American Union, 7 November 1862, WO 33/12, National Archives.

80. Spence, *On the Recognition of the Southern Confederation,* 6.

81. Ibid., 4.

82. Spence, *Southern Independence,* 16.

83. Davis, *Messages and Papers of Jefferson Davis,* 2:62, 67.

84. *Hansard* (Commons), 168:511–522 (18 July 1862).

85. *Reynolds's Newspaper,* 26 January 1862, 1.

86. *The Times,* 4 November 1861, 6.

87. John Stuart Mill, "The Contest in America," *Fraser's Magazine* 65 (February 1862), 265.

88. *Daily Telegraph,* 5 November 1862, 4.

89. See the *Daily Telegraph,* 27 September 1864, 4.

90. Corsan, *Two Months in the Confederate States,* 140; *Economist,* 29 June 1861, 702.

91. *Daily Telegraph,* 12 September 1862, 4.

92. *Hansard* (Lords), 173:25 (5 February 1863). Lord Hartington (then an MP for North Lancashire but later the 8th Duke of Devonshire), who also visited the Confederacy, wrote to his father from Charleston that "whatever happens they [the southerners] can never be brought back into the union except as conquered provinces, & I think they will take a great deal of conquering before that is done." Hartington to Devonshire, 21 January 1863, Cavendish Papers, 340.184, Devonshire Collection.

93. *The Times,* 3 July 1862, 10.

94. In January 1862, Bright admitted to Cobden that "you will say that I am enthusiastic . . . but every day I am strengthened in my belief that the Union will be restored, & that the 'inevitable negro' will be a great gainer." Bright's commitment to the northern cause took place very early in the war. Bright claimed he fully embraced the North at an 1861 breakfast with John Lothrop Motley at Austen Henry Layard's home. See Bright to Cobden, 13 January 1862, Bright Papers, British Library, Add. Mss., 43,384.

95. Cairnes, *The Slave Power,* 308–324; Joseph Hernon, review of *John Eliot Cairnes and the American Civil War,* by Adelaide Weinberg, *Civil War History* 21 (September 1975): 283–284

96. John Stuart Mill, "The Contest in America," *Fraser's Magazine* 65 (February 1862), 266–267; Mill to Cairnes, 15 June 1862, and Mill to Cairnes, 24 June 1862, both in Mill-Taylor Papers, vol. 55, London School of Economics Archive and Special Collections.

97. For various references to this specter, see the *Spectator,* 9 March 1861, 242, and the *Economist,* 2 March 1861, 226. See also Adams, *The Slaveholders' War,* 8; Dill, *The American Conflict,* 18; Estcourt, *Rebellion and Recognition,* 6; Hall, *The American War,* 24; Jones, *The Slaveholders' War,* 42; Leng, *The American War,* 30; Newman, *The Good Cause of President Lincoln,* 5; Smith, *The Civil War in America,* 2; Waddington, *The American Crisis,* 26.

98. Cairnes, *The Slave Power,* 304.

99. John Stuart Mill, "The Contest in America," *Fraser's Magazine* 65 (February 1862), 267.

100. *Reynolds's Newspaper,* 26 January 1862, 1; "Moral Aspects of the American Struggle," *British Quarterly Review* (July 1863), 220–233, particularly 233.

101. See Spence, *On the Recognition of the Southern Confederation,* 22; Spence, *Southern Independence,* 20; Beresford Hope, *Social and Political Bearings,* 23–29, 36–39; Beresford Hope, *England, the North, and the South,* 38, 69–70, 75. See also Tocqueville, *Democracy in America,* 1:375, 385–386.

102. Gladstone to Harris, 31 August 1864, Gladstone Papers, British Library, Add. Mss., 44,534.

103. See, for example, Blackett, *Divided Hearts,* 27.

104. Bright, *Speech of Mr. Bright,* 15–16.

105. *The Times,* 28 September 1863, 7.

106. Ibid., 7 November 1862, 6–7.

107. Ibid., 17 November 1862, 9.

108. Sir George Cornewall Lewis, Recognition of the Independence of the Southern States of the North American Union, 7 November 1862, WO 33/12, National Archives.

109. Bernard, *Two Lectures on the Present American War.* Frederick Waymouth Gibbs, the former tutor of Edward, Prince of Wales (later Edward VII), from 1852 to 1858, and a close friend of the great jurist Sir James Fitzjames Stephen, also produced a pamphlet making very similar arguments. See Gibbs, *Recognition.*

110. William Gregory, MP for County Galway, and one of the Confederacy's most prominent supporters in the Commons, was a notable exception in that he seemed especially clear-eyed about these issues. He understood the distinctions between recognition and intervention. He was sure that recognition would not help the Confederacy, and he seemed convinced that unless it was accompanied by force of arms, intervention would be equally useless. See Gregory's notes in July 1862 (?), Gregory Family Papers, Mss. 624, Box 31, Folder 4, Emory University Library Special Collections.

111. Spence, *On the Recognition of the Southern Confederation,* 4–11. Spence did recognize that an important argument against immediate recognition of the South was "by the plea that it is more expedient to allow facts to work themselves out without our incurring responsibility." Spence to Gregory, 14 July 1862, Gregory Family Papers, Mss. 624, Box 24, Folder 2, Emory University Library Special Collections.

112. In the *Index,* Hotze claimed of the South: "They are conscious that they have fulfilled every condition which can justly be required of a new nation claiming admission into the family of nations—extent of territory, sufficiency of population and resources, unanimity of thought and action, resoluteness of purpose, unflinching determination of will." If the Confederacy had met these criteria, it would have been a nation. However, meeting these standards was beside the point when it came time to discuss recognition of the Confederate state. Later, in an essay entitled "What Constitutes a Nation?" Hotze wrote, "Not only has the country [the South] its statesmen and its generals, its triumphs and its reverses, but each family in the land has its hero or its martyr. If the South had not possessed the conditions of a vigorous nationality before, it would have derived them from the events of this war." Again, such an assertion had little to do with recognition. See the *Index,* 15 May 1862, 41; *Index,* 26 February 1863, 282.

113. See *The Times,* 22 October 1862, 8; Sir George Cornewall Lewis, "Recognition of the Independence of the Southern States of the North American Union," 7 November 1862, WO 33/12, National Archives.

114. See Jones, *Union in Peril,* 181–223; Krein, *The Last Palmerston Government,* 62–76.

115. Krein, *The Last Palmerston Government,* 176.

116. Matthew, *Gladstone,* 138.

117. *Spectator,* 18 October 1862, 1152.

118. Speeches by Members of Parliament in *The Times* are striking in that they consistently supported the policy of neutrality. See *The Times,* 21 October 1861, 9 (Major William Beresford); 1 November 1861, 9 (Sir John Pakington); 22 November 1861 (Austen Henry Layard); 23 November 1861, 7 (Lord Stanley); 6 December 1861, 7 (John Harvey Lewis); 11 December 1861, 8 (Edward Horsman); 28 October 1862, 9 (David Salomons); 6 November 1862, 10 (Charles Buxton); 14 January 1863, 5 (Alexander Kinglake); 22 January 1863, 9 (Thomas Milner Gibson); 16 October 1863, 7 (Roundell Palmer); 19 October 1863, 11 (Captain Henry Jervis-White-Jervis); 19 October 1863, 11 (Earl de Grey); 3 January 1864, 10 (David Mure); 13 January 1864, 6 (William Edward Forster); 17 September 1864, 12 (William Edward Baxter); 24 October 1864, 8 (Ralph Bernal Osborne). True, a number of these speakers were members of the government or Radicals who could be expected to support the North, but a number were not. Moreover, the number of MPs calling for recognition appear to have been much smaller.

119. Palmerston to Russell, 14 September 1863, Russell Papers, PRO 30/22/14F, National Archives.

120. *Daily Telegraph,* 7 December 1861, 4. Sir James Fergusson quoted Jefferson Davis approvingly: "Our separation from the North is as complete as if it had been accomplished fifty years [ago]." *The Times* believed the facts of the case proved "not that Jefferson Davis has made a nation of the South, but the South is a nation already, and Jefferson Davis has given it a form and a name." [Sir James Fergusson], "Some Account of Both Sides of the American War," *Blackwood's Edinburgh Magazine* 90 (December 1861), 779; *The Times,* 9 October 1861, 8.

121. *The Times*, 6 December 1861, 6.

122. See [William Forsyth], "The American Crisis," *Quarterly Review* 111 (January 1862), 251–252.

123. Russell to Lyons, 10 January 1861, Russell Papers, PRO 30/22/36, National Archives.

124. Rable, *The Confederate Republic,* 2.

125. [Francis Newman], "The American Quarrel," *Fraser's Magazine* 63 (April 1861), 411, 412. See also *Bee-Hive,* 21 March 1863, 1.

126. Archibald to Russell, 4 September 1862, FO 5/842, National Archives.

127. Hammond to Layard, 17 October 1862, Layard Papers, British Library, Add. Mss., 38,951.

128. Hammond to Layard, 26 July 1863, Layard Papers, British Library, Add. Mss., 38,952.

129. Lyons to Russell, 16 February 1863, Russell Papers, PRO 30/22/37, National Archives; Lyons to Russell, 12 June 1863, FO 5/887, National Archives.

130. Lyons to Russell, 2 February 1863, Russell Papers, PRO 30/22/37, National Archives.

131. *Daily Telegraph,* 26 September 1864, 5

132. *Saturday Review,* 15 February 1862, 177.

133. *Economist,* 28 September 1861, 1066.

134. *Spectator,* 8 June 1861, 607.

135. Ibid., 31 January 1863, 1582.

136. X. Y., "Causes of the Disruption of the American Union," *Fraser's Magazine* (August 1861), 234–245.

137. "Moral Aspects of the American Struggle," *British Quarterly Review* 38 (July 1863), 222–223.

138. [Henry Reeve], "The Disunion of America," *Edinburgh Review* 114 (October 1861), 581. Edward Bruce Hamley wrote essentially the same thing in *Blackwood's Edinburgh Magazine:* "A shrewd glance might perceive that the Constitution, framed with a view to common interests and to existing necessities, no longer fulfilled its purpose. The interests of the original consenting parties had ceased to be common—had even become hostile. . . . New states, with different climates and different products, had been joined to the original framework; but while the dominion increased, and with the difficulty of reconciling contending interests, the power of the Government remained as before." [Edward Bruce Hamley], "The Disruption of the Union," *Blackwood's Edinburgh Magazine* 90 (July 1861), 128. Hamley wrote something similar in "Trollope's North America," *Blackwood's Edinburgh Magazine* 92 (September 1862), 384.

139. Sala, *My Diary in America,* 2:64. See also Kershaw, *The Truth of the American Question,* 15. Southerners also tended to think in this fashion. Their explanation of northern politics might have influenced certain observers. William Corsan reported, "to the influx at the North of uneducated masses, saturated with political fallacies and crotchets, who at once acquired the power of voting, and consequently, great weight in the State—to this chiefly do Southern people attribute the steady deterioration in political virtue which, they say, has been going on at the North for years." Corsan, *Two Months in the Confederate States,* 197. See also Russell, *My Diary North and South,* 5.

140. *Economist,* 9 November 1861, 1236.

141. Tocqueville, *Alexis de Tocqueville on Democracy, Revolution, and Society,* 294.

142. *The Times,* 29 April 1861, 8.

143. Ibid., 18 October 1861, 6.

144. Sala, *My Diary in America,* 2:81.

145. [Edward Bruce Hamley], "Spence's American Union," *Blackwood's Edinburgh Magazine* 91 (March 1862), 519. In a review of Anthony Trollope's *North America,* Hamley reiterated this point: "the Government of the Union, or any government that continues to rest on the consent of the governed, is not framed on a basis that can be permanent, and must be condemned because it leads everywhere to illogical results." [Edward Bruce Hamley], "Trollope's North America," *Blackwood's Edinburgh Magazine* 92 (September 1862), 389. See also [Robert Cecil,] "The Confederate Struggle and Recognition," *Quarterly Review* 112 (October 1862), 557.

146. [Sir George Cornewall Lewis], "Election of President Lincoln," *Edinburgh Review* 113 (April 1861), 574.

147. [William Rathbone Greg], "The Civil War in America," *National Review* 13 (July 1861), 158.

148. *Standard,* 20 August 1864, 4. *The Times* unlocked the mystery of the Union by claiming it was part of a corrupt bargain between the two sections: in return for obtaining high tariffs that provided them with a commercial monopoly, northerners recognized the "political ascendancy" of the southern-led Democratic Party. *The Times,* 24 November 1862, 6.

149. *Lloyd's Weekly Newspaper,* 15 September 1861, 1.

150. [Robert Hogarth Patterson], "The Crisis of the American War," *Blackwood's Edinburgh Magazine* 92 (November 1862), 641–643.

151. "The Periodical Press of the United States of America," *Fraser's Magazine* 68 (September 1863), 331–332.

152. *The Times,* 29 June 1862, 9; see also Henry Reeve and his discussion upon "territorial dominion," in "The Disunion of America," *Edinburgh Review* 114 (October 1861), 575.

153. [Robert Cecil], "The United States as an Example," *Quarterly Review* 117 (January 1865), 252.

154. Sala, *My Diary in America,* 1:399.

155. *Saturday Review,* 28 September 1861, 314.

156. Lyons to Russell, 8 April 1862, Russell Papers, PRO 30/22/36, National Archives; Lyons to Russell, 16 September 1864, Russell Papers, PRO 30/22/38, National Archives. See also *The Times,* 23 January 1863, 9.

157. *The Times,* 15 October 1861, 9.

158. Ibid., 16 October 1861, 8. Martin Crawford suggests that Russell's understanding of the northern effort as a battle for empire came from *The Times.* See Crawford, *Anglo-American Crisis of the Mid-Nineteenth Century,* 124–125.

159. *The Times,* 11 December 1861, 8.

160. See Lawley to Hartington, 14 June 1863, Cavendish Papers, 340.199, Devonshire Collection; Lawley to Gregory, 3 November 1861, Gregory Family Papers, Mss. 624, Box 24, Folder 1, Emory University Library Special Collections; Lawley to Gregory, 23 January 1862, Gregory Family Papers, Mss. 624, Box 24, Folder 2, Emory University Library Special Collections; Lawley to Gregory, 26 March 1863, Gregory Family Papers, Mss. 624, Box 24, Folder 3, Emory University Library Special Collections.

161. *The Times,* 23 January 1863, 9.

162. Ibid., 22 January 1864, 8.

163. Ibid., 3 March 1865, 8.

164. Ibid., 22 October 1861, 6.

165. [James Fitzjames Stephen], "England and America," *Fraser's Magazine* 68 (October 1863), 423.

166. [Charles Bowen], "Passing Events—Retrospect of the American Difficulty," *Macmillan's Magazine* 5 (February 1862), 354.

167. E[dward] D[icey], "The Outlook of the War," *Macmillan's Magazine* 6 (September 1862), 411.

168. *Spectator,* 9 August 1862, 883.

169. William Gladstone, "Gladstone's Letter to Schenk," *Harper's New Monthly Magazine* 54 (December 1876), 105.

170. Matthew, *Gladstone,* 190.

171. See Parish, "Gladstone and America," 101–103.

172. Bell, *The Idea of Greater Britain,* 236. For example, John Robert Seeley, whose famous *Expansion of England* (1883) both reflected and influenced British attitudes toward the empire and its governance, expressed a typically "eulogistic" stance toward American federalism.

173. William Gladstone, “Kin Beyond the Sea,” *North American Review* 127 (September–October, 1876), 182–183.

174. Ibid., 183.

175. Ibid., 186.

176. Ibid., 186.

177. Ibid., 184.

178. Ibid., 191.

179. Ibid., 187–189.

180. Ibid., 212.

BIBLIOGRAPHY

MANUSCRIPT SOURCES

Bodleian Library, Oxford, England

- Bryce Papers
- Clarendon Papers
- Harcourt Papers
- Hughenden Papers
- Kimberley Papers

British Library, London, England

- Bright Papers
- Carnarvon Papers
- Cobden Papers
- Dilke Papers
- Gladstone Papers
- Layard Papers
- Macmillan Papers
- Northcote/Iddesleigh Papers
- Palmerston Papers
- Ripon Papers

Cambridge University Library, Cambridge, England

- Acton Papers
- Stephen Papers

Centre for Buckinghamshire Studies, Aylesbury, England

- Somerset Papers

Devon Record Office, Exeter, England

- Somerset Papers

Devonshire Collection, Chatsworth, Bakewell, Derbyshire, England

- Cavendish Papers

Duke University Library Special Collections, Durham, North Carolina

- Malet Papers

Emory University Library Special Collections, Atlanta, Georgia
Gregory Family Papers
Exeter University Library Special Collections, Exeter, England
Northcote/Iddesleigh Collection
Hampshire Archives and Local Studies, Winchester, England
Malmesbury Collection
Hartley Library, University of Southampton, Southampton, England
Palmerston Papers
Library of Congress, Washington, D.C.
Hotze Papers
Mason Papers
Lincolnshire Archives, Lincoln, England
Monson Collection
Liverpool Record Office, Liverpool, England
Stanley Family Papers
London School of Economics Archive and Special Collections, London, England
Taylor-Mill Papers
National Archives, Kew, England
Colonial Office Papers
Foreign Office Papers
Granville Papers
Russell Papers
War Office Papers
National Library of Ireland, Dublin, Ireland
Cairnes Papers
National Library of Scotland, Edinburgh, Scotland
Blackwood Papers
National Library of Wales, Aberystwyth, Wales
Lewis Papers
National Maritime Museum, Greenwich, London, England
Lindsay Papers
News International, plc Archives, London, England
The Times Archive
Rothschild Archive, London, England
Belmont Papers
Somerset Archives and Local Studies, Taunton, England
Malet Papers
Suffolk Record Office, Ipswich, England
Cranbrook Collection

University of Nottingham, Nottingham, England
Papers of the Dukes of Newcastle
West Sussex Record Office, Chichester, England
Lyons Papers
Wren Library, Trinity College, Cambridge University, Cambridge, England
Houghton Collection

PRESS SOURCES

All the Year Around
Anthropological Review
Army and Navy Gazette
Army and Navy Journal
Bee-Hive
Blackwood's Edinburgh Magazine
British Quarterly Review
Colburn's United Service Magazine and Naval Military Review
Cornhill Magazine
Daily News
Daily Telegraph
Dublin University Magazine
Economist
Edinburgh Review
Fraser's Magazine
Harper's New Monthly Magazine
Household Words
Illustrated London News
Index
Journal of the Royal United Service Institution
Lloyd's Weekly Newspaper
London Review
Macmillan's Magazine
Monthly Review
Morning Herald
Morning Star
National Review
New Monthly Magazine and Humorist
North American Review

North British Review
Papers on Subjects Connected with the Duties of the Corps of Royal Engineers
Quarterly Review
Reynolds's Newspaper
Saturday Review
Spectator
Standard
Temple Bar
Times, The
Westminster Review

PUBLISHED PRIMARY SOURCES

Acton, John Dalberg Acton, Baron. *Acton in America: The American Journal of Sir John Acton, 1853.* Edited by S. W. Jackman. Shepherdstown: Patmos Press, 1979.

———. "The Civil War in America." In *Historical Essays and Studies,* edited by John Neville Figgis and Reginald Vere Laurence, 123–142. London: Macmillan, 1907.

———. "Nationality." In *Essays in the Liberal Interpretation of History: Selected Papers by Lord Acton,* edited by William H. McNeill, 131–159. Chicago: Univ. of Chicago Press, 1967.

Adams, Henry. *The Letters of Henry Adams.* Edited by J. C. Levenson. 6 vols. Cambridge, Mass.: Belknap Press of Harvard University Press, 1982–1988.

Adams, W. E. *The Slaveholders' War: An Argument for the North and the Negro.* London: J. Snow, 1863.

Alexander, James Edward. *Transatlantic Sketches, Comprising Visits to the Most Interesting Scenes in North and South America and the West Indies.* London: Bentley, 1833.

Anent the North American Continent. London: William Ridgway, 1864.

Argyll, George Douglas Campbell, Duke of. *Autobiography and Memoirs.* Edited by the Dowager Duchess of Argyll. 2 vols. London: John Murray, 1906.

Arnold, Matthew. *Complete Prose Works.* Edited by R. H. Super. Vol. 2, *Democratic Education.* Ann Arbor: Univ. of Michigan Press, 1963.

Ashworth, Henry. *A Tour of the United States, Cuba and Canada.* London: A. W. Bennett, 1861.

Bagehot, Walter. *The Collected Works of Walter Bagehot.* Edited by Norman St. John-Stevas. 15 vols. Cambridge, Mass.: Harvard Univ. Press, 1965–1986.

———. *The English Constitution.* Ithaca, N.Y.: Cornell Univ. Press, 1981.

———. *Essays on Parliamentary Reform.* London: Kegan Paul, Trench, 1883.

Bell, George, Sir. *Soldier's Glory: Being Rough Notes of an Old Soldier.* London: G. Bell and Sons, 1956.

Belmont, August. *A Few Letters and Speeches of the Late Civil War.* New York: Privately printed, 1870.

Beresford Hope, Alexander James Beresford. *England, the North, and the South: Being a Popular View of the American Civil War.* London: James Ridgway, 1862.

———. *The Results of the American Disruption: The Substance of a Lecture Delivered by Request before the Maidstone's Literary & Mechanics' Institution, in Continuation of a Popular view of the American Civil War, and England, the North and the South.* London: James Ridgway, 1862.

———. *The Social and Political Bearings of the American Disruption.* London: William Ridgway, 1863.

Bernard, Montague, B.C.L. *Two Lectures on the Present American War.* London: J. H. and Jas. Parker, 1861.

Bigelow, John. *Retrospections of an Active Life.* 5 vols. New York: Baker and Taylor, 1909–1913.

Bird, Isabella. *The Englishwoman in America.* London: John Murray, 1856.

Birmingham and Midland Freedmen's-Aid Association. *The Speeches (On Behalf of the Four Millions of Coloured People Freed from Slavery by the Late Civil War in America,) Delivered in the Town Hall, Birmingham, on Wednesday Evening, August 2, 1865.* London: S. W. Partridge, 1865.

Blackman, E. L., Rev. *Our Relations with America.* Manchester: Committee of the Manchester Southern Club, 1863.

Blanc, Louis. *Letters on England.* 2 vols. London: Sampson Low, Son, and Marston, 1866.

Borcke, Heros von. *Memoirs of the Confederate War of Independence.* 2 vols. London: William Blackwood and Sons, 1866.

Bourne, Kenneth, and D. Cameron Watt, eds. *British Documents on Foreign Affairs—Reports and Papers from the Foreign Office Confidential Print, Part 1, Series C, North America, 1837–1914.* Vol. 5, *The Civil War Years, 1859–1861.* Bethesda, Md.: University Publications of America, 1986.

———, eds. *British Documents on Foreign Affairs—Reports and Papers from the Foreign Office Confidential Print, Part 1, Series C, North America, 1837–1914.* Vol. 6, *The Civil War Years, 1862–1865.* Bethesda, Md.: University Publications of America, 1986.

Bright, John. *Speeches of John Bright on the American Question.* Boston: Little, Brown, 1865.

———. *Speeches on Parliamentary Reform, &c., by John Bright Delivered during the Autumn of 1866, to the People of England, Scotland, and Ireland, at Birmingham, Manchester, Leeds, Glasgow, Dublin, and London.* London: Simpkin, Marshall, and Co., 1866.

——. *Speech of Mr. Bright, MP, in the Town Hall, Birmingham.* Birmingham: Joseph Allen, 1862.

Buckingham, James Silk. *The Eastern and Western States of America.* 3 vols. London: Fisher, Son and Co., 1842.

——. *The Slave States of America.* 2 vols. London: Fisher, Son and Co., 1842.

Burn, James Dawson. *Three Years among the Working-Classes in the United States during the War.* London: Smith, Elder and Co., 1865.

Butler, Pierce. *Mr. Butler's Statement; Originally Prepared in Aid of His Professional Counsel.* Philadelphia: John C. Clark, 1850.

Cairnes, John Elliott. *The Revolution in America: A Lecture.* Dublin: Hodges, Smith and Co., 1864.

——. *The Slave Power: Its Character, Career, and Probable Designs: Being an Attempt to Explain the Real Issues Involved in the American Contest.* Columbia: Univ. of South Carolina Press, 2003.

——. *Who Are the Canters?* London: Ladies' London Emancipation Society, 1863.

Campbell, John Francis. *A Short American Tramp in the Fall of 1864.* Edinburgh: Edmonston and Douglas, 1865.

Chesney, Charles Cornwallis. *Essays in Modern Military Biography.* London: Longmans, Green and Co., 1874.

——. *A Military View of Recent Campaigns in Virginia and Maryland.* 2 vols. London: Smith, Elder and Co., 1863–1865.

Chesnut, Mary. *Mary Chesnut's Civil War.* Edited by C. Vann Woodward. New Haven, Conn.: Yale Univ. Press, 1981.

Civis Anglicus. *A Voice from the Motherland, Answering Mrs. H. Beecher Stowe's Appeal.* London: Trubner and Co., 1863.

Cobbe, Frances Power. *The Red Flag in John Bull's Eyes.* London: Ladies' London Emancipation Society, 1863.

Combe, George. *Notes on the United States of North America during a Phrenological Visit in 1838–9–40.* 3 vols. Edinburgh: Machlachlan, Stewart, 1841.

Corbett, James Paul. *An Answer to the Manchester Southern Club, or Southern Independence Association.* Manchester: Abel Heywood and John Heywood, 1863.

Corsan, William. *Two Months in the Confederate States; an Englishman's Travels through the South.* Edited by Benjamin Trask. Baton Rouge: Louisiana State Univ. Press, 1996.

Cossham, Handel. *The American War: Facts and Fallacies.* Bristol: Whereat, 1864.

Davis, Jefferson. *The Messages and Papers of Jefferson Davis and the Confederacy, Including Diplomatic Correspondence, 1861–1865.* Edited by James D. Richardson. 2 vols. New York: Chelsea House–R. Hector, 1966.

Day, Samuel Phillips. *Down South; or, an Englishman's Experience at the Seat of the American War.* 2 vols. London: Hurst and Blackett, 1862.

De Leon, T. C. *Belles, Beaux and Brains of the 60's.* New York: G. W. Dillingham Company, 1909.

Derby, Edward George Smith Stanley, Earl of. *Journal of a Tour in America, 1824–1825.* London: Privately printed, 1930.

Derby, Edward Henry Stanley, Earl of. *Disraeli, Derby and the Conservative Party: Journals and Memoirs of Edward Henry, Lord Stanley 1849–1869.* Edited by John Vincent. Hassocks, England: Harvester Press, 1978.

Dicey, Edward. *Six Months in the Federal States.* 2 vols. London: Macmillan, 1863.

——. *Spectator of America.* Edited by Herbert Mitgang. Athens: Univ. of Georgia Press, 1989.

Dickens, Charles. *The Letters of Charles Dickens.* Edited by Walter Dexter. 3 vols. Bloomsbury: Nonesuch Press, 1938.

——. *The Letters of Charles Dickens.* Edited by Madeline House and Graham Storey. 12 vols. Oxford: Clarendon Press, 1965–2002.

——. *The Works of Charles Dickens.* Vol. 19, *American Notes and Pictures from Italy.* London: Chapman and Hall, 1882.

Dilke, Charles Wentworth. *Greater Britain: A Record of Travel in English-Speaking Countries during 1866 and 1867.* 2 vols. London: Macmillan, 1868.

Dill, Samuel Marcus, Rev. *The American Conflict: A Lecture.* Belfast: Daily Northern Whig, 1863.

Douglass, Frederick. *The Frederick Douglass Papers.* Edited by John W. Blassingame. Series 1 (4 vols.) and Series 2 (2 vols.). New Haven, Conn.: Yale Univ. Press, 1979–1992.

Earl Russell and the Slave Power. Manchester: Union and Emancipation Society, 1863.

Essays on Reform. London: Macmillan, 1867.

Estcourt, J. H. *Rebellion and Recognition: Slavery, Sovereignty, Secession, and Recognition Considered.* Manchester: Union and Emancipation Society of Manchester, 1863.

Featherstonhaugh, George. *Excursion through the Slave States, from Washington on the Potomac, to the Frontier of Mexico.* New York: Harper, 1844.

Ferguson, Robert. *America during and after the War.* London: Longmans, Green, Reader, and Dyer, 1866.

Fergusson, James, Sir. *Notes of a Tour in North America in 1861.* Edinburgh: Privately printed, 1861.

Fletcher, Henry Charles. *History of the American War.* 3 vols. London. Richard Bentley, 1865–1866.

Forster, W. E., and Goldwin Smith. *Speech of Mr. W. E. Forster, M.P., on the Slaveholders' Rebellion; and Professor Goldwin Smith's Letter on the Morality of the Emancipation Proclamation.* Manchester: Union and Emancipation Society, 1863.

Fremantle, Arthur James Lyon, Sir. *Three Months in the Southern States: April–June 1863.* Lincoln: Univ. of Nebraska Press, 1991.

Gibbs, Frederick Waymouth, C.B. *Recognition: A Chapter from the History of the North American and South American States.* London: W. Ridgway, 1863.

Gilzean-Reid, Hugh, Sir, and P. J. Macdonell. "The Press." In *The Civilisation of Our Day. A Series of Original Essays on Some of Its More Important Phases at the Close of the Nineteenth Century, by Expert Writers,* edited by John Samuelson, 276–292. London: Sampson Low, Marston and Company, 1896.

Gladstone, William. *Mr. Gladstone's Address and Speeches at Manchester.* London: John Murray, 1862.

———. *Speeches on Parliamentary Reform in 1866.* London: John Murray, 1866.

Goddard, S. A. *Reply to Mr. Roebuck's Speech at Sheffield, on the American Question.* Birmingham: E. C. Osborne, 1863.

Godkin, E. L. *Life and Letters of Edwin Lawrence Godkin.* Edited by Rollo Ogden. 2 vols. New York: Macmillan, 1907.

Grattan, Thomas Colley. *Civilized America.* 2 vols. London: Bradbury and Evans, 1859.

Gregory, William, Sir. *Sir William Gregory, KCMG, Formerly Member of Parliament and Sometime Governor of Ceylon: An Autobiography.* Edited by Lady Gregory. London: John Murray, 1894.

Grey, Henry George Grey, Earl. *Parliamentary Government Considered with Reference to a Reform of Parliament.* London: Richard Bentley, 1858.

Guttsman, W. L., ed. *A Plea for Democracy: An Edited Selection from the 1867 "Essays on Reform" and "Questions for a Reformed Parliament."* London: MacGibbon and Kee, 1967.

Hall, Basil. *Travels in North America in the Years 1827 and 1828.* 3 vols. Edinburgh: Printed for R. Cadell, 1830.

Hall, Newman. *The American War.* London: James Nisbet and Co., 1862.

Hamilton, Thomas. *Men and Manners in America.* 2 vols. Edinburgh: William Blackwood, 1833.

Hamley, Edward Bruce. *The Operations of War Explained and Illustrated.* London: William Blackwood and Sons, 1866.

Hare, Thomas. *The Machinery of Representation.* London: W. Maxwell, 1857.

[Harcourt, William Vernon]. *Letters by Historicus on Some Questions of International Law.* London: Macmillan, 1863.

Harrison, Burton. *Recollections Grave and Gay.* New York: Charles Scribner's Sons, 1912.

Harrison, Richard, Sir. *Recollections of Life in the British Army during the Latter Half of the 19th Century.* London: Smith, Elder and Co., 1908.

Henderson, G.F.R. *The Science of War: A Collection of Essays and Lectures, 1892–1903.* New York: Longmans. Green, 1905.

——. *Stonewall Jackson and the American Civil War.* New York: Barnes and Noble, 1961.

Hobart-Hampden, Augustus Charles. *Sketches from My Life.* New York: D. Appleton and Company, 1887.

Hopps, John Page. *Southern Independence: A Lecture.* London: Whitfield, Green, and Son, 1865.

Hotze, Henry. *Henry Hotze, Confederate Propagandist: Selected Writings on Revolution, Recognition, and Race.* Edited by Lonnie A. Burnett. Tuscaloosa: Univ. of Alabama Press, 2008.

Hughes, Thomas. *The Cause of Freedom: Which Is Its Champion in America, the North or the South?* London: Emancipation Society, 1863.

Hunt, James. *On the Negro's Place in Nature.* London: Trubner and Co., 1863.

Huxley, Thomas. *Professor Huxley on the Negro Question.* London: Ladies' London Emancipation Society, 1864.

Johnson, James Finlay Weir. *Notes on North America; Agricultural, Economical, and Social.* 2 vols. Boston: C. Little and J. Brown, 1850–1851.

Jones, Ernest. *The Slaveholder's War.* Ashton-under-Lyne: Union and Emancipation Society, 1863.

Kemble, Frances Anne. *Journal of a Residence in America.* Paris: A. and W. Galignani, 1835.

——. *Journal of a Residence on a Georgian Plantation in 1838–1839.* New York: Harper and Brothers, 1863.

Kershaw, T. Bentley. *The Truth of the American Question.* Manchester: Southern Independence Association, 1864.

Lawrence, G. G. *Three Months in America in the Summer of 1863; Two Lectures Given in Huddersfield.* London: Whittaker and Co., 1864.

Lawrence, George Alfred. *Border and Bastille.* New York: W. I. Pooley and Co., 1863.

Leigh, Frances Butler. *Ten Years on a Georgia Plantation since the War.* London: Richard Bentley and Son, 1883.

Leng, William C. *The American War: The Aims, Antecedents, and Principles of the Belligerents.* Dundee: Advertiser Office, 1863.

Letter on the American War by a Northern Sympathiser. London: Nisbet and Co., 1863.

Lewis, George Cornewall, Sir. *A Dialogue on the Best Form of Government.* London: Parker Son and Bourn, 1863.

——. *Letters of the Right Hon. Sir George Cornewall Lewis, Bart. To Various Friends.* Edited by Rev. Sir Gilbert Frankland Lewis. London: Longmans, Green, 1870.

Lothian, William Schomberg Robert Kerr, Marquess of. *The Confederate Secession.* Edinburgh: William Blackwood and Sons, 1864.

Ludlow, J. M. *American Slavery.* London: Ladies' London Emancipation Society, 1864.

———. *The Southern Minister and His Slave-Convert.* Manchester: Emancipation Society, 1863.

Lyell, Charles, Sir. *A Second Visit to the United States of North America.* 2 vols. London: John Murray, 1849.

MacDougall, Patrick Leonard, Sir. *Modern Warfare as Influenced by Modern Artillery.* London: John Murray, 1864.

Mackay, Alexander. *The Western World; or, Travels in the United States in 1846–47.* 3 vols. New York: Negro Universities Press, 1968.

Mackay, Charles. *Forty Years' Recollections of Life, Literature, and Public Affairs from 1830 to 1870.* 2 vols. London: Chapman and Hall, 1870.

———. *Through the Long Day or, Memorials of a Literary Life during Half a Century.* 2 vols. London: W. H. Allen and Co., 1887.

Malet, William Wyndham. *An Errand to the South in the Summer of 1862.* London: Richard Bentley, 1863.

Mallock, W. H., and Lady Guendolen Ramsden, eds. *Letters, Remains, and Memoirs of Edward Adolphus Seymour, Twelfth Duke of Somerset.* London: Richard Bentley and Son, 1893.

Malmesbury, James Howard Harris, 3rd Earl of. *Memoirs of an Ex-Minister: An Autobiography.* 2 vols. London: Longmans, Green, 1884.

Marryat, Frederick. *A Diary in America.* New York: Knopf, 1962.

Martineau, Harriet. *The Collected Letters of Harriet Martineau.* Edited by Deborah Anna Logan. 5 vols. London: Pickering and Chatto, 2007.

———. *Harriet Martineau's Autobiography.* Edited by Maria Weston Chapman. 2 vols. Boston: James R. Osgood and Company, 1877.

———. *Harriet Martineau's Letters to Fanny Wedgwood.* Edited by Elisabeth Sanders Arbuckle. Stanford: Stanford Univ. Press, 1983.

———. *Society in America.* 3 vols. New York: AMS Press, 1966.

The Martyrdom of John Brown. London: Emancipation Society, 1864.

Marx, Karl. *The Civil War in the United States.* New York: International Publishers, 1961.

Mason, Virginia. *The Public Life and Diplomatic Correspondence of James M. Mason.* Roanoke, Va.: Stone Printing and Manufacturing Co., 1903.

Massachusetts Historical Society. "Bright-Sumner Letters, 1861–1872." *Proceedings* 46 (October 1912–June 1913): 93–166.

———. "Letters of the Duke and Duchess of Argyll to Charles Sumner." *Proceedings* 47 (October 1913–June 1914): 66–107.

Massie, James William. *The American Crisis, in Relation to the Anti-Slavery Cause.* London: John Snow, 1862.

———. *Report of the Proceedings at a Conversazione, Held in the Manchester Athenaeum, on Monday Evening, February 1, 1864.* Manchester: Union and Emancipation Society, 1864.

Mill, John Stuart. *On Liberty and Considerations on Representative Government.* New York: Macmillan, 1947.

———. *Thoughts on Parliamentary Reform.* London: John W. Parker and Son, 1859.

Moran, Benjamin. *The Journal of Benjamin Moran, 1857–1865.* 2 vols. Edited by Sarah Agnes Wallace and Frances Elma Gillespie. Chicago: Univ. of Chicago Press, 1948.

Morton, William Lewis, ed. *Monck Letters and Journals, 1863–1868: Canada from Government House at Confederation.* Toronto: McClelland and Stewart, 1970.

Motley, John Lothrop. *The Correspondence of John Lothrop Motley.* Edited by George William Curtis. 2 vols. New York: Harper and Brothers, 1889.

Murray, Amelia. *Letters from the United States, Cuba and Canada.* New York: G. P. Putnam and Company, 1856.

National Committee of British Freed-Men's Aid Societies. *Report of the Proceedings at Meetings Held at the Westminster Palace Hotel, May 17, 1865.* London: S. W. Partridge, 1865.

Nemo. *Remarks on the Policy of Recognizing the Independence of the Southern States of North America and on the Struggle in That Continent.* London: Effingham Wilson, 1863.

Newman, Francis. *Character of the Southern States of America: Letter to a Friend Who Had Joined the Southern Independence Association.* Manchester: Union and Emancipation Society, 1863.

———. *The Good Cause of President Lincoln.* London: Emancipation Society, 1863.

Nightingale, Florence. *Letters from Egypt: A Journey on the Nile, 1849–1850.* New York: Weidenfeld and Nicolson, 1987.

Ozanne, T. D. *The South as It Is, or Twenty-One Years' Experience in the Southern States of America.* London: Saunders, Otley and Co., 1863.

Proceedings at the Public Breakfast Held in Honour of William Lloyd Garrison of Boston, Massachusetts in St. James's Hall, London, on Saturday, June 29, 1867. London: William Tweedie, 1868.

Recognition of the Southern Confederacy, Indispensable for Resolving the American Question. London: William Ridgway, 1863.

Reid, Hugo. *The American Question in a Nut-Shell; or, Why We Should Recognize the Confederates.* London: Robert Hardwicke, 1862.

Ross, Fitzgerald. *Cities and Camps of the Confederate States.* Urbana: Univ. of Illinois Press, 1958.

Russell, John Russell, Earl. *The Later Correspondence of Lord John Russell, 1840–1878.* 2 vols. London: Longmans, Green, 1925.

——. *Recollections and Suggestions, 1813–1873.* Boston: Roberts Brothers, 1875.

——. *Speech of the Earl Russell at Newcastle on Monday, October 14 1861 at the Banquet Given in His Honor.* London: Longman, Green, Longman, and Roberts, 1861.

Russell, William Howard. *My Diary North and South.* Boston: T.O.H.P. Burnham, 1863.

——. *William Howard Russell's Civil War: Private Diary and Letters, 1861–1862.* Edited by Martin Crawford. Athens: Univ. of Georgia Press, 1992.

Sala, George. *The Life and Adventures of George Augustus Sala.* 2 vols. New York: Charles Scribner's Sons, 1895.

——. *My Diary in America in the Midst of War.* 2 vols. London: Tinsley Brothers, 1865.

——. *Things I Have Seen and People I Have Known.* 2 vols. London: Cassell and Company, 1894.

Scheibert, Justus. *Seven Months in the Rebel States during the North American War, 1863.* Tuscaloosa: Confederate Publishing Company, 1958.

Seebohm, Frederic. *The Crisis of Emancipation in America, Being a Review of the History of Emancipation, from the Beginning of the American War to the Assassination of President Lincoln.* London: A. W. Bennett, 1865.

Selbourne, Roundell Palmer, Earl. *Memorials.* 4 vols. London: Macmillan, 1896.

The Slavery Quarrel; with Plans and Prospects of Reconciliation. London: Robert Hardwicke, 1863.

Smith, Goldwin. *The Civil War in America: An Address Read at the Last Meeting of the Manchester Union and Emancipation Society.* London: Simpkin, Marshall and Co., 1866.

——. *England and America: A Lecture Delivered by Goldwin Smith before the Boston Fraternity, during his Recent Visit to the United States.* Manchester: A. Ireland and Co., 1865

——. *A Letter to a Whig Member of the Southern Independence Association.* London: Macmillan, 1864.

——. *Reminiscences.* New York: Macmillan, 1910.

Spence, James *The American Union; Its Effect on National Character and Policy, with an Inquiry into Secession as a Constitutional Right, and the Causes of the Disruption.* London: Richard Bentley, 1862.

——. *On the Recognition of the Southern Confederation.* London: Richard Bentley, 1862.

——. *Southern Independence: An Address Delivered at a Public Meeting in the City Hall, Glasgow.* London: Richard Bentley, 1863.

Stephen, Leslie. *The "Times" on the American War: A Historical Study.* London: William Ridgeway, 1865.

Stevenson, William J. *Thirteen Months in the Rebel Army.* New York: A. S. Barnes and Burr, 1862.

Stirling, James. *Letters from the Slave States.* New York: Negro Universities Press, 1969.

Stuart-Wortley, Emmeline, Lady. *Travels in the United States, etc. during 1849 and 1850.* 3 vols. New York: Harper and Brothers, 1851.

Thomas, Frederick Moy, ed. *Fifty Years of Fleet Street; Being the Life and Recollections of Sir John R. Robinson.* London: Macmillan, 1904.

Thompson, George. *Slavery in America: A Lecture.* London: London Emancipation Committee, 1860.

Tocqueville, Alexis de. *Alexis de Tocqueville on Democracy, Revolution, and Society.* Edited by John Stone and Stephen Mennell. Chicago: Univ. of Chicago Press, 1980.

———. *Democracy in America.* Edited by Erik von Kuehnelt-Leddihn. 2 vols. New Rochelle, N.Y.: Arlington House, 1965.

Trelawny, Sir John. *The Parliamentary Diaries of Sir John Trelawny, 1858–1865.* Edited by T. A. Jenkins. London: Royal Historical Society, 1990.

Trimble, Robert. *The Negro, North and South: The Status of the Coloured Population in the Northern and Southern States of America Compared.* London: Whittaker and Co., 1863.

Trollope, Anthony. *An Autobiography.* 2 vols. Edinburgh: William Blackwood and Sons, 1883.

———. *North America.* New York: Da Capo Press, 1986.

———. *The West Indies and the Spanish Main.* London: Chapman and Hall, 1859.

Trollope, Frances. *Domestic Manners of the Americans.* 2 vols. London: Whittaker, Treacher, and Co., 1832.

United States of America. *The Case of the United States to be Laid before the Tribunal of Arbitration to be Convened at Geneva.* Washington: Government Printing Office, 1872.

United States of America, Navy Dept. *Official Records of the Union and Confederate Navies in the War of Rebellion,* ser. 2, vol. 3. Washington, D.C.: Government Printing Office, 1922.

United States of America, War Dept. *The War of the Rebellion: A Compilation of the Official Records of the Union and Confederate Armies,* ser. 1, vol. 34. Washington, D.C.: Government Printing Office, 1880–1898.

Vizetelly, Henry. *Glances Back through Seventy Years: Autobiographical and Other Reminiscences.* 2 vols. London: Kegan Paul, Trench, Trubner and Co., 1893.

Waddington, John. *The American Crisis in Relation to Slavery.* London: Elliot Stock, 1862.

Wolseley, Garnet, Viscount. *The Story of a Soldier's Life.* 2 vols. London: Archibald Constable and Company, 1903.

Worden, John. *The Plain English of American Affairs.* London: Alfred W. Bennett, 1863.

Secondary Sources

Adams, Ephraim Douglass. *Great Britain and the American Civil War.* New York: Russell and Russell, 1958.

Adams, Michael C. C. *Fighting for Defeat: Union Military Failure in the East, 1861–1865.* Lincoln: Univ. of Nebraska Press, 1978.

Allen, H. C. "Civil War, Reconstruction, and Great Britain." In *Heard Round the World: The Impact Abroad of the Civil War,* edited by Harold Hyman, 3–96. New York: Knopf, 1969.

———. *Great Britain and the United States: A History of Anglo-American Relations (1783–1952).* New York: St. Martin's Press, 1955.

Altick, Richard Daniel. *The English Common Reader: A Social History of the Mass Reading Public, 1800–1900.* Chicago: Univ. of Chicago Press, 1983.

Anderson, Benedict. *Imagined Communities: Reflections on the Origin and Spread of Nationalism.* New York: Verso, 1991.

Andrews, James R. "The Rhetorical Shaping of National Interest: Morality and Contextual Potency in John Bright's Parliamentary Speech against Recognition of the Confederacy." *Quarterly Journal of Speech* 79 (1993): 40–60.

Archibald, Edith. *Life and Letters of Sir Edward Mortimer Archibald, KCMG, CB: A Memoir of Fifty Years of Service.* Toronto: George N. Morang, 1924.

Armitage, David, Thomas Bender, Leslie Butler, Don H. Doyle, Susan-Mary Grant, Charles S. Maier, Jörg Nagler, Paul Quigley, and Jay Sexton. "Interchange: Nationalism and Internationalism in the Era of the Civil War." *Journal of American History* 98 (2011): 455–489.

Armstrong, Margaret. *Fanny Kemble: A Passionate Victorian.* New York: Macmillan, 1938.

Ashley, Evelyn. *The Life of Henry John Temple, Viscount Palmerston; with Selections from His Diaries and Correspondence.* London: Richard Bentley, 1870–1874.

Ash, Stephen. *When the Yankees Came: Conflict and Chaos in the Occupied South, 1861–1865.* Chapel Hill: Univ. of North Carolina Press, 1995.

Atkins, John Black. *The Life of Sir William Howard Russell, the First Special Correspondent.* 2 vols. London: John Murray, 1911.

Augstein, H. F. *James Cowles Prichard's Anthropology: Remaking the Science of Man in Early Nineteenth-Century Britain.* Atlanta: Rodopi, 1999.

Baker, Jean H. *Affairs of Party: The Political Culture of Northern Democrats in the Mid-Nineteenth Century.* Ithaca, N.Y.: Cornell Univ. Press, 1983.

Bakhtin, M. M. *The Dialogic Imagination.* Austin: Univ. of Texas Press, 1981.

Banton, Michael. *The Idea of Race.* London: Tavistock Publications, 1977.

Barker, Francis, Peter Hulme, Margeret Iverson, and Diana Loxley, eds. *Europe and Its Others, Proceedings of the Essex Conferences on the Sociology of Literature.* Colchester: University of Essex, 1985.

——. *Racial Theories.* New York: Cambridge Univ. Press, 1987.

Barker, Hannah. *Newspapers, Politics and English Society, 1695-1855.* New York: Longman, 1999.

Barrow, J. W. "Evolution and Anthropology in the 1860's: The Anthropological Society of London, 1863–1871." *Victorian Studies* 7 (1963): 137–154.

Beach, William Thomas. *The Story of* The Spectator. London: Metheun, 1928.

Beales, Derek. *England and Italy, 1859–60.* New York: Thomas Nelson and Sons, 1961.

Beasley, Edward. *The Victorian Reinvention of Race: New Racisms and the Problem of Grouping in the Human Sciences.* New York: Routledge, 2010.

Beckert, Sven. "Emancipation and Empire: Reconstructing the World Wide Web of Cotton." *American Historical Review* 109 (2004): 1405–1438.

Beeching, Jack. *The Chinese Opium Wars.* New York: Harcourt Brace Jovanovich, 1975.

Belich, James. "Myth, Race, and Identity in New Zealand." *New Zealand Journal of History* 31 (1997): 9–22.

Bell, Duncan. *The Idea of Greater Britain: Empire and the Future of World Order, 1860–1900.* Princeton, N.J.: Princeton Univ. Press, 2007.

Bellows, Donald. "A Study of British Conservative Reaction to the American Civil War." *Journal of Southern History* 51 (1985): 505–526.

Beloff, Max. "Great Britain and the American Civil War." *History* 37 (1952): 40–48.

Belz, Herman. *Emancipation and Equal Rights: Politics and Constitutionalism in the Civil War Era.* New York: Norton, 1978.

——. *Reconstructing the Union: Theory and Policy during the Civil War.* Ithaca, N.Y.: Cornell Univ. Press, 1969.

Bender, Thomas. *A Nation among Nations: America's Place in World History.* New York: Hill and Wang, 2006.

Bennett, Andrew, ed. *Readers and Reading.* New York: Longman, 1995.

Bentley, Michael. *Politics Without Democracy: Great Britain, 1815-1914.* Totowa: Barnes and Noble Books, 1984.

Berger, Max. "American Slavery as Seen by British Visitors, 1836–1860." *Journal of Negro History* 30 (1945): 181–202.

——. *The British Traveller in America, 1836-1860.* Gloucester, Mass.: Peter Smith, 1964.

Beringer, Richard E., Herman Hattaway, Archer Jones, and William Still. *Why the South Lost the Civil War.* Athens: Univ. of Georgia Press, 1986.

Bernath, Michael T. *Confederate Minds: The Struggle for Intellectual Independence in the Civil War South.* Chapel Hill: Univ. of North Carolina Press, 2010.

Bernstein, George. "Special Relationship and Appeasement: Liberal Policy towards America in the Age of Palmerston." *Historical Journal* 41 (1998): 725–750.

Berwanger, Eugene H. *The British Foreign Service and the American Civil War.* Lexington: Univ. Press of Kentucky, 1994.

Bevington, Merle Mowbray. *The Saturday Review, 1855–1868: Representative Educated Opinion in Victorian England.* New York: Columbia Univ. Press, 1941.

Bhabha, Homi K. *The Location of Culture.* New York: Routledge, 2004.

Biagini, Eugenio. *Gladstone.* New York: Macmillan, 2000.

——. *Liberty, Retrenchment and Reform: Popular Liberalism in the Age of Gladstone 1860–1880.* New York: Cambridge Univ. Press, 1992.

Billington, Ray Allen. *Land of Savagery Land of Promise: The European Image of the American Frontier.* New York: Norton, 1981.

Binnington, Ian. *Confederate Visions: Nationalism, Symbolism, and the Imagined South in the Civil War.* Charlottesville: Univ. of Virginia Press, 2013.

Blackett, R.J.M. "African Americans, the British Working Class and the American Civil War." *Slavery and Abolition* 17 (1996): 51–67.

——. "British Views of the Confederacy." In *Britain and the American South: From Colonialism to Rock and Roll,* edited by Joseph Ward, 141–162. Jackson: Univ. Press of Mississippi, 2003.

——. *Building an Antislavery Wall: Black Americans in the Atlantic Abolitionist Movement, 1830–1860.* Baton Rouge: Louisiana State Univ. Press, 1983.

——. *Divided Hearts: Britain and the American Civil War.* Baton Rouge: Louisiana State Univ. Press, 2001.

——. "The Transatlantic Address to Lincoln: Birmingham and the American Civil War." *American Nineteenth Century History* 3 (2002): 29–52.

Black, Robert. *The Conservative Party from Peel to Churchill.* London: Eyre and Spottiswoode, 1970.

Blake, Peter. "George Augustus Sala and the English Middle-Class View of America." *Interdisciplinary Studies in the Long Nineteenth Century* 9 (2009): http://www.19.bbk.ac.uk/articles/10.16995/ntn.509/.

Blake, Robert. *Disraeli.* Garden City, N.Y.: Anchor Books, 1968.

Blumenthal, Henry. "Confederate Diplomacy: Popular Notions and International Realities." *Journal of Southern History* 32 (1966): 151–171.

Bocklehurst, Helen, and Robert Phillips. *History, Nationhood and the Question of Britain.* New York: Palgrave Macmillan, 2004.

Bolt, Christine. *The Anti-Slavery Movement and Reconstruction: A Study in Anglo-American Co-operation, 1833–1877.* New York: Oxford Univ. Press, 1969.

———. "British Attitudes to Reconstruction in the United States, 1863–1877." University of London, D.Phil., 1966.

———. "Race and the Victorians." In *British Imperialism in the Nineteenth Century,* edited by C. C. Eldridge, 126–147. London: Macmillan, 1984.

———. *Victorian Attitudes to Race.* London: Routledge and Kegan Paul, 1971.

Bolton, Charles C. *Poor Whites of the Antebellum South: Tenants and Laborers in Central North Carolina and Northeast Mississippi.* Durham, N.C.: Duke Univ. Press, 1994.

Bond, Bradley G. *Political Culture in the Nineteenth-Century South: Mississippi, 1830–1900.* Baton Rouge: Louisiana State University, 1995.

Bonham, Milledge. *The British Consuls in the Confederacy.* New York: Columbia University, 1911.

Bonner, Robert E. *Mastering America: Southern Slaveholders and the Crisis of American Nationhood.* New York: Cambridge Univ. Press, 2009.

———. "Roundheaded Cavaliers? The Context and Limits of a Confederate Racial Project." *Civil War History* 48 (2002): 34–59.

———. "Slavery, Confederate Diplomacy, and the Racialist Mission of Henry Hotze." *Civil War History* 5 (2005): 288–316.

Bonner-Smith, D., and E.W.R. Lumby, eds. *The Second China War, 1856–1860.* London: Spottiswoode, Ballantyne, 1954.

Borrit, Gabor S. "Punch Lincoln: Some Thoughts on Cartoons in the British Magazine." *Journal of the Abraham Lincoln Association* 15 (1994): 1–21.

———, ed. *Why the Confederacy Lost.* New York: Oxford Univ. Press, 1992.

Bourne, Kenneth. *Britain and the Balance of Power in North America, 1815–1908.* Berkeley: Univ. of California Press, 1967.

———. "British Preparations for War with the North, 1861–1862." *English Historical Review* 76 (1961): 600–632.

Brake, Laurel, Aled Jones, and Lionel Madden, eds. *Investigating Victorian Journalism.* London: Macmillan, 1990.

Brantlinger, Patrick. "Victorians and Africans: The Genealogy of the Myth of the Dark Continent." *Critical Inquiry* 12 (1985): 166–203.

Bratton, J. S. "English Ethiopians: British Audiences and Black-Face Acts, 1835–1865." *Yearbook of English Studies* 11 (1981): 127–142.

Brauer, Kinley J. "British Mediation and the American Civil War: A Reconsideration." *Journal of Southern History* 38 (1972): 49–64.

———. "Seward, American Politics, and Anglo-American Relations: The British Perspective." *American Chronicle* 1 (1972): 48–55.

Breckenridge, Carol A., and Peter van der Veer, eds. *Orientalism and the Postcolonial Predicament: Perspectives on South Asia.* Philadelphia: Univ. of Pennsylvania Press, 1993.

Brewster, David. "Ulysses S. Grant and Newcastle upon Tyne." *Durham University Journal* 30 (1969): 119–128.

Brockliss, Laurence, and David Eastwood, eds. *A Union of Multiple Identities: The British Isles, c. 1750–c. 1850.* New York: Manchester Univ. Press, 1997.

Brogan, Hugh. *Alexis de Tocqueville: A Life.* New Haven, Conn.: Yale Univ. Press, 2006.

——. "America and Walter Bagehot." *American Studies* 11 (1977): 335–356.

Brown, David. "Compelling but not Controlling? Palmerston and the Press, 1846–1855." *History* 86 (2001): 41–61.

——. *Palmerston: A Biography.* New Haven, Conn.: Yale Univ. Press, 2010.

Brown, Lucy. "The Treatment of the News in Mid-Victorian Newspapers." *Transactions of the Royal Historical Society* 27 (1977): 23–39.

——. *Victorian News and Newspapers.* Oxford: Clarendon Press, 1985.

Buchan, Alastair. *The Spare Chancellor: The Life of Walter Bagehot.* East Lansing: Michigan State Univ. Press, 1960.

Bullard, F. Lauriston. *Famous War Correspondents.* Boston: Little, Brown, 1914.

Bunker, Gary L. "The Comic News, Lincoln, and the Civil War." *Journal of the Abraham Lincoln Association* 17 (1996): 53–87.

Burk, Kathleen. *Old World, New World.* New York: Atlantic Monthly Press, 2007.

Burn, W. L. *The Age of Equipoise.* New York: Norton, 1964.

Burnet, Alastair. *America 1843–1993: 150 Years of Reporting the American Connection.* London: Economist Books, 1993.

Burnham, Edward Levy-Lawson, Baron. *Peterborough Court: The Story of the Daily Telegraph.* London: Cassell and Company, 1955.

Burrow, J. W. "Evolution and Anthropology in the 1860's: The Anthropological Society of London, 1863–1871." *Victorian Studies* 7 (1963): 137–154.

Bush, Barbara. *Imperialism and Postcolonialism.* Harlow, UK: Longman, 2006.

Camlot, Jason. *Style and the Nineteenth-Century British Critic: Sincere Mannerisms.* Burlington, Vt.: Ashgate, 2008.

Campbell, Duncan Andrew. *English Public Opinion and the American Civil War.* Rochester, N.Y.: Boydell Press/Royal Historical Society, 2003.

——. "Palmerston and the American Civil War." In *Palmerston Studies II,* edited by David Brown and Miles Taylor, 144–165. Southampton, UK: Hartley Institute, University of Southampton, 2007.

——. *Unlikely Allies: Britain, America and the Victorian Origins of the Special Relationship.* New York: Hambledon Continuum, 2007.

Cannadine, David. *Ornamentalism: How the British Saw Their Empire.* New York: Oxford Univ. Press, 2001.

Carp, Benjamin L. "Nations of American Rebels: Understanding Nationalism in Revolutionary North America and the Civil War South." *Civil War History* 48 (2002): 5–33.

Cash, W. J. *The Mind of the South.* New York: Vintage Books, 1992.

Castillo, Susan. "'The Best of Nations'? Race and Imperial Destinies in Emerson's *English Traits.*" *Yearbook of English Studies* 34 (2004): 100–111.

Chadwick, Owen. *Acton and History.* New York: Cambridge Univ. Press, 1998.

Chalaby, Jean K. *The Invention of Journalism.* New York: St. Martin's Press, 1998.

Channing, Steven A. "Slavery and Confederate Nationalism." In *From the Old South to the New: Essays on the Transitional South,* edited by Walter J. Fraser Jr. and Winfred B. Moore Jr., 219–226. Westport, Conn.: Greenwood Press, 1981.

Churchman, Michael. "Walter Bagehot and the American Civil War." *Dublin Review* 56 (1965): 377–393.

Clarke, J. J. *Oriental Enlightenment: The Encounter Between Asian and Western Thought.* New York: Routledge, 1997.

Clausen, Christopher. "Lord Acton and the Lost Cause." *American Scholar* 69 (2000): 49–58.

Clinton, Catherine. *Fanny Kemble's Civil Wars.* New York: Oxford Univ. Press, 2000.

Clinton, David. "'Dash and Doubt': Walter Bagehot and International Restraint." *Review of Politics* 65 (2003): 89–109.

Cobban, Alfred. *The Social Interpretation of the French Revolution.* New York: Cambridge Univ. Press, 1964.

Colley, Linda. *Acts of Union and Disunion: What Has Held the UK Together—and What Is Dividing It?* London: Profile Books, 2014.

———. "Britishness and Otherness: An Argument." *Journal of British Studies* 31 (1992): 309–329.

———. *Britons: Forging the Nation, 1707–1837.* New Haven, Conn.: Yale Univ. Press, 1992.

Collyer, Cedric. "Gladstone and the American Civil War." *Proceedings of the Leeds Philosophical and Literary Society* 6 (1951): 583–594.

Coltham, Stephen. "George Potter, the Junta, and the *Bee-Hive.*" *International Review of Social History* 9 (1964): 391–432.

Compton, John W. "The Emancipation of the American Mind: J. S. Mill on the Civil War." *Review of Politics* 79 (2008): 221–244.

Conboy, Martin. *Journalism: A Critical History.* Thousand Oaks, Calif.: SAGE Publications, 2004.

———. *The Press and Popular Culture.* Thousand Oaks, Calif.: SAGE Publications, 2002.

Connor, Walker. "A Nation Is a Nation, Is a State, Is an Ethnic Group, Is a. . . ." *Ethnic and Racial Studies* 1 (1978): 377–400.

Coulter, E. Merton. "The Great Georgia Railway Disaster Hoax on the London *Times*." *Georgia Historical Society* 56 (1972): 25–50.

Cowling, Maurice. *1867: Disraeli, Gladstone and Revolution: The Passing of the Second Reform Bill.* London: Cambridge Univ. Press, 1967.

Craitu, Aurelian, and Jeremy Jennings. "The Third Democracy: Tocqueville's Views of America after 1840." *American Political Science Review* 98 (2004): 391–404.

Crangle, John V. "E. A. Freeman and Opposition to Victorian Anglo-Saxonism." *Proceedings of the South Carolina Historical Association* (1991): 88–94.

Crawford, Martin. "The Anglo-American Crisis of the Early 1860's: A Framework for Revision." *South Atlantic Quarterly* 82 (1983): 406–423.

———. *The Anglo-American Crisis of the Mid-Nineteenth Century:* The Times *and America, 1850–1862.* Athens: Univ. of Georgia Press, 1987.

———. "Anglo-American Perspectives: J. C. Bancroft Davis, New York Correspondent of *The Times,* 1854–1861." *New York Historical Society Quarterly* 62 (1978): 191–217.

———. "British Travellers and the Anglo-American Relationship in the 1850s." *Journal of American Studies* 12 (1978): 203–219.

———. "The Great Georgia Railway Disaster Hoax Revisited." *Georgia Historical Quarterly* 58 (1974): 331–339.

———. "William Howard Russell and the Confederacy." *Journal of American Studies* 15 (1981): 191–210.

Crook, David Paul. *American Democracy in English Politics, 1815–1850.* Oxford: Clarendon Press, 1965.

———. *The North, the South, and the Powers.* New York: John Wiley and Sons, 1974.

———. "Portents of War: English Opinion of Secession." *Journal of American Studies* 4 (1971): 163–179.

Cubitt, Geoffrey. *Imagining Nations.* New York: Manchester Univ. Press, 1998.

Cullop, Charles. *Confederate Propaganda in Europe, 1861–1865.* Coral Gables, Fla.: Univ. of Miami Press, 1969.

———. "Edwin De Leon, Jefferson Davis' Propagandist." *Civil War History* 8 (1962): 386–400.

———. "English Reaction to Stonewall Jackson's Death." *West Virginia History* 29 (1967): 1–5.

Curtis, Edith Roelker. "Blood Is Thicker than Water." *American Neptune* 27 (1967): 157–176.

Curtis, L. P. *Anglo-Saxons and Celts: A Study of Anti-Irish Prejudice in Victorian England.* Bridgeport, Conn.: Conference on British Studies at the University of Bridgeport, 1968.

Daniel, W. Harrison. "The Reaction of British Methodism to the Civil War and Reconstruction in America." *Methodist History* 16 (1977): 3–20.

———. "The Response of the Church of England to the Civil War and Reconstruction in America." *Historical Magazine of the Protestant Episcopal Church* 47 (1978): 51–72.

Dasent, Arthur Irwin. *John Thadeus Delane, Editor of "The Times": His Life and Correspondence.* 2 vols. New York: Charles Scribner's Sons, 1908.

Davenport-Hines, Richard. *The Macmillans.* London: Mandarin, 1992.

David, Deirdre. *Fanny Kemble: A Performed Life.* Philadelphia: Univ. of Pennsylvania Press, 2007.

David, Vincent. *Literacy and Popular Culture: England, 1750-1914.* New York: Cambridge Univ. Press, 1989.

Davis, Calvin. "A British Diplomat and the American Civil War: Edward Malet in the States." *South Atlantic Quarterly* 77 (1978): 159–178.

Davis, Michael T., ed. *Radicalism and Revolution in Britain, 1775-1848: Essays in Honour of Malcolm I. Thomis.* New York: St. Martin's Press, 2000.

Davis, Richard. *The English Rothschilds.* London: Collins, 1983.

Davis, William C. *Look Away! A History of the Confederate States of America.* New York: Free Press, 2002.

———. "Lost Will, Lost Causes." In *The Cause Lost: Myths and Realities of the Confederacy,* edited by William C. Davis, 111–126. Lawrence, Kans.: Univ. Press of Kansas, 1996.

Dawson, Jan C. "The Puritan and the Cavalier: The South's Perception of Contrasting Traditions." *Journal of Southern History* 44 (1978): 597–614.

Dawson, Joseph G. *Army Generals and Reconstruction: Louisiana, 1862–1877.* Baton Rouge: Louisiana State Univ. Press, 1982.

Denholm, Anthony. *Lord Ripon, 1827-1909: A Political Biography.* London: Croom Helm, 1982.

De Nie, Michael. "The London Press and the American Civil War." In *Anglo-American Media Interactions, 1850–2000,* edited by Joel H. Wiener and Mark Hampton, 129–154. New York: Palgrave, 2007.

DeVine, Christine, ed. *Nineteenth-Century British Travelers in the New World.* New York: Routledge, 2013.

Dirck, Brian R. *Lincoln and Davis: Imagining America, 1809–1865.* Lawrence: Univ. Press of Kansas, 2001.

Dirks, Nicholas B., ed. *Colonialism and Culture.* Ann Arbor: Univ. of Michigan Press, 1992.

Doyle, Don H. *The Cause of All Nations: An International History of the American Civil War.* New York: Basic Books, 2015.

Doyle, Elisabeth. "A Report on Civil War America: Sir James Fergusson's Five-Week Visit." *Civil War History* 12 (1966): 347–362.

Drescher, Seymour. "The Ending of the Slave Trade and the Evolution of European Scientific Racism." *Social Science History* 14 (1990): 415–450.

——. "Servile Insurrection and John Brown's Body in Europe." *Journal of American History* 80 (1993): 499–524.

Dubrulle, Hugh. "A Military Legacy of the Civil War: The British Inheritance." *Civil War History* 49 (2003): 153–180.

——. "'We Are Threatened with . . . Anarchy and Ruin': Fear of Americanization and the Emergence of an Anglo-Saxon Confederacy during the American Civil War." *Albion* 33 (2001): 583–613.

Dyer, Thomas G. *Secret Yankees: The Union Circle in Confederate Atlanta.* Baltimore: Johns Hopkins Univ. Press, 1999.

Dzelzanis, Ella, and Ruth Livesey, eds. *The American Experiment and the Idea of Democracy in British Culture, 1776–1914.* Burlington, Vt.: Ashgate, 2013.

Edsall, Nicholas C. *Richard Cobden, Independent Radical.* Cambridge, Mass.: Harvard Univ. Press, 1986.

Edwards, Ruth Dudley. *The Pursuit of Reason: The Economist, 1843–1993.* Boston: Harvard Business School Press, 1995.

Ellegård, Alvar. "The Readership of the Periodical Press in Mid-Victorian Britain." Göteborgs, Sweden: *Göteborgs Universitets,* 1957.

Ellison, Mary. *Support for Secession: Lancashire and the American Civil War.* Chicago: Univ. of Chicago Press, 1972.

Ellsworth, Edward. "Anglo-American Affairs in October of 1862." *Lincoln Herald* 66 (1964): 89–96.

——. "British Consuls in the Confederacy during 1862." *Lincoln Herald* 66 (1964): 149–154.

Escott, Paul D. *After Secession: Jefferson Davis and the Failure of Confederate Nationalism.* Baton Rouge: Louisiana State Univ. Press, 1978.

Evans, Richard J. *In Defense of History.* New York: Norton, 1999.

Fahs, Alice. *The Imagined Civil War: Popular Literature of the North and South, 1861–1865.* Chapel Hill: Univ. of North Carolina Press, 2001.

Farley, M. Foster. "Josiah Tattnall: American Sea Dog." *History Today* 29 (1979): 163–171.

——. "Josiah Tattnall: Gallant American." *Georgia Historical Quarterly* 58 (1974): 172–180.

Faust, Drew Giplin. *The Creation of Confederate Nationalism: Ideology and Identity in the Civil War South.* Baton Rouge: Louisiana State Univ. Press, 1988.

Fehrenbacher, Don Edward. *Constitutions and Constitutionalism in the Slaveholding South.* Athens: Univ. of Georgia Press, 1989.

Fenton, Laurence. *Palmerston and* The Times*: Foreign Policy, the Press and Public Opinion in Mid-Victorian Britain.* New York: I. B. Tauris, 2013.

Feuchtwanger, E. J. *Gladstone.* New York: St. Martin's Press, 1975.

Fisch, Audrey. "'Exhibiting Uncle Tom in Some Shape or Other': The Commodificatin and Reception of *Uncle Tom's Cabin* in England." *Nineteenth-Century Contexts* 17 (1993): 145–158.

Fish, Stanley. *Is There a Text in This Class? The Authority of Interpretative Communities.* Cambridge, Mass.: Harvard Univ. Press, 1980.

Fitzmaurice, Edmond, Baron. *The Life of Granville George Leveson Gower, Second Earl Granville, K.G., 1815–1891.* 2 vols. New York: Longmans, Green, 1905.

Fleche, Andre. *The Revolution of 1861: The American Civil War in the Age of Nationalist Conflict.* Chapel Hill: Univ. of North Carolina Press, 2012.

Fogel, Robert William, and Stanley L. Engerman, *Time on the Cross: The Economics of American Negro Slavery.* Boston: Little, Brown, 1974.

Foner, Eric. *Free Soil, Free Labor, Free Men.* New York: Oxford Univ. Press, 1970.

Foner, Philip S. *British Labor and the American Civil War.* New York: Holmes and Meier, 1981.

Foreman, Amanda. *A World on Fire: An Epic History of Two Nations Divided.* London: Allen Lane, 2010.

Förster, Stig, and Jörg Nagler, eds. *On the Road to Total War: The American Civil War and the German Wars of Unification, 1861–1871.* New York: Cambridge Univ. Press, 1997.

Franklin, John Hope. *A Southern Odyssey: Travelers in the Antebellum North.* Baton Rouge: Louisiana State Univ. Press, 1977.

Frawley, Maria H. *A Wider Range: Travel Writing by Women in Victorian England.* Rutherford, N.J.: Farleigh Dickinson Press, 1994.

Fredrickson, George M. *The Comparative Imagination: On the History of Racism, Nationalism, and Social Movements.* Berkeley: Univ. of California Press, 1997.

——. *The Inner Civil War.* Urbana: Univ. of Illinois Press, 1993.

——. *Racism: A Short History.* Princeton, N.J.: Princeton Univ. Press, 2002.

Freund, Elizabeth. *The Return of the Reader: Reader-Response Criticism.* New York: Methuen, 1987.

Fulton, Richard D. "Now Only the *Times* Is on Our Side: The London *Times* and America Before the Civil War." *Victorian Review* 16 (1990): 48–58.

Gallagher, Gary W. *The Confederate War.* Cambridge, Mass.: Harvard Univ. Press, 1997.

——. *The Union War.* Cambridge, Mass.: Harvard Univ. Press, 2001.

Gallas, Stanley. "Lord Lyons and the Civil War, 1859–1865." Ph.D. diss. University of Illinois at Chicago Circle, 1982.

Gandhi, Leela. *Postcolonial Theory: A Critical Introduction.* New York: Columbia Univ. Press, 1998.

Gardiner, A. G. *The Life of Sir William Harcourt.* 2 vols. New York: George H. Doran, 1923.

Gardner, Lloyd C., and Marilyn B. Young, eds. *Iraq and the Lessons of Vietnam: Or, How Not to Learn from the Past.* New York: New Press, 2007.

Gellner, Ernest. *Nations and Nationalism.* Ithaca, N.Y.: Cornell Univ. Press, 1983.

Gentry, Judith. "A Confederate Success in Europe: The Erlanger Loan." *Journal of Southern History* 36 (1970): 157–188.

Gerster, Patrick, and Nicholas Cords. "The Northern Origins of Southern Mythology." *Journal of Southern History* 43 (1977): 567–582.

Gerteis, Louis. *From Contraband to Freedom: Federal Policy toward Southern Blacks, 1861–1865.* Westport, Conn.: Greenwood Press, 1973

Gettman, Royal Alfred. *A Victorian Publisher: A Study of the Bentley Papers.* Cambridge: Cambridge Univ. Press, 1960.

Goldberg, David Theo. "Liberalism's Limits: Carlyle and Mill on 'The Negro Question.'" *Nineteenth-Century Contexts* 22 (2000): 203–216.

Gordon, Lesley J., and John C. Inscoe, eds. *Inside the Confederate Nation: Essays in Honor of Emory M. Thomas.* Baton Rouge: Louisiana State Univ. Press, 2005.

Grant, Susan-Mary. *North Over South: Northern Nationalism and American Identity in the Antebellum Era.* Lawrence: Univ. Press of Kansas, 2000.

Griest, Guinevere L. *Mudie's Circulating Library and the Victorian Novel.* Bloomington: Indiana Univ. Press, 1970.

Griffiths, Dennis. *Plant Here* The Standard. London: Macmillan, 1996.

Grimsley, Mark. *The Hard Hand of War: Union Military Policy toward Southern Civilians 1861–1865.* New York: Cambridge Univ. Press, 1996.

Gurowich, P. M. "The Continuation of War by Other Means: Party and Politics, 1866–1865." *Historical Journal* 27 (1984): 603–631.

Hagerman, Edward. *The American Civil War and the Origins of Modern Warfare.* Bloomington: Indiana Univ. Press, 1992.

Hall, Catherine. *Civilising Subjects: Metropole and Colony in the English Imagination 1830–1867.* Cambridge, UK: Polity, 2002.

———. "'From Greenland's Icy Mountains . . . to Afric's Golden Sand': Ethnicity Race and Nation in Mid-Nineteenth-Century England." *Gender and History* 5 (1993): 212–230.

Hall, Catherine, Keith McClelland, and Jane Rendall. *Defining the Victorian Nation: Class, Race, Gender and the Reform Act of 1867.* New York: Cambridge Univ. Press, 2000.

Halperin, John. "Trollope and the American Civil War." *Clio* 13 (1984): 149–155.

Hampton, Mark. *Visions of the Press in Britain, 1850–1950.* Urbana: Univ. of Illinois Press, 2004.

Hankinson, Alan. *Man of Wars: William Howard Russell of* The Times. London: Heinemann Educational Books, 1982.

Hanlon, Christopher. *America's England: Antebellum Literature and Atlantic Sectionalism.* New York: Oxford Univ. Press, 2013.

Hannay, David. *Life of Frederick Marryat.* New York: Haskell House, 1973.

Harrison, Royden. *Before the Socialists: Studies in Labour and Politics, 1861–1881.* Toronto: Univ. of Toronto Press, 1965.

———. "British Labour and American Slavery." *Science and Society* 25 (1961): 291–319.

———. "British Labour and the Confederacy." *International Review of Social History* 2 (1957): 78–105.

Haultain, Arnold. *Goldwin Smith: His Life and Opinions.* New York: Duffield, 1914.

Hawkins, Angus. *British Party Politics, 1852–1886.* New York: St. Martin's Press, 1998.

———. *The Forgotten Prime Minister: The 14th Earl of Derby.* 2 vols. New York: Oxford Univ. Press, 2007–2008.

Heckman, Richard A. "British Press Reaction to the Emancipation Proclamation." *Lincoln Herald* 71 (1969): 150–153.

Heineman, Helen K. *Three Victorians in the New World: Interpretations of the New World in the Works of Frances Trollope, Charles Dickens, and Anthony Trollope.* New York: Peter Lang, 1992.

Hernon, Joseph M., Jr. "British Sympathies in the American Civil War: A Reconsideration." *Journal of Southern History* 33 (1967): 356–367.

———. *Celts, Catholics, and Copperheads: Ireland Views the American Civil War.* Columbus: Ohio State Univ. Press, 1968.

———. "The Irish Nationalists and Southern Secession." *Civil War History* 12 (1966): 43–53.

Herrick, Francis. "Gladstone and the Concept of the 'English-Speaking Peoples.'" *Journal of British Studies* 12 (1972): 150–156.

Hess, Earl J. *Liberty, Virtue, and Progress: Northerners and Their War for the Union.* New York: New York Univ. Press, 1988.

Hill, Roland. *Lord Acton.* New Haven, Conn.: Yale Univ. Press, 2000.

Himmelfarb, Gertrude. *Victorian Minds.* Gloucester, Mass.: Peter Smith, 1975.

Hinde, Wendy. *Richard Cobden: A Victorian Outsider.* New Haven, Conn.: Yale Univ. Press, 1987.

Hitsman, J. Mackay. "Winter Troop Movement to Canada, 1862." *Canadian Historical Review* 43 (1962): 127–135.

Hobsbawm, Eric. *Nations and Nationalism since 1780: Programme, Myth, Reality.* New York: Cambridge Univ. Press, 1992.

———. *On History.* New York: New Press, 1997.

Hodder, Edwin. *The Life and Work of the Seventh Earl of Shaftesbury, K.G.* 3 vols. London: Cassell, 1892.

Holland, Bernard. *The Life of Spencer Compton, Eighth Duke of Devonshire.* 2 vols. London: Longmans, Green, 1911.

Holt, Edgar. *The Opium Wars in China.* London: Putnam, 1964.

Hoole, William. *Lawley Covers the Confederacy.* Tuscaloosa: Confederate Publishing, 1964.

———. *Vizetelly Covers the Confederacy.* Tuscaloosa: Confederate Publishing, 1957.

Hopkins, A. G. "Back to the Future: From National History to Imperial History." *Past and Present* 164 (1999): 198–243.

Hoppen, K. Theodore. *The Mid-Victorian Generation 1846–1886.* New York: Oxford Univ. Press, 2003.

Horsman, Reginald. "Origins of Racial Anglo-Saxonism in Great Britain Before 1850." *Journal of the History of Ideas* 37 (1976): 387–410.

Hougton, Walter. *The Victorian Frame of Mind, 1830–1870.* New Haven, Conn.: Yale Univ. Press, 1985.

Howe, Anthony, and Simon Morgan, eds. *Rethinking Nineteenth-Century Liberalism: Richard Cobden Bicentenary Essays.* Burlington, Vt.: Ashgate, 2006.

Hubbard, Charles M. *The Burden of Confederate Diplomacy.* Knoxville: Univ. of Tennessee Press, 1998.

———. "James Mason, the Confederate Lobby and the Blockade Debate of March 1862." *Civil War History* 45 (1999): 223–237.

Hudson, Nicholas. "Nation to 'Race': The Origin of Racial Classification in Eighteenth-Century Thought." *Eighteenth-Century Studies* 29 (1996): 247–264.

Hughes, Michael F. "'The Personal Observations of a Man of Intelligence': Sir James Fergusson's Visit to North America, 1861." *Civil War History* 45 (1999): 238–247.

Hulme, Peter. *Colonial Encounters: Europe and the Native Caribbean, 1492–1797.* New York: Routledge, 1992.

———. "Including America." *Ariel* 26 (1995): 117–123.

Humphreys, Anne, and Louis James, eds. *G.W.M. Reynolds: Nineteenth-Century Fiction, Politics, and the Press.* Burlington, Vt.: Ashgate, 2008.

Hurd, Douglas. *The Arrow War: An Anglo-Chinese Confusion, 1856–1860.* New York: Macmillan, 1967.

Hutchinson, Coleman. *Apples and Ashes: Literature, Nationalism, and the Confederate States of America.* Athens: Univ. of Georgia Press, 2012.

Huzzey, Richard. *Freedom Burning: Anti-Slavery and Empire in Victorian Britain.* Ithaca, N.Y.: Cornell Univ. Press, 2012.

Hynes, Samuel W. *Unfinished Revolution: The Early American Republic in a British World.* Charlottesville: Univ. of Virginia Press, 2010.

Innes, Joanna, and Mark Philip, eds. *Re-Imagining Democracy in the Age of Revolutions: America, France, Britain, Ireland 1750–1850.* New York: Oxford Univ. Press, 2013.

Irschick, Eugene F. *Dialogue and History: Constructing South India, 1795–1895.* Berkeley: Univ. of California Press, 1994.

Jackson, Patrick. *The Last of the Whigs: A Political Biography of Lord Hartington, Later Eighth Duke of Devonshire (1833–1908)*. Rutherford: Fairleigh Dickinson Univ. Press, 1994.

Jacoby, Russell. "Marginal Returns: The Trouble with Post-Colonial Theory." *Lingua Franca* 5 (1995): 30–37.

Jauss, Hans Robert. *Toward an Aesthetic of Reception*. Minneapolis: Univ. of Minnesota Press, 1982.

Jenkins, Brian. *Britain and the War for the Union*. 2 vols. Montreal: McGill-Queen's Univ. Press, 1974.

———. "Frank Lawley and the Confederacy." *Civil War History* 23 (1977): 144–160.

———. *Lord Lyons: A Diplomat in an Age of Nationalism and War*. Montreal: McGill-Queen's Univ. Press, 2014.

———. "William Gregory: Champion of the Confederacy." *History Today* 28 (1978): 322–330.

Jenkins, Keith, ed. *The Post-Modern History Reader*. New York: Routledge, 1997.

Jenkins, Rebecca. *Fanny Kemble: A Reluctant Celebrity*. New York: Simon and Schuster, 2005.

Jenkins, T. A. *Disraeli and Victorian Conservatism*. New York: St. Martin's Press, 1996.

———. *The Liberal Ascendancy, 1830–1886*. London: Macmillan, 1994.

———. *Parliament, Party and Politics in Victorian Britain*. New York: Manchester Univ. Press, 1996.

Jervis, Robert. *Perception and Misperception in International Politics*. Princeton, N.J.: Princeton Univ. Press, 1976.

Jones, Aled. *Powers of the Press: Newspapers, Power and the Public in Nineteenth-Century England*. Aldershot: Scolar Press, 1996.

Jones, Charles Colcock. *The Life and Services of Commodore Josiah Tattnall*. Savannah: Morning News Steam Printing House, 1878.

Jones, Howard. *Union in Peril: The Crisis Over British Intervention in the Civil War*. Chapel Hill: Univ. of North Carolina Press, 1992.

Jones, Robert Huhn. "Anglo-American Relations, 1861–1865, Reconsidered." *Mid-America: An Historical Review* 45 (1963): 36–49.

Jones, Wilbur Devereux. *The American Problem in British Diplomacy, 1841–1861*. London: Macmillan, 1974.

———. "British Conservatives and the American Civil War." *American Historical Review* 58 (1953): 527–543.

Jordan, Donaldson, and Edwin Pratt. *Europe and the American Civil War*. New York: Houghton Mifflin, 1933.

Jordan, John O., and Robert L. Patten, eds. *Literature in the Marketplace: Nineteenth-Century British Publishing and Reading Practices*. New York: Cambridge Univ. Press, 1995.

Joyce, Davis D. "Pro-Confederate Sympathy in the British Parliament." *Social Science* 44 (1969): 95–100.

Karras, Mead Smith. *Commodore Josiah Tattnall: From Pirates to Ironclads, Half a Century in the Old Navy.* N.p.: Authorhouse, 2011.

Katz, Irving. *August Belmont: A Political Biography.* New York: Columbia Univ. Press, 1968.

Keiser, Thomas. "The Prince of Wales in the United States: A Harbinger of English Opinion of the Civil War." *Illinois Historical Journal* 83 (1990): 235–246.

Kennedy, Dane. "Imperial History and Post-Colonial Theory." *Journal of Imperial and Commonwealth History* 24 (1996): 345–363.

Kersh, Rogan. *Dreams of a More Perfect Union.* Ithaca, N.Y.: Cornell Univ. Press, 2001.

Khong, Yuen Foong. *Analogies at War: Korea, Munich, Dien Bien Phu, and the Vietnam Decisions of 1965.* Princeton, N.J.: Princeton Univ. Press, 1992.

Kinser, Brent E. *The American Civil War in the Shaping of British Democracy.* Burlington, Vt.: Ashgate, 2011.

Kohn, Hans. *American Nationalism: An Interpretive Essay.* New York: Macmillan, 1957.

Koss, Stephen E. *The Rise and Fall of the Political Press in Britain.* 2 vols. London: Hamish Hamilton, 1981–1984.

Krein, David F. *The Last Palmerston Government: Foreign Policy, Domestic Politics, and the Genesis of "Splendid Isolation."* Ames: Iowa State Univ. Press, 1978.

Kumar, Krishan. *The Making of English National Identity.* New York: Cambridge Univ. Press, 2003.

Lang, Timothy. "Lord Acton and 'The Insanity of Nationality.'" *Journal of the History of Ideas* 63 (2002): 129–149.

Langdon, Robert M. "Josiah Tattnall—Blood Is Thicker than Water." *Proceedings of the United States Naval Institute* 85 (1959): 156–158.

Lawson, Melinda. *Patriot Fires: Forging a New American Nationalism in the Civil War North.* Lawrence: Univ. Press of Kansas, 2002.

Leader, Robert E. *Life and Letters of John Arthur Roebuck.* London: Edward Arnold, 1897.

Lee, Alan J. *The Origins of the Popular Press in England, 1855–1914.* London: Croom Helm, 1976.

Leventhal, Fred, and Roland Quinault. *Anglo-American Attitudes: From Revolution to Partnership.* Burlington, Vt.: Ashgate, 2000.

Lhamon, W. T., Jr. *Raising Cain: Blackface Performance from Jim Crow to Hip Hop.* Cambridge, Mass.: Harvard Univ. Press, 1998.

Lillibridge, G. D. *Beacon of Freedom: The Impact of American Democracy Upon Great Britain, 1830–1870.* Philadelphia: Univ. of Pennsylvania Press, 1955.

Logan, Deborah Anna. *The Hour and the Woman: Harriet Martineau's "Somewhat Remarkable" Life.* Dekalb: Northern Illinois Univ. Press, 2002.

Logan, Kevin. "The *Bee-Hive* Newspaper and British Working Class Attitudes toward the American Civil War." *Civil War History* 24 (1976): 337–348.

Loomba, Ania. *Colonialism/Postcolonialism.* New York: Routledge, 2005.

Lorimer, Douglas A. "Bibles, Banjoes and Bones: Images of the Negro in Popular Culture in Victorian England." In *In Search of a Visible Past: History Lectures at Wilfrid Laurier University, 1973–1974,* edited by Barry M. Gough, 31–50. Waterloo, Ont.: Wilfrid Laurier Univ. Press, 1975.

———. *Colour, Class and the Victorians: English Attitudes to the Negro in the Mid-Nineteenth Century.* New York: Holmes and Meier, 1978.

———. "Nature, Racism, and Late Victorian Science." *Canadian Journal of History* 25 (1990): 369–385.

———. "Reconstructing Victorian Racial Discourse: Images of Race, the Language of Race Relations, and the Context of Black Resistance." In *Black Victorians/Black Victoriana,* edited by Gretchen Holbrook Gerzina, 187–207. New Brunswick, N.J.: Rutgers Univ. Press, 2003.

———. "The Role of Anti-Slavery Sentiment in English Reactions to the American Civil War." *Historical Journal* 19 (1976): 405–420.

Lott, Eric. *Love and Theft: Blackface Minstrelsy and the American Working Class.* New York: Oxford Univ. Press, 1993.

Lowenthal, David. *The Past Is a Foreign Country.* New York: Cambridge Univ. Press, 1985.

Lucas, Reginald. *Lord Glenesk and the "Morning Post."* London: Alston Rivers, 1910.

Luvaas, Jay. "G.F.R. Henderson and the American Civil War." *Military Affairs* 20 (1956): 139–153.

———. *The Military Legacy of the Civil War: The European Inheritance.* Lawrence: Univ. Press of Kansas, 1988.

Lynn, Martin. "British Policy, Trade, and Informal Empire in the Mid-Nineteenth Century." In *The Oxford History of the British Empire,* edited by William Roger Louis, vol. 3, *The Nineteenth Century,* 101–121. New York: Oxford Univ. Press, 1999.

Macfie, A. L. *Orientalism.* New York: Longman, 2002.

Machin, Ian. *The Rise of Democracy in Britain, 1830–1918.* New York: St. Martin's Press, 2001.

Machor, James L., ed. *Readers in History: Nineteenth-Century American Literature and the Contexts of Response.* Baltimore: Johns Hopkins Univ. Press, 1993.

Machor, James L., and Philip Goldstein, eds. *Reception Study: From Literary Theory to Cultural Studies.* New York: Routledge, 2001.

MacKenzie, John M. "Edward Said and the Historians." *Nineteenth-Century Contexts* 18 (1994): 9–25.

——. *Orientalism: History, Theory, and the Arts*. New York: St. Martin's Press, 1995.

MacMillan, Margaret. *Dangerous Games: The Uses and Abuses of History*. New York: Modern Library, 2009.

Mandler, Peter. *The English National Character: The History of an Idea from Edmund Burke to Tony Blair*. New Haven, Conn.: Yale Univ. Press, 2006.

——. "'Race' and 'Nation' in Mid-Victorian Thought." In *History, Religion, and Culture: British Intellectual History, 1750–1850*, edited by Stefan Collini, Richard Whatmore, and Brian Young, 224–244. Cambridge: Cambridge Univ. Press, 2000.

Marryat, Florence. *The Life and Letters of Captain Marryat*. 2 vols. London: Richard Bentley and Son, 1872.

Mason, J.F.A. "The Third Marquess of Salisbury and the *Saturday Review*." *Bulletin of the Institute of Historical Research* 34 (1961): 36–54.

Massey, Hector. "Lord Acton's Theory of Nationality." *Review of Politics* 31 (1969): 495–508.

Matthew, H.C.G. *Gladstone 1809–1898*. Oxford: Clarendon Press, 1997.

Maurer, Oscar. "*Punch* on Slavery and the Civil War in America, 1841–1865." *Victorian Studies* 1 (1957): 5–28.

Maxwell, Herbert, Sir. *Life and Letters of the Fourth Earl of Clarendon*. 2 vols. London: Edward Arnold, 1913.

May, Robert E., ed. *The Union, the Confederacy, and the Atlantic Rim*. West Lafayette, Ind.: Purdue Univ. Press, 1995.

McCardell, John. *The Idea of a Southern Nation: Southern Nationalists and Southern Nationalism, 1830–1860*. New York: Norton, 1979.

McLeod, John. *Beginning Postcolonialism*. New York: St. Martin's Press, 2000.

McPherson, James. *For Cause and Comrades: Why Men Fought in the Civil War*. New York: Oxford Univ. Press, 1997.

McWhiney, Grady. *Southerners and Other Americans*. New York: Basic Books, 1973.

McWilliam, Rohan. *Popular Politics in Nineteenth-Century England. New York: Routledge, 1998.*

Meckier, Jerome. *Innocent Abroad: Charles Dickens's American Engagements*. Lexington: Univ. Press of Kentucky, 1990.

Meer, Sarah. *Uncle Tom Mania: Slavery, Minstrelsy and Transatlantic Culture in the 1850s*. Athens: Univ. of Georgia Press, 2005.

Meisel, Joseph S. *Public Speech and the Culture of Public Life in the Age of Gladstone*. New York: Columbia Univ. Press, 2001.

Melman, Billie. "Claiming the Nation's Past: The Invention of an Anglo-Saxon Tradition." *Journal of Contemporary History* 26 (1991): 575–595.

——. *Women's Orients: English Women and the Middle East, 1718–1918*. Ann Arbor: Univ. of Michigan Press, 1995.

Merli, Frank J. *Great Britain and the Confederate Navy, 1861–1865.* Bloomington: Indiana University, 1970.

Merli, Frank J., and Theodore A. Wilson. "The British Cabinet and the Confederacy: Autumn 1862." *Maryland Historical Magazine* 65 (1970): 239–262.

Midgley, Clare, ed. *Gender and Imperialism.* New York: Manchester Univ. Press, 1998.

Miller, Frank Lorenz. *Britain and the German Question: Perceptions of Nationalism and Political Reform, 1830–63.* Basingstoke, UK: Palgrave, 2002.

Miller, William L. "J. E. Cairnes on the Economics of American Negro Slavery." *Southern Economic Journal* 30 (1964): 333–341.

Mills, Sara. *Discourses of Difference: An Analysis of Women's Travel Writing and Colonialism.* New York: Routledge, 1993.

Monypenny, William, and G. E. Buckle. *The Life of Benjamin Disraeli, Earl of Beaconsfield.* 6 vols. London: John Murray, 1910–1920.

Moore-Gilbert, B. J. *Postcolonial Theory: Contexts, Practices, Politics.* New York: Verso, 1997.

Morely, John. *The Life of Richard Cobden.* London: T. Fisher Unwin, 1920.

———. *The Life of William Ewart Gladstone.* 3 vols. London: Macmillan, 1903.

Morgan, Charles. *The House of Macmillan (1843–1943).* New York: Macmillan, 1944.

Morgan, Marjorie. *National Identities and Travel in Victorian Britain.* Palgrave: New York, 2001.

Morgan, Peter F. *Literary Critics and Reviewers in Early 19th-Century Britain.* London: Croom Helm, 1983.

Morgan, Phillip D. "British Encounters with Africans and African-Americans, circa 1600–1780." In *Strangers Within the Realm: Cultural Margins of the First British Empire,* edited by Bernard Bailyn and Phillip D. Morgan, 157–219. Chapel Hill: Univ. of North Carolina Press, 1991.

Moss, Sidney P. *Charles Dickens' Quarrel with America.* Troy, N.Y.: Whitson, 1984.

Mullen, Richard. *Birds of Passage: Five Englishwomen in Search of America.* New York: St. Martin's Press, 1994.

Mulvey, Christopher. *Transatlantic Manners: Social Patterns in Nineteenth-Century Anglo-American Travel Literature.* New York: Cambridge Univ. Press, 1990.

Munsell, F. Darrell. *The Unfortunate Duke: Henry Pelham, Fifth Duke of Newcatle, 1811–1864.* Columbia: Univ. of Missouri Press, 1985.

Munslow, Alun. *Deconstructing History.* New York: Routledge, 2006.

Murray, Nicholas. *A Life of Matthew Arnold.* New York: St. Martin's Press, 1996.

Myers, Phillip E. *Caution and Cooperation: The American Civil War in British-American Relations.* Kent, Ohio: Kent State Univ. Press, 2008.

Nagle, Paul C. *One Nation Indivisible: The Union in American Thought, 1776–1861.* New York: Oxford Univ. Press, 1964.

———. *This Sacred Trust: American Nationality, 1798–1898*. New York: Oxford Univ. Press, 1971.

Neely, Mark E., Jr. *The Civil War and the Limits of Destruction*. Cambridge, Mass.: Harvard Univ. Press, 2007.

———. *The Fate of Liberty*. New York: Oxford Univ. Press, 1991.

———. *Lincoln and the Triumph of the Nation: Constitutional Conflict in the American Civil War*. Chapel Hill: Univ. of North Carolina Press, 2011.

———. "Was the Civil War a Total War?" *Civil War History* 37 (1991): 5–28.

Neville-Sington, Pamela. *Fanny Trollope: The Life and Adventures of a Clever Woman*. New York: Viking, 1997.

Nevins, Allan, ed. *America through British Eyes*. New York: Oxford Univ. Press, 1948.

Newton, Thomas Wodehouse Legh, Baron. *Lord Lyons: A Record of British Diplomacy*. 2 vols. New York: Longmans, Green, 1913.

Oakes, James. *The Ruling Race: A History of American Slaveholders*. New York: Norton, 1998.

———. *Slavery and Freedom: An Interpretation of the Old South*. New York: Knopf, 1990.

Oates, Stephen. "Henry Hotze: Confederate Agent Abroad." *Historian* 27 (1965): 131–154.

O'Leary, Cecilia Elizabeth. *To Die For: The Paradox of American Patriotism*. Princeton, N.J.: Princeton Univ. Press, 1999.

Oliphant, Margaret. *Annals of a Publishing House: William Blackwood and His Sons, Their Magazine and Friends*. 2 vols. Edinburgh, UK: William Blackwood and Sons, 1897.

Osterweis, Rollin G. *Romanticism and Nationalism in the Old South*. New Haven, Conn.: Yale Univ. Press, 1949.

Owsley, Frank Lawrence. *King Cotton Diplomacy: Foreign Relations of the Confederate States of America*. Chicago: Univ. of Chicago Press, 1959.

———. *Plain Folk of the Old South*. Baton Rouge: Louisiana State Univ. Press, 1949.

Paludan, Phillip Shaw. *"A People's Contest": The Union and the Civil War, 1861–1865*. New York: Harper and Row, 1988.

Parish, Peter J. "An Exception to Most of the Rules: What Made American Nationalism Different in the Mid-Nineteenth Century?" *Prologue* 27 (1995): 219–229.

———. "Gladstone and America." In *Gladstone*, edited by Peter J. Jagger, 85–103. London: Hambledon Press, 1998.

———. *The North and the Nation in the Era of the Civil War*. New York: Fordham Univ. Press, 2003.

Park, Peter T. "John Stuart Mill, Thomas Carlyle, and the U.S. Civil War." *Historian* 54 (1991): 93–106.

Parker, C.J.W. "The Failure of Liberal Racialism: The Racial Ideas of E. A. Freeman." *Historical Journal* 24 (1981): 825–846.

Parry, Jonathan. *The Politics of Patriotism: English Liberalism, National Identity and Europe, 1830–1886*. New York: Cambridge Univ. Press, 2006.

———. *The Rise and Fall of Liberal Government in Victorian Britain*. New Haven, Conn.: Yale Univ. Press, 1993.

Partridge, Michael. *Gladstone*. New York: Routledge, 2003.

Patten, Robert L. *Charles Dickens and His Publishers*. Oxford: Clarendon Press, 1978.

Pessen, Edward. "How Different from Each Other Were the Antebellum North and South?" *American Historical Review* 85 (1980): 1119–1149.

Peterson, Linda H. "Harriet Martineau: Masculine Discourse, Female Sage." In *Victorian Sages and Cultural Discourse: Renegotiating Gender and Power*, edited by Thaïs E. Morgan, 171–186. New Brunswick, N.J.: Rutgers Univ. Press, 1990.

Peyre, Henri. *Historical and Critical Essays*. Lincoln: Univ. of Nebraska Press, 1968.

Pickering, Michael. "'A Jet Ornament to Society': Black Music in Nineteenth-Century Britain." In *Black Music in Britain: Essays on the Afro-Asian Contribution to Popular Music*, edited by Paul Oliver, 16–33. Philadelphia: Open Univ. Press, 1990.

———. "Mock Blacks and Racial Mockery: The 'Nigger' Minstrel and British Imperialism." In *Acts of Supremacy: The British Empire and the Stage, 1790–1930*, edited by J. S. Bratton, 179–236. New York: Manchester Univ. Press, 1991.

———. "White Skin, Black Masks: 'Nigger' Minstrelsy in Victorian England." In *Music Hall: Performance and Style*, edited by J. S. Bratton, 70–91. Philadelphia: Open Univ. Press, 1986.

Platt, D.C.M. *The Cinderella Service: British Consuls since 1825*. London: Longman, 1971.

Platt, Stephen R. *Autumn in the Heavenly Kingdom: China, the West, and the Epic Story of the Taiping Civil War*. New York: Vintage Books, 2012.

Pocock, Tom. *Captain Marryat: Seaman, Writer and Adventurer*. London: Chatham Publishing, 2000.

Pole, J. R. "Walter Bagehot on Deference: An American Source?" *American Nineteenth Century* History 2 (2001): 104–109.

Porter, Andrew. "Trusteeship, Anti-Slavery, and Humanitarianism." In *The Oxford History of the British Empire*, edited by William Roger Louis, vol. 3, *The Nineteenth Century*, 198–221. New York: Oxford Univ. Press, 1999.

Porter, Dennis. "Orientalism and Its Problems." In *The Politics of Theory: Proceedings of the Essex Conference on the Sociology of Literature*, edited by Francis Barker, 179–193. Colchester: University of Essex, 1983.

Potter, David M. "The Historian's Use of Nationalism and Vice Versa." *American Historical Review* 67 (1962): 924–950.

Pratt, Mary Louise. *Imperial Eyes: Travel Writing and Transculturation.* New York: Routledge, 2008.

Prest, John. *Lord John Russell.* Columbia: Univ. of South Carolina Press, 1972.

Preston, Richard Arthur. *Canada's R.M.C.: A History of the Royal Military College.* Toronto: Univ. of Toronto Press, 1969.

———. "The Impact of the American Civil War on British Military Training." *Military Review* 33 (1953): 96–101.

———. "A Letter from a British Military Observer of the American Civil War." *Military Affairs* 16 (1952): 49–60.

———. "Military Lessons of the American Civil War: The Influence of Observers from the British Army in Canada on Training the British Army." *Army Quarterly* 65 (1953). 229–237.

Prochaska, Frank. *Eminent Victorians on American Democracy: The View from Albion.* New York: Oxford Univ. Press, 2011.

Proudman, Max F. "Disraeli as an 'Orientalist': The Polemical Errors of Edward Said." *Journal of the Historical Society* 5 (2005): 547–568.

Quigley, Paul. *Shifting Grounds: Nationalism and the American South, 1848–1865.* New York: Oxford Univ. Press, 2012.

Rable, George C. *Civil Wars: Women and the Crisis of Southern Nationalism.* Urbana: Univ. of Illinois Press, 1991.

———. *The Confederate Republic: A Revolution Against Politics.* Chapel Hill: Univ. of North Carolina Press, 1994.

Racevskis, Karlis. "Edward Said and Michel Foucault: Affinities and Dissonances." *Research in African Literatures* 36 (2005): 83–97.

Rainger, Ronald. "Race, Politics, and Science: The Anthropological Society of London in the 1860s." *Victorian Studies* 22 (1978): 51–70.

Ransom, Roger L. *Conflict and Compromise: The Political Economy of Slavery, Emancipation, and the American Civil War.* New York: Cambridge Univ. Press, 1989.

Ransom, Teresa. *Fanny Trollope: A Remarkable Life.* New York: St. Martin's Press, 1995.

Rapson, Richard. *Britons View America, 1860–1935.* Seattle: Univ. of Washington Press, 1971.

Rehin, George F. "Blackface Street Minstrels in Victorian London and Its Resorts: Popular Culture and Its Racial Connotations as Revealed in Polite Opinion." *Journal of Popular Culture* 15 (1981): 19–38.

———. "Harlequin Jim Crow: Continuity and Convergence in Blackface Clowning." *Journal of Popular Culture* 9 (1975): 682–701.

Reid, Brian Holden. "Power, Sovereignty, and the Great Republic: Anglo-American Diplomatic Relations in the Era of the Civil War." *Diplomacy and Statecraft* 14 (2003): 45–76.

———. "'A Signpost That Was Missed'? Reconsidering British Lessons from the American Civil War." *Journal of Military History* 70 (2006): 385–414.

Reid, Robert, ed. "William Gladstone's 'Insincere Neutrality' during the Civil War." *Civil War History* 15 (1969): 293–307.

Reid, T. Wemyss. *Life of the Honourable William Edward Forster.* 2 vols. London: Chapman and Hall, 1888.

Rich, Paul B. *Race and Empire in British Politics.* New York: Cambridge Univ. Press, 1990.

Richardson, Michael. "Enough Said: Reflections on Orientalism." *Anthropology Today* 6 (1990): 16–19.

Ridley, Jasper. *Lord Palmerston.* London: Constable, 1970.

Ripley, C. Peter. *Slaves and Freedmen in Civil War Louisiana.* Baton Rouge: Louisiana State Univ. Press, 1976.

Robbins, Keith. *Great Britain: Identities, Institutions and the Idea of Britishness.* New York: Longman, 1998.

———. *John Bright.* Boston: Routledge and Kegan Paul, 1979.

———. *Nineteenth-Century Britain: England, Scotland, and Wales; The Making of a Nation.* New York: Oxford Univ. Press, 1989.

Rose, Anne C. *Victorian America and the Civil War.* New York: Cambridge Univ. Press, 1992.

Royster, Charles. *The Destructive War: William Tecumseh Sherman, Stonewall Jackson, and the Americans.* New York: Knopf, 1991.

Rubin, Anne S. *A Shattered Nation: The Rise and Fall of the Confederacy, 1861–1868.* Chapel Hill: Univ. of North Carolina Press, 2005.

Said, Edward. *Orientalism.* New York: Vintage Books, 1979.

St. John, Ian. *Disraeli and the Art of Victorian Politics.* New York: Anthem Press, 2005.

———. *Gladstone and the Logic of Victorian Politics.* New York: Anthem Press, 2010.

St. John-Stevas, Norman. *Walter Bagehot: A Study of His Life and Thought Together with a Selection from His Political Writings.* Bloomington: Indiana Univ. Press, 1959.

Saunders, Robert. *Democracy and the Vote in British Politics, 1848–1867: The Making of the Second Reform Act.* Burlington, Vt.: Ashgate, 2011.

Scherer, Paul. *Lord John Russell: A Biography.* Selinsgrove, Pa.: Susquehanna Univ. Press, 1996.

———. "Partner or Puppet? Lord John Russell at the Foreign Office, 1859–1862." *Albion* 19 (1987): 347–371.

Schleifer, James T. *The Making of Tocqueville's* Democracy in America. Chapel Hill: Univ. of North Carolina Press, 1980.

Schneider, Thomas E. "J. S. Mill and Fitzjames Stephen on the American Civil War." *History of Political Thought* 28 (2007): 290–304.

Semmel, Bernard. *Jamaican Blood and Victorian Conscience.* Westport, Conn.: Greenwood Press, 1976.

Shain, Charles. "The English Novelists and the American Civil War." *American Quarterly* 14 (1962): 399–421.

Shannon, Richard. *Gladstone.* 2 vols. London: H. Hamilton, 1982, 1999.

Shattock, Joanne. *Politics and Reviewers: The* Edinburgh *and the* Quarterly. New York: Leicester Univ. Press, 1989.

Sheehan-Dean, Aaron. *Why Confederates Fought: Family and Nation in Civil War Virginia.* Chapel Hill: Univ. of North Carolina Press, 2007.

Shirley, Michael H., and Todd E. A. Larson, eds. *Splendidly Victorian: Essays in Nineteenth- and Twentieth-Century British History in Honour of Walter Arnstein.* Burlington, Vt.: Ashgate, 2001.

Showalter, Elaine, ed. *The New Feminist Criticism: Essays on Women, Literature, and Theory.* New York: Pantheon, 1985.

Silbey, Joel. *A Respectable Minority: The Democratic Party in the Civil War Era, 1860–1868.* New York: Norton, 1977.

Simpson, David. "Literary Criticism and the Return to 'History.'" *Critical Inquiry* 14 (1988): 721–747.

Sisson, C. H. *The Case of Walter Bagehot.* London: Faber and Faber, 1972.

Smith, Anthony D. *National Identity.* Reno: Univ. of Nevada Press, 1993.

——. *Nationalism: Theory, Ideology, History.* Malden, Mass.: Blackwell, 2001.

——. *The Nation in History: Historiographical Debates About Ethnicity and Nationalism.* Hanover, N.H.: Univ. Press of New England, 2000.

Smith, F. B. "Democracy in the Second Reform Debates." *Historical Studies* 11 (1964): 306–323.

——. *The Making of the Second Reform Bill.* Cambridge: Cambridge Univ. Press, 1966.

Southgate, Donald, ed. *The Conservative Leadership, 1832–1932.* New York: St. Martin's Press, 1974.

——. *"The Most English Minister . . .": The Policies and Politics of Palmerston.* New York: St. Martin's Press, 1966.

——. *The Passing of the Whigs, 1832–1886.* London: Macmillan, 1962.

Spiers, Edward M. *The Late Victorian Army, 1868–1902.* Manchester, UK: Manchester Univ. Press, 1992.

Spring, David. "Walter Bagehot and Deference." *American Historical Review* 81 (1976): 524–531.

Stacey, C. P. "Britain's Withdrawal from North America, 1864–1867." *Canadian Historical Review* 26 (1955): 185–198.

——. *Canada and the British Army, 1846–1867.* Toronto: Univ. of Toronto Press, 1963.

Stampp, Kenneth M. *The Imperiled Union: Essays on the Background of the Civil War.* New York: Oxford Univ. Press, 1980.

Stapleton, Julia. "James Fitzjames Stephen: Liberalism, Patriotism, and English Liberty." *Victorian Studies* 41 (1998): 243–263.

Steele, E. D. *Palmerston and Liberalism, 1855–1865.* New York: Cambridge Univ. Press, 1991.

Stewart, Robert. *The Foundation of the Conservative Party, 1830–1867.* New York: Longman, 1978.

Stocking, George W. *Victorian Anthropology.* New York: Free Press, 1987.

———. "What's In a Name? The Origins of the Royal Anthropological Institute." *Man* 6 (1971): 369–390.

Stone, Harry. "Charles Dickens and Harriet Beecher Stowe." *Nineteenth-Century Fiction* 12 (1957): 188–202.

Straus, Ralph. *Sala: The Portrait of an Eminent Victorian.* London: Constable, 1942.

Suleiman, Susan R., and Inge Crosman, eds. *The Reader in the Text: Essays on Audience and Interpretation.* Princeton, N.J.: Princeton Univ. Press, 1980.

Sullivan, Eileen P. "Liberalism and Imperialism: J. S. Mill's Defense of the British Empire." *Journal of the History of Ideas* 44 (1983): 599–617.

Sutherland, Daniel. "Abraham Lincoln, John Pope, and the Origins of Total War." *Journal of Military History* 56 (1992): 567–586.

Sutherland, John. *Victorian Novelists and Publishers.* Chicago: Univ. of Chicago Press, 1976.

———. *Victorian Fiction: Writers, Publishers, Readers.* New York: Palgrave Macmillan, 1995.

Tamarkin, Elisa. *Anglophilia: Deference, Devotion, and Antebellum America.* Chicago: Univ. of Chicago Press, 2008.

Taylor, Antony. "Palmerston and Radicalism, 1847–1865." *Journal of British Studies* 33 (1994): 157–179.

Taylor, William. *Cavalier and Yankee: The Old South and American National Character.* New York: George Braziller, 1961.

Thistlethwaite, Frank. *America and the Atlantic Community: Anglo-American Aspects, 1790–1850.* New York: Harper and Row, 1959.

Thomas, Deborah. *Thackeray and Slavery.* Athens: Ohio State Univ. Press, 1993.

Thomas, Emory M. *The Confederacy as a Revolutionary Experience.* Columbia: Univ. of South Carolina Press, 1991.

———. *The Confederate Nation: 1861–1865.* San Francisco: Harper and Row, 1979.

Thornton, J. Mills, III. *Politics and Power in a Slave Society: Alabama, 1800–1860.* Baton Rouge: Louisiana State Univ. Press, 1978.

The Times. The History of The Times. Vol. 2, *The Tradition Established, 1841–1884.* London: Office of *The Times,* 1939.

Tompkins, Jane P., ed. *Reader-Response Criticism: From Formalism to Post-Structuralism.* Baltimore: Johns Hopkins Univ. Press, 1980.

Trefousse, Hans. *The Radical Republicans: Lincoln's Vanguard for Racial Justice.* New York: Knopf, 1969.

Trevelyan, George Macaulay. *The Life of John Bright.* Boston: Houghton Mifflin, 1925.

Tunnell, Ted. *Crucible of Reconstruction: War, Radicalism and Race in Louisiana.* Baton Rouge: Louisiana State Univ. Press, 1984.

Tuttle, William M., Jr. "Forerunners of Frederick Jackson Turner: Nineteenth-Century British Conservatives and the Frontier Thesis." *Agricultural History* 41 (1967): 219–227.

Vanauken, Sheldon. *The Glittering Illusion: English Sympathy for the Southern Confederacy.* Washington, D.C.: Regnery Gateway, 1989.

Van Deusen, Glyndon G. *Thurlow Weed: Wizard of the Lobby.* New York: Da Capo Press, 1969.

Varouxakis, Georgios. *Mill on Nationality.* New York: Routledge, 2002.

Vincent, J. R. *The Formation of the British Liberal Party 1857–1868.* New York: Harvester Press, 1976.

Viroli, Maurizio. *For Love of Country: An Essay on Patriotism and Nationalism.* New York: Clarendon Press, 1995.

Wade, Richard C. *Slavery in the Cities: The South 1820–1860.* New York: Oxford Univ. Press, 1964.

Walker, Ernestein. *Struggle for the Reform of Parliament, 1853–1867.* New York: Vantage Press, 1977.

Waller, John O. "Charles Dickens and the American Civil War." *Studies in Philology* 57 (1960): 535–548.

———. "Charles Kingsley and the American Civil War." *Studies in Philology* 60 (1963): 554–568.

Walther, Eric H. *The Fire-Eaters.* Baton Rouge: Louisiana State Univ. Press, 1992.

Ward, Paul. *Britishness since 1870.* New York: Routledge, 2004.

Warner, Oliver. *Captain Marryat: A Rediscovery.* London: Constable, 1953.

Washbrook, D. A. "Orients and Occidents: Colonial Discourse Theory and the Historiography of the British Empire." In *The Oxford History of the British Empire,* edited by William Roger Louis, vol. 5, *Historiography,* 596–611. New York: Oxford Univ. Press, 1999.

Waterfield, Gordon. *Layard of Nineveh.* New York: Frederick A. Praeger, 1968.

Waters, Hazel. *Racism on the Victorian Stage: Representation of Slavery and the Black Character.* Cambridge, UK: Cambridge Univ. Press, 2007.

Watson, Ritchie Devon, Jr. *Normans and Saxons: Southern Race Mythology and the Intellectual History of the American Civil War.* Baton Rouge: Louisiana State Univ. Press, 2008.

Webb, R. K. *Harriet Martineau: A Radical Victorian.* London: Heinemann, 1960.

Weedon, Alexis. *Victorian Publishing: The Economics of Book Production for a Mass Market, 1836–1916.* Burlington, Vt.: Ashgate, 2003.

Weinberg, Adelaide. *John Elliott Cairnes and the American Civil War: A Study in Anglo-American Relations.* London: Kingswood Press, 1968.

Wheare, K. C. "Walter Bagehot." *Proceedings of the British Academy* 60 (1974): 173–198.

White, Laura A. "The United States in the 1850's as Seen by British Consuls." *Mississippi Valley Historical Review* 19 (1933): 509–536.

Whitridge, Arnold. "Anglo-American Trouble-Makers: J. G. Bennett and J. T. Delane." *History Today* 6 (1956): 88–95.

———. "British Liberals and the American Civil War." *History Today* 12 (1962): 688–695.

———. "The Peaceable Ambassadors." *American Heritage* 8 (1953): 40–43, 89–103.

Williams, Patrick, and Laura Chrisman, eds. *Colonial Discourse and Post-Colonial Theory: A Reader.* New York: Columbia Univ. Press, 1994.

Winks, Robin. *Canada and the United States: The Civil War Years.* Montreal: Harvest Press, 1971.

Winstanley, Michael. *Gladstone and the Liberal Party.* New York: Routledge, 1990.

Wolf, Lucien. *Life of the First Marquess of Ripon.* 2 vols. London: John Murray, 1921.

Wolfe, Patrick. "History and Imperialism: A Century of Theory, from Marx to Postcolonialism." *American Historical Review* 102 (1997): 388–420.

Wolseley, Garnet Wolseley, Viscount. *The Story of a Soldier's Life.* 2 vols. Westminster, UK: Archibald Constable, 1903.

Wood, Gordon S. *Purpose of the Past: Reflections on the Uses of History.* New York: Penguin Press, 2008.

Wood, Marcus. "The American South and English Print Satire, 1760–1865." In *Britain and the American South: From Colonialism to Rock and Roll,* edited by Joseph Ward, 107–140. Jackson: Univ. Press of Mississippi, 2003.

———. *Blind Memory: Visual Representations of Slavery in England and America, 1780–1865.* New York: Routledge, 2000.

Woollacott, Angela. *Gender and Empire.* New York: Palgrave Macmillan, 2006.

Worth, George J. "Alexander Macmillan and His Magazine." *Victorian Periodicals Review* 36 (1993): 105–107.

———. "Macmillan's Magazine and the American Civil War: A Reconsideration." *Victorian Periodicals Review* 36 (1993): 193–198.

Wright, D. G. "Bradford and the American Civil War." *Journal of British Studies* 8 (1969): 69–85.

——. "English Opinion on Secession: A Note." *Journal of American Studies* 5 (1971): 151–154.

Wright, Gavin. *The Political Economy of the Cotton South: Households, Markets, and Wealth in the Nineteenth Century.* New York: Norton, 1978.

Wyatt-Brown, Bertram. *Southern Honor.* New York: Oxford Univ. Press, 1982.

Wykoff, George. "Charles Mackay: England's Forgotten Civil War Correspondent." *South Atlantic Monthly* 76 (1927): 50–62.

Yokota, Kariann. *Unbecoming British: How Revolutionary America Became a Postcolonial Nation.* Oxford, UK: Oxford Univ. Press, 2011.

Young, Robert. *Colonial Desire: Hybridity in Theory, Culture, Race.* New York: Routledge, 2000.

——. *Postcolonialism.* New York: Oxford Univ. Press, 2003.

——. *White Mythologies.* New York: Routledge, 2004.

Zimmerman, Kristen. "Liberal Speech, Palmerstonian Delay, and the Passage of the Second Reform Act." *English Historical Review* 118 (2003): 1176–1207.

INDEX